The Di [barcode] 9

D0390342

EDITED BY

GORDON A. CRAIG

AND

FELIX GILBERT

VOLUME 2: THE THIRTIES

ORIGINALLY PUBLISHED BY
PRINCETON UNIVERSITY PRESS

ATHENEUM

NEW YORK   1974

TO THE MEMORY OF

THEODOR ERNST MOMMSEN, 1905-1958

AND

FRANK MANSFIELD CRAIG, 1882-1952

Published by Atheneum
Reprinted by arrangement with Princeton University Press
Copyright 1953 by Princeton University Press
All rights reserved
ISBN 0-689-70055-5
Manufactured in the United States of America by
The Murray Printing Company, Forge Village, Massachusetts
Published in Canada by McClelland & Stewart Ltd.
First Atheneum Printing August 1963
Second Printing January 1965
Third Printing December 1965
Fourth Printing April 1967
Fifth Printing August 1968
Sixth Printing March 1971
Seventh Printing September 1972
Eighth Printing August 1974

ACKNOWLEDGMENTS

THE EDITORS and contributors wish to express their gratitude to:

Theodor Ernst Mommsen, for having first suggested to the editors the usefulness of a symposium on interwar diplomacy, and Datus C. Smith and Joseph R. Strayer for having seconded the suggestion so enthusiastically;

the Research Committee of Princeton University, the Rutgers University Research Council, the Board of Directors of the American Philosophical Society, and Edward F. D'Arms and the Board of Directors of the Rockefeller Foundation for grants in aid of research and assistance in meeting necessary travel and conference expenses;

Bernard C. Noble and Bernadotte Schmitt of the Division of Historical Policy Research, the Department of State, for permitting the use of certain papers bearing on the Japanese problem; the Swedish Foreign Office for allowing one of the contributors to have access to its files; and Herman Kahn, Director of the Franklin D. Roosevelt Library, Hyde Park, N.Y., for assistance and advice to several of the contributors;

Alexis Saint-Léger Léger and Joseph Clark Grew for their interest and counsel; and Walter Johnson and the Directors of Houghton Mifflin Company for having made available to the editors the proofs of Mr. Grew's *Turbulent Era: A Diplomatic Record of Forty Years*, which has now been published under the editorship of Professor Johnson;

Allen Macy Dulles, for information included in his unpublished Princeton B.A. thesis on the British Foreign Office; and Robert B. Glynn, for permitting the use of his unpublished Harvard honors thesis on Nevile Henderson;

Fred Aandahl, Gerald Aylmer, Cyril E. Black, Percy Corbett, Edward Mead Earle, Carl Hillger, Leonard Krieger, Philip Noel Buxton, E. S. Passant, Raymond J. Sontag, Jacob Viner, John W. Wheeler-Bennett and Sir Llewellyn Woodward for information and advice; and

Elizabeth D'Arcy and Mrs. Benton Schrader of Princeton, N.J., Joan Connolly of Bryn Mawr College, and Patricia and Gordon Decato of Keene, N.H. for typing, and retyping, the manuscript; and Harriet Anderson for seeing it through the press.

For the shortcomings of the book, none of the individuals or institutions mentioned above can be held accountable; but, if this volume makes any contribution to our knowledge of the recent past, they deserve much of the credit.

LIST OF CONTRIBUTORS

ELIZABETH R. CAMERON is a former teacher of European history at Bryn Mawr College. She is author of *Prologue to Appeasement* and translator of *And There Was Light*, by Jacques Lusseyran.

GORDON A. CRAIG is Professor of History at Stanford University. He is author of *Politics of the Prussian Army, 1640-1945; From Bismarck to Adenauer; Europe Since 1815*. He was collaborating editor of and contributor to *Makers of Modern Strategy: Military Thought from Machiavelli to Hitler*.

FRANKLIN L. FORD is Professor of History and Dean of the Faculty of Arts and Sciences, Harvard University. He is author of *Robe and Sword: The Re-Grouping of the French Aristocracy after Louis XIV* and *Strasbourg in Transition*.

FELIX GILBERT is Professor in the School of Historical Studies at The Institute for Advanced Study, Princeton. He is author of *To the Farewell Address: Ideas of Early American Foreign Policy* and was collaborating editor of and contributor to *Makers of Modern Strategy;* editor of *Hitler Directs His War*.

JOHN HUIZENGA was a member of the Board of Editors of *Documents on German Foreign Policy, 1918-1945*.

WILLIAM W. KAUFMANN is Professor of Political Science at the Massachusetts Institute of Technology. He is author of *British Policy and the Independence of Latin America, 1804-1828*. He was the editor of *Military Policy and National Security*.

HENRY L. ROBERTS is Professor of History and Director of the Russian Institute at Columbia University. He is author of *Rumania: The Political Problems of an Agrarian State; Russia and America: Dangers and Prospects;* (with Paul A. Wilson) *Britain and the United States: Problems in Cooperation;* and other historical books.

CARL E. SCHORSKE is Professor of History at the University of California, Berkeley. He is author of *German Social Democracy, 1905-1917;* (with Hoyt Price) *The Problem of Germany*.

HENRY R. WINKLER is Professor of History at Rutgers University. He is author of *The League of Nations Movement in Great Britain, 1914-1919*. He was editor (with K. M. Setton) of *Great Problems in European Civilization*.

CONTENTS

A NOTE ON ABBREVIATIONS

The most frequently cited collections of printed diplomatic correspondence and other documents are consistently referred to in the footnotes by short titles. For the convenience of the reader, the abbreviated title employed and the full titles of the collections follow.

BRITISH DOCUMENTS. *Documents on British Foreign Policy, 1919-1939*, edited by E. L. Woodward and Rohan Butler (London, H. M. Stationery Office, 1949 and continuing).

CONSPIRACY AND AGGRESSION. *Nazi Conspiracy and Aggression* (8 vols. and 2 supplements, Washington, Government Printing Office, 1946-1949).

DEGRAS. Jane Degras, ed., *Soviet Documents on Foreign Policy*, Volume I, 1917-24 (Oxford, 1951); Volume II, 1925-32 (Oxford, 1952).

DIRKSEN PAPERS. Ministry of Foreign Affairs of the USSR, *Documents and Materials Relating to the Eve of the Second World War*. Volume II, Dirksen Papers, 1938-1939 (Moscow, 1949).

DOCUMENTS AND MATERIALS. Ministry of Foreign Affairs of the USSR, *Documents and Materials Relating to the Eve of the Second World War*. Volume I, November 1937-1938 (Moscow, 1949).

DOCUMENTI ITALIANI. Ministero degli Affari Esteri, *I Documenti Diplomatici Italiani* (Rome, La Libreria dello Stato, 1952 and continuing).

FOREIGN RELATIONS. *Foreign Relations of the United States* (Department of State, Washington).

GERMAN DOCUMENTS. *Documents on German Foreign Policy, 1918-1945: From the Archives of the German Foreign Ministry* (Washington, Government Printing Office, 1949 and continuing).

NAZI-SOVIET RELATIONS. *Nazi-Soviet Relations 1939-1941: Documents from the Archives of the German Foreign Office*, edited by R. J. Sontag and J. S. Beddie (Washington, 1948).

POLISH WHITE BOOK. Republic of Poland, Ministry for Foreign Affairs, *Official Documents concerning Polish-German and Polish-Soviet Relations, 1933-1939* (London, 1940).

TRIAL OF MAJOR CRIMINALS. *The Trial of the Major War Criminals* (42 vols., Nuremberg, 1947-1949).

TRIALS OF WAR CRIMINALS. *Trials of War Criminals before the Nuernberg Military Tribunals under Control Council Law No. 10* (14 volumes, Nuremberg, 1946-1949).

VORGESCHICHTE. *Dokumente zur Vorgeschichte des Krieges*, herausgegeben vom Auswärtigen Amt der deutschen Regierung (Basel, 1940).

All other works are cited by their full title on the first reference in any chapter. Thereafter, short—but, it is to be hoped, easily recognizable—titles are used.

10

Arthur Henderson

BY HENRY R. WINKLER

WHEN ARTHUR HENDERSON came to the British Foreign Office in the summer of 1929, prospects for a European pacification appeared better than at any time since the end of the war. Locarno had been followed by Germany's entrance into the League of Nations, Russia was participating in the Preparatory Commission for the Disarmament Conference, and the Pact of Paris, if it did no more, seemed to symbolize a genuine will to achieve a lasting settlement of international tensions on a new basis.[1] In such a setting, Henderson prepared with characteristic directness to carry out the foreign policy advocated by the Labor party in the decade since Versailles. Two years later, when he was swept aside in the Labor debacle of 1931, the auguries for permanent peace were grim. In the wake of world economic crisis, the explosion of German nationalism was a striking repudiation of the policy of conciliation he had patiently undertaken. And in the aftermath, his experience as President of the Disarmament Conference was a tragic epilogue to the program he had attempted. Yet when he stepped down, the prestige of Great Britain was perhaps at its height and his tenure of office appeared to have been fruitful of real results. His approach to foreign affairs, despite the fate for which it was destined, had captured the imagination of large sections of the British public. It had, indeed, made a profound, if not always a convincing, impression on his European colleagues. Since that time, however, critics have divided sharply on the merits of his policy. His reputation among Labor writers as the greatest Foreign Secretary of the twentieth century is challenged by the picture of a well-meaning, bumbling amateur, blindly following the will-of-the-wisp of disarmament and conciliation in a world that was ready for neither.[2]

---

[1] This view was held in both the major British parties. See Anthony Eden's speech in the Debate on the Address, Parliamentary Debates: Commons, 5th series, CCXXIX, 425-426; and Margaret Cole, *Growing Up into Revolution* (London, 1949), p. 133.

[2] Harold J. Laski, "Ramsay MacDonald," *Harpers*, CLXIV (May 1932), 749; C. M.

While neither portrait is entirely accurate, the aims and nature of Henderson's policy form one of the more revealing chapters in the history of interwar diplomacy. He was in a sense a watershed figure and a survey of his role throws considerable light on the position of Britain as the hopes of the 1920's changed slowly into the fears and disillusionment of the 1930's.

I

Henderson's conduct of foreign affairs must be assessed in the light of his attitudes during the preceding decade. The British Labor party, within whose ranks he worked them out, moved slowly in developing its approach to foreign policy. Its reaction to the peace settlement was bitter. The unilateral disarmament of Germany was damned as unjust. The implication was drawn that other countries had both a legal and a moral obligation to scale down their armaments to the German level. France was accused of harboring aggressive intentions and German grievances were considered a major possible source of a new war. The redress of these grievances and the revision of the peace treaties became therefore a prime element in Labor policy.[3] Labor had been in the forefront of the campaign for a League of Nations, but the actual organization that came into being profoundly disappointed its hopes.[4] In the first shock of disillusionment, substantial groups within the party rejected the League as a coalition of the Allies whose main purpose was the maintenance of their own predominance. While the rank-and-file did not accept the left-wing thesis that peaceful international cooperation could not in any circumstances be organized by an alliance of capitalist governments, there was considerable feeling that the League as it existed fell far short of the genuine internationalism which Labor had demanded. Nevertheless, as time went on, the conviction grew that a reformed and strengthened League could be made to work in the interests of European conciliation and international peace.[5]

That Labor, despite its suspicions, came gradually to support a "League of Nations policy" as its first principle for the conduct of

Lloyd, "Uncle Arthur," *New Statesman and Nation*, x (October 26, 1935), 591. Cf., D. C. Somervell, *British Politics since 1900* (New York, 1950), pp. 186-187, 210; Quintin Hogg, *The Left Was Never Right* (London, 1945), pp. 121-123.

[3] W. R. Tucker, *The Attitude of the British Labour Party Towards European and Collective Security Problems*, 1920-1939 (Geneva, 1950), pp. 244-246.

[4] See Henry R. Winkler, "The Development of the League of Nations Idea in Great Britain, 1914-1919," *Journal of Modern History*, xx (June 1948), 107-109, 112.

[5] Maxine Whitney, *The Attitude of British Labor Toward the League of Nations, 1919-1924* (unpublished M. A. thesis, Stanford University, 1930), pp. 130, 144-145.

foreign affairs was in part at least the work of Arthur Henderson. The simplicity and directness which were his distinguishing marks in the eyes of his contemporaries concealed a very complex personality.[6] Until the war Henderson's career had glided steadily along in the grooves of trade union activities and Labor party organization. He had displayed little interest in and perhaps less knowledge of British relations with the rest of the world. The coming of the war marked the turning point of his career. Unlike Ramsay MacDonald and a sizable group within the party, Henderson supported the war once Great Britain was involved. At the same time, he soon became one of the leaders in the search for means to prevent its recurrence. While his aspiration was genuine, he made it clear that he realized, as perhaps few within the Labor movement did, that the organization of peace must be attempted within the limits of the possible. As a Methodist lay preacher, he was emotionally attached to the pacific ideal, but his years of experience as a trade union official and party worker offered unmistakable evidence of the practical day-to-day need for negotiation and compromise. His speeches and his tactics even in this early period demonstrate that he was convinced that the will to peace was not enough, that real results must be sought within the framework of generally accepted machinery and techniques of international organization.

During the war Henderson had worked closely with Sidney Webb and Ramsay MacDonald on the important "Memorandum on War Aims" which defined Labor's demands for the postwar settlement. As the outstanding official Labor spokesman in the campaign for a League of Nations and a moderate peace, he shared the disappointment of the party with the results of Versailles. Nevertheless, from the very start he urged the Labor movement to accept the machinery which existed and to work for its improvement in order that it might be used effectively in the construction of a viable international order.

The Labor policy in the early postwar years was essentially one of conciliation. Its details, as outlined by Henderson, were relatively simple. He insisted that the burden of reparations be reduced and that Germany and Russia be admitted as equals into the League. The authority of the Assembly should be increased, with the Council becoming primarily an executive body. The rule of unanimity, which in his view reduced the League to impotence, should give way in most cases to a system based

---

[6] For an assessment of Henderson by a close collaborator, see Mary Agnes Hamilton, *Arthur Henderson* (London, 1938). See also her *Remembering My Good Friends* (London, 1944), especially pp. 251-252; C. M. Lloyd in *New Statesman*, X, 591-592; and Margaret Cole, *Makers of the Labour Movement* (London, 1940), pp. 256, 260.

on majority decision. Some of these demands were eventually brought to fruition. Others were quietly dropped as adjustments were made to the environment of the postwar world.

Changes in the composition and structure of the League, however, were not really the major theme of his policy. To achieve a true pacification it was necessary to deal with the basic causes of war. Militarism must be attacked at its roots by a progressive limitation of armaments in all the states. But Henderson recognized, as he indicated in a speech before the World Peace Congress in December 1922, that disarmament was hardly an adequate guarantee for the maintenance of peace. Each nation, in his view, must find such a guarantee in the League of Nations itself. To that end, he proposed to amend the Covenant so as to make compulsory the submission of every dispute, whatever its nature, for inquiry and decision to the Council, the Assembly, or the Permanent Court of International Justice. Not only should arbitration be required in certain types of disputes, but decisions in such cases must be binding. Once such a system was in full use, the League could more effectively take the lead in promoting the economic, no less than the political, cooperation of the nations of the world.

The development of this approach as early as 1922 revealed the road that the Labor party and Henderson were to follow with considerable consistency for the next decade. It has been customary to emphasize this aspect of the policy and to point out that in contrast Labor opinion gave very little thought, and Labor spokesmen very little emphasis, to the means by which such a system was to be enforced. It is true that a large part of the Labor party shrank from sanctions with an unrealistic aversion to the use of force under any circumstances. It is equally evident that Ramsay MacDonald, the party's leader, displayed a rather vague reliance on the development of the international spirit far more often than he revealed any genuine willingness to face the unpalatable realities that characterized postwar Europe.[7] But it is also clear—and this has often been neglected—that Henderson, who was increasingly to become a major architect of Labor policy, recognized quite early that disarmament, arbitration, the use of the League to promote peaceful settlement, in the final reckoning depended on the willingness of the Powers to commit themselves to the task of enforcement. From the beginning he warned his party that an essential preliminary to disarmament was the assurance that all members of the League would come to the assistance of any

---

[7] See, for example, J. R. MacDonald, *The Foreign Policy of the Labour Party* (London, 1923), pp. 20-24; Hamilton, *Remembering My Good Friends*, p. 104.

victim of aggression.[8] In so arguing, he was, of course, leading the party closer to the conception of security which had from the first been urged by France. Quite clearly, he did not share the French view that preponderant power must be retained by the beneficiaries of the postwar settlement. At the same time, he saw that the ideal of a European community based on friendly understanding might be long in coming. Meanwhile he accepted the need of making at least some concessions to the requirements of security. He was, in a word, preparing the way for the Geneva Protocol in whose formulation he played a significant part.

The first Labor government, despite MacDonald's success in conciliating France and in ending the Ruhr impasse, had little time to promote its positive program for European pacification. Actually, a major plank in Labor's foreign policy, the revision of the Versailles Treaty, was dropped with the assumption of the responsibilities of office.[9] The question continued to be raised by the left-wing minority, but the leaders of the party came to accept Article 19 of the League Covenant as a sufficient vehicle for possible change. This turn from treaty revision was one aspect of a policy which saw the Labor government draw closer to France. Although it rejected the Draft Treaty of Mutual Assistance, in part because the all-too-concrete guarantees of military support were not combined with any clear-cut definition of aggression, its delegation proceeded at the Fifth Assembly of the League to cooperate with the French in the development of the Geneva Protocol. As a member of the Third Committee of the Assembly, Henderson took a leading part in hammering out its details.[10] Stripped to its simplest terms, this complex proposal made provision for the use of "arbitration," that is, some kind of peaceful settlement, as a key to the equation of disarmament with security.

The Geneva Protocol was a logical application of the policy Henderson had been advocating for several years. It provided for the growth of the machinery of international conciliation along the lines that he had proposed in 1922. In order to achieve this development of the League system, he was willing to make concessions to the French demand for hard-and-fast military commitments, particularly since the Protocol was not to

[8] Arthur Henderson, *Labour and Foreign Affairs* (London, 1922), pp. 6-11 and "War against War. Political Action for Peace," *Labour Magazine*, 1 (January, 1923), 392-393; Tucker, *Attitude of Labour Party*, pp. 94-95, 99.

[9] W. M. Jordan, *Great Britain, France and the German Problem* (London, 1943), p. 207; Tucker, *Attitude of Labour Party*, pp. 99, 103.

[10] Lord Parmoor, *A Retrospect, Looking Back over a Life of More than Eighty Years* (London, 1936), p. 241; Cole, *Makers of the Labour Movement*, p. 261; W. N. Medlicott, *British Foreign Policy since Versailles* (London, 1940), pp. 93-94.

come into force until its signatories had agreed upon a scheme to limit national armaments. Within the Labor party, however, there was considerable doubt as to its wisdom. Some groups were disturbed over its implied support of the post-Versailles *status quo*. Others, probably a substantial majority within the party, suspected a system of security based upon armaments and looked askance at its emphasis on sanctions. MacDonald himself minimized the possibility of the use of force. He referred to the sanctions provisions as a "harmless drug to soothe nerves" and underlined their purely deterrent aspect.[11] The terms of the Protocol were never formally accepted by the Cabinet, and there are observers who believe that the Labor government, had it remained in office, would not have adopted them without serious revision.[12]

Even Henderson argued that if the nations could be persuaded to use arbitration there would eventually be little need for military force. He stressed the role of the Protocol in developing methods of peaceful settlement and in making possible a move in the direction of disarmament. But with a realism relatively rare in Great Britain at the time, he refused to neglect its security features. In October 1924, for example, he commented on the provisions for sanctions in a speech at Burnley. He insisted quite categorically that "we are solemnly pledged that our force shall be used to make the decisions come to effective, if sanity, reason, right and justice fail and these sanctions have to be employed. Let that be clear."[13] This was as close to the concept of collective security as any important group in Britain ever came in the years before the emergence of the Nazi power. It was closer, as has been noted, than the bulk of the Labor movement was prepared to go. For the thought of the Labor party, no less than that of its rivals, was attuned to a popular opinion that had not yet learned to accept the thesis that "if peace is to be obtained, it must be paid for by certain sacrifices, the assumption of certain obligations."[14] The fact that Henderson went as far as he did in accepting the coercive features of the Protocol, rather than his obvious emphasis on its value in fostering arbitration and disarmament, is the most striking element in his position.

[11] Arnold Wolfers, *Britain and France between Two Wars* (New York, 1940), pp. 347-353; Jordan, *Great Britain, France and the German Question*, pp. 208-209; Tucker, *Attitude of Labour Party*, pp. 102-106, 246-248.

[12] See, for example, C. E. Sipple, *British Foreign Policy since the World War*. University of Iowa Studies in the Social Sciences, x, No. 1 (Iowa City, 1932), 85-86.

[13] Arthur Henderson, *The New Peace Plan* (London, 1924), pp. 14-15. See also *idem, Labour and the Geneva Protocol* (London, 1925), pp. 5-16. This is a reprint of his speech in the House of Commons on March 24, 1925.

[14] Quoted in Jordan, *Great Britain, France and the German Question*, p. 207.

Whatever may have been Labor's interpretation of the Protocol, its fate was sealed when the Baldwin government assumed office. The substitution of the Locarno treaties for the Protocol posed a serious dilemma. The Labor party was suspicious of a policy which appeared to turn from the League toward individual agreements between individual nations. It was perturbed because Locarno made no specific provision for disarmament and did not commit Great Britain to the fullest use of arbitration procedures. In addition, Labor spokesmen argued that the new treaties contained military obligations in some ways more binding than those which the Conservatives had rejected in the Geneva Protocol. Moreover, they reasoned, the chances of war, since Austen Chamberlain had deliberately renounced British participation in the stabilization of eastern Europe, were perhaps greater than ever. On the other hand, there was real satisfaction over the arbitration treaties which had been signed and, above all, over German entry into the League of Nations. In the event, therefore, the Labor movement accepted Locarno as a first step toward the conciliation of Europe. In the years that followed, however, that acceptance was tempered by the belief that the Conservative government was throwing away the opportunity to build a genuine peace. When Hugh Dalton later referred to the policy of "the fumbling fingers and the faltering feet," he was reflecting Labor's conviction that Chamberlain could have taken advantage of the "spirit of Locarno" to strengthen the League and obtain substantial disarmament.[15]

During the Locarno era, the Labor party continued to advocate its own prescription for the organization of peace. The apparent return of some measure of economic stability and the presumed reconciliation of Germany and France made the time seem ripe for a further development of the international system. In principle, the Geneva Protocol was proclaimed to be at the core of Labor policy, but emphasis tended to shift more and more to the aspect of the Protocol which had provided for the development of the machinery of arbitration.[16] At its annual conference in 1926, the party demanded that the government sign the Optional Clause of the Permanent Court, which pledged its signatories to submit justiciable disputes for settlement at The Hague. A pamphlet explaining the resolution pointed out that Labor believed all dangerous quarrels

[15] Hugh Dalton, "British Foreign Policy, 1929-1931," *Political Quarterly*, II (1931), 505; C. R. Attlee, *The Labour Party in Perspective—And Twelve Years Later* (London, 1949), p. 150; J. R. MacDonald, foreword to George Glasgow, *From Dawes to Locarno* (New York and London, 1926), pp. ix-xi; Tucker, *Attitude of Labour Party*, pp. 110-115, 145.
[16] Arthur Henderson, "The Principles of the Protocol," *Labour Magazine*, VI (November, 1927), 298-300.

[317]

should be submitted either to arbitral decision or conciliation. If conciliation broke down then in the last resort the nations should be bound to accept "compulsory arbitration." This was the program of the Geneva Protocol, but Labor recognized that such a general treaty might take some time to bring into operation. Meanwhile, in its place but as an immediate practicable step toward the same end, it supported the signature of the Optional Clause.[17]

Within the next two years, other elements were added to the Labor scheme for the conduct of international affairs. The adoption of the Kellogg-Briand Pact was hailed as a positive step toward the outlawry of war. When MacDonald warned the party that the "public sanctions" of the League were not acts of war and must be maintained, he was hinting at the future Labor program of bringing the Pact of Paris and the League Covenant into closer conformity with each other. The renunciation of war, in the Labor view, must be accompanied by the progressive development of substitutes for war. This was a postulate upon which pacifists and those who accepted the role of compulsion could unite. Hence the emphasis which was placed on the promotion of the policies embodied in the Optional Clause and the General Act of Arbitration, Conciliation and Judicial Settlement proposed in 1928 by the League Assembly.[18]

By 1928 the party had prepared a full-dress statement on international affairs. The Birmingham Conference of that year was one of the most important in its history. After an acrimonious debate, a document called "Labour and the Nation" was adopted. While historians of the Labor party have been concerned with the domestic aspects of this policy statement, it was actually more important in the field of foreign affairs. Its social and economic clauses were never considered seriously by the Labor government after 1929. In contrast, its international section came to be the program upon which Arthur Henderson later based his foreign policy. As a consequence, it merits some attention.

It is stretching a point too far to insist, as has recently been done,[19] that the international section of "Labour and the Nation" contained conflicting statements on the organization of peace. Superficially, there was perhaps a contradiction. The manifesto laid stress, on the one hand, upon the collective renunciation of war as an instrument of national policy and upon disarmament and arbitration, while on the other it supported the

[17] Labour Party, *Arbitrate! Arbitrate! Arbitrate!* (London, 1927), pp. 1-11.
[18] *Report of the Annual Conference of the Labour Party* (1928), pp. 183-184.
[19] Tucker, *Attitude of Labour Party*, p. 145.

concept of "pooled security" against aggression. But in the minds of Labor leaders like Henderson, it is clear, the problem was resolved by the belief that such security must be looked for within the framework of the League of Nations. They saw a significant difference between war as an instrument of national policy and sanctions as a bulwark of League guarantees. It may be that this was a naive reading of the realities of the international scene and it is certain that many in the party did not share this view, but it was at least a conscious effort to relate the vague promises of the Pact of Paris to the presumably more substantial machinery of the League Covenant. At any rate, "Labour and the Nation" pledged the party to try to implement the renunciation of war by the signature of the Optional Clause, by the international reduction of armaments, by the promotion of international economic cooperation, and by the systematic use of the League to achieve those ends. When, a short time later, the party urged acceptance of the General Act, it had laid down the program which Henderson was subsequently to follow, for his one remaining aim, the conciliation of Germany and Russia, had long been an element of Labor policy.[20]

II

When the Labor government was formed in June 1929, Henderson insisted upon the Foreign Office. He was given the post despite the reluctance of Ramsay MacDonald, who seems to have had the curious notion that in some way J. H. Thomas was qualified for the position. But Henderson, who had taken the leading role in hammering out the international program of "Labour and the Nation," was unquestionably looked upon as the man to carry it out. As we have seen, he had been one of the major architects of Labor's foreign policy. If, therefore, the press expressed some surprise at his appointment, this was an indication not so much of his ignorance of foreign affairs as it was of the press's un-awareness of developments within the Labor party since the war. Mac-Donald made no secret of his resentment, but the new Foreign Secretary held to the objective of carrying through the decisions of the party.[21]

The policy of drift which seemed to characterize the domestic side of

[20] *Report of the Annual Conference of the Labour Party* (1928), pp. 196-200, 264-266; Labour Party, *Labour and the Nation* (London, 1928), pp. 41-49; *Labour's Appeal to the Nation* (London, 1929), p. 3; *Arbitration: Tory Record and Labour Policy* (London, 1929), p. 5. The latter two were campaign leaflets in 1929.

[21] For views of Henderson's appointment and his relations with MacDonald, see Philip Snowden, *An Autobiography* (2 vols., London, 1934), II, 760-764, 767; Laski in *Harpers*, CLXIV, 749, 752; Viscount Cecil, *A Great Experiment* (New York, 1941), p. 207; Parmoor, *Retrospect*, p. 296; Hamilton, *Remembering My Good Friends*, p. 250.

the Labor government's program was certainly not apparent at the Foreign Office. Henderson made it clear from the beginning that he had firm conceptions of his general aims and that he intended to take full responsibility for implementing them. He apparently found it possible to work within the framework of the Foreign Office. For, despite Labor criticism of its organization in past years, he seems to have made no substantial change in either its routine or its structure during these years. His absolute honesty, which a recent writer has summed up as that of a man who was "an almost solid block of integrity,"[22] strikes one as a major element in his conduct of his office. The opinion of those closest to him at this time is that he quickly gained the affection of his subordinates. Often enough, however, civil servants may feel well-disposed to a minister who is sufficiently weak and malleable to be influenced towards positions which they, rather than he, determine. But there is no evidence to indicate such a relationship. Henderson seems to have won the respect as well as the affection of his permanent staff. As one of his associates has put it, they understood that, when he had heard the evidence on any given matter, it was his views and not theirs that were going to prevail.

At the same time, Henderson had a real consciousness of his personal limitations. He showed no feeling of inferiority about surrounding himself with first-rate advisers of whose training and abilities he made the fullest use. The Foreign Office staff under Henderson was surely one of the most competent of its period. In the position of Permanent Under-Secretary, Sir Robert Vansittart succeeded Sir Ronald Lindsay (who went to Washington) early in 1930. The Parliamentary Under-Secretary, Hugh Dalton, and the Parliamentary Private Secretary, Philip Noel Baker, had the background and the brilliance which Henderson lacked. He depended heavily on them, and especially on Dalton, for advice. But in the final analysis, he made the basic decisions, and it reveals much that these products of the best in English (and American) education should have respected the judgment of an almost uneducated ironfounder with a conviction that apparently still persists. Equally striking is the attitude of Viscount Cecil, whom he brought into the Foreign Office to help pursue his League of Nations policy.

His methods of work were singular. He spent little time reading long memoranda or other papers. He preferred to listen to oral explanation of a subject, to ask questions, and to reach his conclusions on the basis of such conversation. Such methods quite obviously have their dangers, but those who worked with him have described his grasp of the problems

[22] Raymond Postgate, *Life of George Lansbury* (London, 1951), p. 171.

which he faced and his ability to cut to the heart of an issue without burying himself in the minutiae of detail. Whatever its defects, the system seems to have worked quite well for him.[23]

While Henderson settled easily into the routine of the Foreign Office, his relations with Ramsay MacDonald were a constant irritant and often a positive deterrent to the efficient conduct of foreign relations. From the start he encountered, as one journalist has described it, "a steady stream of criticism, disparagement and, what was far more galling to the new Foreign Secretary, of contemptuous indifference from No. 10 Downing Street."[24] MacDonald's personal antipathy has been documented again and again, but its effect on the pursuit of a consistent foreign policy requires some comment. In a sense, Great Britain had two foreign policies from 1929 to 1931. MacDonald jealously kept virtually every aspect of American relations in his own hands. From his well-staged trip to America in 1929 through the negotiations which followed the announcement of the Hoover moratorium in 1931, he was almost exclusively in control of this important aspect of British policy. Henderson was deliberately kept in the background and was, apparently, left to keep the rest of his policy consistent with MacDonald's American program as best he could.

In other spheres, MacDonald was difficult to work with. His extraordinary sensitivity to public criticism and his tendency to make ill-considered public statements without consulting his colleagues often caused embarrassment where they did not do worse. Two examples will perhaps reveal how difficult was the position of a Foreign Minister under so perplexing a personality. Scarcely more than a week after he had taken office, MacDonald permitted the publication of an article in the *Sunday Times*, in which he castigated the treatment of minorities in various European countries. With almost breathtaking lack of tact—if one considers that cooperation with France was to be one of the central pivots of his Foreign Minister's policy—he included Alsace and the Saar in his catalogue of minority problems. The explanation that the article had been written before he had assumed office hardly was sufficient to assuage irritation on the Continent or to make the position of Henderson any less difficult.[25]

---

[23] I am indebted to the Rt. Hon. Philip Noel Baker (letter of February 22, 1952) and the Rt. Hon. Hugh Dalton (letter of March 22, 1952) for informative and sympathetic accounts of Henderson at the Foreign Office. See also Hamilton, *Henderson*, pp. 285-286; Major General A. C. Temperley, *The Whispering Gallery of Europe* (London, 1939), p. 163; Cecil, *A Great Experiment*, p. 200.

[24] George Slocombe, *A Mirror to Geneva. Its Growth, Grandeur and Decay* (New York, 1938), p. 239.

[25] Tucker, *Attitude of Labour Party*, p. 118.

Several months later, Henderson was at Geneva supporting British adherence to the Convention for Financial Assistance. The Foreign Office had examined it carefully and had decided that it involved no dangerous new commitments. But MacDonald became frightened by the opposition of a section of the press, and just before Henderson was ready to deposit the signature of Great Britain he wrote the Foreign Secretary a "not very temperate letter," in which the implications pointed quite clearly to a repudiation of Henderson's policy.[26] Henderson struck back with some heat. After tracing the way in which the British decision to sign had been reached and pointing out that MacDonald himself had agreed, he expressed himself in blunt terms to the Prime Minister. "Surely, we shall stultify our whole attitude, if, on being confronted by the first issue that gives us an opportunity of giving some effect to our policy, we turn back because a few hostile and ill-informed critics elect to make a fuss. If we give way to the stunt Press on this, they will seek to make the Government position on Russia, Egypt, etc. impossible.

"I wrote strongly, because . . . there is not that confidence when working in the international sphere one is entitled to expect."[27]

These examples illustrate a situation which continued as long as the Labor government remained in office. On the other hand, despite the problems caused by MacDonald's unreliability, Henderson was from the beginning determined to carry through his program. That program has already been described. At the suggestion of Hugh Dalton, he circulated "Labour and the Nation" among the principal officials. This was perhaps a unique method of explaining his policy, but his Under-Secretary was later to testify to the loyalty and helpfulness with which officials and diplomatic representatives pursued that general policy.[28] Parenthetically, it should be noted that Henderson was well served by his diplomats abroad, particularly by Sir Horace Rumbold and Basil Newton at Berlin and by Lord Tyrrell at Paris. The Berlin embassy was alert to the rising current of German nationalism and the dangerous development of Nazi strength.[29] It recognized the complex difficulties—and also the tortured maneuvering for position—of the Brüning regime and reported what it saw to London. At Paris, Tyrrell outlined with sympathy, but with considerable insight, the French reaction to the changing spirit in Germany which soon cast its shadow over Henderson's entire program.[30]

[26] Hamilton, *Henderson*, p. 326.

[27] Henderson to MacDonald, September 12, 1929. *Ibid.*, pp. 327-328.

[28] Dalton to author, March 22, 1952; Dalton in *Political Quarterly*, II, 489.

[29] See below, Chapter 14, § 1.

[30] See, in particular, *British Documents*, 2nd series, I, chapter VI, and II, chapter IV.

When Henderson felt that his representatives could not give him loyal service, he acted with firmness. Soon after coming to the Foreign Office he became convinced that Lord Lloyd, the High Commissioner of Egypt, was unalterably opposed to the policy he intended to pursue. He demanded and received Lord Lloyd's resignation. A parliamentary attempt, led by Winston Churchill, to make it appear that he had brutally dismissed the High Commissioner for political reasons, reacted in his favor. He was able to document the difficulties which Sir Austen Chamberlain had had with Lord Lloyd and to maintain the obvious position that representatives abroad must be willing, whatever their own views, to carry out the policy determined by the government.[31]

With the Egyptian policy itself, he had less success. Although he recognized that Chamberlain had made a start in erasing the bitterness which had followed the murder of Sir Lee Stack, he hoped by extending the policy of cooperation to create an entirely new atmosphere. Working closely with the Cabinet, he took the opportunity of an Egyptian initiative to reopen negotiations for a treaty. He explained the spirit in which he approached the question in a statement to the Commons on December 23, 1929. Irritating restrictions, he remarked, "have been removed, because of the conviction that such restrictions, sought to be imposed from without, can only defeat the main purpose which both countries had in view. That purpose, as far as His Majesty's Government are concerned, is the establishment of a firm and lasting friendship with the Egyptian people, by the removal of those sources of suspicion which in the past have been the cause of so much damage to the interests of both peoples."[32] In contrast was the reaction of Sir Austen Chamberlain to the proposal that both Egypt and Great Britain should undertake not to adopt in foreign countries an attitude which was inconsistent with the alliance or would create difficulties for the other party to it. Chamberlain poured ridicule on the idea that the foreign policy of Great Britain should be governed by the interests and circumstances of Egypt. "The elephant undertakes to protect the mouse, and thereafter the elephant's march is to be conditioned by the mouse's trot."[33] The difference in approach was considerable.

In any event, Henderson's proposals went substantially beyond those made by Chamberlain in 1927 and 1928. He was willing to withdraw troops to the region of the Suez Canal, but refused to accept the Egyptian

[31] Parliamentary Debates: Commons, 5th series, CCXXX, 1301, 1635-1646.
[32] *ibid.*, CCXXXIII, 1977.
[33] *ibid.*, 1959-1960.

demand for control of immigration into the Sudan.[34] Although Henderson was eager to achieve a *détente* in Anglo-Egyptian relations, he declined to sacrifice important British interests in order to accomplish his purpose. Nevertheless, the contrast between the spirit of his policy and that of Chamberlain affords an interesting insight into his approach to other questions of perhaps greater significance.

III

Prominent among those other questions were relations with Germany and Russia. Reconciliation with Germany and closer relations with Russia were of course standing tenets of the Labor creed. The party had long argued that such a policy was an indispensable prelude to the constructive development of international cooperation. Henderson and his advisers believed, in these last days before the onset of the world depression, that there was at last an opportunity to establish an enduring peace in Europe. Hugh Dalton reflected this optimism when he explained the government's policy during the debate on the Address from the Throne. "I myself hope and believe that we are now entering upon a new and more hopeful phase of history," he said. "I think we now have an opportunity to go forward which, if we miss it, may not come again in our own day. Therefore, I hope and believe that we shall be able, in the months and years that lie ahead, to make a forward movement in the direction of arbitration, disarmament, the better economic organization of the life of the world, and the general establishment of reconciliation between old enemies and firmer friendship between old friends."[35] This was more than rhetoric. In 1929, Henderson, like Dalton, saw the Labor government's main problem of foreign policy as the removal of the political antagonisms that stood in the way of a peaceful international order. He was convinced that it could not be solved until Germany and Russia participated as equals in the development of disarmament, machinery for pacific settlement, and the rational economic organization of the world. In retrospect it seems clear that, whatever the possibilities when Henderson took office, the conditions for such a policy were swept away after 1930 by the great depression, which precipitated the trend toward political conflict and eventual war.[36] In the atmosphere of 1929, however, the policy appeared sound. If it was stubbornly maintained even when the German challenge made it unrealistic, it should be remembered that few policy-

---

[34] The Egyptian negotiations are summarized in Arnold J. Toynbee, *Survey of International Affairs*, 1930 (London, 1931), pp. 188-222.
[35] Parliamentary Debates: Commons, 5th series, CCXXIX, 457-458.
[36] Medlicott, *British Foreign Policy*, pp. 107-108.

makers indeed were perceptive enough before 1931 to understand the changes that had come upon the world of the 1920's. Henderson, as we have said, stood at the watershed and the fate of his policy reflected the end of the old era as it symbolized the tragic emergence of the new.

The first step in the reconciliation of Germany was taken almost immediately after the Labor government took office. Henderson was determined to heal the German "wound in the west" by promoting the early evacuation of the Rhineland. He announced his policy to the House of Commons on July 5, 1929, when he declared that the Germans had carried out, so far as he was able to see, the conditions imposed upon them by the Versailles Treaty. The evacuation, therefore, should be carried out as quickly as possible.[37] But his attitude toward the German question was a good deal more complex than has sometimes been represented.[38] He realized that it was not primarily a matter of Anglo-German relations. It meant above all a reconciliation between Germany and France. And while suspicion of France still maintained a strong hold on the Labor party, he was as convinced of the necessity of working closely with France as he was that Germany must have her legitimate demands satisfied. While he was prepared as a last resort to withdraw British troops independently, he realized that such a move might mean a more galling occupation under Belgian and French forces and the increase of tension between Britain and France. On this matter, at least, he received the wholehearted concurrence of Sir Austen Chamberlain, who shared his belief in the desirability of a collective withdrawal.[39]

Henderson's discussion of his plans was in anticipation of the conference which had been scheduled to deal with the experts' report on reparations and the future of the Rhineland. At The Hague in August, he undertook, as chairman of the Political Commission, to promote withdrawal by fostering a Franco-German agreement. Stresemann was insistent that Germany would accept the Young Plan only on condition of a Rhineland evacuation. Briand for his part put the financial settlement first and demanded guarantees of German performance. During the course of the negotiations, Henderson announced explicitly that British troops would be withdrawn beginning in September regardless of the decision on the Young Plan. This pressure on the French, although he worked closely with Briand, apparently had much to do with the successful outcome of

---

[37] Parliamentary Debates: Commons, 5th series, CCXXIX, 417.

[38] See the comments on this in Floris Delattre, "La Psychologie de la diplomatie britannique depuis la guerre," *L'Année politique française et étrangère*, VI (October 1931), p. 279.

[39] Parliamentary Debates: Commons, 5th series, CCXXIX, 406, 416.

the political negotiations. Actually, the political problem was not the most difficult at the conference. Philip Snowden threw the discussions into an impasse by demanding a greater share of the reparation annuities than had been recommended in the experts' report. Although his stand was hailed with delight in Great Britain, it seems clear that he helped create needless tension in Anglo-French relations, to say nothing of jeopardizing the outcome of negotiations. In the light of the later history of reparations, of course, Snowden's insistence on a share of payments that were never to be made seems like one of the more trivial aspects of the problem. For the moment, the Rhineland settlement appeared about to be shattered in the ruin of the financial negotiations, but in the long run a compromise, rather favorable to Snowden's demands, was reached. Snowden later paid tribute to Henderson's support, but the documents are not yet available by which to judge his role in the financial struggle.[40] In any case, the final agreement called for evacuation to begin in September and to be completed by the French within eight months. In the event, although there were a few qualms about French intentions,[41] the withdrawal went off on schedule. Henderson's policy had been a success at The Hague. He believed it to be a final step for bringing the world war to an end.[42] Its effect in Germany will have to be looked at later.[43]

The Labor movement had insisted for years on the importance of proper relations with Russia. Although the majority of organized labor had little illusion about the nature of the Soviet regime, it is possible to discern, as one French scholar puts it, a kind of "socialist mystique" in the promotion of this demand.[44] But the Foreign Office felt that there were imperative reasons for the resumption of diplomatic intercourse. Henderson accepted a doctrine of recognition that has become unfashionable in recent years. He contended that unsatisfactory relations, far from being an argument for the abolition of normal diplomatic machinery, were a further reason for more regular contact. Acting on the information of his legal advisers that diplomatic relations had never been severed but merely suspended, he proceeded to negotiate for their reestablishment. The Russian refusal to accept responsibility for the activities of the

[40] Compare Snowden, *Autobiography*, II, 819, with the account in Hamilton, *Henderson*, p. 316.

[41] See *British Documents*, 2nd series, I, 475-478.

[42] *Verbatim Record of the Eleventh Ordinary Session of the Assembly of the League of Nations*, first plenary meeting, September 10, 1930, p. 5.

[43] For an account of the first Hague Conference, based on press reports and Commons debates, see *Survey of International Affairs, 1929*, pp. 180-188. Also Tucker, *Attitude of Labour Party*, pp. 119-121.

[44] Delattre in *L'Année politique*, II, 278.

Third International proved a particular source of difficulty, but finally on October 3, 1929, an accord was signed which simply confirmed the article in the treaty of 1924 which had prohibited propaganda.

During the course of the next year, the policy of the government was under constant attack in the House of Commons, particularly on the issue of the continuation of Soviet propaganda. In defending his position, Henderson argued that normal relations at least provided a mechanism through which the problem could be discussed. He did not deny that propaganda was going on, but he failed to see how cutting off relations could improve the situation. He was especially anxious for better relations in order to promote British trade in Russian markets.[45] But perhaps an even more important reason of the government was revealed by Philip Noel Baker, who took a major part in defending its policy in the House. Noel Baker laid stress on its value in the maintenance of peace. The prevention of another war, he declared, depended on two things: the realization of the government's policy of disarmament and the spread throughout the world of the spirit of peace. The world knew that unless Russia was brought in, a policy of general disarmament was impossible. Negotiations at Geneva made it clear that in every circumstance the attitude of Russia had to be considered. In Central Europe, where disarmament was vital, nothing was possible without Russian help. It was imperative to resume relations in order to exorcise the suspicion of Britain which existed in Russia and thus work together more effectively for world disarmament.[46] Whatever its purpose, the Russian rapprochement was a disappointment. The problem of propaganda was never solved, as the Conservative press and politicians continued to point out. The best that Henderson's colleague, Hugh Dalton, was later able to say for the policy was that it had succeeded in making Anglo-Russian relations less unsatisfactory than they would otherwise have been.[47] In a sense, however, it did serve as a symbol of the desire for fuller Russian collaboration in the work of European pacification and so formed an integral part of the program which Henderson was attempting to achieve.

IV

The major element in that program, beyond any question, was the changed British attitude toward the League of Nations. In essence, the Rhineland withdrawal and the resumption of relations with Russia aimed

[45] Parliamentary Debates: Commons, 5th series, CCXXIX, 418, 466; CCXXXI, 900-902; CCXXXIII, 1447-1498; CCXXXIX, 2581-2633.

[46] *ibid.*, CCXXXI, 920-921.

[47] Dalton in *Political Quarterly*, II, 499-500.

at European appeasement as a preliminary to disarmament and the development of a real collective system through the League.[48] No more than the Conservatives, however, were the Labor leaders ready to consider collective security in terms of the French thesis of automatic sanctions and mutual assistance. Firm in the belief that the war had been liquidated and that it was now imperative to foster a spirit of cooperation, the Labor party, even after conditions had changed radically in 1930 and 1931, clung to the illusion that the collective organization of substitutes for war was more immediately pressing than a collective stand against the unilateral transformation of the European system. This policy, with its emphasis upon disarmament, the use of arbitration in international disputes, and the promotion of measures of economic cooperation, was so tragically divorced from the realities of 1931 that it is somewhat too easy to forget that in 1929 it represented a bold, and on the whole a relatively well-founded, approach to international affairs. Its strength was in its recognition that the problem of maintaining a healthy Europe was more than a problem of military alliance to prevent the disruption of the *status quo*. Labor recognized more clearly than its opponents the imperative need for erecting the framework in which the tensions leading to war might be kept at a minimum. On the other hand, it is essential to point out that so long as the tensions existed, as they did in this period, it was disastrous to act as though they were unimportant or as though some vague spirit of good will would dissolve them. While it was desirable to work for the fullest development of a system of real international law, it was even more essential to recognize that law must be enforced. This was the corollary which many within the Labor party were unwilling to face. Even Henderson, who accepted the need for a system of sanctions, never really faced up to the problem of power relationships in Europe. So long as Germany, for example, had the military and industrial potentialities which she possessed, it was folly to expect France and her allies to agree to substantial disarmament which would leave them at a comparative disadvantage. The French policy, understandable as it was, remained curiously negative. It offered little hope for a progressive development of genuine cooperation. But the British Labor position, correct in its assessment of the long-term goal to be sought, vitiated its usefulness by the optimistic belief that the Europe of the depression and the explosion of German nationalism was a suitable starting place for the inauguration of the millennium.

[48] A. L. Rowse, *The End of an Epoch. Reflections on Contemporary History* (London, 1948), pp. 50-51.

In 1929, however, when Henderson went to Geneva as the working head of the British delegation to the Tenth Assembly of the League, the prospects for the success of his policy appeared promising. The delegation, which included William Graham of the Board of Trade, Cecil, Dalton, and Baker, was an able one. Henderson himself felt at home in Geneva. He got on well with Briand and the dying Stresemann and quite clearly hoped that his close contact with them would promote the fuller development of the League, which was central to his program of action. As a result, he kept himself free for the kind of consultation and conversation that had virtually become the hallmarks of postwar diplomacy.[49] He would probably have agreed with Briand, who explained to the Assembly: "I have often been told that I am rather too fond of conversations. After drafting dispatches and reading dispatches from other people, I soon felt that this method was out of harmony with the modern love of speed. It seemed to me that many difficulties might be solved by a personal conversation—You understand one another, or at least try to understand one another. You make an effort to find a solution, and in the end do find a solution for a situation which appeared to admit of none."[50] Such diplomacy had its dangers, as was strikingly illustrated by the experiences of Lloyd George or MacDonald or even Briand himself. In the case of Henderson there is some doubt. Certainly he was a practitioner of the method. The agreement to resume relations with Russia had been reached at an informal meeting in a little inn at Lewes. At Geneva he pursued his policy in much the same fashion. But he was not particularly flexible nor did he have the capacity for brilliant improvisation which rested on little more substantial than the inspiration of the moment. He came to his "friendly talks" with Briand well prepared, and while the records are not fully available, the documents for the later stages of his Foreign Office tenure show that at such occasions he hewed closely to the fundamentals of his program. There is no indication that at any time the Foreign Office was confused as to the nature or the direction of his personal negotiations.

Actually, there was little need for subtle negotiation with France or Germany about the major item of the British program at the Tenth Assembly. Both states welcomed the new British view of the value of the Optional Clause. The real difficulty came from the British Dominions. They were particularly concerned, as their attitude toward the Geneva

[49] For descriptions of Henderson at Geneva, see Hamilton, *Henderson*, pp. 319-323, 330; Temperley, *Whispering Gallery*, pp. 116-117; Slocombe, *Mirror to Geneva*, pp. 228-229.
[50] *Record of the Tenth Assembly*, sixth plenary meeting, September 5, 1929, p. 5.

Protocol had demonstrated earlier, that their signature should not involve them unnecessarily in continental quarrels and that intra-Imperial questions should be kept from the jurisdiction of the court. Henderson and his advisers worked hard in London and later at Geneva to achieve a compromise which might satisfy the Dominions. The solution was reached in the decision to reserve certain types of questions, even of a justiciable nature, from the province of compulsory arbitration.[51] Here again was another illustration of the complexity of the British position as the center of the empire on the one hand and as a part of the European system on the other.

In his speech to the Assembly on September 3, Ramsay MacDonald announced the intention of the British and the Dominion governments to sign the Optional Clause.[52] Henderson, a few days later, explained to the Assembly what he hoped to accomplish by this move. The British government, he pointed out, believed arbitration to be more likely to bring about a wise and just settlement of a dispute than any other method. It was the true alternative to war for the solution of international quarrels. Above all, it was important because of the new spirit it would bring to the relations between the governments of the world. "A nation which relies on arbitration and is ready to accept the verdict of an impartial judge," he declared, "does not rely on the use of armed force. Its national mind is turned in a new direction, and it is precisely in this new spirit which the practice of arbitration may induce that lies perhaps the most powerful single factor in bringing to the nations security from war." He emphasized that the signature of the Optional Clause was only a first step in the direction of real peace. On the basis of an expanded system of arbitration it would be possible to move ahead to the next step, the formulation of a general treaty of disarmament.[53]

Although he based his hopes on the development of substitutes for war and the consequent disarmament it might make possible, Henderson had some conception of the difficulties of the program. At the annual conference of the Labor party in October he rebuked the delegates who proposed immediate and complete British disarmament—disarmament by example—as the proper road to world peace. "We will not attempt that which is practically impossible," he warned. "The world will have

---

[51] *Survey of International Affairs, 1929*, p. 75; Dalton in *Political Quarterly*, II, 496. The reservations concerned intra-Imperial questions, disputes in which the parties had recourse to other means of settlement, disputes arising out of questions posed before British ratification (i.e. questions arising out of the peace treaties), and those in which one of the parties preferred to refer the case to the League Council first.

[52] *Record of the Tenth Assembly*, third plenary session, September 3, 1929, pp. 2-5.

[53] *ibid.*, seventh plenary session, September 6, 1929, pp. 5-6.

to be very much more advanced and human nature very much more perfect before you will be able to do without policing forces."[54] Such "policing forces," whatever they might have been, were clearly rather far removed from the sort of security arrangements the French insisted upon. Henderson, like other British Foreign Secretaries before him, was not convinced that the French reading of security was accurate. Unlike them, at least, he had a positive program for achieving it. His policy marked a significant change in attitude on the part of the British government. It might have succeeded if Europe had been favored with years of relative prosperity and quiet. It had little if any chance in the Europe of the 1930's.

At the Tenth Assembly, however, it would have been a prescient observer who could have predicted the cataclysm of the 1930's. The British position on the Optional Clause was almost symbolic of the changed atmosphere. The British plans for future development—Henderson's proposals for a reform of the Secretariat, Willie Graham's appeal for economic cooperation and for a tariff truce, plans to harmonize the League Covenant with the Pact of Paris—testified to the optimism at Geneva about the future. When its work was finished the Tenth Assembly appeared to have made a real start—certainly the most impressive since the Fifth Assembly of 1924—toward the imperative task of rebuilding the political stability of Europe.[55]

At the Tenth Assembly, Aristide Briand broached his tentative scheme for the formation of a European Federal Union. Couched in vague terms, it laid particular stress on the economic association of the European nations.[56] By the time Briand circulated his proposals to the European governments in May 1930, the emphasis had been changed to subordinate economic to political problems.[57] Although Henderson had assured Briand that he would give it his greatest interest, the British reaction to the scheme was not enthusiastic. A Foreign Office memorandum, circulated on May 30, analyzed the basis for criticism. It pointed out that the proposed federation might be regarded as hostile to the American or other continents and might weaken the political cooperation of Britain with other members of the Commonwealth. Above all, the European Union might become a rival of the League of Nations and thus adversely

[54] *Report of the Annual Conference of the Labour Party* (1929), pp. 215-216.
[55] F. P. Walters, *A History of the League of Nations* (2 vols., London, 1952), I, 430.
[56] *Record of the Tenth Assembly*, sixth plenary meeting, September 5, 1929, p. 6.
[57] "Mémorandum sur l'organisation d'un régime d'union fédérale européenne," in *British Documents*, 2nd series, I, 320.

affect its prestige and utility. While the memorandum recognized that Briand's plan could be construed as an attempt to stereotype the territorial *status quo*, it suggested that since Briand was a "good European" the sincerity of his desire for fuller European cooperation should be assumed. It proposed, therefore, that the plan be received with general sympathy and with a promise to give the French proposals the fullest consideration in consultation with the Dominions. At the same time, however, it suggested that Briand be made cognizant of the British criticism of the methods which he had proposed.[58] In somewhat amended form the memorandum was presented to the Cabinet in explanation of a proposed draft reply which was then approved.[59] The British note to France emphasized in particular that the European Union would set up new and independent international institutions as possible rivals of the League of Nations. It recommended that Briand submit his memorandum to the next Assembly for its consideration.[60] After a meeting of delegates from some twenty-seven European states, the plan was discussed at the Eleventh Assembly, approved in general terms, and referred to a Commission of Enquiry for European Union to draw up definite proposals. The action of the Assembly effectively pigeonholed the project. It has often been alleged that the action of the British government was the kiss of death for the Briand plan.[61] Actually, Henderson knew that Italy was opposed to the proposal and that Germany was cool.[62] It is possible that if it had been elaborated earlier there might have been some chance of a limited accomplishment. But by the fall of 1930, the project for a European federation, which offered no special concessions to Germany, was almost inevitably greeted with suspicion in revisionist circles. Whatever the attitude of the British government, the Briand plan had little prospect of success. From the point of view of Henderson's policy, the consistency of his approach to the problems of Europe is the significant thing. His coolness to the idea, despite his real confidence in Briand, was motivated, not only by the unique relations of Britain to the Dominions and the United States, but above all by his conception of the League as the central instrument for the promotion of real international cooperation.

[58] *British Documents*, 2nd series, I, 313, 330-331.
[59] *ibid.*, pp. 336-345.   [60] *ibid.*, pp. 345-347.
[61] Jacques Bardoux, *L'Ile et l'Europe, la politique anglaise, 1930-1932* (Paris, 1933), pp. 294-299; Jean-Felix Charvet, *L'Influence britannique dans la S. D. N. (Des origines de la S. D. N. jusqu'à nos jours)* (Paris, 1938), pp. 134-135.
[62] *British Documents*, 2nd series, I, 334 (Graham to Henderson, May 31, 1930) and 335 (Newton to Henderson, July 26, 1930). Newton's dispatch was received after the British note to France had been sent. But see, also, *ibid.*, pp. 324-326 (Rumbold to Henderson, May 28) for a conversation on the Briand plan with Brüning.

Henderson's conception of constructive British leadership was to co-operate in strengthening the League Covenant. This—and of course disarmament[63]—was at the heart of his approach. "We have always believed," he told the Eleventh Assembly, "that true security can only be obtained by a cooperative action through the machinery of the League. We are equally certain that this purpose can far more effectively be sought through measures designed to prevent the outbreak of war, rather than through measures designed to suppress war once it has begun.[64] He proposed accordingly to push on from the Optional Clause, in particular by harmonizing the League Covenant with the Pact of Paris and by signing the General Act of Arbitration, Conciliation, and Judicial Settlement.

The first of these measures was held to be necessary because of the "gap" in the Covenant which permitted members of the League to go to war after having fulfilled the requirements for delay. Since most states had accepted the Pact of Paris and thus presumably had repudiated the right of "private war," Henderson proposed to amend the Covenant so as to ban a right which was now obsolete.[65] This was not a move to do away with sanctions, as a discussion of the amendments in the Labor party's magazine was careful to point out. Acceptance of the new pledges, an article in the *Labour Magazine* declared, would imply acceptance of the obligation to enforce them. Most of the opposition to the draft amendments came from people who were really opposed to the principle of sanctions. "But it must be applied as loyally as any other principle of the Covenant, for it is an integral part of the whole edifice."[66] Despite Henderson's efforts the draft amendments were never accepted. What they would have accomplished, in any case, is difficult to see, for, as Lord Cecil later pointed out, war, when it did erupt, came each time in defiance of the League and not by creeping through the celebrated "gap" in the Covenant.[67]

With the General Act Henderson had more success. The Labor party was pledged to accede to it, but he moved slowly. Once again, it was the problem of the Dominions which posed the difficulties. In September

[63] See below §v.

[64] *Record of the Eleventh Assembly*, fourth plenary meeting, September 11, 1930, p. 3.

[65] *League of Nations Official Journal*, xi (February, 1930), 78-79. An attempt to work out an agreement between France and Britain to ensure the incorporation of the amendments into the Covenant foundered in the general failure to reconcile Franco-Italian differences at the London Naval Conference. Actually, the discussion of this issue revealed once again the difference between the British and the French concept of security. *British Documents*, 2nd series, I, 293-301.

[66] *Labour Magazine*, viii (April, 1930), 540.

[67] Cecil, *A Great Experiment*, pp. 204-205.

1930, he announced to the Assembly the British intention to sign, but indicated that the government wished to proceed in close accord with the members of the Commonwealth.[68] The subsequent Imperial Conference finally reached agreement—except for South Africa—but, as in the case of the Optional Clause, insisted on the usual reservations. Henderson was anxious for accession. The Optional Clause and the General Act were in his view the prelude to effective disarmament. By early 1931 the date for the Disarmament Conference had been set and he himself had been chosen its president. He was convinced, he told the House of Commons, that at the Conference "nations will be prepared to reduce and limit their national forces in proportion to the measure of their confidence in the constructive machinery of peace. If they are convinced that Governments have renounced war, not in name only, but in real intention, as shown by their willingness to support the League proposals for peace, they will be more ready to dispense with the machinery of war."[69] Accession to the General Act came at the Sixty-third Council on May 21, 1931. With the British signature virtually the whole of Henderson's program that had any chance of success had been carried out. Now, as he saw it, he had laid the foundations for a substantial measure of disarmament.

V

Disarmament had of course been in the forefront of his program from the beginning. At the Tenth Assembly, the question had been shelved pending the results of the naval conversations among the major Powers. The London Naval Conference was largely Ramsay MacDonald's show. Henderson participated, but his role was not decisive. He looked upon a naval agreement, in much the same way that he considered his steps at Geneva, as one of the necessary preludes to a

[68] *Record of the Eleventh Assembly*, fourth plenary meeting, p. 3.
[69] Parliamentary Debates: Commons, 5th series, CCXLIX, 825-831. Henderson was clearly most concerned with convincing France of British intention to fulfill the obligations implied in his program. A draft declaration, drawn up at the London Naval Conference, had pledged Britain (and France) to make fullest use of the Covenant (including Article 16), the Optional Clause, the General Act, and to work to close the "gap" in the Covenant. It had included a declaration that "Our Governments are convinced that this declaration will dissipate all uncertainty regarding their common intention fully to carry out, should need arise, the duty which the Covenant of the League of Nations lays upon them; and that by so doing it will effectively help to prevent any situation arising in which, as the result of the failure of preventive action, the question for the community of nations would be no longer the maintenance but the reestablishment of peace." The declaration was never issued, but Henderson's subsequent policy was in part at least directed to assure the French of British intention to carry out the provisions of the Covenant in order to promote French acceptance of disarmament. *British Documents*, 2nd series, I, 300-301.

successful world disarmament conference. The French position at London disturbed him. The European situation, he insisted, had improved in recent years. Germany was a member of the League. She was to be subjected to even firmer control since he and Briand had decided to work toward incorporating the Kellogg Pact into the machinery of the League. Moreover, the Optional Clause had now been ratified. All in all, he professed not to understand the caution of the French delegates.[70] But European agreement was not possible. Although the United States, Japan, and Great Britain signed an accord which provided little in the way of naval disarmament, France and Italy could not see eye to eye on the Italian demand for theoretical parity with France. After the Conference adjourned, Henderson worked to bring the two together. As at London, he continued to deprecate the French attitude. Tyrrell warned him not to undercut Briand's position in France, for "you will achieve more by cooperation with Briand than you will by any appeal to Caesar, or in other words, public opinion."[71] Henderson acted on the same assumption, though he was later to comment that the underlying difficulty in reaching an agreement was that France was evidently determined to effect a rapid and substantial increase in naval armament at a time when all other Powers were attempting to make reductions.[72] By that time, it should be noted, the German touchstone of French policy was as real as the Italian rivalry.[73] For a brief moment in March 1931, it appeared that real progress had been made. The story of the "Bases of an Agreement" and their subsequent fate is well enough known and the recently published documents do no more than fill in some of the details of Henderson's single-mindedness on the issue. Throughout the complicated negotiations his main purpose was to facilitate the holding of the Disarmament Conference. He insisted to Grandi and especially to Briand that a compromise was essential before the Preparatory Commission could complete its task with any hope of success.[74] Despite his efforts, however, when the Disarmament Conference met in 1932 the French and Italian governments were as far apart on the issue as they had ever been.

His diplomatic pressure on France and Italy was paralleled by his more public exhortations. On the issue of disarmament he came as close

[70] *British Documents*, 2nd series, I, 213-214.

[71] *ibid.*, pp. 390 (Tyrrell to Henderson, July 11, 1930) and 456 (Tyrrell to Henderson, February 20, 1931).

[72] *ibid.*, II, 417 (Henderson to Lindsay, May 3, 1931).

[73] See, for example, Vansittart to Rumbold, December 20, 1930, *ibid.*, I, 544.

[74] *ibid.*, pp. 359-360 (Henderson to Graham, May 7, 1930) and 401-402 (Henderson to Tyrrell, October 1, 1930).

to eloquence as was ever possible for him. Beginning with the meeting of the League Assembly in September 1930, he joined the German campaign for a rapid termination of preparatory work and for calling the long-delayed Disarmament Conference. Even if his reports from Germany had not documented the dangerous flaring of nationalist impatience, the position of the German representatives at Geneva testified to the German temper. But Henderson, instead of reassessing the bases of his policy, continued to hope that Germany might be appeased by adequate concessions. He lectured the Eleventh Assembly on the long delay in fulfilling the intentions of the Covenant. Its authors, he declared, never believed that international cooperation could succeed if national armaments remained unrestricted and if armament competition revived. Article 8 contained quite definite pledges for a general reduction and limitation of national forces. Britain had undertaken significant new obligations, but was determined to go no further until disarmament became a reality. "The pace is slow," he warned, "and the peoples of the world are growing impatient and doubtful, in many cases, of our good faith."[75] At the Council meeting the following January he took issue with the growing certainty of the French leaders that the changing temper in Germany posed a real threat that must be met. "It may be true," he declared, "that anxiety and fears do exist. But what I want to ask is this: In how great a measure is this anxiety, this fear, the result of the armaments that now exist? How far is it the result of the uncertainties as to whether war can be prevented by the League of Nations?" Given disarmament, the League could enforce the peace. No government, however powerful, could then flout it and violate the obligations it had undertaken.[76] Finally, in November the draft convention of the Preparatory Commission, vague as it was, was adopted. The date for the Disarmament Conference was set for February 1932. For the next year, Henderson continued to pin his hopes on what it would accomplish, despite the rapid deterioration of the European situation.

Henderson's disarmament policy depended to a large extent on his assessment of the German situation as the shadow of the depression lengthened in Europe. From the beginning, the German response to his program of appeasement was not encouraging. The evacuation of the Rhineland, far from being welcomed with enthusiasm, was a signal for raising other demands. Dr. Curtius, who had suc-

[75] *Record of the Eleventh Assembly*, fourth plenary meeting, September 11, 1930, pp. 3-4.
[76] *League of Nations Official Journal*, XII (February 1931), pp. 159-160.

ceeded Stresemann at the Ministry of Foreign Affairs, almost immediately brought up the issue of the Saar.[77] In August, Herr Treviranus, a Cabinet minister, created something of a panic by the incendiary speech in which he brought to the fore the question of the eastern frontier. This German intransigence was not unanticipated in London. In May, Sir Robert Vansittart pointed out in a memorandum that all the German objectives had not been achieved by the Hague settlement. These he defined as the reestablishment of Germany as a world Power, the *Anschluss* with Austria, rearmament so as to obtain at least parity with Poland, and a drastic modification of the German-Polish frontier. These objectives must be assumed to be "inevitable," whatever the urgency with which they were pressed.[78] Even earlier, a memorandum from the Chief of the Imperial General Staff had described in some detail the German contravention of the military terms of the Versailles Treaty. But the report concluded that the German army was not a menace to the peace of Europe. Germany was rather trying secretly to lay the foundations for a large expansion at some future date, when the political situation might permit it.[79]

In the light of such information, Henderson apparently acted on the assumption that he was racing for time against the extreme elements in Germany. On occasion he could be firm. When Curtius sounded out Rumbold, toward the end of the year, on a possible moratorium or revision of the Young Plan, Henderson quashed the idea. Pointing out that the depression had probably hit England harder than Germany, he warned Curtius that to raise the question would frighten foreign investors from Germany and, by inflaming nationalist hopes in Germany and fears elsewhere, might cause serious tension in Europe.[80] Perhaps he occasionally shared the feeling of Rumbold, who had wryly commented: "It is an unattractive feature of the German character to display little gratitude for favours received, but when the receipt of favours is followed up by fresh demands, there are grounds for feeling impatient."[81] But even after the ominous revelation of Nazi strength in the election of September 1930, Henderson hewed to his main course. He remained convinced that by granting concessions to Germany—as in his disarmament program—he might strengthen the moderate elements and preserve their collaboration in working toward European pacification. "The fall of the Brüning Government," he explained to Rumbold in February 1931, "might easily have far-reaching detrimental effects on interna-

---

[77] *British Documents*, 2nd series, I, 489.   [78] *ibid.*, p. 501, note 5.
[79] *ibid.*, pp. 598-603.   [80] *ibid.*, pp. 536-538.   [81] *ibid.*, p. 486.

tional relationships. If, therefore, there is a real danger of its not being able to weather the storm to which it is likely to be exposed in the near future, it ought, I consider, to be the policy of His Majesty's Government to give it such support and encouragement as they properly can, in order to fortify its position."[82]

The German government, pressed as it was by its domestic critics, did not make Henderson's position any easier. Its growing impatience on the disarmament issue had been apparent for some time. In February, he instructed Rumbold to tell Curtius quite plainly that he expected full cooperation in preparing for the Disarmament Conference. He denounced the view that Germany, being virtually disarmed, had no role to fill beyond that of complainant. Curtius was to be warned that it was essential to restrain the responsible leaders of German opinion from provocative utterance and action and to try to create "that atmosphere of international loyalty and confidence in which alone the conference can hope to succeed."[83]

How well Curtius heeded his advice was revealed in March, when the project of an Austro-German customs union burst upon the European scene. To France and the Little Entente the customs union seemed a clear portent of the *Anschluss* that had been prohibited at Paris and again in the Austrian Reconstruction Protocol of 1922. Their reaction was agitated and immediate. While Henderson refused to go along with a joint *démarche* at Berlin and Vienna, he was seriously disturbed. It is a striking misreading of the implications of his position to write that he "gave no signs of disapproval of the customs union."[84] He received the project with "reserve," but he made his attitude clear in his instructions to his representatives at Vienna and Berlin. His first reaction was that if nothing were done to calm existing fears the task of those who were anxious for the Disarmament Conference to meet under the most favorable circumstances would be seriously compromised. He instructed Rumbold and Phipps to emphasize that the position of Briand in France had become extremely difficult, and that his influence "in controlling more extreme tendencies among his own countrymen" would be unquestionably affected. He appealed to the two governments to give the League Council the opportunity to judge whether the treaty was compatible with the Protocol of 1922 before proceeding further.[85] At Paris,

[82] *ibid.*, p. 559.   [83] *ibid.*, pp. 554-555.
[84] Tucker, *Attitude of Labour Party*, p. 125.
[85] *British Documents*, 2nd series, II, 12-13. In the House of Commons on March 30, Henderson repeated almost verbatim the instructions, omitting only the reference to Briand's position. Parliamentary Debates: Commons, 5th series, CCL, 717-720.

where he had gone for a meeting of the Organization Committee of the Commission of Enquiry for European Union, he quickly found that Briand appreciated his intent. On the evening of March 25 a statement was issued from the British embassy indicating that the two Foreign Ministers were in consultation and announcing that Henderson would ask the Council to take up the question at its May meeting.[86] Meanwhile, although both the German and Austrian Foreign Ministers had replied that in their view there was no incompatibility with the 1922 commitment, Phipps was reporting from Vienna that the Austrians were showing signs of wanting to back down.[87] In the event, both accepted the appeal to the Council, despite the fact that Germany kept insisting that the proposal was really an implementation of the Briand plan for European Union. Henderson, for his part, sat tight. Eventually, the Council took up the question and in turn requested an advisory opinion from the Permanent Court of International Justice. By the time a split opinion unfavorable to the customs union was handed down on September 5, Henderson was out of office and the Austrian government, under severe financial pressure from France, had declared its intention not to proceed.[88] The entire incident had embittered the European atmosphere, already tense with the strain of the economic crisis, and was an ominous prelude to the Disarmament Conference. That Conference, it is clear, was Henderson's main concern in the matter. He resented the method chosen by Germany to foster economic union and felt strongly that he must protect Briand's position in France. If his public position was cautious and legalistic, it was because he judged such tactics to be best suited to keep the way open for cooperation in disarmament. He did not want the German government, desperate for a success in foreign affairs to silence its domestic critics, to lose face. He believed that his proposal gave it a way out while at the same time it would satisfy opinion in France. That he was not entirely successful was almost entirely a function of the deteriorating economic situation in Central Europe and above all in Germany.

The summer months of 1931 were taken up, in large part, with the problem of the financial difficulties of Germany. The complicated negotiations, highlighted by President Hoover's proposal of a moratorium on intergovernmental debts and culminating in the unsuccessful London Conference of July 20 to 23, need only be mentioned, since in the final

[86] *Survey of International Affairs, 1931*, pp. 305-307; *British Documents*, 2nd series, II, 17-18.
[87] *ibid.*, p. 31.　　　　[88] *Survey of International Affairs*, 1931, pp. 318-321.

reckoning their results were negative. MacDonald played a much more prominent role than Henderson in the discussions and in any case Great Britain was hardly in a position to be of much real assistance. Henderson, however, continued to be optimistic. As late as July 30, after he and MacDonald had made a quick visit to Berlin, he wrote to Briand that the Brüning government was receiving an increasing amount of support at home for its handling of the very serious financial situation.[89] Actually, he seemed as much concerned, during this period, to persuade the Germans to give up plans to construct a second pocket battleship.[90] More and more, disarmament had become the touchstone of his policy.

By the time the Disarmament Conference met in February 1932, the foundations for its work had long since been eaten away. In the face of the deterioration of the German situation, it would have been difficult to persuade France to reduce her military superiority except in return for rigid guarantees of collective support to compensate for the sacrifice. Henderson's policy in part had aimed to provide such guarantees, but even his position was not entirely satisfactory to France. When the National government took over, the greater reluctance of Great Britain to make such commitments became quickly apparent. In any case, it is not easy to see how the triangular struggle between Britain, France, and Germany could have ended otherwise than in failure. The German Nazis and their Nationalist allies were not really concerned with disarmament. By 1932 they were well on their way to power. A compromise on disarmament might have permitted Brüning to hang on a little longer. But he too was committed to a demand for equality which the French could not accept. The disintegration of the German political system in the solvent of the economic depression was the final precipitant of the collapse of the disarmament dream.

To recapitulate the history of the Disarmament Conference would have no purpose. But a word on Henderson's role is necessary. The meeting of some sixty-odd nations at Geneva should have been the fulfillment of his career. Instead, it came as a personal tragedy. He had been elected President in May and was grimly determined to take the chair even though the collapse of the Labor government had driven him from the Foreign Office. From the beginning, his position was impossible. The bitterness of the political cleavage at home was reflected in the hostility of the British delegation. He himself was seriously ill. But he kept doggedly to his task, never missing a meeting of the General Commis-

[89] *British Documents*, 2nd series, II, 245.
[90] See, for example, *ibid.*, pp. 115, 119, 161.

sion, working stubbornly with the Bureau, endeavoring by sheer force of will to extract an agreement that had become patently impossible. By exhortation and persuasion he attempted to make up for the fact that he no longer had the authority and bargaining power of a Foreign Secretary. He had no other weapon at his disposal.

The sheer horror of any future war made it inconceivable to him that a treaty would not be achieved. In his speech at the opening of the Conference he elaborated the familiar arguments for disarmament—the expense of huge military establishments, the insecurity caused by arms competition, and the rest. Almost passionately he pleaded: "The world wants disarmament. The world needs disarmament. We have it in our power to help fashion the pattern of future history. Behind all the technical complexities regarding man-power, gun-power, tonnage, categories, and the like, is the well-being of mankind, the future of our developing civilisation."[91] But behind the technical complexities also was the growing reality of the Franco-German antagonism. The French demand for security, the German claim to equality added up to a dilemma for which the Conference had no solution.

The almost interminable haggling of the first six months of the Conference set the tone for its labors. By July, all that had been accomplished was the drafting of a general resolution as a proposed basis for further negotiation. When the resolution was presented, the German delegate, Herr Nadolny, made it clear that he could not accept a formula which made no provision for equality of armaments.[92] Henderson did not conceal his disappointment with the resolution. He tried, however, to salvage something from the wreckage. Whatever its defects, he argued, it would put the Conference on the right road to disarmament. Eventually, success would come and he pledged himself to lose no time in getting on with the task. Nevertheless, Germany, along with the USSR, voted against the resolution.[93] Although it was carried, the fate of the Conference was clear. Thereafter, from the first German withdrawal through her final departure on October 14, 1933, its work went on in a vacuum of unreality. The triumph of the National Socialists should have been proof enough of the failure of its efforts. But Henderson, at least, continued to hope against hope. He literally grasped at every straw. In May 1933, he seized upon President Roosevelt's proposals to the Conference to suggest a compromise which might be ac-

---

[91] *League of Nations, Records of the Conference for the Reduction and Limitation of Armaments*, series A, Plenary Meetings, I, 40-47.
[92] *ibid.*, series B, Minutes of the General Commission, II, 186-188.
[93] *ibid.*, pp. 204-205.

ceptable to Germany.[94] The next month he was in London, trying to convince the heads of governments assembled for the World Monetary and Economic Conference to break the deadlock at Geneva. Again, he had little success. A sketch of his activities at London is surely one of the tragic portraits of this period. John W. Wheeler Bennett wrote: ". . . there have been few more pathetic figures than that of Mr. Henderson sitting alone in one of the lounges in the delegates' *foyer* and gazing enviously at the milling groups of representatives who surged up and down the floor and cast not a glance at the lonely, rubicund, kindly figure in the corner. On the outskirts of these scrimmages hung, like a half-back, Mr. Henderson's faithful Achates, M. Aghnides, Director of the Disarmament Secretariat, who spared no effort to 'collar' delegates as they broke away from their groups and to transform the picture of Mr. Henderson from 'Solitaire' into 'Conversation Piece.' But even when M. Aghnides' efforts were crowned with success, his prey would vanish from his clutches into another group before they had crossed the brief distance to Mr. Henderson's sofa."[95]

Nevertheless, a little later, he was making a swing around the circle of the major European countries to seek a way out of the impasse. He brought back to the Conference only a greater awareness of the real difficulties to be faced, though he still hoped they might be overcome.[96] Even after the final German break he continued his efforts. He met with the Bureau and various committees in 1934 and 1935, but the Conference was finished, although its formal existence dragged on almost without end. The award of the Nobel Peace Prize in 1935 must have been scant recompense for his labor. When he died on October 20, 1935, the world which had come into being furnished a bitter testimony to the failure of his hopes.

VI

The temptation is great to let the final tragedy of Henderson's efforts obscure the full picture of what he tried to achieve. His last-ditch stand for disarmament by exhortation has captured the imagination of admirers who have seen him as the archetype of the aspiration of all men for peace—and of critics who have summed him up as a sentimentalist, if not a well-intentioned fool. But seen as a whole, as we have tried to see it here, his program comes into a different focus. More than most states-

[94] *ibid.*, II, 462-464.
[95] John W. Wheeler Bennett, *The Disarmament Deadlock*, p. 164, quoted in William E. Rappard, *The Quest for Peace since the World War* (Cambridge, 1940), pp. 459-460.
[96] *League of Nations, Records of the Conference for the Reduction and Limitation of Armaments*, series C, Minutes of the Bureau, II, 178-179.

men in British public life, he had a surprising conception of the issues posed by the catchwords of disarmament and security. He accepted the thesis that it was necessary to strike at the tensions caused by the post-war settlement in order to prepare the way for a viable international order. But at a time when the British people felt themselves secure and most British leaders were unwilling to make any sizable commitments in Europe, he had some sense of the real difficulties faced by the bene-ficiaries of the Versailles system on the continent. While he was perhaps never willing to go as far in the direction of explicit military guarantees as the French might have wished, he collaborated fully in trying to erect a genuine structure of international guarantees through the League of Nations in order to make disarmament possible. He realized that armed forces would be necessary, but he hoped that they might be re-duced as security came more and more to rest upon the collective action of the League. His policy of appeasement, the development of the League, and then disarmament came closer to being one of effective col-lective security before 1930 than any within the realm of serious possi-bility. Seen in the light of the 1920's, it was a thoughtful, perceptive, and practicable line of approach. It is tempting, also, to commit the cardinal sin and to speculate, unhistorically, on what might have been if the world had not plunged into economic disaster. Temptation aside, the cataclysm of 1930 and 1931 turned a practical program of action into a shambles. By 1932, all the basic assumptions of the campaign which was supposedly to culminate in the progressive reduction of armaments had disappeared. It was now time for rigid resistance to the demands of an importunate German nationalism—and time also for equally firm support of France and the European order. The threat to the stability of Europe itself was too great to be ignored. In such a pattern, there was little place for the chimera of disarmament by international agreement. To change a way of thinking overnight, however, was difficult, and there were few who saw the issues clearly. If Henderson did not have the insight of a Winston Churchill after 1932, he had at least, in the brief hopeful era before the decade of nemesis, opened up to Europe some of the avenues for a constructive approach to the problem of an enduring peace. That was the significance of his role in international affairs, and this, rather than his tragic part at the Disarmament Conference, should be the balance in which to weigh his diplomatic career.

11

Maxim Litvinov

BY HENRY L. ROBERTS

MAXIM LITVINOV, Peoples Commissar for Foreign Affairs from 1930 to 1939, was undoubtedly the Soviet diplomat most widely and familiarly known in the West during the interwar period. At international conferences and at sessions of the League of Nations his chubby and unproletarian figure radiated an aura of robust and businesslike common sense that was in striking contrast to the enigmatic brutality of the Politburo or the conspiratorial noisiness of the Comintern. Although he was an old revolutionary—he was born Meyer Wallach in 1876 and like Lenin, six years his senior, and Stalin, three years his junior, he assumed a *nom de guerre* while dodging the Tsarist police—to him perhaps more than to any other single person may be traced the impression that revolutionary Russia was returning to the family of nations and could be counted upon as a force for stability and peace. Indeed, the most perplexing problem in Litvinov's career is that of the relation of his role to the totality of aims and intentions of the Soviet regime.

This problem was most sharply posed in the blatant contrast between Litvinov's appeals after 1933 for collective security against Nazi Germany and the provisions of the German-Soviet agreement of August 23, 1939. Was Litvinov really striving for the determined cooperation of the peacefully inclined Powers or was Lord Lothian right in his belief that the ulterior aim of Litvinov's policy was "to maintain discord in Europe?"[1] Is it correct to assume that there was a distinctive "Litvinov policy"[2] or was his role throughout an essentially subordinate one in the Soviet hierarchy?[3] Were there important differences between Lit-

---

[1] See his speech of April 2, 1936, in *Germany and the Rhineland* (London, Royal Institute of International Affairs, 1936), p. 55.

[2] "Soviet foreign policy between 1929 and May 1939 followed the pattern of Litvinov's mind more than of his chief's." Louis Fischer, *Men and Politics* (New York, 1941), p. 127.

[3] Max Beloff, reflecting on his study of Soviet foreign policy, commented, in 1950:

vinov's outlook and that of the Politburo? If so, how did he survive the great purges which decimated the Foreign Commissariat; if not, why was he so abruptly retired in May 1939? Finally, did his retirement represent a real turning point in Soviet policy or was it only a tactical shift, the importance of which should not be overrated?

In attempting to come to closer grips with these questions—their definitive resolution seems impossible in the absence of evidence from the Soviet archives—this paper will consider in turn three topics: (1) the content of Litvinov's diplomatic policy, so far as it can be ascertained from his public pronouncements and recorded conversations; (2) the connection of this policy with the aims of the Politburo; (3) the relations between Litvinov, the Foreign Commissariat, and the Bolshevist high command.

I

Although it may be a matter of temperament one can detect a definite and largely consistent flavor in Litvinov's diplomatic attitude and behavior. Never the firebrand or the theoretician, he was always valued for his efficiency and practical abilities. Before the 1905 Revolution, the nickname Papasha (little father) was given to him by party comrades. In 1918, when hopes of general revolution were running high, when Chicherin was suggesting that the League of Nations be based on the expropriation of the capitalists of all countries and was intimating to President Wilson that the latter's government was to be replaced by a Council of Peoples Commissars,[4] Litvinov, writing to Wilson two months later, struck a quite different note. He attempted to explain the Red Terror as a defensive measure, protested against the intervention as leading only to the final devastation of Russia, and concluded: "The dictatorship of toilers and producers is not an aim in itself, but the means of building up a new social system under which useful work and equal rights would be provided for all citizens, irrespective of the class to which they had formerly belonged. One may believe in this ideal or not, but it surely gives no justification for sending foreign troops to fight against it, or for arming and supporting classes interested in the restoration of the old system of exploitation of man by man."[5]

One cannot be sure, of course, whether Litvinov's moderation was

---

"It is probable, too, that I did not lay enough stress upon the essentially subordinate nature of Litvinov's role." "Soviet Foreign Policy, 1929-1941: Some Notes," *Soviet Studies* (Oxford), II (October 1950), 127.

[4] See his note to Wilson of October 24, 1918 in Degras, I, 112-120.

[5] Telegram from Litvinov to Wilson, December 24, 1918, *ibid.*, pp. 129-133.

merely adroit diplomatic address—it was clearly to the advantage of the struggling regime to persuade the Western Powers to give up their intervention—or whether it actually reflects the absence of revolutionary expectation and belligerence. Louis Fischer reported Litvinov as saying to him some years later, "The prospect of world revolution disappeared on November 11, 1918."[6] In any event, this tone of unrevolutionary reasonableness remained a permanent trade mark of Litvinov's dealings with the outside world.

During the years when Litvinov served as Chicherin's second in the Narkomindel, the principal goals of Soviet diplomacy were, after the flurry of revolution and civil war, to achieve recognition and to increase the security of the Soviet Union by means of treaties of neutrality and nonaggression. The reason for these goals is evident and requires no discussion. Less evident is the Soviet purpose in entering the League discussions concerning disarmament, discussions which first brought Litvinov's name to general prominence.

The initial Soviet attitude on the subject of war and peace is stated in the Narkomindel's Appeal to the Toiling, Oppressed and Exhausted Peoples of Europe, of December 19, 1917: "We do not attempt to conceal the fact that we do not consider the existing capitalist Governments capable of making a democratic peace. The revolutionary struggle of the toiling masses against the existing Governments can alone bring Europe nearer to such a peace. Its full realization can only be guaranteed by the victorious proletarian revolution in all capitalist countries."[7] As a logical consequence the League of Nations was viewed as a "mere mask, designed to deceive the broad masses, for the aggressive aims of the imperialist policy of certain Great Powers or their vassals."[8] Despite this hostile attitude, Litvinov appeared at the Preparatory Commission of the Disarmament Conference to propose "the complete abolition of all land, marine, and air forces."

Litvinov never denied these Soviet views concerning peace under capitalism. In 1922 he granted that the present social-economic structures of the majority of countries made the removal of the possibility of armed international conflict "unthinkable."[9] In 1927 he reiterated the Soviet Union's lack of confidence in the readiness and capability of capitalist countries to destroy the system of war between nations.[10] Nevertheless,

[6] Fischer, *Men and Politics*, p. 127. Litvinov's American biographer, Arthur Upham Pope, states that as early as 1920 Litvinov had declared that the project of world revolution was impossible. (*Maxim Litvinoff*, New York, 1943, p. 334).
[7] Degras, I, 19.   [8] *ibid.*, I, 381.
[9] *The Soviet Union and Peace* (New York, n.d.), p. 117.   [10] *ibid.*, p. 134.

this fundamental skepticism did not, in Litvinov's view, preclude the possibility of negotiating for disarmament. On November 6, 1930, he made this point quite clearly: "To us, the representatives of the Soviet Union, and exponents of definite socio-economic theories, the impossibility of removing the politico-economic antagonisms of capitalist society, and hence the ultimate inevitability of war, is perfectly clear. We believe, however, or we should not be here, that the danger of war might be considerably diminished, or made comparatively remote, by some measure of real disarmament."[11] It would appear that something which is ultimately inevitable may, however, be reduced as an imminent likelihood by appropriate action.

But was the Soviet proposal for complete disarmament such an appropriate action? Did it represent an effort, as Litvinov put it, "to find a common language" with the other Powers? It is easy to understand the embarrassed and irritable reaction of the other nations, which were trying—without notable success—to fit disarmament into a more general program encompassing security and arbitration. But to the charge that the Soviet scheme could not guarantee security or destroy international distrust, Litvinov simply answered that he was not offering a universal remedy ("We cannot recommend you any such panacea, for we know you would not entertain it for a moment.").[12]

The other Powers also had suspicions, though they were reluctant to express them, that the real intent of the Soviets was to weaken other states militarily and increase the effectiveness of the Communist weapons of insurrection and subversion. To this charge Litvinov replied with a mixture of frankness and disingenuousness. He stated that the Soviet government had no intention of participating with any other government in working out questions "regarding the class war or the struggle against revolution," and asked caustically if the purpose of armaments was to put down possible revolution. He also gave the customary Soviet denial of any responsibility for the actions of the Comintern.

A more serious doubt about the sincerity of the Soviet disarmament proposal arises from the basic premises of Leninism. The argument has been advanced that the Soviets by their own theory could not be advocates of disarmament: True peace is achievable only in a classless and stateless world. Such a world cannot come about by a process of peaceful evolution, but involves the establishment of the dictatorship of the proletariat. This dictatorship explicitly rests on force, of which the Red

[11] *The Soviet's Fight for Disarmament* (New York, n.d.), p. 34.
[12] *The Soviet Union and Peace*, pp. 188-189.

Army is, equally explicitly, a vital element. Hence, complete disarmament would be, for the Soviets, a "suicidal act."[13] This argument, however, is not wholly conclusive since the Communist response would be that their analysis and consequent tactics were based on the real nature of modern imperialist states. If these states were to prove capable of overcoming their own nature by the act of disarmament, then the Soviet Union could likewise disarm the Red army. Such indeed was the implication in Litvinov's report to the Fifteenth Congress of the Russian Communist party: "If the capitalist governments doubt our sincerity, they have a simple means of proving it. This means is their adherence to our programme. Let them decide on this. If they do not do this, if they cannot do this, if they do not wish to do this, then, before the whole world, against their will, they testify to the fact that a proposal for full disarmament and abolition of war can emanate only from the Soviet Government; that it can be accepted and executed only when the Soviet system has been adopted by all the countries of the world, when their policies and principles will, of course, be at one with those by which the ussr is guided."[14]

In retrospect the real criticism to be made of Litvinov's stand on disarmament in the 1920's is not that it was insincere propaganda but that by viewing the world in the black and white of Communism versus Capitalist Imperialism it misrepresented the significance of the relations between the non-Communist Powers, and reduced them to the sinful bickerings of reprobates.[15] By making the sweeping generalization that "economic competition is the true cause of war" it falsely placed the issue of security, which could not be separated from disarmament, on an all-or-nothing basis.

With such an outlook collective security was, of course, impossible. In 1924 Chicherin had said: "The Soviet Government therefore rejects any plan for an international organization which implies the possibility of measures of constraint being exercised by any international authority whatsoever against a particular State. . . . In the present international situation, it is impossible in most cases to say which party is the aggressor. Neither the entry into foreign territory nor the scale of war preparations can be regarded as satisfactory criteria. . . . The Soviet Government con-

[13] See T. A. Taracouzio, *War and Peace in Soviet Diplomacy* (New York, 1940), pp. 266-276, for an able expression of this argument.

[14] *The Soviet Union and Peace*, p. 162.

[15] In his report to the Fifteenth Congress Litvinov said: "It may be said that on all questions considered by the Commission, a clear sharp line was drawn between us and the other delegates. It was a case of *we* and *they*. And this is as it should be."

siders, therefore, that it is absolutely impossible to adopt the system of
deciding which State is the aggressor in the case of each conflict and
making definite consequences depend upon such decision."[16] In 1928
Litvinov expressed somewhat the same view: "Owing to the lack of
exact criteria as to what constitutes an offensive and what a defensive
war, the system of regional guarantee pacts based upon mutual assistance . . . may end in something perilously akin to the prewar system
of alliances and other military and political combinations."[17]

Even the innocuous Kellogg Pact was regarded with deep suspicion.
Chicherin, in August 1928, flatly termed it "an organic part of the preparation for war against the USSR." Litvinov, too, intimated that the
proposal to prohibit war as an instrument of national policy implied the
possibility of war as an instrument for the defence of "civilization"
against "barbarism"—i.e. against the Soviet Union.[18] Nevertheless, after
having criticized its origins, its omissions, and its reservations, Litvinov
not only announced that the USSR would subscribe to the pact but then
turned it to advantage by achieving a regional reaffirmation of its terms
through the Litvinov Protocol, signed by the Soviet Union and most
of its Western neighbors, in February 1929. The Protocol, however,
represented "negative security"; it was not a step toward positive cooperative action. When, in 1929, the United States government attempted to invoke the Kellogg Pact in the Russian-Chinese dispute in
Manchuria, Litvinov brusquely rejected all efforts at diplomatic intervention and declared that the Pact did not provide any one of its
signatories with the function of being its guardian. Clearly, he was not
thinking of collective security at this point.

In July 1930, Chicherin, who had been in ill health for some years,
was retired, and Litvinov became chief of the Narkomindel. It is generally agreed that the relations between the two men were far from
friendly. Their temperaments clashed, each was suspicious of the other's
intentions, and Litvinov, who, despite his amiable appearance, was not
an easy person to get on with, appears to have been not overly scrupulous
in his ambitions to become Foreign Commissar.[19]

[16] Degras, I, 432-433.
[17] *The Soviet Union and Peace*, p. 167.
[18] Louis Fischer (*Men and Politics*, pp. 88-89) states that neither Litvinov nor Chicherin really believed that the Soviet Union was threatened with attack in 1927-1928.
Litvinov is quoted as saying, "That was merely idle gossip here of some people and the
press. . . . It is wrong to suppose, as many of us do, that Russia is the center of all
international affairs. . . ."
[19] See A. Barmine, *Memoirs of a Soviet Diplomat* (London, 1938), pp. 217-
218.

With regard to a new course in foreign policy, Litvinov, on July 25, 1930, informed correspondents that his appointment did not imply any change, not only because he had been for ten years a close associate of Chicherin's but because, under the dictatorship of the proletariat, foreign policy was determined by the will of the working masses and hence not subject to fluctuations.[20] Nevertheless, the German ambassador in Moscow, Dirksen, felt, or so he related twenty years later, that his task had become more difficult because Litvinov was not a really convinced adherent of the Rapallo policy but gave it only lip service.[21] Dirksen went on to say, however, that Litvinov did not really deviate from the German orientation until the Nazi seizure of power gave him the perhaps not unhoped for opportunity to be one of the first to abandon the Rapallo connection.

In fact, it was not his new post as Foreign Commissar but rather developments abroad between 1931 and 1933 which led Litvinov to a new course. The process was gradual, but several stages may be observed.

The Soviet Union continued its policy of signing neutrality and non-aggression pacts with its neighbors. Treaties were made with Turkey, Lithuania, Iran, and Afghanistan between 1925 and 1927. A new treaty with Afghanistan was signed on June 24, 1931. Then, in September 1931 Japan launched its attack on Manchuria. On January 21, 1932, the Soviet Union and Finland signed a treaty which resembled its predecessors, but included a significant new clause: "Should either High Contracting Party resort to aggression against a third Power, the other High Contracting Party may denounce the present treaty without notice." This clause appeared in all subsequent Soviet nonaggression treaties up to but definitely not including the pact with Germany of August 1939.[22]

If this double negative—denouncing a nonaggression pact—be considered a positive step, it may be concluded that this initial move toward collective security, at least by indirection, was stimulated by the first overt aggression of the 1930's.

Litvinov, however, still challenged the possibility of improving international relations except by the path of disarmament. On February 11, 1932, at the Disarmament Conference he declared: "Security against

---

[20] M. Litvinov, *Vneshniaia politika* SSSR (Moscow, 1937), p. 59.

[21] Herbert von Dirksen, *Moskau, Tokio, London: Erinnerungen und Betrachtungen zu 20 Jahre deutscher Aussenpolitik, 1919-1939* (Stuttgart, 1950), pp. 94-95. Dirksen also commented: "Although he [Litvinov] almost passionately denied any deviation from the pure Rapallo doctrine, his sympathies were with Great Britain, where he had passed the years of his exile and met his wife. So he had to be earnestly admonished from time to time when he was disposed to deviate from the correct faith to the Western heresy."

[22] Such pacts were signed with Estonia, Latvia, Poland, and France in 1932, and with Italy in 1933.

war must be created. This security can never be achieved by roundabout ways, but only by the direct way of total general disarmament. This is no communist slogan. The Soviet delegation knows that the triumph of socialistic principles, removing the causes giving rise to armed conflicts, is the only absolute guarantee of peace. So long, however, as these principles prevail only in one-sixth of the world, there is only one means of organizing security against war, and that is total and general disarmament."[23]

A year later, on February 6, 1933—that is, after Hitler had come to power—Litvinov took a different line. He expressed, somewhat reluctantly, his willingness to consider the French security proposals, and in conjunction with a French plan submitted a draft definition of aggression. He was now attempting to supply the criteria which in 1928 he had said were lacking. Litvinov's original draft, which defined as aggressions declarations of war, invasions without a declaration, bombardments and naval attacks, landings and unpermitted occupations, and blockades, did not include a notable phrase, subsequently added by a subcommittee of the Disarmament Conference: "Provision of support to armed bands formed on its territory which have invaded the territory of another state, or refusal, notwithstanding the request of the invaded State, to take on its own territory all the measures in its power to deprive these bands of all assistance or protection."[24] Moreover, Litvinov's original draft in its second clause was far more vigorous than the subsequent convention in spelling out the political, military, economic or other considerations which could *not* serve as an excuse or justification for aggression as defined: in substance, revolutionary regimes were not to be subject to retaliation for their revolutionary acts of expropriation and civil violence, "backward areas" were not to be exploited by force or penalized by gunboat assault for their actions against capitalist exploitation. It is interesting to note, in view of the publicity later given to the definition of aggression, that Litvinov said frankly, "I admit, however, that the Soviet delegation itself attributes infinitely greater importance to the second clause in its declaration."[25] Thus, the Soviet Union was at this time definitely less interested in establishing a criterion for aggression—which

[23] *The Soviet Fight for Disarmament*, p. 23.

[24] It is worth noting that when the USSR in November 1950 presented a definition of aggression to the Political Committee of the U.N. General Assembly, it reverted to the original Litvinov formulation—i.e., without mention of indirect aggression by armed bands—and not to the revised formula accepted by the Soviet Union in 1933 and used in its treaties with neighboring powers.

[25] League of Nations, *Records of the Conference for the Reduction and Limitation of Armaments*, Series B, Minutes of General Commission, II, 238.

could provide the basis for collective measures—than in protecting its position as a revolutionary state in a presumably hostile world.

A modification of the convention was proposed by a subcommittee on May 24, 1933, and was accepted by the Soviets. While it fared no further at the Disarmament Conference, at the London Economic Conference Litvinov proposed that Russia and its neighbors sign this convention. The proposal was accepted, and in July 1933 a series of treaties bound the Soviet Union, Afghanistan, Estonia, Latvia, Persia, Poland, Rumania, Czechoslovakia, Turkey, Yugoslavia, Finland, and Lithuania to accept this definition of aggression.

On December 29, 1933, shortly after his return from the United States, where he had successfully negotiated for American recognition,[26] Litvinov delivered an important speech to the Central Executive Committee of the USSR. In this speech a distinct change in outlook was apparent. The era of "bourgeois pacifism" had come to an end; new and dangerous ideologies were arising. But whereas Litvinov had previously tended to lump all capitalist states together, he now differentiated between actively belligerent powers, those that were temporarily passive but that would not mind a bit of fighting in the world, especially if it were directed against the USSR, and those powers actively interested in the preservation of peace. With regard to the latter, "I am not entering into an estimation of the motives for such a policy, but am merely stating a fact which is highly valuable to us." Moreover, while stressing that the Soviet Union was perfectly capable of defending itself, "and even the approaches to it," he went on to say that "the maintenance of peace cannot depend upon our efforts alone. It depends upon the cooperation and assistance of other countries as well. By striving, therefore, toward the establishment and maintenance of friendly relations with all countries we devote particular attention to the strengthening of relations and maximum rapprochement with those countries which, like ourselves, furnish proof of their sincere desire to preserve peace and show that they are prepared to oppose any violators of peace."[27]

[26] For the negotiations leading to the establishment of American-Soviet diplomatic relations and for an account of the mutually disappointing aftermath, see *Foreign Relations: Diplomatic Papers: The Soviet Union, 1933-1939* (Washington, 1952). American-Soviet relations are not discussed here primarily because they were not of great importance to Litvinov's major diplomatic efforts. As George F. Kennan wrote from Moscow in November 1937: "When he can be found in Moscow, Litvinov has frequently shown a reluctance to discuss topics other than those he considers to be major political matters. These seem at present to be the success or failure of efforts to induce other states to take strong measures against Germany, Italy and Japan. The result is that few of the current problems of Soviet-American relations attract his interest." *Ibid.*, p. 447.

[27] *Vneshniaia politika* SSSR (Moscow, 1937), pp. 74-96.

The chief trouble makers, of course, were Germany and Japan, to whom Litvinov devoted a considerable amount of attention. He pointed out that for ten years Germany and Russia had enjoyed particularly close political and economic relations, which were advantageous to both Powers. Nevertheless, relations had deteriorated beyond recognition in the course of the last year. The new German regime was showing itself openly hostile to the Soviet Union; its leaders in the past had frequently advocated an anti-Soviet policy, which they had not disavowed since they had come to power. He denied that the Nazi attack on the German Communists was the source of friction: "We have, of course, our own opinion of the German regime. We are, of course, sensitive to the sufferings of our German comrades, but we Marxists are the last who can be reproached for permitting our feelings to dictate our policy." He emphasized that the Soviet Union desired good relations with Germany, but that the responsibility lay with the new regime to desist from its current attitude. In concluding, Litvinov fell back upon the older view that the USSR was, after all, surrounded by capitalist Powers and had ultimately to rely upon the Red army, navy, and air force.

In passing, it is interesting to compare this speech with the one delivered by Stalin to the Seventeenth Congress of the Communist party a few weeks later, on January 26, 1934.[28] While the main lines of foreign policy were quite similar, there was a certain difference in emphasis. Stalin's speech, naturally, was more pontifical and grimmer in tone. He expounded at greater length on the reasons for the changes in the world scene, stressing, as always, the economic crisis of capitalism (Litvinov had given less weight to this, and suggested such other factors as the rise of a new generation which had not experienced war). His talk was more "revolutionary": "The masses of the people have not yet reached the stage when they are ready to storm capitalism; but the idea of storming it is maturing in the minds of the masses." While criticizing the attitude of the new German regime, he was by no means friendly to the "peaceloving" capitalist Powers. He denied any new orientation: "Our orientation in the past and our orientation at the present time is towards the USSR, and towards the USSR alone."

The year 1933 seems definitely to have marked a major turning point in Litvinov's diplomatic orientation. To be sure, in subsequent years Communist spokesmen would say that the Soviet Union had anticipated the mounting crisis of the 1930's and point to a multitude of statements about the precarious state of the capitalist world and the emergence of

[28] J. Stalin, *Problems of Leninism*, 11th edition (Moscow, 1940), pp. 470-486.

fascism. But in these earlier statements the jeremiads against the capitalist world were general volleys against all the Western Powers, just
as the term fascism was a general epithet for quite indiscriminate use in
domestic politics. The specific menace of a National Socialist Germany
was something else again, and it took the unpleasant experiences of
1933 to bring Litvinov, and the Soviet Union, to the position he adopted
in his speech at the end of the year.

For the next two and a half years, however, Litvinov proceeded in
high gear down the road of collective security and cooperation with the
peace-loving Powers. These were the years when the USSR joined the
League, when mutual assistance pacts were signed with France and
Czechoslovakia, and when Litvinov made some of his most constructive
pronouncements on the means to preserve peace, which he now declared
to be "indivisible."

In the spring of 1934, on May 29, Litvinov was prepared to admit
that "international life and particularly political events in some countries
during recent years had prevented the [Disarmament] Conference from
carrying out its direct task of drawing up a disarmament convention."
After all, however, disarmament, was only a means to an end: "Could
not the Conference feel its way towards other guarantees for peace?"—
a possibility he had categorically denied some years earlier. He then went
on to say that, "Even if there should be dissident States, that should by
no means prevent the remainder from coming still more closely together
to take steps which would strengthen their own security."[29]

In line with this approach was a new and amiable view toward the
League of Nations. As late as December 1933 Litvinov had denied that
Russia was likely to join the League in any foreseeable future, but by
the following spring his attitude was quite different, and in September
the USSR obtained a permanent seat in the Council. Of course, one specific
reason for joining the League was that a mutual assistance pact with
France, the negotiations for which began in 1934, could be reconciled
with the Locarno Treaty only if France's partner were a member of the
League.[30]

Although Litvinov was unsuccessful in persuading Germany to join
in guaranteeing the Eastern European frontiers or in creating an Eastern
Locarno pact, France and Russia did achieve a mutual assistance pact,
which was signed on May 2, 1935. On May 16 was also signed a Soviet-

[29] League of Nations, *Records of the Conference for the Reduction and Limitation of
Armaments*, Series B, III, 657-661.
[30] Max Beloff, *The Foreign Policy of Soviet Russia* (2 vols., London, 1947, 1949),
I, 135.

Czech mutual assistance pact, with provisions similar to those of the French pact, but stipulating that they should come into force only if France gave assistance to the country attacked.

Although the Soviet Union was thus drawing closer to some of the capitalist Powers, at the same time, in 1935 and 1936, the Fascist states struck three decisive blows at the structure of European peace: Germany's repudiation of disarmament, the Italian attack on Abyssinia, and the march into the Rhineland. While each of these events did not directly concern the USSR and while the Soviet government did not actually take any important measures, a good deal of Litvinov's positive reputation rests on the speeches he delivered in response to these actions.

In his speech of April 17, 1935, he stated that while the Soviet Union neither favored the Versailles Treaty nor was bound by it, the German action did violate the Covenant of the League, and "one of the foundations of peace is the observance of international relations directly affecting the security of nations."[31] He agreed in principle to the right of equality of armament, but not "if a country which demands or assumes the right to arm is exclusively led by people who have publicly announced as the programme of their foreign policy a policy which consists, not only in revenge, but in the unrestricted conquest of foreign territory and the destruction of the independence of whole States."

On September 5, 1935, when Italy was threatening Abyssinia, he pointed out that while the USSR had no interests involved, the Italian action could set a dangerous precedent: "The repetition of the precedent would certainly have a cumulative effect and, in its turn, would stimulate new conflicts more directly affecting the whole of Europe."[32]

On September 14, in speaking of the Fascist Powers' technique of advocating bilateral pacts, he stated: "We know of another political conception that is fighting the idea of collective security and advocating bilateral pacts, and this not even between all States but only between States arbitrarily chosen for this purpose. This conception can have nothing in common with peaceful intentions. Not every pact of nonaggression is concluded with a view to strengthening general peace. While nonaggression pacts concluded by the Soviet Union with its neighbors, include a special clause for suspending the pact in cases of aggression committed by one of the parties against any third State, we know of other pacts of nonaggression which have no such clause. This means that a State which has secured by such a pact of nonaggression its rear or its flank, obtains the

[31] Maxim Litvinov, *Against Aggression* (New York, 1939), pp. 18-19.
[32] League of Nations, *Official Journal*, 16th Year, No. 11, November 1935, p. 1142.

facility of attacking with impunity third States."[33] Perhaps this statement indicates why Litvinov was not quite the man to negotiate the German-Soviet pact of August 1939.

When Germany marched into the Rhineland in March 1936, Litvinov again urged collective action: "One cannot fight for the collective organization of security without taking collective measures against the violation of international obligations. We, however, do not count among such measures collective capitulation to the aggressor."[34]

His funeral speech, on July 1, 1936, for the demise of Abyssinia was one of his best. "We are gathered here," he began, "to close a page in the history of the League of Nations, the history of international life, which it will be impossible to read without a feeling of bitterness." The League had been unable to maintain the territorial integrity and political independence of one of its members, and it was possible that the League itself would be declared bankrupt. Litvinov undertook to combat this defeatist mood and to strengthen the collective security provisions of the Covenant: "I say we do not want a League that is safe for aggressors. We do not want that kind of League, even if it is universal, because it would become the very opposite of an instrument of peace. . . .

"We must educate and raise people up to its lofty ideas, not degrade the League. We must seek to make the League universal, but we must not by any means make it safe for the aggressor to this end. On the contrary, all new members and all ex-members wishing to return must read on its portals: 'Abandon all hope of aggression and its impunity all ye who enter here.' . . .

"As for myself, I would rather have a League of Nations that tries to render at least some assistance, even if it proves ineffective, to a victim of aggression, than a League of Nations that closes its eyes to aggression and lets it pass unperturbed. . . .

"In an ideal League of Nations military sanctions, too, should be obligatory for all. But if we are yet unable to rise to such heights of international solidarity, we should make it our concern to have all continents, and for a start, at least all Europe, covered with a system of regional pacts, on the strength of which groups of States would undertake to protect particular sectors from aggression."[35]

Finally, on September 28, 1936, he warned against the sense of apathy that was spreading under the impact of the Axis: "The legend of the invincible aggressor is being created even outside his country; it is

[33] League of Nations, *Official Journal, Special Supplement to No. 138*, p. 73.
[34] *Against Aggression*, p. 23.   [35] *ibid.*, pp. 35-45.

engendering fatalistic and capitulatory sentiments in some countries, which gradually—sometimes even without their noticing it—are beginning to lose their independence and are becoming vassals of the aggressor. Thus begins the process of the formation of a hegemony which is to culminate in the crushing of all refractory countries by force of arms."[36]

Toward the end of 1936, however, there were signs that the Soviet Union's new policy was not proving particularly fruitful. The growing menace of Germany, Italy, and Japan was not being checked. The efforts at collective security did not develop into anything substantial, and indeed the outbreak of the Spanish Civil War introduced new strains in the relations between the Soviets and France and Great Britain. The Popular Front adopted by the Comintern did not diminish the suspicions of the non-Communist states which continued to find that the activities of domestic Communists were a major impediment to collaboration with the Soviet Union. The great purges within Russia were under way and served to weaken Western confidence in the character and stability of the Soviet regime.

In Litvinov's speech before the Extraordinary Eighth Congress of Soviets, on November 28, 1936, a new note, or rather an old one, made its appearance. After commenting on the danger of fascism, not as a form of government but as a source of external aggression, after stressing the specifically anti-Soviet content of the anti-Comintern pact (he clearly had very accurate information on its secret terms), Litvinov waxed bitter over the policy of nonintervention in Spain, and uttered a definite word of warning to the non-Fascist Powers:

"The Soviet Union, however, does not beg to be invited to any unions, any *blocs*, any combinations. She will calmly let other States weigh and evaluate the advantages which can be derived for peace from close cooperation with the Soviet Union, and understand that the Soviet Union can give more than receive. . . .

"Other States, other territories are menaced most. Our security does not depend upon paper documents or upon foreign policy combinations. The Soviet Union is sufficiently strong in herself."[37]

From this time on, in Litvinov's speeches and reported statements two distinct themes are detectable: on the one hand, a continued appeal for collective security; on the other, increasing animus against Great Britain and France and the threat of a Soviet return to isolation. The first theme needs no further development as it is largely the exposition of the prin-

[36] *ibid.*, p. 49.　　　　　　　　　　[37] *ibid.*, pp. 78-79.

ciples set forth in the preceding two or three years. The second and ominous theme tends to become more and more dominant.

On February 4, 1937, Litvinov complained to the United States ambassador, Joseph E. Davies, that "he could not understand why Great Britain could not see that once Hitler dominated Europe he would swallow the British Isles also. He seemed to be very much stirred about this and apprehensive lest there should be some composition of differences between France, England and Germany."[38] On February 15 he said that "Germany was concerned solely with conquest and it was a mistake to magnify Hitler's importance by engaging in discussions of the character which France and England were projecting."[39]

In a speech to the electors of Leningrad, on November 27, 1937, Litvinov reiterated the old theme that imperialism was inherent in all bourgeois states, and was heavily sarcastic about the efforts of France and Britain to pretend that the Fascist Powers were not aggressive: "I see it is a puzzle to you how experienced bourgeois diplomats could fail to understand the meaning of the aggressor's tactics. You think they are only pretending to disbelieve the aggressor's statements and, under cover of negotiations for confirmations and explanations, they are groping for a deal with the aggressor. You can think so if you like, but my position does not allow me to express such doubts, and I must leave them to your responsibility."[40]

In December Litvinov had an interview with a foreign correspondent in which he was reported, some years later, to have made the following significant remarks:

"Anti-Comintern Pact? What nonsense! Can you never look at things without your cheap bourgeois prejudice? The Anti-Comintern Pact is no threat to the Soviet Union. It is dust in the eyes of the Western democracies. . . . Ideologies mean little to the Fascist brigands. The Germans have militarized the Reich and are bent on a brutal policy of gangsterism. Those contemptible peoples, the Japanese and Italians, are following at the German heels, hoping to share in the spoils of German conquest. It is the rich capitalist countries which will fall an easy prey. The British and French peoples are soft under leaders who are blind. The Soviet Union is the last foe to be attacked by the Anti-Comintern powers. They will loot your countries, but we have the Red Army and a vast extent of territory. . . .

"Hitler and the generals who control Germany read history. They

[38] Joseph E. Davies, *Mission to Moscow* (New York, 1941), p. 60.
[39] *ibid.*, p. 79.   [40] *Against Aggression*, pp. 106-107.

know that Bismarck warned against war on two fronts. They know that he urged the reinsurance policy with Russia. They believe the Kaiser lost the first world war because he forgot Bismarck's admonitions. When the Germans are prepared at last to embark upon their new adventures, these bandits will come to Moscow to ask us for a pact."[41] According to this report, he predicted the *Anschluss* and the attack on Czechoslovakia, and pointed out that the Soviet Union need not come to Czechoslovakia's aid unless France did: "Well, France won't fight. France is through."

By the spring of 1938 Litvinov had adopted a comparatively passive role, though still affirming that the Soviet Union was ready to join in collective action to arrest further aggression, and was willing to discuss measures within the League or outside it. In March 1938 he told Davies that Czechoslovakia would probably fall because it lacked confidence in France; for that matter "France has no confidence in the Soviet Union, and the Soviet Union has no confidence in France. . . . The only thing that would prevent a complete Fascist domination of Europe was a change of government or policy in Great Britain." He appeared to envisage within the near future a Europe dominated by fascism and opposed only by Great Britain on the West and the USSR on the East.[42]

The prolonged Czechoslovakian crisis of 1938 is far too complex for even summary discussion here. In general, it may be said that Litvinov, publicly and apparently privately, stood by the position that the Soviet Union would honor its obligations to Czechoslovakia if France came to the latter's aid. On the other hand, he repeatedly indicated that the responsibility for taking the initiative lay with France, and this included the thorny question of obtaining Polish and/or Rumanian permission for Russian troops to come to Czechoslovakia's assistance.

There does not seem to be much evidence, however, that he was expecting Russia to be required to take forceful action. It is striking that neither the British nor the German diplomatic representatives in Moscow felt that the Soviet government showed any sign of preparing itself or the Russian people for the defense of Czechoslovakia. The German ambassador, Schulenburg, commented that Litvinov's speech of June 23, 1938, showed distinct aloofness and a desire to retain freedom of action. Moreover, "the tone of the speech has remarkably little aggressiveness and strives to leave open all possibilities. The attempt to arrive at an objective attitude toward the policy of the Third Reich is striking."[43]

[41] J. T. Whitaker, *We Cannot Escape History* (New York, 1943), pp. 207-208.
[42] Davies, *Mission to Moscow*, p. 291.   [43] *German Documents*, series D, I, 924.

On August 22, 1938, Litvinov, in a conversation with Schulenburg was quite frank in charging Germany with aggression and a desire to destroy Czechoslovakia. He went on to say, however, "If the old democratic Germany still existed, the Czech question would have a quite different aspect for the Soviet Union." While the Soviet Union approved of national self-determination and had had no part in the creation of Czechoslovakia, the threat to its independence affected the balance of power: an increase in Nazi strength would be bad for the Soviet Union.[44] According to a British report the Germans felt that in this conversation Litvinov was opening the door for a possible German-Russian rapprochement.[45] Schulenburg, however, did not thus interpret his conversation, and its content as reported need not lead to such an interpretation.

Was Litvinov considering the possibility of independent Soviet action even if France failed to act? This question remains somewhat obscure. In May 1938 he asked the French ambassador Coulondre what France, the ally of Poland, would do in case the latter, having attacked Czechoslovakia, was itself attacked in turn by the USSR? Coulondre replied that the answer was obvious since France was also allied with Czechoslovakia, and both treaties were defensive. Coulondre also pointed out that France recognized that Russia was not bound to move unless France intervened. Litvinov replied, "That is right, but there is another hypothesis: the case in which the USSR for one reason or another should intervene without France having moved."[46] The question naturally presents itself, as it did to Coulondre at the time, whether the Soviet Union was envisaging military action against Poland and whether such action was possible without a preliminary understanding with Germany.

As far as the Czechs themselves are concerned, it is still not altogether clear whether, and if so how, they were led to believe that Russia would aid them even if France did not. Apparently Litvinov, through the Soviet minister in Prague, Alexandrovsky, did inform the Czech government that if the case were submitted to the League of Nations and Germany were found an aggressor, the Soviet Union would give assistance regardless of France.[47] This was clearly not a very rash promise under the circumstances. It has also been stated, though the evidence seems less satisfactory, that Alexandrovsky later informed the Czech government that the Soviet government would come to the support of Czechoslovakia as soon as Moscow was informed that the League had been

[44] *ibid.*, II, 604, 630.   [45] *British Documents*, 3rd series, II, 141, note 3.
[46] Robert Coulondre, *De Staline à Hitler* (Paris, 1950), p. 153.
[47] Cf. Beloff, *Foreign Policy*, II, 151.

seized of the case and would not wait for a decision to be reached at Geneva.[48] Some years later Benes referred to "the fact that, in spite of the insistence of Moscow, I did not provoke war with Germany in 1938."[49] Some light on this remark may be cast by a statement in a recent Soviet work: "More than that, J. V. Stalin, in conversation with K. Gottwald, said that the Soviet Union was ready to give military aid to Czechoslovakia, even if France did not do this, but on the condition that Czechoslovakia defend itself and ask for Soviet assistance. Gottwald told Benes to that effect."[50] Although this statement requires a good deal of elucidation, it would indicate that such approaches, if made, may not have been through diplomatic channels but through the Communist party. In any event there appears to be no direct evidence connecting Litvinov with any measures more extensive than those to which the USSR was publicly committed: the Czech Treaty and the League of Nations. Furthermore, although Litvinov told the Germans that he thought France and England would assist Czechoslovakia, he seems to have been thoroughly skeptical. On September 16, in discussing with a foreign journalist ways and means of Soviet assistance, he remarked, "This is also unrealistic. . . . They have already sold Czechoslovakia down the river."[51]

In his last major speech in the League, on September 21, 1938, Litvinov bitterly criticized the record of the last few years: "A fire brigade was set up in the innocent hope that, by some lucky chance, there would be no fires. Things turned out differently, however. Fires have broken out in defiance of our hopes, but luckily not in our immediate vicinity: so let us dissolve the fire brigade—of course not forever, but merely temporarily. Directly the danger of any fire disappears, we shall reassemble the fire brigade without a moment's delay." He also carefully relieved the Soviet Union of any responsibility in the debacle: "At a moment when the mines are being laid to blow up the organization on which were fixed the great hopes of our generation, and which stamped a definite character on the international relations of our epoch; at a moment when, by no accidental coincidence, decisions are being taken outside the League which recall to us the international transactions of prewar days, and which are bound to overturn all present conceptions of international morality and treaty obligations; at a moment when there is

---

[48] John W. Wheeler-Bennett, *Munich—Prologue to Tragedy* (New York, 1948), p. 127.

[49] Letter from Eduard Benes to L. B. Namier, in Namier, *Europe in Decay*, p, 284.

[50] *Diplomaticheskii Slovar'* (1950), II, 198.

[51] Fischer, *Men and Politics*, p. 561.

being drawn up a further list of sacrifices to the god of aggression, and a line is being drawn under the annals of all postwar international history, with the sole conclusion that nothing succeeds like aggression—at such a moment, every State must define its role and its responsibility before its contemporaries and before history. That is why I must plainly declare here that the Soviet Government bears no responsibility whatsoever for the events now taking place, and for the fatal consequences which may inexorably ensue."[52] He concluded: "The Soviet Government takes pride in the fact that it has no part in such a policy, and has invariably pursued the principle of the two pacts I have mentioned, which were approved by nearly every nation in the world [the League Covenant and the Briand-Kellogg Pact]. Nor has it any intention of abandoning them for the future, being convinced that in present conditions it is impossible otherwise to safeguard a genuine peace and genuine international justice. It calls upon other Governments likewise to return to this path."

Despite these concluding remarks it was generally felt among European diplomats that the Munich agreement did mark the bankruptcy of the Litvinov policy and that the ussr would inevitably examine other possibilities. The German reaction is particularly interesting. Counselor of embassy in Moscow, von Tippelskirch, on October 3 and 10, 1938, wrote: "That the policy of Litvinov has suffered a complete fiasco, that the war, from which chaos and weakening of Germany were expected, has not broken out, that the policy of pacts and alliances has failed, that the collective idea has collapsed, and that the League of Nations has disappointed the hopes reposed in it, can in my opinion not remain without consequences for Soviet policy. . . .

"In the light of our experiences it seems to me probable that Stalin will draw conclusions about personalities from the failure of Soviet policy. In that connection I naturally think in the first place of Litvinov, who has made fruitless efforts in Geneva throughout the crisis. . . .[53]

"Litvinov will certainly try to convince the Soviet Government that the policy hitherto pursued by him was the only right one and that it must be continued in the future as well. . . . If I judge Litvinov correctly, he will continue to defend his policy of collective action in the conviction that Germany's growth of power . . . will lead to a change in the European balance of power in which sooner or later a definite role must quite automatically fall to the Soviet Union. . . . In other words he will con-

[52] *Against Aggression*, p. 127.
[53] *German Documents*, series D, IV, 602-605.

tinue to recommend measures against the aggressors in the hope of having more success next time."[54]

This German observer was, perhaps, unduly persuaded that Litvinov still had the opportunity to pursue his policy, or that he really felt capable of pressing it vigorously any longer. Shortly after Munich, Potemkin, Litvinov's assistant, after coldly receiving Coulondre, burst out: "My poor friend, what have you done? As for us I do not see any other outcome than a fourth partition of Poland."[55] And on October 16, Litvinov himself said: "Henceforth the USSR has only to watch, from the shelter of its frontiers, the establishment of German hegemony over the center and southeast of Europe. And if by chance the Western Powers finally decide to wish to stop it, they must address themselves to us, for— he added throwing me a sharp look—we shall have our word to say."[56] He then went on to remark that he had made the following declaration to Lord Halifax: "Once its hegemony is solidly established in Europe, and France neutralized, Hitler will be able to attack either Great Britain or the USSR. He will choose the first solution because it will offer him much greater advantages with the possibility of substituting the German Empire for the British Empire, and, to succeed in this undertaking, he will prefer to reach an understanding with the USSR."

In his discussions with the British after Munich Litvinov was distinctly cool; he saw no evidence that the Western Powers would cease their policy of capitulation, and said that the Soviet Union would probably remain "aloof" henceforth, since its interests were not directly threatened.[57] In late March 1939, in a conversation with R. S. Hudson, Litvinov was reported as saying: "He foresaw in the not far-distant future a Europe entirely German from the Bay of Biscay to the Soviet frontier and bounded, as it were, simply by Great Britain and the Soviet Union. Even that would not satisfy German ambitions, but the attack, he said smiling happily, would not be directed to the East."[58]

It is true that Litvinov was willing to embark on the final round of fruitless negotiations after the German march into Prague, but it was

[54] *ibid.*, p. 605.
[55] Coulondre, *De Staline à Hitler*, p. 165. On September 29, 1938, Potemkin said to Schulenburg: "The Powers now taking part in the destruction of Czechoslovakia would bitterly regret their submission to militant nationalism. In the first place, Poland, for there were a 'great many' Germans in Poland; in particular it must not be forgotten that several million Ukrainians were living in Poland, who were already beginning to 'move'." *German Documents*, series D, II, 998.
[56] Coulondre, *De Staline à Hitler*, p. 171.
[57] E.g., his conversation with Sir William Seeds, February 19, 1939. *British Documents*, 3rd series, IV, 124.
[58] *ibid.*, p. 585.

clear that he displayed no confidence in the Western Powers. On May 3, 1939, he was relieved of his post.

From this review of Litvinov's diplomatic career several general observations may be made. In the first place, his advocacy of collective security was limited in time: before the rise of the Fascist Powers, he denied the possibility of such methods of providing international security. Moreover, from 1936 on there is an increasing note of isolationism: if the other Powers would not cooperate the Soviet Union could follow its own interests independently. In the second place, the idea of collective security was restricted conceptually. Basically the world was still divided into two camps and the Fascist Powers belonged to the capitalist camp. "Peaceful coexistence" was not in the permanent order of things, nor were the motives inducing certain capitalist Powers to be peaceloving necessarily fundamental or enduring. Litvinov's collective security is not to be identified with the idealism of some of his Western admirers.

On the other hand, it is difficult to find evidence that Litvinov had any revolutionary expectations in these years or that by his diplomacy he was bent on fomenting strife. To be sure, the Soviet Union's total impact abroad, its unofficial as well as its official activities, remained troublesome and disturbing. It is also true that Litvinov's speeches to Soviet audiences displayed a truculent and scornful attitude toward the capitalist world which was moderated though not entirely eliminated in his diplomatic addresses to the League. Even so, his speeches on collective security in the League and elsewhere do have a most convincing ring of sincerity and urgency. By 1938 most foreign diplomatic observers in Moscow—Germans as well as French and English—seem to have felt that Litvinov was an ardent supporter of the course he had advocated since 1933.

If, with the above-mentioned qualifications, Litvinov's campaign for collective security was something real and not merely misleading oratory on his part, then the question arises whether his views and those of the Politburo coincided.

II

From all that is known of the structure of the Soviet state and the Communist party it would be absurd to assume that Litvinov could have pursued a diplomatic course at odds with that desired by Stalin and the inner circle of the Politburo. Clearly the general lines of his foreign policy had the official blessing. Nevertheless, an examination of the available record does reveal a number of instances during his career in which Litvinov was reportedly not in agreement with his superiors. Some of the more illuminating examples may be given, in chronological sequence:

In 1919 a British naval officer, who had an interview with Litvinov in Reval, reported that "M. Litvinoff stated that from the first he had opposed his Government's repudiation of their external debt, as he felt certain that such a course would tend to unify the resistance of other nations against them."[59]

In 1924, according to Christian Rakovsky, Litvinov wished to recognize Rumanian sovereignty over Bessarabia in order to settle the matter. Opposed to his view were Rakovsky, Chicherin, and Stalin, who felt it desirable to maintain Bessarabia as a "Soviet irredenta."[60]

Litvinov seems not to have been convinced of the value of Soviet and Comintern maneuvers in the colonial and Asiatic world at the expense of relations with the Western Powers. He is reported as having said, in March 1929, "I think an agreement with England about Afghanistan and the East generally is possible, but the government takes a different view."[61]

In 1938 it was the opinion of the German ambassador that the new evidence of Soviet antiforeign feeling shown in the closing of numerous consulates was not Litvinov's doing: "Litvinov has to accommodate himself to this predominance of domestic policy."[62]

In January 1938 both Zhdanov and Molotov publicly criticized the Foreign Commissariat, though not Litvinov in person, for its presumed lenience with France, which was accused of harboring anti-Soviet elements, terrorists, and diversionists.[63]

In the summer of 1938 Coulondre told Schulenburg that Litvinov was willing to agree to Soviet participation in defraying expenses occasioned by the withdrawal of volunteer troops from Spain, but had encountered opposition in the Politburo. Litvinov seemed willing to cut losses in the Spanish affair, but the Politburo had prestige considerations.[64]

On March 1, 1939, Schulenburg, referring to Soviet economic negotiations with Germany and Japan, remarked that "M. Litvinov does not regard M. Mikoyan's negotiations with a friendly eye at all. If by obstinacy toward Japan he can sabotage the zealous activities of the Commissar for Foreign Trade, he will intensify rather than moderate this line of action.[65]

[59] *British Documents*, 1st series, III, 659.   [60] Fischer, *Men and Politics*, p. 135.
[61] *ibid.*, p. 128. See also David Dallin, *The Rise of Russia in Asia* (New York, 1949), p. 240.
[62] *German Documents*, series D, I, 905.   [63] Beloff, *Foreign Policy*, II, 113-114
[64] *German Documents*, series D, III, 714.   [65] *ibid.*, IV, 628.

Louis Fischer has remarked that Litvinov "has never by word or hint approved of Stalin's pact policy with Hitler."[66] It is obvious, of course, that the German-Soviet rapprochement of 1939 was hardly in the spirit of collective security, that the nonaggression pact of August 23 did not contain the escape clause in the event one of the signatories attacked a third Power. On the other hand, as should be apparent from the above, it is not difficult to find a number of hints of a possible German-Soviet agreement in Litvinov's private remarks from 1937 on. Still, it is worth noting that after the German attack on the USSR in June 1941, and after Stalin in his speech of July 3 had defended the wisdom of the nonaggression pact, Litvinov, in a broadcast in English on July 8, indicated that agreements of any sort with Hitler were worthless because the Nazi gang considered themselves above all conceptions of international obligations. While commenting on the failure to organize collective resistance, he stressed Hitler's technique of dividing his prospective victims: "His strategy is to knock down his victims and strike them one by one in an order prompted by circumstances. He intended first to deal with the Western countries so that he would be free to fall on the Soviet Union." Not only was this no defense of the German-Soviet pact—which would hardly have been a tactful approach to the British and American audience at whom the broadcast was directed—but the whole line of argument was that Hitler's treachery was inevitable and predictable.[67]

Finally, evidence of Litvinov's disapproval of Soviet policy following World War II has been provided by two American reporters writing shortly after his death. C. L. Sulzberger stated that on April 5, 1945, Litvinov, then an isolated figure in Moscow, expressed his pessimism about East-West relations: "The situation is developing badly. First, the Western Powers make a mistake and rub us the wrong way. Then we make a mistake and rub you the wrong way."[68] Richard C. Hottelet wrote that in June 1946 Litvinov indicated to him that the Soviets would continue pressing demands on the West. "As far as I am concerned the root cause is the ideological conception prevailing here that conflict between the Communist and capitalist worlds is inevitable." He declared that the Soviet rulers would not call on him for advice and had reverted to the outmoded concept of security in terms of territory.[69]

While it is difficult to weigh the importance of these scattered examples, they do seem to have a certain consistency: in each case Litvinov

[66] Louis Fischer, *The Great Challenge* (New York, 1946), p. 46.

[67] *New York Times*, July 9, 1941.   [68] *New York Times*, January 3, 1952.

[69] *New York World-Telegram*, January 28-February 1, 1952.

appears to have favored practical accommodation with the Western Powers as against moves to create or abet revolution, disturbance, or international disorder. To be sure, such an attitude would be part of his diplomatic function: his job as Foreign Commissar was not made easier by the Communist temptation to kick things around.

Less tangible than these evidences of disagreements on policy but perhaps as important are the subtler indications of a difference in emphasis and interpretation. In a political system where all action and policy is dependent upon a "party line" enunciated by the supreme authority, emphasis and interpretation are all-important, especially since the "line" is often not wholly unambiguous. For example, the theme which underlies Soviet diplomacy throughout most of the interwar period—"the temporary coexistence of the two systems"—can in practice be given two entirely different meanings depending upon the emphasis accorded "temporary" or "coexistence." Although it is perilous to draw conclusions from purely external evidence, there appear to be a number of respects in which Litvinov's interpretation differed from that of the Politburo—Stalin and the rather murky figures of his inner circle.

While Litvinov always acknowledged that the possibilities of cooperation with the capitalist Powers were temporary, that ultimately the capitalist system was doomed to destruction, in the period after Hitler came to power he recognized the Nazi menace as something requiring the cooperative resistance of the peace-loving Powers, not as the turbulent prologue to the victory of Communism. This mood is quite apparent in his speech of December 29, 1933. Yet at the same time, on December 31, 1933, the official journal *Bolshevik* could still give the following interpretation of the German situation: "In Germany the proletarian revolution is nearer to realization than in any other country; and victory of the proletariat in Germany means victory of proletarian revolution throughout Europe, since capitalist Europe cannot exist if it loses its heart. . . . He who does not understand the German question does not understand the path of the development of proletarian revolution in Europe."[70] Stalin's speech of January 26, 1934, while less far out on the limb, is much more revolution-conscious than Litvinov's.[71] One receives the impression that the Politburo was reluctant and regretful in accepting the new course.

Indeed, Litvinov as a diplomat seems always to have found the irrepressible revolutionary yearnings of the Bolsheviks an uncomfortable

[70] Quoted in David Dallin, *Russia and Post-War Europe* (New Haven, 1943), p. 62.
[71] See above, §1.

problem. In a letter to an English negotiator in December 1919, he said: "From the point of view of the vital interests of both countries there should be no obstacle to the establishment of real peace, excepting the bogey of revolutionary propaganda. If formal guarantees from the Soviet Government on this point be considered insufficient, could not means of preventing this propaganda be devised without barring the way to mutual representation?"[72]

The change in the Comintern line at the Seventh Congress in 1935 did not really eradicate this difference. Although Litvinov's diplomatic policy of "collective security" and the Popular Front are often identified, it is doubtful whether this identification should be pressed too far, even though both had Stalin's approval in some fashion. A reasonably attentive reading of Dimitrov's speeches at the Seventh Congress can dispel the popular notion that the Comintern had now really concealed its hard revolutionary core. Certainly, the energetic behavior of the comrades under the new line caused Litvinov perpetual embarrassment. In 1936, for example, Coulondre pointed out to him that the interference of the Comintern in French internal affairs was imperiling the Franco-Soviet pact. In response, Litvinov, after assuring him that the Soviet Union had no intention of interfering and that the Soviet ambassador in Paris had received instructions to that effect—which he would make even more precise—was obliged to fall back on the old claim that the Comintern had nothing to do with the foreign policy of the Soviet government. Coulondre felt, however, that Litvinov was fully aware that this customary disclaimer of responsibility for the Comintern carried no conviction. "But the question went beyond him. It concerned the other side of the double ladder on the top of which sat Stalin alone."[73]

Although Litvinov frequently expressed disapproval and suspicion of the capitalist nations and, in the years after 1936, was extremely critical of the policies of France and Great Britain, he does not seem to have been so deeply imbued with that xenophobia which has increasingly blighted the perception of Soviet leaders. It should not be forgotten that he lived a decade in England, from 1908 to 1918, during which time he settled rather thoroughly into a middle-class existence and married an English wife.

With regard to Germany, while Litvinov certainly subscribed to the general line that the Soviet Union did not desire bad relations with Germany and would welcome a resumption of cordial relations should

---

[72] *British Documents*, 1st series, III, 740.
[73] Coulondre, *De Staline à Hitler*, pp. 32-33.

the German government drop its menacing attitude, he does not seem to have shared the enthusiasm which a number of Russians and Germans had for the Russo-German connection. Dirksen, as mentioned earlier, felt that Litvinov was not a true believer in the Rapallo policy and was pro-English at heart. In March 1936, following the march into the Rhineland, the Soviet statements concerning Germany seemed to display some confusion. On the one hand, Litvinov in the League castigated Germany's recent actions in very sharp terms; on the other, Molotov said to a French editor: "The main trend among our people, the trend which determines the policy of the Soviet Government, considers an improvement in relations between Germany and the Soviet Union possible. . . . The participation of Germany in the League of Nations would be in the interest of peace and would be favorably regarded by us." "Even of Hitler Germany?", asked the French journalist. "Yes, even of Hitler Germany."[74] While there may be no logical contradiction between the two Soviet statements, they have a quite different flavor.

The German-Soviet pact of 1939 inevitably created the suspicion that some Soviet leaders, including Stalin, were always eager for a rapprochement with Germany and had made secret contacts with Hitler even during the period of so-called collective security. Coulondre, who said that he was convinced that Litvinov was, like himself, "a sincere worker for the Franco-Soviet entente within the framework of the League of Nations,"[75] also commented, "I am not even sure that during all that period of my mission in the ussr, certain clandestine contacts had ever ceased between Moscow and Berlin."[76] He was of the opinion that something was definitely in preparation in the spring of 1937, only to be dropped in April.[77] The former Soviet intelligence officer, Krivitsky, professed to know that in the spring of 1937 an agreement had been drafted by Stalin and Hitler, with one David Kandelaki as the intermediary, but had broken down.[78] This source also stated, however, that the Commissariat for Foreign Affairs had no part whatever in this undertaking.

[74] See Beloff, *Foreign Policy*, II, 51-54.   [75] Coulondre, *De Staline à Hitler*, p. 32.
[76] *ibid.*, p. 45.   [77] *ibid.*, p. 125.
[78] W. G. Krivitsky, *In Stalin's Secret Service* (New York, 1939), pp. 225-226. The thesis that Stalin was, all along, seeking for a deal with Hitler encounters difficulties in having to explain all the anti-German steps taken by the Soviet Union between 1933 and 1938. Krivitsky contended that the entry into the League, collective security, the pact with France, the intervention in Spain were all undertaken with a view to making Hitler find it "advantageous to meet his [Stalin's] advances." This seems a singularly round-about way to achieve a rapprochement. Still, this tactic of trying to win an ally by making things uncomfortable for him is not unknown in the history of diplomacy. William II and Holstein tried to woo Britain by the threat of a continental bloc against it.

In general, even after one has made deductions for the fact that Litvinov, as a diplomat dealing with the outside, capitalist world, was likely to adopt a less revolutionary stance than Communists dealing with Communists or, perhaps, dictators with dictators, there still seems to remain a not unimportant difference between the diplomatic policy advocated or desired by him and the temper of the Politburo, a difference occasionally showing up in specific disagreements but more persistently if less tangibly in shadings of interpretation and emphasis. These, however, form a sufficiently coherent pattern to warrant the conclusion that there was a tension of ideas within the monolithic framework of the Soviet government. If so, is it possible to form any notion of the political or bureaucratic relations behind this tension?

III

A preceding chapter has shown that diplomacy as such did not stand very high in the hierarchy of instruments developed or revamped by the new Soviet order. Foreign considerations tended to rank below domestic considerations during most of the interwar period, and even in the field of foreign relations the diplomatic arm lacked the prestige of the revolutionary and the military arms. At the same time, because of the peculiar sensitiveness attaching to foreign policy decisions there came to be "a particularly close, direct, and continual relationship . . . between the Politburo and the Narkomindel in the conduct and control of foreign affairs."[79] Consequently the post as Peoples Commissar for Foreign Affairs did not, in itself, carry a great deal of weight in the Soviet system.

Nor did Litvinov, despite the fact that he was an "old Bolshevik,"[80] rank high in the Party. He was never in the all-important Politburo, though he was a member of the Party's Central Committee for a number of years. Two reasons may help to explain why he was never admitted to the inner circle despite his obvious ability and long record as a party member. He had not returned to Russia from England to participate in the Bolshevik revolution. From the very first he was concerned not with the establishment of the revolutionary state but with its relations abroad. Moreover, even before the revolution he seems to have been valued pri-

[79] Julian Towster, *Political Power in the* USSR., *1917-1947* (New York, 1948), p. 162. Towster points out that in the late 1920's while nearly all the governmental organs were scheduled to report before the Politburo, the Narkomindel apparently was not, presumably because decisions concerning foreign issues were continuously on the agenda of the Politburo itself.

[80] He joined the Russian Social Democratic Labor party in 1898 and was on Lenin's side when the latter formed the Bolshevik faction against the Mensheviks in 1903.

marily as a competent technician. In Lenin's references to him during the war as "our legal representative in the International Socialist Bureau," the term "legal" is charged with the characteristic double meaning of being official and public but not really part of the illegal or extralegal revolutionary core. While part of his function as Chicherin's second in the 1920's may have been as Bolshevik guardian over a former Menshevik,[81] it is doubtful whether in the long run his party status was any higher than that of his predecessor; in the opinion of the German ambassador who worked with both men, it was lower.[82]

Consequently, neither as Peoples Commissar nor as a party member was Litvinov in a position to follow his own policy or even to initiate policy. Indeed, late in his career he is reported as remarking rather sourly: "You know what I am. I merely hand on diplomatic documents."[83]

It is, therefore, difficult to see just how Litvinov was in any position to differ significantly with the Politburo. Moreover, Litvinov's term in office overlapped the years of the Great Purges, in which, so it seems, even half-formed or possibly-to-be-formed disagreements were sufficient to destroy a man. Yet Litvinov retained not only his health but his post.

His success in surviving the purges was something of a surprise and miracle to contemporary observers. He was an old Bolshevik; old Bolsheviks were dropping like flies. He headed the Foreign Commissariat; the Foreign Commissariat and the embassies abroad were swept clean. The former Soviet diplomat, Alexander Barmine, comments on Litvinov's "inexplicably surviving all his friends and collaborators": "Two of Litvinov's four assistants were executed, the third was put in prison and the fourth disappeared. His old friends and personal protégés, Ambassadors Yurenev and Rosenberg, disappeared also. Almost all the heads of departments of his ministry and the leading diplomatic personnel abroad, gathered and trained by him over fifteen years, were shot. But Litvinov continued to smile enigmatically. 'They were traitors; all is well!' Was he so confident because he deemed himself indispensable, or did he have to keep a good face because his family were held as hostages?"[84] Litvinov does seem to have been jolted by the arrest of his assistant Krestinsky,[85] but in general his recorded remarks indicate approval of the purges as a necessity to rid the Soviet Union of treasonous elements.

---

[81] See, for example, Simon Liberman, *Building Lenin's Russia* (Chicago, 1945), p. 111.
[82] Dirksen, *Moskau, Tokio, London*, p. 94.
[83] Fischer, *Men and Politics*, p. 497.
[84] Alexander Barmine, *One Who Survived* (New York, 1945), p. 121.
[85] Davies, *Mission to Moscow*, p. 262.

Inasmuch as the underlying intent of the purges remains one of the major riddles of Soviet history,[86] it is impossible here to unravel their meaning in the Foreign Commissariat. While some observers have been inclined to regard the diplomatic housecleaning as a preparation for the agreement with Hitler, the part played by foreign policy considerations is by no means clear beyond the fairly obvious fact that people with foreign contacts and foreign experiences were frequent victims, but this may have been for reasons other than the direction of foreign policy itself. The effect of the purge was to reduce even further any independence of action or decision on the part of foreign service officials, an increasing number of whom apparently were attached to the NKVD, and to leave Litvinov a general without an army.

As to Litvinov's own survival, a few comments may be made. In the first place, he may have been fortunate in the fact that while an old Bolshevik he had *not* been one of the inner circle which made the revolution, and consequently had not become enmeshed in the struggle for power within the party, a struggle which produced a very high death rate among the contestants. Moreover, so long as the policy of "collective security" was officially upheld by the Soviet Union, Litvinov's removal or disappearance would have had unfavorable foreign repercussions. By the time he was dropped the purges had subsided. Finally, it is clear that Litvinov must have possessed in some sense or another Stalin's confidence. It is difficult to believe that for all his international political value he could have survived those years of unimaginable suspicion had Stalin not had confidence in his personal as well as his political loyalty. The thesis, however, that Litvinov really believed that Stalin was purging the Foreign Commissariat to rid it of a Fascist fifth column seems quite unlikely, especially since the course of the purges generally started with a suspected chief and spread out through the ranks of his associates and subordinates. Nor does the contrary thesis that Litvinov and Stalin were clandestinely retooling the Narkomindel for a German rapprochement carry conviction; besides making utter nonsense of Litvinov's public policy it increases the difficulty of accounting for his dismissal.

The conclusion that seems able to deal with these confused and contradictory problems most satisfactorily is the one which sees Stalin as always having several strings to his bow. If one assumes that he was capable of considering simultaneously two separate and even conflicting

---

[86] Two authors, with firsthand experience in the purges, have recently enumerated seventeen theories which have been advanced to explain the purges: F. Beck and W. Godin, *Russian Purge and the Extraction of Confession* (New York, 1951). With unusual reserve they do not pretend to know the answer.

lines of policy, not making up his mind in advance but waiting to see how events developed, then it is possible, perhaps, to reconcile the elements of difference discussed above and the fact that Litvinov was not a victim of the purge.

According to this interpretation, which is the most this paper can attempt to offer, there were at least two contending lines of foreign policy within the Politburo, and perhaps within Stalin's own mind, in the 1930's: one, the "Litvinov policy," of which Litvinov himself was not only the agent but probably also the advocate and possibly even the formulator (even in a monolithic state ideas cannot all originate at the apex of the pyramid); the other, the policy which emerged with the pact of August 23, 1939, and acquired explicit characteristics in the two years following. Stalin, while perhaps inclined toward the second, was willing to give the first a trial, especially since no other alternative appeared profitable after 1933: the revolutionary line had brought few results and did not fit well with domestic developments, the Rapallo connection seemed impossible with Hitler's Germany behaving in an exceedingly unfriendly fashion. On the other hand the "Litvinov policy" depended upon achieving results. When these failed to come about the balance—whether between persons in the Politburo or between ideas in Stalin's own mind—would swing away from it. Thus, Litvinov's warnings after 1936 that "collective security" could be wrecked if the Western Powers did not change their ways may be regarded as a reflection of a decision still in suspension in the Politburo, a forewarning of a course which he himself may not have favored but which was in the cards if collective security failed.[87]

This interpretation also seems able to meet the question of Litvinov's resignation on May 3, 1939. The terse Soviet announcement merely stated that his resignation had been at his request because of ill health. Since the war, however, the official Soviet explanation has been that in the spring of 1939, when the international situation was deteriorating, when the Soviet Union was threatened with a hostile combination of capitalist Powers, "it was necessary to have in such a responsible post as that of Peoples Commissar for Foreign Affairs, a political leader of

[87] When discussing the possible failure of collective security, Litvinov often indicated that the USSR might do well to return to isolation. Now the Molotov-Ribbentrop Pact was scarcely a return to isolation but, as it proved, a decision to collaborate in aggression (the purely defensive interpretation of Russia's advances during the period of the pact seems inadequate in light of the documents published in *Nazi-Soviet Relations*, esp. pp. 258-259). Hence in his occasional predictions that the Germans would seek a pact with the Soviet Union, Litvinov may have been predicting a development which he himself did not approve.

greater experience and greater popularity in the country than M. M. Litvinov."[88]

While this statement is true in the sense that the authority of the Politburo was now concerned with the immediate direction of foreign relations, it does not suggest the possibility of a change in policy. At the time, quite naturally, the Soviet government and its representatives abroad assured the other Powers that the switch in Foreign Commissars meant no alteration in the direction of Soviet policy. These assurances were received with justified skepticism, however, and one of the most interested parties, Hitler, later said, "Litvinov's dismissal was decisive."[89] To be sure, Stalin's speech of March 10 at the Eighteenth Congress of the Communist Party had served to pave the way, as had the remarks on April 17 by the Soviet ambassador in Berlin.[90] Nevertheless, it can be concluded that Litvinov's retirement was a very important step in the German-Soviet rapprochement, if only because he was a Jew and had come to symbolize the effort at collective security against German aggression.

While Litvinov's retirement certainly facilitated the German-Soviet negotiations which led to the pact, was it a mark of "no confidence" in him or his diplomacy? His American biographer, whose account of the event was obtained directly from Litvinov during the latter's ambassadorship in the United States during the war, denies that he was discharged or abruptly dismissed. According to this account, Litvinov, after Munich, decided that a rapprochement with Germany was necessary, that he was an obstacle, and suggested his own retirement. The resignation took place untheatrically after a series of conferences with Stalin, and Litvinov himself proposed his friend Molotov as a successor.[91]

This interpretation has Litvinov's authority for its authenticity. And while it is true that he was, in 1942-1943, an official representative of the Soviet government and therefore not likely to stress conflicts in the conduct of Soviet diplomacy, it is also true that he was often surprisingly frank in such matters and not inclined to allow personal concerns to flavor his thinking. Nevertheless, there are certain difficulties with this interpretation. The postwar Soviet explanation seems to imply, quite ungraciously if the change had been marked by full harmony, that Litvinov was not a

---

[88] *Falsifiers of History*, Supplement to "New Times" (Moscow), No. 8, February 18, 1948, p. 9. See also *Diplomaticheskii Slovar'*, II, 162 and 675.

[89] "Notes on Hitler's Conference with his Commanders-in-Chief, August 22, 1939," *Documents on International Affairs 1939-46*, I, 446.

[90] *Nazi-Soviet Relations*, pp. 1-2.

[91] Pope, *Litvinoff*, pp. 441-442. The author is grateful to Mr. Pope for his letter explaining that Litvinov had personally confirmed this account of his resignation.

big enough man for the job. The picture of Litvinov, not a member of the Politburo, nominating the powerful Molotov to be his successor, appears incongruous. Moreover, there is some evidence that Litvinov was in disgrace with fortune and Stalin's eyes. Early in May 1939 the unusually communicative, and perhaps unreliable, Soviet chargé in Berlin, Astakhov, told Coulondre that for six months Litvinov's fall had been foreseeable, since he and Molotov were no longer in accord, and Stalin, while esteeming him, did not like him.[92] After his retirement he seems to have received a cold shoulder at Soviet public functions.[93] In a speech on August 31, 1939, Molotov criticized those "short-sighted people even in our own country who, carried away by oversimplified anti-Fascist propaganda, forgot about this provocative work of our enemies [the machinating Western European politicians],"[94] a remark that may be interpreted as a slap at Litvinov. On February 20, 1941, Litvinov was dropped from the Central Committee of the Communist party for "inability to discharge obligations."[95]

It is possible, then, that Litvinov was under a cloud; that Stalin had weighed his policy and found it wanting. At the same time he was not officially damned, partly because the policy connected with his name had been Stalin's also, at least nominally; partly, it would seem, because he might still be useful should circumstances change, as they did in June 1941. Still, the remainder of his career is an anticlimax. During his brief ambassadorship in the United States from 1941 to 1943 he was not the leading figure he had been in the 1930's. After the war he sank again into obscurity. At his death on December 31, 1951, he was a minor Soviet hero—with members of the Foreign Ministry as pallbearers, but no one from the Politburo. In the second volume of the Soviet Diplomatic Dictionary, published in 1950, the favorable but brief biography of Litvinov occupies 92 lines, as compared with 54 for Chicherin and 292 for Molotov. Stalin's accomplishments as a diplomat were, of course, too vast for inclusion or comparison.

[92] Quoted in Georges Bonnet, *Fin d'une Europe* (Paris, 1946), p. 184.

[93] It may be worth mentioning that the daughter of a former NKVD official attached to the Foreign Commissariat has recently written that immediately after Litvinov's resignation and replacement by Molotov her father was purged as a part of a general, though unexplained, house cleaning in that ministry. Nora Murray (née Korzhenko), *I Spied for Stalin* (New York, 1951), pp. 116-129.

[94] V. M. Molotov, *The Meaning of the Soviet-German Non-Aggression Pact* (New York, 1939), p. 8.

[95] According to Pope, *Litvinoff*, p. 460, this step was taken because "Stalin was determined to give no offense to the Germans." In that case it is difficult to see why Maisky, Soviet ambassador to Great Britain, should have been elevated to alternate membership on the Central Committee at the same time.

IV

In retrospect Litvinov's "collective security" can be seen to have been largely a phrase, never a reality. Neither the Soviet Union nor the Western Powers were ever really guided by the principle of common action against the rising danger from Germany; both ardently hoped that the hurricane, if it developed, would not come in their direction. The "appeasement" policies of France and Great Britain have been thoroughly criticized by disapproving citizens of those states. There was also, however, a corresponding tendency in Russia which sought a reconciliation with Nazi Germany. This tendency was naturally less apparent so long as the major force of Hitler's propaganda was directed against Soviet Communism.

Even Litvinov's position appears reasonably clear and unambiguous only during the short span from 1933 to 1936—before Germany was equipped to fight a war. After it was clear that the Third Reich was, willy-nilly, going to become a powerful military state, his pleas for collective measures were interspersed with warnings of a Soviet return to isolation. By the time of the Munich crisis his support of collective security was form without content: he was sure that France and England would not move; the French, the British—and the Germans—were equally convinced the Russians would not move.

Nor, in the long run, did Litvinov's efforts to "find a common language" between the Soviet Union and the rest of the world succeed. This failure needs no emphasis today. Indeed Litvinov may have been a cause for deepening the rift. The atmosphere of practical cooperativeness which he created partly concealed but in no way softened the hard core of the Stalinist regime. As a result, collisions with that hard core were not only bruising but carried the additional sting of disillusion.

Still, after this has been said and after one recognizes that future documentary revelations may further darken the picture of Soviet policy between the wars and present Litvinov in a more doubtful light, the late Foreign Commissar does have claim to two things of lasting significance: his ideas and his acumen as a diplomat. Regardless of the aims of Soviet foreign policy or of Litvinov's connection with those aims, the ideas he expressed in his major League speeches are important in themselves. Indeed, whole paragraphs describe, in mood as in content, the tasks facing the world today in its effort to check the new danger of Soviet expansion. His ability to detect the major trends in the 1930's and to anticipate the course of events indicates an extraordinary understanding of that decade.

The most recent historian of the League of Nations has remarked on Litvinov's role in that organization: "No future historian will lightly disagree with any views expressed by Litvinov on international questions. Whatever may be thought of the policy and purposes of his government, the long series of his statements and speeches in the Assembly, the Council, the Conferences, and Committees of which he was a member between 1927 and 1939 can hardly be read today without an astonished admiration. Nothing in the annals of the League can compare with them in frankness, in debating power, in the acute diagnosis of each situation. No contemporary statesman could point to such a record of criticisms justified and prophecies fulfilled."[96]

While one might quarrel with the inclusion of the years 1927-1933, it is difficult to disagree with this conclusion for the six years between Hitler's coming to power and Litvinov's retirement from the diplomatic scene.

[96] F. P. Walters, *A History of the League of Nations* (2 vols., London, 1952), II, 712.

12

Alexis Saint-Léger Léger

BY ELIZABETH R. CAMERON

DIPLOMACY, says Alexis Léger, is imagination, foresight, suggestion, representation, execution. The diplomat is the master of critical analysis and the creator of large designs. He must have courage, he must have patience, he must accept humbly the limits of the possible. In disagreement with his ministers, he must combat the false to the best of his ability, but always as their loyal subordinate. In construction and prevention alike, his role remains hermetic and anonymous. This is Léger's conception of the diplomat: he is an innovator, but also an executor bound by the disciplines of the civil servant.[1]

Léger's career as a diplomat spans the quarter of a century from 1914 to 1940. He entered the service at the beginning of the first world war. He was dismissed from the highest post in the French Foreign Office only a few weeks before the defeat of France by Nazi Germany.

From the start he was no ordinary diplomat. He was a poet, and, as a poet, lived in a world not much frequented by other diplomats. But he was also capable of their world, experienced in many worlds, and not least in the worldly society of the French capital. His courtesy was famous though not always comfortable, and often of a kind to put him out of

[1] The story of Léger's diplomatic career as found in French and foreign sources is extremely fragmentary. The available British and German documents cover only a fraction of the period, and in them the role of the permanent services remains, for the most part, anonymous. The *French Yellow Book*, the only official publication of the Ministry of Foreign Affairs for the period just before the war, has been carefully tailored and contains nothing on the work of Léger. A large part of the archives of the Quai d'Orsay was burned in Paris in May 1940, and of the part saved still more was afterwards lost at sea. There are memoirs, in profusion, by French politicians, soldiers and journalists, and despite their controversial character, they yield some valuable information on Léger's attitudes and accomplishments. There is further evidence, unfortunately not free of political bias, in the report and hearings of the French parliamentary commission charged with investigating the events of the war and prewar years in France. But the reader will see how important Léger's personal testimony is in this study. Wherever references to his record and opinions are not documented, they are taken from conversations between Léger and the writer in Washington in December 1951.

reach.[2] Many, and most of all the worldly and the ambitious, were made uneasy by his aloofness, the subtleties of his language, and the sinuous progressions of his thought.

Léger's life presents a series of contrasts, and it does not yield to simple analysis. As one writer has said, he is a man of East and West, and of both shores of the Atlantic; he is a man also of silence and of the word; a man of worldly possessions and a man stripped of them; a solitary and a lover of the human race; a man of pleasure and an ascetic; a man of culture and a man at home with the elements.[3] These contrasts suggest deep layers in Léger's character and experience. And in their own way, they help to explain his loyalties, the friends and enemies he made through his long and critical course in French foreign policy.

Léger was born in the late 1880's on a small coral island in the Antilles, "the son of a family French as only the colonials are French." From the age of eleven, when he left the scene of an idyllic childhood in the tropics, he was educated in Paris, in literature, medicine, and the law. He completed his training for the Diplomatic Service, and went out to China in 1916 as a junior secretary. Here he lived in Peking in a rented temple, "sat with the philosophers and sages," and broke the life of diplomatic conversations and official cables with journeys overland across the Gobi Desert, and overseas to the far islands of the Pacific. In the East, writes another poet, Léger "learned the art by which a man defends his life from others and even from himself."[4]

The China post was his only foreign service, a fact always held against him by his colleagues in the field. The rest of his professional life was spent within the walls of the Quai d'Orsay. He served first on the Asiatic desk, and later went to the political and commercial division, of which he became chief in 1929. He succeeded to the office of Secretary General with the rank of ambassador of France in 1933, following Philippe Berthelot.

From the mid-1920's, when Léger's rapid rise in the diplomatic hierarchy began, his professional career falls into two periods of equal length: seven years of service under Briand (1925-1932), and seven years as "the permanent master of French foreign policy" (1933-1940). The first was a period of design and realization. The second was "*décadence*," a phase

[2] André Gide in *Les Cahiers de la Pléiade* (St-Jean Perse issue), Summer-Autumn 1950, pp. 23-24.
[3] Gabriel Bounoure, *ibid.*, pp. 107-108.
[4] Archibald MacLeish in *Exil and other Poems*, by St-Jean Perse (New York, 1949), pp. 143-144.

of contraction when all diplomatic operations were conducted on a steadily narrowing base.

The long contact with Briand began in 1921 at the Washington Disarmament Conference, to which Léger was called as a Far Eastern expert. Impressed by the insight of the young diplomat, Briand later invited him to join his personal secretariat, and in 1925 Léger became Briand's *chef de cabinet*. This was a political appointment, and in it Léger had great influence on the shaping of French foreign policy. In effect, he became the intimate collaborator in all Briand's plans for peace and security.

Léger, by 1925, was already a poet of reputation, though under a different name. But when he took service with Briand, he turned himself over completely to diplomacy. He published no verse from 1924 until the years of his exile from France in the 1940's, and the story goes that when Briand asked Léger about the early works of "St-Jean Perse," Léger refused to claim their authorship.[5] He never allowed the private labors or public acclaim of the poet to impinge on the professional dedication of the diplomat.

In Briand Léger found many of the qualities upon which he has always patterned himself: "the boldness of the dream . . . tempered . . . by the dictates of common sense"; the speed of suggestion and retort equaled only by "indifference to the exploitation of success." Briand, he writes, "had no need of duplicity or violence to win. . . . He hated equally stupidity, cowardice, clumsiness and vulgarity. . . . He hunted with the lightest arms, and fished with the finest lines. . . . He brought the refinement of the artist to the handling of men."[6] The skills of the master entered deeply into the consciousness of the pupil, and in Léger they were reflected in a subtlety and complexity often misunderstood by the diplomats and politicians with whom he worked.

From Briand Léger had also learned the rules which guided French diplomacy in the period of construction, and in a published tribute to Briand they are stated in Léger's own words:

First: "To insure for France in particular all possible elements of immediate security."

Second: "Under cover of this immediate security, and in rhythm with its development, to seek the broader bases of European peace."

Third: "To extend beyond Europe the solidarity of nations against war."

Fourth: "In case of pressing risks, to put aside the ambitious plans, and

[5] Louis-Marcel Raymond in *Cahiers de la Pléiade*, p. 125.
[6] Alexis Léger, *Briand* (Aurora, N.Y., 1943), pp. 6-7.

to concentrate exclusively upon assembling all the forces necessary for the exercise of collective action in prevention."[7]

In Briand's time, says Léger, "these directives were followed so clearly that French foreign policy could never be accused of the least ambiguity."[8] For her own "immediate security," France had her pacts of mutual assistance with Poland and Czechoslovakia. And in the West, Briand had finally succeeded in winning British recognition of the principle of shared responsibility. The Locarno Pact of 1925 was his contribution to the insurance of the critical Rhineland area, and in it Léger had worked with him in all the difficult preparatory stages and in the drafting of the final texts. To its designers, the peculiar virtue of Locarno was that it was both "collective" and "automatic," committing the guarantors to defend the Rhine, committing them further to act in case Germany violated the forbidden demilitarized zone.

With this agreement as the solid base of French security, Briand and Léger moved on to explore "the broader bases of European peace." Together they drafted a plan for an organic statute of Europe, and this plan was first rehearsed in Briand's Commission for European Union. Outside Europe, their device for drawing America in, to make her "first gesture of moral and psychological solidarity," was the Kellogg-Briand Pact.

Taken as a whole, it was an ambitious scheme of diplomacy, ranging from precise guarantees at the chief danger point, to long-range planning for new international ties and institutions. But by 1930, political danger signals in Germany had begun already to expose France to the "pressing risks" which Briand had foreseen. And, as Léger points out, the last painful efforts of Briand's life were expended in the "most urgent of diplomatic campaigns,"[9] the effort to alert the Powers to real and pressing danger.

When Briand died in 1932, Léger was in the small circle which stood beside his deathbed. He inherited many things from Briand which were deep and lasting in their effect on his diplomacy. But the immediate inheritance, the thing that came to Léger most directly, something to which he felt an almost personal commitment, was the burden of the watch on security. In the year of Briand's death, a member of the British embassy had a long conversation with Léger, who was deeply depressed about the prevalence in Germany of what he called the "mentality of prewar imperialist Germany." "What was so alarming, M. Léger continued, was that it seemed impossible to reach finality; each concession,

[7] *ibid.*, p. 13.   [8] *ibid.*   [9] *ibid.*, p. 16.

freely granted in the desire to conciliate, was promptly followed by fresh and yet more extravagant demands. If Germany were now to take the law into her own hands in the armament question, and were not brought to book, her next move would assuredly be to proceed to some flagrant act in the demilitarized zone which might even bring into play the Treaty of Locarno. The only way, in M. Léger's opinion, to meet this situation which he considered fraught with great danger, was for the British and French Governments to unite in saying to Germany: 'Thus far and no further.' They must speak their mind clearly and make it plain that there would be no wavering. Otherwise a situation would develop in which war in the relatively near future was absolutely inevitable."[10]

From the moment when he took over the highest post in the French Foreign Office, Léger became a fighter for lost causes. His chief function now was a function of prevention. It fell to him to guard the guarantees of the 1920's. It fell to him also to stand in the way of policies prompted by new threats of violence against France. Léger says of Briand that "he would never have committed the psychological error of practising, at the wrong moment, the policy called appeasement."[11] And this too was Léger's intent.

II

With Briand gone, the task of the Secretary General was complicated by differences which divided him from his Foreign Ministers: in succession, from 1933 to 1940, Paul-Boncour, Barthou, Laval, Flandin, Delbos, Bonnet, Daladier and Reynaud. The list speaks for itself. After Briand, with the single exception of Barthou in 1934, Léger never had a minister who combined, as he says, the vision with the will to carry on "the great rules of French diplomacy." Boncour was a man of integrity but not strong; Delbos was a man of narrow vision and distrustful of himself. Of the rest, all contributed sooner or later to the abandonment of safeguards and the snow-balling of appeasement.

Léger had always regarded Briand's attempt to conciliate republican Germany as the most courageous act of his diplomacy. But after the Nazi revolution the setting itself was changed, and Léger saw no chance of agreement with the new masters of the Reich. The problem now was a problem of containment: of mobilizing, by diplomatic action, the force needed to hold Germany to the terms imposed on her at Versailles; above all, to the contract she had freely agreed to at Locarno. "The

[10] *British Documents*, 2nd series, IV, 101-102.   [11] Léger, *Briand*, p. 16.

structure of Locarno," says Léger, "was for a decade our only corner-stone in Europe; the only one which inspired the respect of Hitler by the precision and strictness of its mechanism, the only one which he felt obliged to acknowledge officially and repeatedly until the moment when he discerned the inner weaknesses of the beneficiaries of the system."[12]

But in France, already in the year when Hitler became Chancellor of the Reich, internal weakness began to show itself in alarming outbreaks of political strife. Trouble came to a head in serious riots in Paris in February 1934, and here the evidence suggests an actual conspiracy, a prepared plan to seize the Chamber, disperse the deputies and proclaim an authoritarian government.[13]

Though the attack came close to succeeding, at the last moment the Chamber was defended against the rioters, and the government of the Republic was saved. But in the years ahead, political crosscurrents ran stronger and deeper under the disturbed surface of a shaken republican system and ideal. And having only narrowly escaped a revolution in 1934, France continued to live under stresses and strains which unsettled her diplomacy. The Foreign Ministers whom the Quai d'Orsay now served were personally involved in the sharpening conflict between profascist Right and procommunist Left in their own country. And, at the same time, they were swayed, one way or another, by the political and diplo-matic experiments of Italy, Germany, and the Soviet Union abroad.

Léger was not blind to these pressures, but his was not a politically oriented diplomacy. And conscious as he was of the need for a wider circle of allies, for him there was one ruling principle in foreign policy. No new ally was worth the price of estrangement from Britain. Her position must be reckoned with, her confidence maintained against all odds, even if necessary at the high cost of sacrificing the initiative for France.

In his relations with the totalitarian states, Léger was never one to think in terms of hand-to-mouth agreements. On the contrary, through all efforts made to woo them by politicians of differing political per-suasions in France, he stubbornly resisted the bait of hasty deals and undercover bargains. And as late as the dark spring of 1940, when Sumner Welles made his tour of exploration in Europe, he was struck by the "magnificent clarity and logic" which Léger "as always" showed, and no less by the "innately liberal nature of his political philosophy."[14] Yet

[12] *ibid.*, p. 15.
[13] *Commission d'Enquête parlementaire sur les événements survenus en France de 1933 à 1945, Rapport de M. Charles Serre, député au nom de la Commission d'Enquête parlementaire* (Paris, 1951), I, 13-14.
[14] Sumner Welles, *The Time for Decision* (New York, 1944), p. 125.

none of these qualities were to spare the civil servant the execution of policy decisions which he disapproved.

The first overture of the 1930's which led away from the settled course of French diplomacy came from Italy in a proposal for a Four Power Pact. The French government was reluctant to turn the cold shoulder to Italy, but it was forced also to consider the suspicions of its small allies. In this dilemma, the permanent services of the Foreign Office played a restraining part. The Four Power Pact was concluded in 1933, but by their efforts to emasculate the revisionist clauses suggested by Italy, the French diplomats succeeded in rendering the pact harmless.[15]

This kind of check exercised by the Quai d'Orsay was one basis for the legend, which grew up later, that Léger was the saboteur of all attempts to reach an understanding with Italy. An exaggerated charge, says Paul-Boncour who was Léger's minister in 1933, and one motivated chiefly by political prejudice: "It is a legend, exploited today for reasons of party politics, which attributes to the Quai d'Orsay, and particularly to Alexis Léger . . . an indefinable hostility toward Italy." In Boncour's opinion, "the mind of Léger, supple to excess, was incapable of any kind of phobia," and he adds that he always found him, "like all my collaborators of the Ministry of Foreign Affairs, the intelligent and loyal executor of the directives transmitted to him."[16]

In 1935 Léger appears again in negotiations with Italy, this time with Laval as his minister. The Quai d'Orsay had been working on the draft of an agreement to adjust unsettled Italian claims against France in Africa. But Léger found that Laval cared nothing for the substance of the contract, only for the sensational *voyage de Rome*, which he insisted on carrying through before the diplomats had completed their interminable arrangements, their endless *"chinoiseries."* This time friction between Léger and the Foreign Minister reached the point where Léger threatened to resign. Laval, fearful that Léger's withdrawal would compromise the negotiations with Mussolini, was reluctant to part with him, and here, as at other later critical junctures, the civil servant made the decision to remain.

In many precarious exchanges between French ministers and the heads of foreign states, the known integrity of the French Secretary General served as a cover. His presence was used to disarm suspicion that secret commitments had been made or rights signed away in some se-

---

[15] John Wheeler-Bennett, *The Pipe Dream of Peace* (New York, 1935), pp. 134ff.

[16] Joseph Paul-Boncour, *Entre deux guerres: souvenirs sur la troisième république* (Paris, 1946), II, 339.

cluded corner of Roman parks, Polish railway stations, or Paris museums. Yet in the case of the Rome interviews Léger has asserted that he had no idea of the extent of Laval's private concessions to Mussolini.[17] He was certain however that they existed, and would be used by Italy in preparing her dangerous adventure in East Africa. He was also sure that France would never make an ally of Italy on the basis of such bargains as Laval's.

Since Léger became Secretary General, France had also been approached by the Soviet Union. And, for the record, it should be said again that Léger was no more inclined toward the Left deviation than toward the Right in diplomacy, no more ready for a communist than a fascist orientation in foreign policy. Indeed, Léger regards the Russian proposal of 1933 as "the most cynical of all projects": a top-secret plan for bilateral agreement with France outside the League, devised as a shield for Soviet imperialism in Asia. At first, at the suggestion of the Russians, the secret was carefully guarded in a locked iron box, whose contents were known only to Paul-Boncour, Léger, and the Russian ambassador.[18] Hoping to persuade the Russians to negotiate on a different base, Léger set to work to remove "the inadmissible conditions." Drafts and counterdrafts were worked out between himself and Potemkin over long months, and, as Léger describes it, the Russian negotiator "visited the dentist twice a week." Little by little, progress was made, and the victim responded to repeated extractions, to "moral embarrassment" and "hard usage."

When Barthou succeeded Paul-Boncour in 1934, he first told Léger that he would be dropped from the service. The suspicion was then that Léger was too soft with the Russians. But, after listening to Léger's progress report, Barthou reversed himself, refused to remain in the ministry unless Léger stayed, and gave him a free hand in the negotiations ahead.

Characteristically, Léger first made it his business to set British suspicions at rest. He went to London with Barthou in the summer of 1934, took the British into his confidence on the French tête-à-tête with the Russians, and pressed his case on the merits of drawing Russia into the collective circle.

Léger's design now took shape as an elaborate dual scheme: first, a regional agreement (Germany, Russia, Poland, Czechoslovakia, and the Baltic states); second, a Franco-Soviet Pact of mutual assistance, open also to Germany if she wished to adhere to it. The regional proposal was

[17] Général M. Gamelin, *Servir* (Paris, 1946), II, 172.
[18] Paul-Boncour, *Entre deux guerres*, II, 366-369.

Léger's most ambitious effort of the 1930's, a plan for insuring Eastern Europe as Western Europe had been insured in the 1920's at Locarno. No commitment was asked of the British in the East, and after the London conference with the French, they approved the proposals. Meanwhile, Litvinov had yielded on the principle of a multilateral pact, and, more important, he had agreed to Russia's prior entry into the League.

But how to overcome the obstacles still standing in the way of an Eastern Locarno? Germany and Poland were both hostile for their own reasons, and in view of their obstruction, time and effort expended in the furtherance of the scheme appears essentially unrealistic on the part of its designer. Yet for months Léger persisted in the pursuit of his goal.

The assassination of Barthou in October 1934 deprived Léger of his strongest backer, and with Laval in Barthou's place, there was an immediate demand for a tactical victory. Laval's *voyage de Moscou*, which followed within a few months his journey to Rome was, as Léger says, a *voyage de cabotin*, a stage on the circuit of the strolling player. The permanent services of the Quai d'Orsay opposed Laval's contracting in haste for this engagement. But when Léger objected to the plan for an insufficiently prepared visit to Moscow, Laval only replied: "Vous couchez avec les affaires." He then summoned Potemkin, and Potemkin, seeing the rift which divided the diplomat from the minister, was able to advise his government that the time was ripe for a deal with the French.

In practical terms, what emerged from the Moscow journey was the most realistic part of the complex dual design. Léger's Eastern Locarno, for reasons which seem obvious, had fallen by the way, but a treaty of mutual assistance was concluded between France and Russia in the spring of 1935. The signature of the pact was an important step, but in the last analysis its effectiveness depended on staff talks between the military of the two countries. These were indispensable to common action, and they were never to materialize.

Léger's chief object in the Franco-Soviet Pact was to drive a wedge between Moscow and Berlin, to divorce Russia from her old military liaison with Germany. But for France he was never convinced of the wisdom of a policy which would throw her into too close and exclusive a dependence on Moscow.[19] As late as December 1938, during the conversations held between Bonnet and Ribbentrop in Paris, Léger told the Germans that "the bilateral nature of the Franco-Russian Pact had not

---

[19] Pertinax, *The Gravediggers of France* (New York, 1944), p. 245.

been designed by the French partner. . . . It was only through the development of circumstances that the pact had become a purely bilateral affair."[20]

For all the agreements made with Rome and with Moscow, 1935 had been a bad year for French diplomacy, and there was reason enough for the pessimism which Léger expressed to Gamelin at the end of the year: "If France commits herself definitely to Russia, [Germany] will reply by occupying the left bank of the Rhine; if Italy emerges weakened from her current difficulties [in Abyssinia] that means *Anschluss*; if there is war between Britain and Italy [in the Mediterranean] and we come in, Germany is prepared to move against us. Only the closest understanding between France and Britain can keep the peace from now on." And he added that even that insurance was in doubt.[21] In effect, the search for allies had accomplished no closing of the ranks. On the contrary, it seemed only to accentuate divergences of interest and purpose, and Léger saw these divergences as dangerous obstacles to common action against the main enemy, the Reich.

III

In the spate of *ex post facto* polemics which in recent years have been centered on the progress of German rearmament, there has been a race on all sides in France to pass the buck. And many have tried to make the Quai d'Orsay the ultimate recipient. For one, the French ambassador to Berlin, M. François-Poncet, maintains that he tried repeatedly to find out what measures the Ministry of Foreign Affairs had prepared to counter treaty violations by Germany. To no avail, he says, since all warnings delivered, all questions asked, all suggestions offered resulted only in the refusal to consider any preventive or punitive measures outside the League.[22] François-Poncet adds that he favored the application of "drastic sanctions" when Germany reintroduced conscription in 1935,[23] but recognizing his government's unwillingness, suggested that efforts be made to seek a compromise with the Reich on the status of the Rhineland. "The Quai d'Orsay, however, replied that it would be rash to admit that the Locarno contract could be modified in any of its details, since there was

---

[20] *German Documents*, series D, IV, 476.

[21] Gamelin, *Servir*, II, 177. Throughout his service as Chief of the General Staff, Gamelin testifies to free and frank exchange of information between himself and Léger. They often conferred, and Gamelin trusted both Léger's integrity and his judgment on foreign affairs.

[22] *Commission d'Enquête parlementaire, Témoignages et Documents recueillis par la Commission d'Enquête parlementaire* (Paris, 1951), III, 762.

[23] *ibid.*, III, 764.

always the danger that England and Italy as guarantors might seize the occasion to draw out."[24]

The French consul general in the Rhineland, M. Dobler, has also some harsh things to say of the negligence, the obstinacy, and the inexperience of the permanent services: "It is the inadequate professional training of the diplomats at home (he cites specifically the fact that Léger had never served abroad except in a junior post in China twenty years earlier); it is the barrier which they opposed to the diffusion in France of information from their foreign agents; it is this deplorable state of affairs which in my opinion was the initial cause of the French government's disastrous failure to act against Germany before March 1936 and at that time."[25]

Dobler cites a number of examples to prove his point. Each is designed to show that reports from Germany to the Quai d'Orsay, all of them containing alarming information on German preparations for remilitarization, had never reached the responsible authorities in Paris. Various excuses had been made and obstacles raised: either the Foreign Minister had been too busy to read the dispatches;[26] or foreign service agents, attempting to bring their reports directly to the Minister, had been turned aside by high officials of the permanent services, and made to understand that their jurisdiction did not extend to political questions.[27]

But other witnesses are more guarded in their judgment of the methods and policies of the Quai d'Orsay. Léger was accused of working too much with the ambassadors of foreign Powers in Paris, doing so in order to exclude his own agents from their proper share in policy decisions. The investigating commission questioned the secretary of the Berlin embassy, M. Tarbe de Saint-Hardouin, on this point but, under pressure of interrogation, he refused to commit himself: "It is certain that there was a tendency to take action on the ground [in Paris] wherever possible. But I think it would be a mistake to generalize or treat this assertion as an indictment."[28]

[24] *ibid.*, III, 766.
[25] *ibid.*, II, 500-502.
[26] *ibid.*
[27] *ibid.*, II, 503-504. Yet Dobler claims that Léger's predecessor, Philippe Berthelot, had intended the Cologne consulate to serve as an outpost of political intelligence in the Rhineland (*ibid.*, II, 470).
[28] *ibid.*, VI, 1526. In an interview with the author in December 1952, Robert Coulondre, former ambassador in Moscow and Berlin, expressed little sympathy for the view that the permanent services had put up a screen between the ministers and the envoys in the field. In Coulondre's view, failure to reach the ministers was always the fault of the ambassador. See, however, Chapter 2, note 34, above. On the methods of the Quai d'Orsay, see also Chapter 2 at note 53.

No doubt, in France as elsewhere, there were sharp jealousies between the foreign and sedentary services, and inadequacies in the diffusion of intelligence.[29] But these in themselves are not sufficient to place the responsibility for the confusions which hampered decision when Germany made her crucial move in the Rhineland. In Paris, it appeared that the professional diplomats, the responsible ministers, and the General Staff were not agreed on the rights to independent action which French diplomacy claimed to have won at Locarno. Gamelin and the Minister of War were both uncertain on this point,[30] whereas others, including Léger and Sarraut, who headed the government, insisted that France had the clear right to move without waiting for the verdict of Geneva.[31]

The possibilities of military reprisals against Germany were also shrouded in doubts and confusion. The fact is that the French army had neither the plan nor the organization to enforce the treaties by military action. And after Germany announced remilitarization on March 7, it became clear that any deep penetration of the Rhineland by the French would involve nothing less than a general mobilization.[32] This fact certainly came as a shock to those who had thought a simple police operation would suffice. Léger had no such illusions. He recognized that heavy sacrifices would be called for to meet the risk of German resistance on the Rhine.

Even severe critics recognize that Léger and the permanent services were determined to preserve demilitarization at whatever cost.[33] Unfortunately, they did not succeed in overcoming the confusions and hesitations which prevailed at the top level. After three days of ministerial conference and consultation in Paris, Léger accompanied his minister to the meetings of the League Council in London in mid-March. And it is worth noting that it was at this moment, so critical for the policy of con-

---

[29] In 1932, Léger had served on an interministerial commission to study the reorganization of the Ministry of Foreign Affairs. The parliamentary report on the foreign affairs budget for 1933 also concerned itself with the lack of cohesion in the permanent services, the inadequacy of Quai d'Orsay intelligence, and the poverty of diplomatic information sent to French representatives abroad. The report, however, suggested that what foreign policy most needed was to be taken out of the realm of political *sautes d'humeur*, and placed in the hands of professional diplomats, *Journal Officiel de la République Française, Chambre des Députés, Documents parlementaires*, Annexe 1535 (March 9, 1933), pp. 510-525. See also Chapter 2, §1 above.

[30] See note of March 11, 1936, from the Ministry of War, Gamelin, *Servir*, II, 208.

[31] *Témoignages et Documents*, III, 574. Yet Sarraut asserts that rights aside, his government had decided before Germany acted that France could not afford to reply without consulting the Locarno guarantors (*ibid.*).

[32] Gamelin, *Servir*, II, 209.

[33] See Dobler in *Témoignages et Documents*, II, 505.

tainment, that Léger was first locked out of the decisive conversations. Léger believes that Flandin followed the *politique de complaisance* from the start, and if this judgment is correct, it is not hard to see how Léger's presence would stand in Flandin's way. As Léger says, it is true that the British encouraged French inaction by rolling out "a velvet carpet for retreat,"[34] and he could see how relieved they were that the French had not ventured to act before them or without them. Still, he remained convinced that, had France moved, the British would have followed. Britain had given her pledge to the French on the Rhineland, and it was a principle of Léger's diplomacy that one could always count on the British to honor their commitments.

For Léger, the decision to leave Germany in military control of the Rhineland spelled the collapse of the whole structure of security: "It was the London Conference of March 1936, not Munich, which must bear the responsibility for Hitler's flooding over the banks."[35] This decision lost France the buffer which protected her from direct attack; it also seriously compromised her power to check Germany's Eastern adventures by threats of counterattack in the West. After the return of the French mission from London, Léger told his subordinates that war was inevitable. It was only a matter of time and of Germany's choosing. And the significance he attached to this warning is indicated by the fact that he has called it his "political testament."

This was the end of Locarno, and it brought Europe to the watershed in the precarious diplomacy of the 1930's. From the start of Léger's regime at the Quai d'Orsay, French diplomacy had fought a losing campaign of prevention. After 1936, he felt that the battle was lost. Yet despite his pessimism, Léger continued in an attitude which he describes as "irréductible dans l'irréductibilité." In this intransigence he became a thorn in the side of all politicians and journalists who favored solutions by compromise. And it was at this time that the pro-appeasement press began to attack him systematically.

The years 1936 and 1937 were the years of the Front Populaire. Léger was now in the service of governments of the Left, and his enemies, ever since, have tried to link his name with all that they found to excoriate in its policies. He was, he claims, a man of the Left, "an

---

[34] Winston Churchill, *The Gathering Storm* (Boston, 1948), p. 194. Léger holds that Churchill, who gave Flandin the benefit of the doubt in writing of his attitude in March 1936, was perhaps influenced to some degree by his expectation that he might, at a future date, have to work again with representatives of the French Right.

[35] Léger, *Briand*, p. 15.

opponent of everything antirepublican." But under governments of Right and Left alike, it was his settled purpose to keep his judgment clear of political sympathies—a purpose well illustrated in his attitude toward the war in Spain.

When war broke out in the peninsula in the summer of 1936, once more Léger's first concern was with the state of opinion in Britain. He saw with alarm that the new socialist government in France, the turmoil of French strikes and workers' agitation, had raised a red scare across the Channel. Accordingly, he persuaded Blum to accompany him to the diplomatic conferences scheduled for London.[36] Léger's *cauchemar* was nothing short of a British alignment with White Spain, Germany, and Italy "in a new Holy Alliance in the style of Metternich." And however right or wrong his judgment, he was convinced that British neutrality could not be assured unless the French government agreed to forego the shipment of arms and volunteers to the legal government of Spain. Therefore, against all Blum's sympathies, he got him to propose nonintervention as the best available insurance against the spread of conflict.

For the obvious reasons, nonintervention placed Blum in the direct line of fire from his supporters on the Left in France, and it often fell to Léger to defend it on behalf of his ministers. Thus, in the Spanish question, Léger became the scapegoat of the communist Left, while at the same time, on other counts, he was still under attack by the profascist Right.

In January 1937, the Spanish crisis gave Léger the chance to show his hand once more, at a critical moment in French relations with Germany. Rumors of German troop movements in Spanish Morocco had started a scare, and Léger, acting in the absence of Blum and Delbos, protested to the German ambassador in Paris. At the same time, the French ambassador in London, M. Corbin, an agent with whom Léger always maintained relations of confidence, secured, at Léger's instance, a promise of energetic support from Vansittart of the British Foreign Office. Such steps Léger regards as only the routine procedures of his office. The Germans, however, thought differently, as their reports on the Quai d'Orsay *démarche* clearly show.[37] They had felt a strong hand at the helm of French foreign policy, and they didn't like it. Thus, the incident

[36] Léger was anxious to show the British conservatives what kind of a man the new head of the French government really was. And one incident, reported by Léger, shows the kind of thing which he did to make his point: as the French delegation passed through the corridor which led to the conference room at 10 Downing Street, Léger deliberately held Blum in conversation beside the statue of Disraeli, a Jew, but obviously a gentleman and a statesman.

[37] *German Documents*, series D, III, 223-224.

added another black mark to their dossier on Léger as a public enemy of the Reich.

With the Blum government, Léger, and to a far greater extent than with those who came before or after Blum, was in a position to exert a decisive influence on foreign policy. Yet with this influence in his hands, it cannot be said that he made a positive approach to the complex issues of the war in Spain. The ideological conflicts were already deep, but he still clung to the view that security could be defended as an interest independent of ideological concerns. A more flexible policy in a rapidly changing world would surely have sought the balance between national security, insurance against war, and the political realities. Léger declares that nonintervention was always distasteful to him politically, but he persisted in upholding it through all the later and more dangerous developments of the Spanish crisis. This he did in the conviction that England would still separate herself from France if France reversed her course.[38]

There is good reason to believe that Spain was the last important issue of the 1930's on which the Quai d'Orsay had sufficient weight with its government to make policy, and its influence here is to be attributed to the confidence and respect in which Léger was held by Blum and his Foreign Minister. Blum, for one, has denied the charges leveled at the Quai d'Orsay for a deliberate blackout of political intelligence: "During this entire period, I myself read all the diplomatic correspondence including the mails from Berlin."[39] And his testimony certainly suggests that the "ignorance" of other ministers had causes more complex than the "screening" of field reports by the home services.

But with Chautemps in Blum's place, relations between the Foreign Office and the government were more strained. Late in 1937 Delbos and the Quai were still advocating the fulfillment of treaty obligations in the East, while Chautemps was inclined to be "soft."[40] But Delbos himself was "terribly tired and fearful," and Léger and Massigli were hard put to it to prop him up.[41] To the British, at least, there was no doubt that Léger was "much more powerful" than his ministers.[42]

After *Anschluss* in March 1938, the whole question of the French alliances was brought up for debate at the Quai d'Orsay. The French ambassadors in Central and Eastern Europe were summoned to Paris

[38] See *Procès-verbal du Comité de la Défense Nationale* (March 15, 1938) in Gamelin, *Servir*, II, 322-328.

[39] *Témoignages et Documents*, I, 126.

[40] *German Documents*, series D, I, 83.   [41] *Documents and Materials*, p. 70.

[42] Keith Feiling, *The Life of Neville Chamberlain* (London, 1946), p. 333.

for consultation for the first and only time in Léger's term as Secretary General, a point on which some of them were sensitive.[43] They were in the mood to blame the Foreign Office for all the trials of their missions, and the debate between the two sides of the service was acrimonious. When, for instance, Noël, the ambassador to Poland, took the position that France could do nothing for her allies while she was so weak in arms and so disturbed internally, he says that one of the principal chiefs of service of the Quai d'Orsay replied by crying "defeatism." Noël has subsequently retaliated by a bitter indictment of the policies of his accuser, and though Léger is not mentioned by name, it seems clear that he is the target of Noël's attack: "Shot through with generous but disastrous illusions; led astray by unbounded confidence . . . in the principle of collective security and the multiplication of international agreements; convinced that it was possible, then and there, to block Hitlerism and defeat it, my colleague revealed the profound lack of realism which afflicted our diplomacy."[44]

Quite apart from the motivation of this attack, Léger admits some grounds for complaint on the crucial question of the alliances. He acknowledges that the disparity between diplomatic commitments and military potentialities was the cardinal weakness of French diplomacy after 1936. However, he argues that it was not the diplomats but the military in France who held most tightly to the Eastern allies. Treaty obligations which the diplomats had come to regard as "charges," both "morally and juridically embarrassing," the military still looked upon as assets. They thought, he says, in terms of Poland and Czechoslovakia holding a large number of German divisions in a part of Europe remote from the Rhine.

These considerations reveal the desperate hand-to-mouth planning of the military at this late stage in French unpreparedness. But they hardly absolve the diplomats of their share of responsibility for a system conceived too much in the abstract, too little in terms of the power to act. This, in effect, is the burden of the accusation which the postwar investigating commission has laid to the charge of the French Foreign Office.[45]

[43] This conference occurred in the short Foreign Ministry of Paul-Boncour (March-April 1938). François-Poncet was apparently not present, and he claims that he was summoned only once, by Flandin, when the ambassadors of the threatened Locarno Powers met after German remilitarization of the Rhineland (*Témoignages et Documents*, III, 767).

[44] Léon Noël, *L'agression allemande contre la Pologne* (Paris, 1946), pp. 196-197. In 1940 Noël served on the French commission to negotiate an armistice with Germany; and, for a short period, he was Vichy's first delegate general to the German military administration in occupied France.

[45] *Commission d'Enquête, Rapport*, I, 86: "The diplomats negotiated. They arrived

There is no doubt, however, that there were strong incentives to begging the question of the alliances at this late date. Had France publicly renounced her commitments in Eastern Europe, while German pressure was rising ominously in this area, her renunciation would have amounted to a public declaration of bankruptcy, to open admission that she no longer regarded herself as a first-class Power. This was certainly the position in which M. Bonnet found himself when trouble started in Czechoslovakia in the spring of 1938. Officially, he stated and restated his government's determination to honor its foreign commitments. At the same time, and increasingly without the knowledge and participation of the permanent services, he was on the look-out for ways of avoiding the fatal contingency.

Léger was no willing accomplice of the champions of appeasement. He was their enemy in 1938, and has remained so ever since. Yet hating both the tawdry politics and the foreseen damages of further surrender to Nazi demands, he nevertheless followed a line which hewed closely to that of the appeasers on the need for concessions to Germany in Czechoslovakia. At the time he was convinced that even a French government dedicated to resistance would have had no alternative to diplomacy by conference. For he believed that France stood alone, without allies among the Great Powers, and that alone it would have been nothing short of folly for her to fight. Here, once again, his judgment was swayed by his analysis of the position of Great Britain. Britain had consistently refused to commit herself to support France in a war for Czechoslovakia,[46] and with Léger the conviction that Britain would not move held even through the disputed British Foreign Office communiqué of late September. As to Russia, he maintains that his doubts of Russian aid antedate Munich by a year. And on this point, at least, the latest evidence appears to confirm his judgment.[47]

The part which Léger took in the Munich negotiations has given rise

---

at juridical constructions, which reflected rigid adherence to a system rather than political views grounded on realities." And in a recent summary of the findings published in the Paris press, the *rapporteur général* of the Commission refers again to the "intellectual acrobatics of M. Alexis Léger and his small coterie." (*Libération*, January 18, 1952.)

[46] More than once the British had thrown cold water on the French by warning them not to overinterpret Britain's concern for the fate of Czechoslovakia (*British Documents*, 3rd series, I, 346-347).

[47] See W. L. Langer and S. E. Gleason, *The Challenge to Isolation* (New York, 1952), p. 56. It is still, however, dangerous to be categorical about Russian intentions in 1938. France's ambassador to Moscow, Coulondre, believes that an effective agreement—that is, one which could have prevented Munich—could have been made as late as March 1938, if the Western Powers had been more responsive to Russian proposals then.

to charges against him of aiding and abetting the dismemberment of Czechoslovakia.[48] By his own admission, he felt that his country was in no position to fight, and, in the end, on September 28, after a long night of argument with Bonnet over the issue of his instructions to act as negotiator for the French government, Léger complied with his minister's orders to board the plane for Munich.

But on arrival, there is no doubt that he did all he could to stand out for the best possible terms for the Czechs. Indeed, it is from German and Italian reports that we learn how important a part he played in stiffening the resistance of Daladier. An Italian account describes Daladier refusing to start operations without Léger: "But where is Léger? I won't begin if Léger is not there. . . . He knows all the tricks of the trade and I know nothing."[49] And Paul Schmidt, who was Hitler's interpreter, tells how Léger sat by Daladier's side, prompting him to raise objections.[50]

In these perilous negotiations, Léger claims to have made headway by stubborn insistence on a line which would make the rump state of Czechoslovakia a reasonable risk for international guarantee. He also claims to have embarrassed Hitler, in the midst of one of his irrational seizures, by asking the direct question whether he was for or against the survival of Czechoslovakia. In the upshot, the Munich agreement upheld the geographical as against the ethnic principle, and the British concede that it was the French delegation which obtained "a form of words" which took some account of Czechoslovakia's economic needs and fortified areas.[51] Hitler's resentment against Léger was expressed on the evening of the conference, when he declared that Léger was a *martiniquais*, a black man, and that it was unthinkable that the French should have sent such a person to represent them.[52]

According to the French Secretary General, it was not the decisions taken at the Munich conference which were disastrous in their consequences but what happened afterwards, when the International Commission of Ambassadors yielded to Hitler's most extreme demands for the transfer of debatable zones in Czechoslovakia.

After Munich, two important officials of the Quai d'Orsay, its political director, Massigli, and the head of its press section, Comert, lost their

[48] Paul Reynaud, *La France a sauvé l'Europe* (Paris, 1947), II, 129. Charles Serre also points the finger at those who preferred the plane for Munich to the plane for Moscow (*Libération*, January 18, 1952).

[49] Filippo Anfuso, *Roma Berlino Salò* (Milan, 1950), p. 94.

[50] Paul Schmidt, *Statist auf diplomatischer Bühne, 1923-45* (Bonn, 1949), p. 414.

[51] See Horace Wilson's account of the Munich conference, *British Documents*, 3rd series, II, 632.

[52] Anfuso, *Roma Berlino Salò*, p. 98.

jobs.[53] Both were recognized opponents of the Munich policy. Léger remained, some say "because the fish was too big," others because Bonnet needed him as a front of firmness. Plainly, he did not remain because they were in agreement. And at the half-way mark between Munich and Prague, when Ribbentrop made his controversial visit to Paris to negotiate a Franco-German agreement, the Germans saw clearly the differences between Bonnet and his Secretary General. At these meetings, as the Germans themselves report them, Léger laid "great stress" on the promised four Power guarantee of Czechoslovakia. Bonnet, on the other hand, suggested that France had been maneuvered into the offer "by force of circumstances."[54] In other words, he was not prepared to insist.

In the end, no guarantee was given the Czechs, and the Germans entered Prague in March 1939. Léger, at this time, urged the recall of Coulondre from Berlin, as a sign to the Germans of the "seriousness of the situation." He also complained to Daladier, "evidently against what he thought the weak attitude and hesitancy of M. Bonnet, and against his being himself 'surrounded with reticence.' "[55] It was therefore no accident that when Bonnet went to London for conferences four days later Léger did not accompany him.

In his analysis of the possibilities of resistance in the spring of 1939, Léger appears to have misjudged the "probable attitude" of Britain and Poland. As to Poland, he had always regarded the policy of M. Beck as entirely "cynical and false." He guessed that Beck would ask the British for an alliance, but he believed that the British would still refuse to "undertake a definite commitment," and that Poland, in her "hand-to-mouth policy," would choose the alternative of leaning on Germany.[56] He saw that "France and Great Britain were at the turning of the road," but he told Sir Ronald Campbell of the British embassy that he hoped Britain would not "put the cart before the horse," by subordinating her decision to the demands of small Eastern Powers like Rumania: "These governments would decide their attitude in accordance with the intentions of France and Great Britain. In any case, they were only what he called 'corollaries.' "[57]

Contrary to Léger's expectations, Britain did reverse her policy of "no commitments beyond the Rhine," and gave her first guarantee, to Poland, on March 31. Here Léger had guessed wrong, but this was not nearly

[53] Reynaud blames Léger for allowing the removal of his "rival," Massigli, on the count of *bellicisme. La France*, II, 129.
[54] *German Documents*, series D, IV, 474.
[55] *British Documents*, 3rd series, IV, 382.
[56] *ibid.*, IV, 373.   [57] *ibid.*, IV, 382.

so serious as the charge brought against him for misjudging the position of the Soviet Union. He has been accused of contributing directly to the "diplomatic Waterloo of French history, the Stalin-Hitler Pact of August 23, 1939." The Quai d'Orsay, says Reynaud, gave no help in the laborious negotiations for a French and British agreement with Russia, but Léger did worse. It was he who was chiefly to blame for "blocking," "taking lightly" and "denying" reports that Moscow and Berlin were preparing a pact of nonaggression."[58] In this attack on Léger, Reynaud cites in evidence reports from the French consul in Hamburg, and here again the substance of the charge, highhanded treatment of field subordinates who were discouraged from passing on field intelligence to the authorities in Paris, agrees with Dobler's testimony on the Rhineland. The Foreign Office may or may not have been ignorant of secret exchanges between Germany and Russia, but it seems clear that Léger was overoptimistic for the British and the French. He told Bullitt at the end of June that "there were eighty chances in a hundred" that Anglo-French talks with the Russians "would be successfully concluded in the near future.[59]

As to the old charge of making trouble with the Italians, there is nothing in the record to bear it out. Since the breakdown of the Stresa front in 1935, when Italy became involved in Abyssinia, the French Foreign Office had searched every possible ground for cooperation with Italy. And at the end of 1938, the British ambassador in Paris made his report on the stalemate which had been reached: "In taking stock of Franco-Italian relations as they now are, the French government feel that they have made repeated and persistent efforts during the past two years to improve the atmosphere, only to be met with a rebuff on each occasion."[60]

By 1939, Léger was persuaded that further British or French efforts to win the Italians would be worse than useless. He insisted that they must be allowed to carry their experiment to the end: "Every effort to bring them back to us is destined to fail; it will only encourage them in their two-faced policy, leading them to name the highest price for their

[58] Reynaud, *La France*, II, 132-135.

[59] Charles Callan Tansill, *Back Door to War, Roosevelt Foreign Policy, 1933-1941* (Chicago, 1952), pp. 533-534. Tansill cites an unpublished despatch of Bullitt to Hull, June 28, 1939, 740.00/1822, *Confidential File*, MS, Department of State.

[60] *British Documents*, 3rd series, III, 480. To illustrate the French "examen de conscience," the ambassador enclosed a detailed memorandum from Léger demonstrating in parallel columns that every concession Paris had offered had served as a spring-board for hostile words or actions from Rome: *ibid.*, pp. 484-486. But see also *ibid.*, pp. 506-507 for Perth's objections to Léger's memorandum.

assets, and making them value even more highly the benefits the Axis can offer them."[61]

While the Quai d'Orsay stood out against further concessions, pro-Italian politicians like M. de Monzie were still promoting unofficial Roman missions, conducted without the knowledge or blessing of the permanent services. And François-Poncet, who had asked for transfer to the Rome embassy in the vain hope of "detaching" the Italians, urged that fresh efforts be made with Rome after Prague. Again, he says the Quai d'Orsay rebuked him, telling him to stick to his day-to-day business.[62] This, to François-Poncet, was only another instance of Foreign Office obstruction of the proper function of the ambassadors. He never forgave Léger, and two weeks before Italy entered the war in 1940 he told Ciano that a great part of the responsibility for the errors of French foreign policy lay with Léger, calling him a "sinister man."[63] There can be no doubt that, in the spring of 1939, Léger was fundamentally opposed to concessions to Italy; he does not seem to have believed that Italy could be "bought off."[64] Yet the fact that, without Franco-Italian agreement, Italy stayed neutral in 1939 and entered the war only when France had been defeated can be regarded as a justification of Léger's attitude. He had been entirely right in his judgment of Italy's role, as right as François-Poncet was wrong. And this particular attack, far from implicating Léger, succeeds only in drawing attention to the confusions of his attacker.

As the Polish crisis deepened in the summer of 1939, Léger took a position quite different from his position in 1938. Britain's guarantees to Poland and other small states threatened by Germany had brought to an end the isolation which had made earlier action "impossible" for France. France had now a sure partner in arms, and resistance became a collective enterprise containing, in Léger's eyes, the possibility of ultimate success. And he was anxious that British and French loans and planes should be given to Poland "at once in order to convince the Germans that France and England are determined to support Poland if Poland should become involved in war with Germany."[65]

[61] Grégoire Gafencu, *Derniers jours de l'Europe, un voyage diplomatique en 1939* (Paris, 1946), p. 209. Gafencu was the Rumanian Foreign Minister. The English edition is Grigore Gafencu, *The Last Days of Europe* (London, 1947).

[62] *Témoignages et Documents*, III, 778.

[63] Galeazzo Ciano, *Diario* (Milan, 1948), I, 271.

[64] See *British Documents*, 3rd series, IV, 335-337 and 353 where Lord Halifax expresses his fear that "M. Léger may be exercising his influence to prevent any response" to Mussolini.

[65] Bullitt to Hull, June 28, 1939, as quoted by Tansill, *Back Door*, p. 534.

The *French Yellow Book* shows only how tightly Bonnet tried to hold the reins in the eleventh hour negotiations which preceded the outbreak of the war.[66] The fact that Léger hardly appears in the *Yellow Book* is in itself no proof of his exclusion, but from other sources we learn that the Secretary General was deliberately shut out of the final negotiations, and that Bonnet took pains to avoid him both before and after the German attack on Poland on September 1. Yet on the next day Bonnet made an occasion at his press conference to suggest that it was Léger who had made it impossible to stave off the struggle.[67]

In one sense, though not in the sense in which he intended it, Bonnet was right on Léger's attitude at the moment of decision. Léger was convinced now that there was no way out, but he was still afraid that his minister would try to find one, where none existed. When he learned on the last day of August that the Italians had proposed another conference to save the peace, he said at once that the English were right, that the conference could not take place with German troops on Polish soil: "If such negotiations were to be started by a retreat on the part of the allies and under threat of German force, the democracies would soon find themselves faced with wholly unacceptable Axis terms. There would be war anyway, and under especially unfavorable conditions. No, the trap is too obvious."[68]

IV

After the war was on, Bonnet was forced out of the Foreign Ministry, and Daladier replaced him. Much less confident than Bonnet of his ability to handle the complexities of diplomacy, he made a practice of reviewing foreign policy in daily conference with Léger and Coulondre.[69] At every turn, freedom of action was hampered by military weakness, and once more the French government was forced to take refuge in a calculated ambiguity. The policy that Daladier decided on, says Léger, was to delude Hitler into thinking that France would entertain proposals for an early peace; and at the same time to pursue rearmament. Active prosecution of the war was to be postponed until France could give a better account of herself. It was a dangerous game, as Léger saw, but he believes that Daladier chose the only course open to him.

The coming of the war, far from putting the quietus on quarrels be-

---

[66] Ministère des Affaires Etrangères: *Le Livre Jaune Français. Documents diplomatiques, 1938-1939* (Paris, 1939).

[67] Pertinax, *Gravediggers*, pp. 408-410.

[68] Pierre Lazareff, *Deadline* (New York, 1942), pp. 239-240.

[69] Pertinax, *Gravediggers*, p. 103. During these conferences, Daladier, like Blum, had the diplomatic correspondence "methodically laid before him by the career diplomats."

tween conflicting factions in France, served only to intensify them, and in the spring both Daladier and Léger were caught in the currents of political intrigue. The Daladier government fell on bad days over the failure of allied aid to Finland, and Daladier's enemies found it a convenient handle for pulling him down. His government resigned in March, and Reynaud succeeded Daladier as Prime Minister and Minister of Foreign Affairs.

This change of government produced the most paradoxical situation of Léger's career as Secretary General. Why was he kept on by such partisans of appeasement as Bonnet and Laval, only to be dismissed by the man who had a long and famous record as the voice of resistance?

Reynaud was a man of many abilities, but he was vain, impatient and uncertain in his judgment of situations and men. Moreover, from the start, his government was in an extremely precarious position politically, and Reynaud was unable to divorce himself from the intrigues and pressures which surrounded it. He felt that his only hope was an immediate and demonstrable victory in foreign policy. And it was this which dictated his first dealings with the British. Drafts of an agreement pledging France and Britain to full cooperation in the war, above all pledging them not to entertain proposals for a separate peace, had been worked on by Léger and the British Foreign Office during the winter, and after long delay, the Franco-British alliance was concluded in London on March 28.

But this, for Reynaud, was not enough. He knew even better than Daladier the weakness of the military position, but he felt that he could no longer delay the activation of the war. Consequently, what he insisted on with the British in London was that steps be taken to retrieve the Finnish fiasco by an expedition to Norway. Léger, on the other hand, recognizing that the Chamberlain government was already politically embarrassed by the recent government upset in France, begged Reynaud not to press the British too hard. He saw that they were anxious and reluctant, and he himself was anxious at all costs to avoid any possible disagreement between the Allies. But in the end Reynaud had his way. The British agreed to the Norwegian expedition, but only with the gravest misgivings.

Léger says that he was on good terms with Reynaud until he took office, and that they had seen eye to eye on many important issues. But there were differences of method and temperament, and in the balance they weighed more heavily with Reynaud than agreement on ultimate goals. These differences first came to the surface in friction over the plan for Norway, with Reynaud in London arguing his case with the ruthlessness of a lawyer in court, impatient of delay and resentful of Léger's cautions and warnings. One day, when someone in Paris asked Reynaud if things were not going well with Léger, he is said to have replied: "Yes, but we haven't the same kind of mind. I don't know how to deal with his infernal socratic method."[70]

Léger's preoccupation with what he calls the "lightning of syntax,"[71] his tireless search for an expression precise and pure of the banal, his refusal to compromise his integrity—all, in the end, acted as intolerable goads to politicians who found him an uneasy presence both in the methods and substance of his diplomacy. And Léger had made many enemies.

How extensive this hostility was is reflected by Elie Bois. As editor of *Le Petit Parisien*, Bois had fought many of the same battles in the press which Léger had fought in the government service. Léger, he says, had against him all the former ministers, deputies, senators, journalists, financiers, and industrialists "who made up the party which Georges Bonnet defined to Sumner Welles as the party of peace." They never pardoned Léger for standing guard over the Franco-British partnership, indeed many hoped by his removal to deal it a blow; and, indifferent to the record, they consistently represented him as the wrecker of agreement with Italy. "Wherever difficulties arose he was blamed, even if he had foreseen them and warned his governments to take action in prevention. But if a desired goal was achieved, he had no part in it, even if he had prepared the way with infinite pains. . . . He was not even in a position to defend himself or take pride in his accomplishments. The nature of his task condemned him to silence and impassivity."[72]

As things went from bad to worse for the French and British in April and May, Reynaud became more and more erratic, and it became more and more difficult for the permanent services to hold his policy on an even keel.[73] With one ear he listened to the counsels of patriots like Mandel and de Gaulle, but "his house, his Cabinet, his anterooms were soon transformed into the most active and dangerous cell where defeatists of all kinds were to attack the nerve centers of the state."[74]

And here there was an actual conspiracy. At the center were Paul Baudouin, secretary of Reynaud's War Cabinet, and Reynaud's mistress,

[70] Elie J. Bois, *Le Malheur de la France* (London, 1941), p. 192.

[71] *Exil and other Poems*, by St-Jean Perse, p. 27.

[72] Bois, *Le Malheur*, p. 189.

[73] Pertinax, *Gravediggers*, p. 241.

[74] Bois, *Le Malheur*, p. 175.

the Comtesse Hélène de Portes. Both were prime movers in the campaign to unseat Léger.[75] To them and their circle, he was the creature of the Front Populaire, the accomplice of Daladier and Gamelin, the prop of the Russians, the willing vassal of the British.

Léger's dismissal came eight days after the German attack on Holland and Belgium, three days after the break through into France. On May 16, Paris was thrown into panic, expecting the arrival of the Germans from hour to hour. On the afternoon of that day, the archives of the Ministry of Foreign Affairs were set on fire in the garden of the Quai d'Orsay.[76]

In the vain hope of restoring public confidence, Reynaud decided to call on Pétain and Weygand. In a Cabinet reshuffle, he himself would take the key Ministry of National Defense, while Daladier would go to the Quai d'Orsay. Therefore, in order to make sure of Léger's removal, Mme. de Portes and the politicians in Reynaud's personal secretariat, using every device of threat and persuasion, got him to sign the decree of replacement before he left the Foreign Ministry on the night of the 18th. Mme. de Portes boasted that "Léger's scalp" was worth over seventy votes to Reynaud in the Chamber.[77]

In the landslide of bad news, Léger's dismissal was only another item. But it did not pass unnoticed. Berlin was triumphant, as were all Léger's enemies in Paris. On the other hand, he still had the confidence of such important Frenchmen as Blum, Herriot, and Daladier, and strong supporters in the London government. Mandel had warned Reynaud in advance that Léger's dismissal would be interpreted as a first step toward policies which he, Reynaud, had fought consistently ever since the appearance of Hitler. And Lazareff of *Paris Soir* wrote in his diary: "The ouster of Alexis Léger has certainly not been well received. The very circumstances of the dismissal of the Secretary General of Foreign Affairs are particularly alarming because they reveal a new Paul Rey-

[75] Pertinax, *Gravediggers*, pp. 244 and 246. According to Pertinax, Baudouin had been talking of reversing the French alliances and urged that "a Secretary General less firmly rooted in the tradition of the British entente should be appointed."

[76] Pertinax maintains that the order for the destruction of the archives was given by Reynaud himself, and that Léger did all he could to prevent the measure from being carried out, yielding only after he had telephoned his minister "and received direct instructions" (*Gravediggers*, p. 238). On the other hand, both Baudouin (*The Private Diaries of Paul Baudouin*, London, 1946, p. 31) and Reynaud (*La France*, II, 131) claim that the destruction took place on Léger's initiative. This charge is repeated in some of Vichy's most vituperative propaganda against the discredited officials of the Third Republic.

[77] Pertinax, *Gravediggers*, p. 246.

naud. One cannot help wondering what this man might be planning to do."[78]

Léger only learned the news on the morning of the 19th, when members of his staff brought the published announcement to his attic room in the Quai d'Orsay. There followed a meeting with Reynaud in which Reynaud was thoroughly ill at ease. According to report, he tried first to persuade Léger that, far from being humiliated, he was slated for the honors of the Washington embassy, where he was to perform the miracle of persuading the United States to immediate action in Europe. But Léger refused to lend himself to this maneuver, insisting that if Reynaud had intended him for Washington, he had surely wrecked the chances of a difficult mission by disgracing his agent in advance. And nothing could be more in character than Léger's final words to Reynaud: "I have the right to the whole injustice."[79]

Reynaud, in his memoirs, has tried to incriminate Léger on a variety of counts. His accusations range from Léger's alleged pacifism in the Briand period, through support of appeasement at Munich, to the turncoat *bellicisme* of post-Munich days, "when the wind had changed." Léger is blamed for the failure to foresee and forestall the Nazi-Soviet Pact, and for ordering the state archives burned to destroy the evidence of gross mistakes in foreign policy. He is further charged with calculated leaks to the press, which insured him a following among such powerful journalists as Lazareff, Pertinax, and Bois. François-Poncet is quoted against him to prove the dictatorial nature of his regime at the Quai d'Orsay. Finally, Reynaud accuses Léger of offering his services to Pétain in the Vichy period.[80]

How much substance there is in this last charge can be seen from the action of the Vichy government. It passed against Léger the sentence of "national indignity," and, as a result, Léger lost his citizenship and all his property in France. He lost too the manuscripts of his unpublished verse which fell into the hands of the Germans in his apartment in Paris, and on the table it is said that there was left only a copy of the Versailles Treaty, inscribed by the Germans with the words, "Much good may it do you now, last defender of the last French victory."[81]

---

[78] Lazareff, *Deadline*, pp. 289-290.
[79] Pertinax, *Gravediggers*, p. 247. Léger holds that Reynaud's last minute appeals for U. S. aid were only for the record: Reynaud did not expect them to succeed, but believed that refusal would give him an easy out. On this question, and for Bullitt's corroboration of Léger's views, see the *Memoirs of Cordell Hull* (New York, 1948), I, 767-768.
[80] Reynaud, *La France*, II, 129-132.
[81] Louis-Marcel Raymond in *Cahiers de la Pléiade*, p. 125.

During the years which followed his dismissal and the defeat and occupation of France, Léger has lived in retirement in the United States. In his retirement he has been deeply concerned with the fate of his country, more so indeed "than many of the extravagant partisans who noisily occupied the center of the stage."[82] He never touched Vichy or Pétain, but he also refused to join de Gaulle. Yet, in a letter to Léger— a piece of evidence whose authenticity Reynaud has since tried to impugn—de Gaulle has asserted that "the grave injustice" committed against Léger was "one of the worst results of the bad influences" which surrounded Reynaud in 1940.[83]

Many of Reynaud's charges against Léger are patently false, and are all vitiated by the animus of the accuser. Léger has never answered his enemies publicly. It has been said that he spoke frankly to Reynaud on the day of his dismissal, accusing him of going to pieces and debasing himself in the hour of his country's greatest danger.[84] And Léger is convinced that Reynaud, as early as May 19, 1940, had decided to reverse himself, to direct his whole policy toward liquidation of French commitments in the war. The removal of Léger has always been one of the blackest marks on Reynaud's record in the eyes of those who have come to regard him as the fallen angel of French resistance.

V

But how are we to judge Léger's own place in the "decadent" diplomacy of the 1930's? Were his methods, more or less than others of the period, equal to the task of coping with a new situation and meeting the accumulation of new threats? And if not equal to the challenge, what were the shortcomings of these methods, and where precisely did they fall down? At times he was too much the disciple of concepts better adapted to the emotional climate of the 1920's, counting too heavily on the ambitious collective design, or bound by too narrow a vision of national security. Again he was too fearful of striking out for France on the gamble of British support. There was something unyielding in the pattern of this diplomacy, a lack of the resilience, perhaps even of the nerve needed to complement the high qualities of his integrity. Léger's resources as an innovator would appear to have been depleted after the failure of his Eastern Locarno in 1935; and virtually exhausted after 1936, with the collapse of the Western Locarno which had been his

---

[82] Denis de Rougemont, *ibid.*, p. 136.
[83] *Journal Officiel de la République Française, Débats de l'Assemblée Nationale Constituante*, 1946, III, 2623.
[84] Lazareff, *Deadline*, pp. 293-294.

master plan for the containment of Germany. As violence mounted, a lead in dealing with it was desperately needed, but the lack of it was certainly not confined to the French Foreign Office. Léger was always out of sympathy with the worst causes of the 1930's, but like so many of his colleagues powerless to salvage the good ones. And at the last what distinguished him from many diplomats in the democracies was a kind of dogged intractability in the delaying actions of retreat.

It can be argued that Léger, at odds with the trimming policies of successive Foreign Ministers, should have resigned his post, before Rome in 1935, before London in 1936, or before Munich in 1938. Since he was compelled as a civil servant to execute the decisions of these ministers if he remained, the only possible protest against counsels overborne was resignation. Yet it can also be argued, and perhaps with greater cogency, that by remaining he could still hope to exercise a restraining influence, a small but valid function of prevention even on the road to surrender.

Since 1940 the end of Léger's life as a diplomat has served as a release for Léger as a poet. At first, as he told a literary colleague in America, "there could be no thought, no possibility of poetry again." Yet within a short time, "he faced not only his exile from his country, but the demand upon him" of creative powers long held in reserve.[85] Since then, with the verse published in the last decade, he has found a secure place among living poets.

This poetry of exile brings to light Léger's vision of the universe and the part that man plays in it. It is a world of great designs constantly renewing themselves from the "abyss" of failure and catastrophe. The innovator and the guardian are familiar figures in his *Exil*. Both are exiles, and both touch nearly Léger's experience in the world of politics. Here he had labored for "the new idea," and here it had fallen to him "to stand guard over the purity of great crystal lenses between two wars."[86] But in the *décadence* of diplomacy, the innovator is caught in the storm of "partiality" and "secession," and the guardian finds himself barred from "the threshold of Lloyd's" where his "gold has no standard," and his "word no currency."[87] But man's design and man himself persist. In the East in his youth Léger had learned early the art of self-defense; he had maintained it later through the heavy pressures of his service as a diplomat; and, in the sequel, it is this persistence of man and the idea which lies at the heart of his poetry.

[85] MacLeish in *Cahiers de la Pléiade*, p. 118.
[86] *Exil and other Poems*, p. 22.   [87] *ibid.*, p. 26.

13

The German Foreign Office from Neurath to Ribbentrop

BY GORDON A. CRAIG

Adolf Hitler's appointment, on January 30, 1933, to the position of Chancellor of the German Reich caused what used, in a more elegant age, to be described as a twittering in the diplomatic dovecotes. The Fuehrer's assumption of office quite clearly forecast a revolution in Germany's domestic affairs. If there were any doubts on this score, they were resolved before the winter of 1932-1933 had turned to spring. But did it also presage a revolution in German foreign policy? Could Hitler be expected to act in that spirit of intransigent nationalism which had characterized his speeches when he was merely a struggling politician? Would he, indeed, revert to the grandiose ambitions expressed in the pages of *Mein Kampf*, and seek to overthrow the accepted diplomatic conventions and the public law of Europe in order to fulfill them? Or would power bring a new sense of responsibility, convert the demagogue into a statesman, and induce him to seek his objectives by peaceful negotiation and collaboration with the other Powers?

If these questions were debated in the Foreign Offices of Germany's neighbors, they caused no less speculation in Germany's own legations and embassies abroad and in the Wilhelmstrasse itself. But, naturally enough, there was yet another question which was of even more pressing concern to the staffs of those establishments. How was the coming of Hitler to affect their own careers? Would the new Chancellor dispense with their services in favor of the men who had fought with him in the streets, or could they expect to have an honorable and influential role in the new order? One German diplomat, at least, viewed the future unhappily. In Washington, Ambassador von Prittwitz, in a conversation with Under-Secretary of State Castle on February 2, spoke in terms of unrelieved gloom and expressed the opinion that, if the new government became entrenched in power, "his days as ambassador would be numbered," and all diplomats "with a Stresemann taint" would lose their positions.[1]

This pessimism was not, however, generally shared. In the embassy at Ankara, the staff members were advised by a visiting party official from Germany that it would be wise for them to join the National Socialist movement as quickly as possible; but they were simultaneously reassured by his statement that Hitler was not as wild a man as he sometimes sounded and that much of his talk about radical change was mere election propaganda which need not worry them overmuch, since "the soup is never eaten as hot as it is cooked."[2] In Geneva, the members of the German delegation to the Conference on Disarmament listened to an informal lecture by one of their number on the attitude of professional diplomats in times of revolutionary change. Referring to the attempt of the Russian diplomatic corps to embarrass the Bolshevist regime in 1917 by refusing to serve it,[3] he argued that this gesture had served no useful purpose. The German diplomats and Foreign Office officials of 1918, he said, had followed a wiser course by remaining at their posts, where their services were soon recognized as indispensable by the revolutionaries and where, incidentally, they had been able to prevent dangerous adventures in foreign policy. More recently, the professional diplomats of Italy had enjoyed similar success in convincing Mussolini that it was well to leave foreign affairs in the hands of experts. There was no reason to suppose that Hitler could not be persuaded of the same truth, provided the professionals did their jobs with their customary efficiency and were sufficiently firm with the Chancellor.[4]

This cheerful belief was probably more representative of the reaction of the foreign service to the *Machtübernahme* of January 1933 than were the prognostications of Prittwitz in Washington. It was certainly a belief that was strongly held in the German Foreign Office. The permanent head of that establishment in 1933 was the Secretary of State Bernhard von Bülow. Member of a family which had supplied the German state with many servants, including Emperor Wilhelm II's favorite Chancellor, Bülow was a precise, methodical, and tireless official, a mas-

[1] *Foreign Relations*, 1933, II, 187. Prittwitz seems, however, to have regarded Hugenberg, rather than Hitler, as the man who would clean house.

[2] Rudolf Rahn, *Ruheloses Leben* (Düsseldorf, 1950), pp. 95-96.

[3] For a description of the situation in the Narkomindel in 1917, see Chapter 8, § 1 above.

[4] Erich Kordt, *Nicht aus den Akten* (Stuttgart, 1950), pp. 51-52. On the situation in the German Foreign Office in 1918-1919, see also Chapter 5, § III above.

ter especially of the legal aspects of diplomacy, and a man who disliked amateur dabblers in foreign affairs.[5] It was perhaps his family pride which prevented him from taking Hitler and his movement very seriously. Throughout the latter half of 1932, and as late as January 1933, Bülow had refused to believe that the former corporal could ever attain the Chancellorship, and he had sent reassuring circulars to the missions abroad predicting the imminent destruction of Hitler's "splinter party."[6] When these prophecies proved false, the Secretary of State was not particularly discomfited. It was, in his eyes, inconceivable that the new Chancellor would attempt to disregard Foreign Office advice in matters in which he had no experience whatsoever. Bülow was forced, before the end of his career, to correct these initial impressions, but there is no evidence that he foresaw trouble in the opening months of 1933; and the opinions of the diplomatic corps were naturally colored by his attitude of calm.[7]

Bülow's opinion was matched by that of the Foreign Minister, Freiherr Konstantin von Neurath. A professional diplomat since the first world war, Neurath had served successively as minister to Copenhagen from 1919 to 1922, ambassador in Rome from 1922 to 1930 and ambassador in London from 1930 until the formation of the Papen Cabinet in June 1932, when he was recalled to Berlin and made Foreign Minister. He had apparently accepted this post because of an urgent personal appeal by President von Hindenburg;[8] but—as Neurath told the British Foreign Secretary at the time—in the political discussions which had preceded the formation of Papen's government, the Nazis had also urged his appointment, "which, he understood, was not intended to be a stop-gap but was made with the intention of leaving foreign affairs in his hands after the German elections."[9] A man of no very penetrating political insight and possessed of an inflexibly sanguine temperament,[10] Neurath comforted himself during the turbulent events of January 1933 with the thought that the Nazis respected him and that, if they showed signs of ceasing to do so, he would be protected by the President's authority. This conviction doubtless inspired his con-

[5] On Bülow, see André François-Poncet, *Souvenirs d'une ambassade à Berlin* (Paris, 1946), pp. 240-241.

[6] See *British Documents*, 2nd series, III, 160; Rahn, *Ruheloses Leben*, p. 95.

[7] Thus, Ambassador Hoesch in London told Sir John Simon on January 31 that "these domestic changes did not betoken any change in the line of German foreign policy." *British Documents*, 2nd series, IV, 401.

[8] *ibid.*, III, 149-150; *Conspiracy and Aggression*, Supplement B, p. 966.

[9] *British Documents*, 2nd series, III, 152-153.

[10] See the analysis of his character in François-Poncet, *Souvenirs*, p. 49.

fident statements to Sir Horace Rumbold on February 4. His first impressions of Hitler, he said, were favorable. The Chancellor was "proving reasonable"; he did not always agree with the other Nazi members of his Cabinet; and he had, on various occasions, "spontaneously" solicited Neurath's advice. As for his own position, Neurath said that "the President had made a point of his being included in the new government, and that he had only accepted on condition that he was given a free hand and that no experiments in foreign policy were to be tried. He knew that he had the President's full support."[11]

In the light of our present knowledge of the history of the Third Reich, Neurath's attitude and that of his colleagues in the Foreign Office and the diplomatic corps appear to have been singularly feckless. Hitler was not to prove as amenable to instruction as the professionals believed. The Foreign Office, indeed, was entering an era in which its formerly proud position was to be systematically destroyed, in which its hitherto uncontested right to advise the government in foreign affairs was to be ignored and its legitimate functions usurped by other agencies, in which the Foreign Minister and the Secretary of State were often kept ignorant of pending political actions, and in which the Wilhelmstrasse was to be degraded to the role of a mere "technical apparatus,"[12] to carry out decisions in the formulation of which its staff had had no share.

The confidence which the professionals expressed was not, however, entirely unreasonable, considering the situation which confronted Hitler in the first months of 1933. For the Fuehrer was in no position to set forth on a foreign policy which was radically different from that of the past. His most urgent consideration was the task of consolidating his power within Germany itself. Until that was accomplished, his steps in foreign policy were necessarily conservative and in line with precedents already established; and for that very reason they not only won the approval of the professional diplomats but strengthened their belief that the Chancellor was a reasonable, and a manageable, man. It was not, indeed, until the beginning of 1934 that the first serious doubts began to creep in.

II

The first subject of international importance to engage the new government's attention was the problem of disarmament. At the end of

---

[11] *British Documents*, 2nd series, IV, 406-407.
[12] The phrase is that of Ernst von Weizsäcker, Secretary of State from 1938 to 1943. *Erinnerungen* (Munich, 1950), p. 129.

January 1933, the delegates to the Conference on Disarmament re-assembled at Geneva, to grapple once more with the questions that had proven so intractable the year before. Remembering Hitler's frequent assertions, in the days before he attained power, that he would end the shame of Versailles and rebuild the German army,[13] the Conference would probably not have been surprised if the Fuehrer had appeared personally on the scene to issue a cease and desist order and to march his delegation back to Berlin. In fact, nothing of the sort happened. The German representatives remained at Geneva and remained, moreover, under the direction of Rudolf Nadolny, the former ambassador to Turkey, who had headed the group during 1932. Nadolny's complete authority over his delegation was, furthermore, strikingly vindicated shortly after the resumption of negotiations when he peremptorily ordered two Nazi dignitaries to return to Berlin because they were attempting to negotiate behind his back and were indulging in undignified political gestures, and when his action was approved personally by the Fuehrer.[14] Meanwhile, in Berlin, Hitler assured visitors that "there would be no change in the policy Neurath had laid down" in 1932;[15] and for the most part he seems to have left the direction of Conference strategy to the Foreign Minister and his Secretary of State, intervening rarely and then only to moderate views expressed by them.

In the course of the first year's negotiations at Geneva, Germany had won important concessions from the other Powers. At the very outset of the Conference, Brüning had made it clear that "the German people look to the present Conference to solve the problem of general disarmament on the basis of equal rights and equal security for all peoples";[16]

---

[13] These promises were made so frequently that they had a perceptible influence in weakening the allegiance of the officers—and especially the junior officers—of the *Reichswehr* to the Weimar Republic; and there is little doubt that the bulk of the army expected that rearmament would follow Hitler's victory and supported him for that reason. See, *inter alia*, Friedrich Hossbach, *Zwischen Wehrmacht und Hitler, 1934-1938* (Wolfenbüttel and Hannover, 1949), p. 9; Friedrich Meinecke, *Die deutsche Katastrophe: Betrachtungen und Erinnerungen* (Wiesbaden, 1947), especially Chapter VI; Ignaz Pollmüller, "Die Rolle der Reichswehr von 1918 bis 1933," *Frankfurter Hefte*, 1. Jahrg., Heft 9 (December 1946), *passim.*; and Gordon A. Craig, "Reichswehr and National Socialism: The Policy of Wilhelm Groener, 1928-1932," *Political Science Quarterly*, LXIII (1948), 199-200, 205-208, 213, 228-229.

[14] These amateur diplomats were Reinhard Heydrich and a certain Krüger who, among other things, insisted on hoisting a swastika banner over the German delegation's hotel. Kordt, *Nicht aus den Akten*, p. 53.

[15] *Foreign Relations*, 1933, II, 218. Statement to Norman Davis in April.

[16] The protocols of the early meetings of the Conference can be conveniently located in *British Documents*, 2nd series, III, 505ff. For an excellent short account, see John W. Wheeler-Bennett, *The Disarmament Deadlock* (London, 1934). See also F. P. Walters, *A History of the League of Nations* (2 volumes, London, 1952), II, 500-516, 541-555.

THE GERMAN FOREIGN OFFICE

and, after Brüning's disappearance from the political scene, this theme had continued to be reiterated by his successors, although, it is true, with increasingly menacing overtones. Attempts to satisfy the Germans by means of qualitative limitations on the armed establishments of all Powers had broken down because of France's reluctance to make concessions to a country in which extreme nationalism was patently on the increase and her suspicion, moreover, that concessions would merely lead to new German demands.[17] The first six months of negotiation had resulted only in an eloquent but innocuous draft resolution which Germany, seconded by the Soviet Union, promptly rejected; and, in July 1932, as the Conference prepared to adjourn for a period of some months, Nadolny had informed the startled delegates that, unless the Powers gave clear recognition of "the equality of all States in the matter of national security" before they reassembled, Germany could not "undertake to continue its collaboration."[18]

This announcement caused general consternation and, in the months that followed, the Western Powers sought to convince themselves that the Germans really didn't mean it. The British and French ambassadors in Berlin believed, at least temporarily, that the hardening of the German line was the result of the increase of *Reichswehr* influence in government counsels;[19] and Rumbold suggested that the Foreign Office did not approve of the new course and would seek, under Neurath's leadership, to check "the ebullitions of General Schleicher," who, as Papen's Defense Minister, had been making minatory speeches about Germany's right to rearm.[20] In reality, both Neurath and Bülow, who was specially charged with the guidance of disarmament policy,[21] soon proved themselves to be convinced and intransigent supporters of the position taken in July; and they steadfastly refused to engage in renewed discussions of any kind until the British government had persuaded the French to give them what they wanted.[22] In December, having apparently been assured beforehand that his case was won,[23] Neurath went to Geneva to meet with the other Powers and to receive, from the British, French, and Italian governments, the assurance that "one of the

---

[17] See Alexis Léger's views on this matter, Chapter 12, § 1 above.

[18] *British Documents*, 2nd series, III, 589.

[19] *ibid.*, IV, 178. The American ambassador, Frederic M. Sackett, also believed in September that Germany was "now being governed virtually by a military directorate." *Foreign Relations*, 1932, II, 314.

[20] *British Documents*, 2nd series, IV, 201.   [21] *ibid.*, pp. 195-196.

[22] Rumbold, who was inclined to think of Neurath as a "reasonable man," found Bülow "suspicious and unhelpful." *Ibid.*, pp. 178, 272.

[23] *ibid.*, pp. 285-286.

principles that should guide the Conference on Disarmament should be the grant to Germany . . . of equality of rights in a system that would provide security for all nations."[24] In return for this first clear recognition of the German claim to equality, Neurath promised that Germany would resume her participation in the Conference.

By January 1933, then, Germany was in a much stronger position at Geneva than she had been when the Conference opened, and Neurath and Bülow were determined now to make the most of their victory. Even if he had wished to do so, there was little reason for Hitler to take personal charge of the negotiations which followed, as the Powers tried to translate the formula of December into regulations governing the armed forces of the signatories. With a dialectical skill which he could not have improved upon, the German diplomats, having achieved recognition of Germany's right to equality, now fought stubbornly to assure her right to achieve that equality in her own way. Between January and March, Nadolny rejected all plans for implementing the December formula, arguing that the French were seeking to repudiate their pledge by giving precedence to security issues and insisting that the only way in which progress could be made was for the other Powers to begin forthwith to reduce their armed forces.[25] When, however, the British government, in order to forestall another deadlock, came forward on March 16 with a plan which actually did envisage a general reduction of armaments but which provided also for effective supervision and investigation of German armaments for a period of five years,[26] Nadolny reacted with suspicion and coldness, and his attitude was reflected by that of his superiors in the Wilhelmstrasse. Although Neurath told Norman Davis in April that he was willing to accept the British plan as a basis for future discussion,[27] he permitted his delegation chief to use tactics which seemed clearly designed to make such acceptance impossible.[28] Moreover, on May 11, the Foreign Minister himself cast serious doubts on Germany's willingness to admit any limitations on her future progress in armaments. In an article in the *Leipziger Illustrierte Zeitung*, Neurath wrote that, whatever the result of the Conference, Germany intended to rearm in military and naval aircraft, heavy artillery, and manpower. "Germany's standpoint is morally and legally beyond criticism," he added. "What is right for others is right for Germany.

[24] *ibid.*, pp. 328ff.   [25] Wheeler-Bennett, *Disarmament Deadlock*, pp. 86-98.
[26] *British Documents*, 2nd series, IV, 539ff.; Walters, *History of the League*, II, 542-544.
[27] *Foreign Relations*, 1933, II, 218-219.
[28] Wheeler-Bennett, *Disarmament Deadlock*, p. 113.

Such weapons and armaments as others hold to be necessary for their security can no longer be dispensed with for Germany's security."[29]

The sharp reaction to this in London and Paris, coupled as it was with growing horror and indignation at the excesses which the Nazis were perpetrating inside Germany, induced Hitler now to intervene openly in the disarmament question for the first time. Sensing that the tactics of his diplomats were placing Germany in the position of being responsible for sabotaging the Conference, the Fuehrer, in a speech to the *Reichstag* on May 17 which has since, by collectors of Hitler's works, been solemnly entitled the *Friedensrede*, obliquely repudiated his Foreign Minister's words of the previous week. With certain conditions which did not at the time seem serious, he announced his acceptance of the British plan as a starting point for the solution of the disarmament problem, his readiness to agree to a transitional period of five years in which Germany would not enjoy full equality, and his willingness to forswear the use of instruments of aggression, and to admit international supervision even over his storm troops and other party formations, during that period.[30] As an essay in appeasement, the speech, it has been said, "could scarcely have been equalled by Stresemann or Bruening"[31] and, if it fell on skeptical ears in Paris, in other capitals it aroused an enthusiasm which confounded the critics of the Nazi regime.[32] As a diplomatic stroke, the speech was masterly, for it effectively passed the responsibility for making the Conference on Disarmament a success, or a failure, back to the French.

In the general euphoria that followed the speech, the Conference adjourned its labors for three months. Part of the interval was employed by Mr. Arthur Henderson, its President, to visit the capitals of the Great Powers and exhort their statesmen to heightened efforts in the approaching session.[33] In Berlin, Henderson had interviews with both Hitler and Neurath. In the first of these—to which the Fuehrer came, rather disconcertingly, armed with a large whip[34]—no matters of great

[29] *ibid.*, p. 115.
[30] The complete text is in *Dokumente der deutschen Politik*, I (Berlin, 1935), 92-103. The greater part of the speech, in translation, is in *The Speeches of Adolf Hitler*, edited by Norman H. Baynes (2 volumes, Oxford, 1942), II, 1041-1058.
[31] Wheeler-Bennett, *Disarmament Deadlock*, p. 118.
[32] The speech, says Walters, "comforted the hearts of all who were still hoping, against their own instinctive convictions, that the new Germany might become part of a tranquil Europe." *History of the League*, II, 547.
[33] See above, Chapter 10, § IV.
[34] Kordt, *Nicht aus den Akten*, p. 65. The whip was apparently a relic of Hitler's Munich days. See Alan Bullock, *Hitler: A Study in Tyranny* (New York, 1953), pp. 349-350.

moment seem to have been discussed. In his talk with the Foreign Minister, however, Henderson had to listen to professions of Germany's desire to cooperate tempered by dark hints concerning the wrecking policy of other Powers.[35] When the recess had passed and the Conference was scheduled to resume its work, Neurath was more open in his language. On September 15, he announced bluntly that it was time now for the Conference to produce equality for Germany or to see the utter collapse of the idea of disarmament.[36]

It seems clear that the Foreign Minister confidently expected that the French would raise new objections to the British plan of March and that he was preparing the ground for the most vigorous kind of retaliation. His expectations were soon confirmed, for the French government, alarmed by growing evidence of illegal military activities inside Germany, were no longer prepared to consider weakening their own military establishment. Instead, they proposed the stabilization of existing forces under strict supervision for a period of at least four years, at the end of which time gradual disarmament might begin; and they succeeded in persuading the American, British, and Italian governments to modify the original British proposals in this sense. Thus, when the Conference convened at the end of September the delegates were handed a plan which departed sharply from the proposals so generously accepted by Hitler in May.

It was this turn of events which prompted Germany's second and final withdrawal from the Conference and her simultaneous resignation from the League of Nations on October 14, 1933. The gravity of this step was not lost upon the German diplomats who effected it. Nadolny, for one, seems to have doubted its wisdom and to have gone to the President's Palace to try to persuade Hindenburg that the new Four Power Plan be provisionally accepted for consideration.[37] But the very fact that he took this unusual course indicates that his views were not shared by his superiors in the Foreign Office. Of Bülow's opinions at this time, we know nothing; but he had always had strong nationalist views on the disarmament question and was a bitter critic of the Geneva system, and there is no reason to suppose that he opposed the October decision. As for Neurath, it is perfectly clear that he greeted the severance with enthusiasm. In pre-trial testimony at Nuremberg, after the

---

[35] Wheeler-Bennett, *Disarmament Deadlock*, p. 165.   [36] *ibid.*, p. 175.

[37] Speaking of this in May 1942, Hitler said that when Nadolny, who had just been appointed ambassador to the Soviet Union, finished his remarks, Hindenburg answered curtly: "You're slated for Moscow. Get yourself there!" Henry Picker, *Hitlers Tischgespräche im Führerhauptquartier, 1941-1942* (Bonn, 1951), p. 432.

second world war, Neurath not only defended the departure from the Conference and the League, but admitted freely that he had advised Hitler in September that no further results could be expected in Geneva and that the break should be made.[38]

It is wholly likely, of course, that Hitler would have taken this action regardless of the advice given him by his diplomatic advisers. The important point here, however, is that in this first marked sally of Nazi foreign policy, the Foreign Office and the Fuehrer were at one. The diplomats had, indeed, every reason for satisfaction. They had, for the most part, been left free to follow to its logical end the line they had laid down in 1932; the cooperation between the *Reichskanzlei* and the Wilhelmstrasse had at all times been amicable and effective; Hitler had preferred the services and advice of the professionals to those of party diplomats like the two Nadolny had expelled from Geneva; and the result of the joint effort had been a diplomatic success, or at least a diplomatic sensation.

The enthusiasm of the professionals for this stroke of policy rested in part, of course, on the conviction that it involved no serious risks. Existing differences between the Great Powers of Europe suggested no possibility of a union on their part against Germany. A period of strained relations with London and Paris could be expected; but Germany was on cordial terms with the other Powers and need not fear isolation. Italy had always been sympathetic to the German claim to equality in arms, and Mussolini was himself so critical of the Geneva system that it was improbable that Germany's repudiation of it would trouble him. As for the Soviet Union, the Treaty of Berlin of 1926 was still in force, and, despite certain signs of Soviet uneasiness—like their request in June that the hitherto close liaison between the *Reichswehr* and the Red Army be discontinued[39]—the Soviets were apparently anxious to preserve their ties with Germany and had sent one of their ablest diplomats, the former ambassador to Ankara, Suritz, to work to this end.[40]

---

[38] *Conspiracy and Aggression*, Supplement B, p. 1504. This advice formed the basis for the first charge in the indictment of Neurath at Nuremberg, and he was adjudged guilty of it. Papen, a member of the Cabinet in October 1933, says that he opposed the withdrawal from the League and that he tried to persuade the Foreign Minister that it was a mistake but that "Neurath was very little help." Franz von Papen, *Memoirs* (London, 1952), p. 297.

[39] Herbert von Dirksen, *Moskau, Tokio, London: Erinnerungen und Betrachtungen zu 20 Jahren deutscher Aussenpolitik, 1919-1939* (Stuttgart, 1950), pp. 124-125.

[40] Erich Kordt, *Wahn und Wirklichkeit* (Stuttgart, 1947), p. 62. Hitler's conclusion in July 1933 of a Concordat with the Papacy—the first Reich concordat since the Reformation—also seemed a sign that Germany's external relations were in good condition. Mussolini, for instance, had said: "The signing of this agreement with the Vatican

Yet, almost before the initial exaltation had died away, German diplomats were confronted with two disturbing developments which led some of them at least to revise their opinion of the new Chancellor. In the first place, Hitler had become increasingly interested in the possibility of a National Socialist revolution in Austria which would promote a union of that country with Germany; and the obvious aid and encouragement sent to the Austrian Nazis from party headquarters in Munich produced a progressive deterioration of relations between the Austrian and German governments. In the late fall of 1933, Franz von Papen had become sufficiently alarmed over this to go, with General von Blomberg, to Hitler and to urge the advisability of a gesture of friendship to the Dollfuss government, so that the tension—which was attracting the anxious attention of other Powers—might be relaxed. This advice Hitler rejected, and he proceeded to commit himself definitely to the course which was to precipitate the disorders in Vienna in 1934.[41] Thus, at the very moment when he was antagonizing the Western Powers by withdrawing from Geneva, the Fuehrer was embarking on a policy admirably designed to alienate Mussolini.

The second development was even more serious. Throughout 1933, Hitler had been considering, in fits and starts, the possibility of a rapprochement with his fellow dictator in Warsaw, Pilsudski;[42] and, at the end of September, he had instructed Neurath to talk with the Polish Foreign Minister Beck about "the best means of creating a better atmosphere in the relations between the two states." Two months later—after the break with Geneva had been effected—the Fuehrer authorized the negotiations which eventuated in the famous Declaration of January 26, 1934, whereby Germany and Poland undertook to refrain for a period of ten years from the use of force in the settlement of disputes between them.[43]

---

will establish the credit of your Government abroad for the first time." Papen, *Memoirs*, pp. 280-281.

[41] *ibid.*, pp. 299-300. Papen claims that his efforts were defeated primarily by Neurath, who convinced Hitler that he could not stab the Austrian Nazis in the back. Papen's animus against Neurath is so strong, however (see, for instance, his remarks on Neurath in the apologia which he wrote at Nuremberg, in *Conspiracy and Aggression*, Supplement A, p. 447), that this need not be accepted as wholly reliable. In general, Papen's *Memoirs* must be used with caution. Some doubt, for instance, is cast on the accuracy of the incident mentioned above by Herman Rauschning's recollection of a remark by Blomberg, who told him that he would "never dream of saying anything to [Hitler] about Austria. . . . It is a point on which he is not quite sane." Rauschning, *Germany's Revolution of Nihilism* (New York, 1939), p. 153. Rauschning indicates, however, that Blomberg said this sometime in 1934.

[42] Dirksen says that Hitler spoke to him of the possibility of a treaty with Poland as

However much this agreement could be praised as a shrewd blow against France's eastern alliance system, it was obvious that it could not help but be disturbing to the Soviet Union and that it might even be the decisive factor in persuading the Soviets to turn to the West. This was all the more likely since Hitler's speeches immediately after the conclusion of the Declaration began to contain open references to the Bolshevist menace. And if Russia turned to the West, Germany, in view of developments on other fronts, would be effectively isolated.

This danger was probably realized by many members of the German diplomatic corps; it was strenuously combatted by only one. Rudolf Nadolny, who had gone to Moscow as ambassador after Germany's departure from the Conference on Disarmament, bombarded Berlin with warning despatches, statistics on the size of the Red Army and recommendations that something be done to reassure the Soviet government.[44] During trips to Germany, he delivered lectures to the officers of the East Prussian military district, urging the importance of cooperation with Russia.[45] And finally he carried his case directly to the Chancellor.

According to Nadolny's friend and former colleague, Rudolf Rahn, the interview with Hitler was a stormy one. The ambassador pointed out that German isolation was imminent and might, in time, lead to a disastrous war. If Hitler were not prepared to remain within the Geneva system, as Nadolny had previously urged, then it was absolutely essential that he preserve the tie with Russia, who protected Germany's rear. Hitler answered that no compromise was possible with Bolshevism and that the Western Powers were not prepared to satisfy Germany's just claims. There was, therefore, only one course left: for Germany to break loose from all international obligations and to become so strong, militarily and economically, that she could attain her goals by her own power. "I am not mistaken," Hitler said angrily. "For fourteen years I have predicted developments accurately." "And I," Nadolny answered, "have been making foreign policy for thirty-two years, and there is no man living who can point to a mistake that I have made in that time." "As far as I am concerned," said the Fuehrer, "this con-

---

early as April 1933. *Moskau, Tokio, London*, p. 123. See also DeWitt C. Poole, "Light on Nazi Foreign Policy," *Foreign Affairs*, xxv (1946), 134.

[43] The pertinent documents will be found in *Polish White Book*, pp. 11-24, and *Vorgeschichte*, pp. 54-66. A convenient chronological record of Polish-German relations will be found in *Speeches of Hitler*, II, 1029-1038. For Polish motives in concluding the agreement, see Chapter 19, § VII below.

[44] Kordt, *Wahn und Wirklichkeit*, p. 63.

[45] Hossbach, *Zwischen Wehrmacht und Hitler*, pp. 37-38.

versation is finished." "As far as I am concerned," the ambassador answered, "it is only beginning"; and he proceeded to repeat his arguments.[46] They did not, however, convince the Fuehrer, and led only to Nadolny's resignation, or dismissal, a few weeks later.

Nadolny's position was almost certainly supported by Bülow, for the Secretary of State knew the importance of the Russian connection, and it had been on his personal initiative that the term of the Berlin Treaty had been prolonged, when it came up for renewal in May 1933.[47] But Neurath had vigorously combatted Nadolny's point of view from the beginning, denying flatly that there was any danger of a. Russian rapprochement with the West.[48] In his decision to ignore realities—for Russia, after all, did change her policy and had, by the end of 1934, become a member of the League—we can detect some of the basic weaknesses of Neurath as a Foreign Minister. The French ambassador in Berlin has written of him that he was not a strong man but gave in easily to pressure, and that he was a covetous man and one desirous of holding on to his office.[49] It seems clear—we have Hitler's own testimony on the point[50]—that Neurath had by now decided to cast his lot completely with Hitler; and, despite his efforts to prove the contrary at Nuremberg, he does not seem to have opposed the Fuehrer on any major issue from this time on. In the dispute with Nadolny, moreover, there were other motives at work. There was a long record of hostility between the two men;[51] Nadolny had been a competitor for the post of Foreign Minister in 1932;[52] and, if his arguments were accepted, he might become so again. Neurath's advocacy of Hitler's policy was in all likelihood determined more by personal considerations than by an objective appraisal of the international situation.

It cannot be said, however, that his attitude enhanced his reputation, or that of the Foreign Office, in Hitler's eyes. It was, indeed, precisely at this point that the decline of the Foreign Office began. It may have been the brush with Nadolny which awakened all of Hitler's latent distrust of the aristocrats who filled the offices of the Wilhelmstrasse, although it would be unwise to attribute too much importance to that incident. It is safer to say that, by the middle of 1934, Hitler had inaugurated a foreign policy of his own, a policy which defied the cautious canons of professional diplomacy, and that he was inclined to place its implementation in the hands of new men.

[46] Rahn, *Ruheloses Leben*, pp. 83-84.
[48] *ibid.*
[50] *Hitlers Tischgespräche*, p. 431.
[52] Rahn, *Ruheloses Leben*, p. 83.

[47] Kordt, *Wahn und Wirklichkeit*, p. 63.
[49] François-Poncet, *Souvenirs*, p. 49.
[51] Kordt, *Nicht aus den Akten*, p. 49.

III

Until the middle of 1934, the Foreign Office had had little reason to complain of party interference or of illegitimate usurpation of functions reserved to it. There had, it is true, been some annoying incidents. The empire-building proclivities of Joseph Goebbels had early become apparent and, in the course of 1933, he had annexed most of the staff and the duties of the press section of the Foreign Office, leaving it only a skeleton force with little responsibility. The new Propaganda Ministry had at the same time arrogated to itself the dissemination of cultural information, which had been within the jurisdiction of the Wilhelmstrasse before 1933.[53] But the loss of these prerogatives, which had always been regarded as of minor importance, was not considered very serious. The core of the Foreign Office's functions and by far the greatest part of its personnel had remained unaffected by the first eighteen months of National Socialist rule; and, in comparison with other Reich agencies, the foreign establishment had reason to be thankful.[54] Whatever satisfaction there might have been, however, was now marred by the sudden irruption of Joachim von Ribbentrop into the field of foreign policy.

It is impossible to write anything but a damaging portrait of Ribbentrop, for there is no evidence upon which to base a charitable account of his activities. Except for some fragmentary, incoherent, and contradictory reports written at Nuremberg, he has left no memoirs;[55] and his former colleagues have been uniformly contemptuous in their appraisals.[56] Geyr von Schweppenburg, who served as military attaché during his mission in London, has admitted grudgingly that Ribbentrop was reputed to have been a brave officer in the first world war; the wife of Italian ambassador Cerruti in Paris has called him "one of the most diverting of the Nazis." These are perhaps the kindest references to Ribbentrop in diplomatic literature, and even their weight is diminished by the fact that Geyr proceeds to excoriate Ribbentrop's conduct of

[53] Kordt, *Nicht aus den Akten*, pp. 91-92.

[54] See H. Gerth, "The Nazi Party: Its Leadership and Composition," *American Journal of Sociology*, XLV (1940), 517-541.

[55] When Ribbentrop was sentenced at Nuremberg, he murmured, "Death! Now I won't be able to write my beautiful memoirs." G. M. Gilbert, *Nuremberg Diary* (New York, 1947), p. 432. Considering his mental state in those last months, it may be doubted that the world has lost anything of value. Extracts from his testimony, which may be considered an apologia for his career, can be found in *Conspiracy and Aggression*, Supplement B, pp. 1177-1251.

[56] See the comments of his fellow prisoners at Nuremberg in Gilbert, *Nuremberg Diary*, *passim*. Neurath's views are on pp. 201, 225, 229-230.

embassy business, while Mme. Cerruti says that only in Nazi Germany could a man of his superficiality have attained high office.[57]

The subject of these unkind remarks had, in the period between the wars, been a *marchand de vins*, the head of Ribbentrop and Co., and allied by marriage to Henkell and Co., the foremost German manufacturer of sparkling wines.[58] This pleasant calling allowed him to live in affluence and to visit foreign capitals frequently; he had a more than superficial acquaintance with London and Paris, some influential friends in business circles, and a good command of languages. It seems probable that these evidences of cosmopolitanism impressed Hitler when he was entertained by the Ribbentrops for the first time in the spring of 1932; and the Fuehrer was further flattered by the attentions of Ribbentrop's wife, who catered to his unorthodox dietary habits, talked to him about landscape painting, and listened raptly to his interminable political monologues. By 1932, the Ribbentrops had developed political ambitions and, although they could not be described as old party comrades, they came into Hitler's life at a crucial point and had the wit to recognize him as the coming man in Germany.

Once Hitler had become Chancellor, he did not forget the pleasant household at Dahlem and Ribbentrop did not give him an opportunity to do so. Indeed, he became the most constant attendant in the Chancellor's anteroom, where, by the simple expedient of making a fine art of hanging around, he managed to have frequent talks with Germany's new ruler. In these conversations à *deux*, he stumbled on the technique that was to be the foundation stone of his career. This was the gift of storing away in his memory pet ideas of the Fuehrer and then introducing them on later occasions as ideas of his own—a procedure which could not help but persuade Hitler that Ribbentrop was a man of discernment and judgment. To this he added the further talent of being more Hitlerian than Hitler himself and encouraging the Fuehrer in those moments when he developed doubts about the possible success of his plans. This coarse form of flattery might have proved obnoxious to a man of finer sensibilities than Hitler; the Fuehrer, however, never fully recovered from the conviction that Ribbentrop was a man of parts.[59]

[57] Freiherr Geyr von Schweppenburg, *Erinnerungen eines Militärattachés: London, 1933-37* (Stuttgart, 1949), p. 112; Elisabetta Cerruti, *Visti da vicino* (Milan, 1951), p. 241.
[58] See Paul Schwarz, *This Man Ribbentrop: His Life and Times* (New York, 1943), pp. 54-70. Dr. Schwarz, a former member of the Foreign Office, knew Ribbentrop before he entered politics. His book is interesting but is filled with such startling inaccuracies that it must be used with extreme caution.
[59] This paragraph follows closely an eloquent passage in François-Poncet, *Souvenirs*, p. 291.

Ribbentrop chose the field of foreign policy as the one in which he could most easily make himself indispensable to Hitler, for it was a sphere in which none of the other leading men of the Third Reich possessed his own dubious qualifications.[60] The man who had been widely considered as Hitler's expert in foreign affairs before the *Macht-übernahme*—Alfred Rosenberg—was already a spent force, because, on a visit to London in the summer of 1933, he had discredited himself and his master by painfully maladroit attempts to get into the good graces of the "English ruling class"—attempts in which, it should be added, he was encouraged by the London embassy staff in the hope that he would, as he did, cover himself with ridicule. With Rosenberg out of the way, Ribbentrop had a clear field as far as the National Socialist party was concerned.

He had now, of course, to contend with the official foreign policy agencies of the state, and this at first promised to be difficult. Throughout 1933, as Hitler and the Foreign Office seemed to work in perfect harmony, he made little headway in establishing his claims to competence in foreign affairs. In 1934, however, a more favorable wind arose. As the professional diplomats began to express their first doubts about Hitler's course and to betray a pessimistic belief that he had, by injudicious behavior, isolated Germany, Ribbentrop undertook to prove to Hitler that these doubts and fears were groundless and that the Chancellor—and he himself—had a more realistic view of the international situation than the gentlemen in the Foreign Office.

Perhaps the most astonishing feature of this experiment was the temerity which Ribbentrop displayed in attempting it. In the spring of 1934, for instance, the French government lost patience with the long-distance correspondence between Berlin and the Western capitals concerning the possible resumption of disarmament talks; and on April 17, in the so-called Barthou note, they accused Germany of bad faith and declared that they would henceforth look to their own security. The menacing tone of this communication seems to have made Hitler nervous; he feared the possibility of a French attempt to persuade the other Powers, at the forthcoming meeting of the Bureau of the Disarmament Conference, to concert on retaliatory action against Germany. Ribbentrop offered to persuade the other governments to postpone their meeting at Geneva; and, with Hitler's permission, he set forth on a whirlwind trip

[60] At Nuremberg, Goering, who yielded to no man in his contempt for Ribbentrop, admitted that, in 1933-1934, his qualifications impressed most of the Nazi leaders. See Poole in *Foreign Affairs*, XXV, 133.

to London and Rome. It was from the outset a hopeless undertaking. In their respective capitals, Sir John Simon and Mussolini listened politely to this extraordinary envoy who came armed with nothing but a proposal that they adjourn the meeting of an organization of which Germany was no longer a member, and went ahead with their plans.[61] Ribbentrop's debut as negotiator was therefore a failure, but it was not one which handicapped him in any way. The fact that nothing eventful transpired when the Bureau of the Disarmament Conference held its meeting may have persuaded Hitler that Ribbentrop's wanderings had not been without result. In any event, he encouraged his eager friend to extend his activities.

Ribbentrop did this by establishing an agency of his own—the so-called *Dienststelle* (or *Büro*) *Ribbentrop*—in a building that faced the Foreign Office across the Wilhelmstrasse and staffing it with a horde of exjournalists, disappointed businessmen, graduates from the *Hitler-jugend*, and aspiring party members who had hitched their wagons to his star. This organization was presumably intended to collect and analyze foreign intelligence, but it tried whenever possible to absorb other Foreign Office functions as well. Before his trip to London, Ribbentrop had been appointed Special Commissioner for Disarmament Questions and had been given the right to see all diplomatic correspondence dealing with this subject. This privilege was now widened, on Hitler's express orders, to include all dispatches which were not specially marked "For the Foreign Minister" or "For the Secretary of State." The former wine merchant developed a habit of scanning the incoming correspondence, seizing upon telegrams which required action and securing Hitler's assent to replies which he had himself drafted, before the Foreign Office had had time to consider the cases.[62]

The *Büro Ribbentrop* took the whole world for its province; its chief, on the other hand, was especially interested in Anglo-German relations, which he knew to be a subject close to Hitler's own heart. The possibility of achieving that natural combination with Britain of which Hitler had written so warmly in *Mein Kampf* seemed to have become extremely remote by the fall of 1934, when the continuing reaction to the Blood Purge of June 30 and to the abortive *Putsch* in Vienna in July seemed to confirm the isolation of Germany which had been predicted by Nadolny. But here again Ribbentrop elected to disregard what the professionals considered to be realities and to persuade Hitler that what

---

[61] For further details, see Kordt, *Nicht aus den Akten*, pp. 69-73.
[62] *ibid.*, pp. 79-80.

the Fuehrer wanted to believe was true: namely, that Germany's isolation was more apparent than real and that the British government was yearning for a comprehensive agreement with Germany. In November he made another journey to London where he talked with such notables as Lord Cecil and Sir Austen Chamberlain, who were decidedly cool, and George Bernard Shaw, who was sardonic; but where he also encountered persons, like Lord Lothian, who expressed their complete sympathy with Germany's right to rearm and their belief in the natural affinity of the two countries. In high good humor, Ribbentrop returned to Berlin and told Hitler that all classes of English society—members of Parliament, journalists, businessmen, and ordinary citizens—desired close collaboration with Germany. Hitler was delighted to have his hopes confirmed so authoritatively. He is reported to have remarked that Ribbentrop was the only man who told him the truth about foreign countries; and he made available to his informant increased funds for the expansion of his Bureau.[63]

The Foreign Office would have been well-advised at this juncture to take some kind of a stand against the interloper. Nothing of the sort, however, could be expected from the Foreign Minister. Neurath had, indeed, helped give Ribbentrop his *entrée* into the sphere of foreign affairs when, in deference to Hitler's wishes, he had overcome President von Hindenburg's resistance to Ribbentrop's appointment as Special Commissioner for Disarmament Questions in the spring of 1934.[64] Aside from this, Neurath had developed a nimbleness in side-stepping awkward questions of competence. He absented himself from Berlin for long periods during hunting season,[65] and—as he explained solemnly at Nuremberg—went to bed early when he was in the capital.[66] The job of dealing with Ribbentrop's incursions into the Foreign Office domain was therefore left to Secretary of State Bülow, and Bülow was betrayed once more by his tendency to underestimate his adversaries. Bülow could not regard as a serious competitor a man who had had no formal training in diplomacy, who could not write a report in correct German, who did not listen carefully enough to the remarks of foreign statesmen to interpret them correctly, and who insisted upon seeing possibilities of alliance where none existed. He took the line, therefore, that no formal

[63] *ibid.*, pp. 83-88.

[64] Kordt, *Wahn und Wirklichkeit*, p. 95.

[65] Dirksen, *Moskau, Tokio, London*, p. 184.

[66] Professing ignorance of many of Hitler's plans, Neurath told the prison psychiatrist: "He must have done his conspiring with his little group of henchmen late at night. But I couldn't stay up so late." Gilbert, *Nuremberg Diary*, pp. 75-76.

protest against Ribbentrop's activities was necessary, since their patent foolishness could not long be hidden even from Hitler.

It would be unfair to be too critical of Bülow's tactics in this matter. Who after all could have foreseen that the British government would act in a manner which seemed to confirm Ribbentrop's wildest statements and that this would make his position unassailable? Yet that is precisely what happened in the spring of 1935.

The events of these months are well enough known to make unnecessary any detailed description of them. This was the spring when Europe first experienced Hitler's "Saturday Surprises," as the Fuehrer countered a final Anglo-French attempt to secure agreement on an armament convention by announcing, first, the creation of a German air force and, second, the complete repudiation of the military clauses of the Versailles Treaty and the institution of universal military service in his country. The second announcement, which was made on March 16, created a situation in which momentarily the isolation of Germany seemed to be confirmed, for in April representatives of the British, French, and Italian governments met at Stresa and agreed that further aggression must be resisted. Yet, as subsequent events showed, only the French government took this plain warning to Germany seriously and continued to act in its spirit. Mussolini's attention was already wandering off in the direction of Africa. As for the British, within six weeks of the Stresa meeting, they had so far forgiven Hitler's violation of the military clauses of the Versailles Treaty that they were willing to authorize him to disregard its naval clauses as well. In June 1935, they concluded a naval pact with Germany, permitting her to build up to 35 per cent of British strength in capital ships and to build submarines virtually without restriction.

The conclusion of this agreement, which effectively destroyed the Stresa front, was Hitler's greatest victory to date, and it was one which redounded especially to Ribbentrop's credit. This was due less to the fact that he had negotiated the agreement personally—although that, of course, had its importance—than to the fact that he had done so after the professional diplomats had declared categorically that an agreement was impossible. The London embassy and the Foreign Office were in complete agreement on this point[67] and, far from being indignant over the choice of Ribbentrop as negotiator, they seem to have welcomed it, in the certain assurance that the amateur would now discredit himself totally. In the memoirs of the German diplomats who had an opportunity to observe Ribbentrop's diplomacy in London, some traces of this attitude

[67] *Conspiracy and Aggression,* Supplement B, pp. 144-145.

are still to be found, for their authors have carefully recorded all of his *gaffes* and discourtesies and breaches of diplomatic usage.[68] This latterday jeering has a rather hollow sound. As negotiator, Ribbentrop had few of the qualities which are considered indispensable by Callières and Sir Ernest Satow; but he did, after all, come back from London with his treaty.

That he had confirmed Hitler's high opinion of him, there is no doubt. For some time now, the idea had been growing in Hitler's mind that the career diplomats were blind to realities (*Wirklichkeitsfremd*)[69] and over-cautious. Years later he was to say: "In 1933-34 the reports of the Foreign Office were miserable. They always had the same quintessence: that we ought to do nothing."[70] Now he had found a man who possessed the dynamic spirit which should characterize a revolutionary regime and whose judgment equalled his energy. He tended, therefore, increasingly to give Ribbentrop his head, using him as his Special Ambassador on all sorts of mysterious missions in the months that followed. In a Europe which in the last part of 1935 was distracted by the tensions engendered by the Abyssinian crisis, Ribbentrop darted busily from capital to capital, seeking to register new triumphs and startling foreign statesmen with ingenious schemes, like his offer to the Belgian government of a solemn renunciation of Germany's claims to Eupen and Malmédy in return for a Belgian declaration of neutrality in any future conflict.[71]

The Foreign Office found itself more and more in the position of not knowing what the Special Ambassador was up to—a situation which was embarrassing when foreign governments directed questions to it—and increasingly uncertain concerning the direction of Hitler's policy as a whole. Even before Ribbentrop's London triumph, communication between the Wilhelmstrasse and the *Reichskanzlei* had become intermittent, and the Foreign Office had learned, for instance, of the projected repudiation of the military clauses too late to express any opinion on its political consequences.[72] As 1935 gave way to 1936, this situation grew progressively worse. Hitler's personal liking for Neurath apparently continued, but he had lost confidence in his organization. It is significant that the working up of the legal case which was to justify Hitler's next

---

[68] See especially Paul Schmidt, *Statist auf diplomatischer Bühne, 1923-1945* (Bonn, 1949), pp. 311-316; and Kordt, *Nicht aus den Akten*, pp. 98-113.

[69] The phrase is taken from a conversation in 1942. *Hitlers Tischgespräche*, p. 86.

[70] *ibid.*, p. 97.

[71] See Kordt, *Wahn und Wirklichkeit*, p. 119.

[72] Kordt, *Nicht aus den Akten*, p. 93. But the leaders of the army do not seem to have been consulted until the eve of the declaration either. See Hossbach, *Zwischen Wehrmacht und Hitler*, pp. 94-96.

adventure in foreign policy—the entry into the Rhineland and the repudiation of Locarno in March 1936—seems to have been handled in the *Büro Ribbentrop* rather than in the Foreign Office.[73]

When the Rhineland invasion was launched, it gave rise to an incident which was scarcely designed to increase Hitler's respect for professional diplomats. In the anxious pause which followed the march-in of the troops, the staff of the London embassy became convinced that military action by Britain was highly likely and, with the apparent approval of Ambassador von Hoesch, the military attachés sent reports home underlining this possibility. Hitler was in an extremely nervous state—in contrast to Neurath, who said phlegmatically, "Jetzt sind mer drinne und bleibet drinne"—and his nervousness increased perceptibly when the reports from London were communicated to him by General von Blomberg.[74] He resented this unnecessary, and undignified, strain and did not forget it when the crisis had passed; the attachés were severely reprimanded, and it seems likely that Hoesch would have suffered also had he not died in April, worn out by his exertions during the crisis.

To Hitler the incident was additional proof of a lack of healthy realism on the part of career diplomats, and there is some indication that, at this moment, he considered a thoroughgoing shake-up of the diplomatic establishment. An opportunity was provided for such a step by the sudden death, in June 1936, of Bernhard von Bülow, and Hitler's first intention seems to have been to make Ribbentrop Secretary of State.[75] His desire for a comprehensive settlement with Great Britain was still, however, unfulfilled, despite the notable advance made toward it in the previous year; and it appeared that Ribbentrop's talents would be better used in London. The creator of the naval pact was, therefore, appointed to succeed Hoesch, a preferment which—having come so close to his real goal—he resisted vigorously, but in vain.[76]

With Ribbentrop's posting to London, the Foreign Office secured a

---

[73] Kordt, *Nicht aus den Akten*, pp. 129-130. How much the Foreign Office knew about Hitler's exact intentions is not clear. At Nuremberg, Neurath admitted that he knew and approved of the step but did not say whether his permanent officials had been consulted in any way. *Conspiracy and Aggression*, Supplement B, p. 1495. In conversations with François-Poncet in January 1936, Bülow stated flatly that Germany had no intention of denouncing the Locarno Treaties. The former ambassador believes that this was merely an evasion, but it may not have been. *Souvenirs*, p. 249.

[74] Geyr von Schweppenburg, *Erinnerungen*, pp. 87-88; Hossbach, *Zwischen Wehrmacht und Hitler*, pp. 97-98.

[75] Neurath claimed that Hitler had suggested this and that he himself had flatly refused to accept Ribbentrop's appointment. Gilbert, *Nuremberg Diary*, pp. 229-230. Neurath was not, however, by this time given to strong stands against Hitler and, if the Fuehrer changed his mind, it was probably for reasons other than Neurath's opposition.

[76] Kordt, *Nicht aus den Akten*, pp. 149-150.

respite, but nothing more. In the eighteen months that followed, its prestige and influence sank to their nadir, new aspirants to its privileges and functions appeared, and the administration of German foreign policy became completely chaotic.

IV

In illustrating the serious diminution of Foreign Office influence in this period, it may be noted at the outset that, in two important areas of Germany's foreign relations, the Wilhelmstrasse now had no effective role. Ribbentrop was not, like other ambassadors, subordinate to the Foreign Office and, while that office was informed of his activities, it had no power to issue instructions to him and found it useless to submit advice. Anglo-German relations thus became a private preserve of the Special Ambassador and the Fuehrer. An exactly similar situation obtained in matters affecting Austria. After the murder of Dollfuss in July 1934, Hitler had appointed Franz von Papen as minister to Vienna. Papen made his acceptance of the post conditional upon his being "free from the jurisdiction of the Foreign Office but . . . responsible to Hitler alone."[77] He was expected to send copies of all his reports to the Foreign Office, and he probably did so; but the personal coolness which existed between him and Neurath probably kept his consultation with the Foreign Minister at a minimum. Moreover, Papen staffed his Vienna legation with men who had been his aides when he was Vice Chancellor,[78] a circumstance which certainly weakened the normal liaison between the legation and the home office. Even in such an important development as the negotiations leading to the Austro-German agreement of July 1936, the Foreign Office played no part, and the drafting of that treaty was Papen's work alone.[79]

At the same time, Foreign Office control over all embassies was affected by another development. This was the growth in influence of the National Socialist party's Foreign Organization (*Auslandsorganisation*).[80] The AO, as it was usually called, had been established in 1931 and was originally concerned only with maintaining contact with party members who resided abroad. After 1933, however, it rapidly developed a kind of foreign service of its own, sending agents abroad to spread National Socialist propaganda, maintain contact with subversive elements and extend party discipline over German nationals. Between these agents

[77] Papen, *Memoirs*, pp. 340-341.   [78] *ibid.*, p. 365.
[79] *ibid.*, pp. 362-364; Weizsäcker, *Erinnerungen*, p. 130.
[80] A convenient outline of the origins and activities of the organization will be found in *Hitler's Speeches*, II, 1063-1079. See also *Trials of War Criminals*, XII, 220-221.

and the official diplomatic representatives of the Reich there was continual friction. Foreign Office protests against the embarrassment caused by AO activities had no result, however; and it finally became injudicious for it to raise any objections. For on January 30, 1937 Hitler issued an order which stated that "in order to unify the care of German citizens living abroad there is created the post of Head of the AO in the Foreign Office, to whom at the same time the conduct and administration of all matters affecting German citizens living abroad falling within the competence of the Foreign Office are entrusted."

This sweeping ukase was a grievous blow to the independence of the foreign service as a whole. In a public interpretation, Neurath sought to explain that the AO would henceforth operate within lines set by him. This was contradicted by the fact that, while E. W. Bohle, the appointee to the new post, was nominally subordinated to Neurath, he remained, in his capacity as Head of the AO of the party, responsible to the Fuehrer's Deputy Rudolf Hess and was furthermore, in all matters touching his sphere of competence, a member of the Cabinet of the Reich. Later in the year, a Foreign Office circular to the field advised Germany's diplomats, in rather obscure language, that Bohle was in fact independent of the Foreign Minister's control.

The net result of Hitler's order, then, was, first, that the AO received jurisdiction over all Germans residing abroad and, second, that it was placed in a position to pass judgment on the loyalty and efficiency of Germany's diplomatic representatives. As one newspaper expressed it: "Henceforth, no German diplomat or consul can be employed who has not given proof of his National Socialist attitude in the closest cooperation with the *Auslandsorganisation*."[81] The effect of this on the morale of the foreign service can easily be imagined. While Bohle prowled about the corridors of the Wilhelmstrasse, accosting officials who were not wearing the party insignia in their lapels, his agents abroad exercised surveillance over the mission chiefs and their staffs and often sought to undermine their reputation and authority.

In addition to this, the AO undertook to make policy on its own. In Austria, for instance, AO agents were active as early as 1935 and were indulging in undercover maneuvers which Papen believed, or claims to have believed, jeopardized the fulfilment of the policy upon which he had agreed with Hitler.[82] In Spain, they were laying the basis for German support of General Franco even before the outbreak of the civil

---

[81] The *Allgemeine Zeitung*, cited in *Hitler's Speeches*, II, 1068.
[82] Papen, *Memoirs*, pp. 355-356; *Trials of War Criminals*, XII, 221.

war, as was later proved when Loyalist authorities raided the AO headquarters in Barcelona and seized their files.[83] It is not too much to say
that the policy adopted by Germany in Spain was an AO policy. Immediately after the beginning of hostilities, two of Bohle's agents traveled from Spain to Berlin with a letter from Franco to Hitler. Through
Bohle's influence, they were received by the Fuehrer and, as a result of
this conversation, Hitler summoned Goering, Blomberg, and a member
of his naval staff to a meeting which agreed in principle to the support
of the rebel forces.[84] It is significant that the Foreign Minister was not
present at these deliberations, and the head of the Political Department
of the Foreign Office has written that the decision took the Foreign
Office completely by surprise.[85]

The surprise was accompanied by a feeling of dismay which grew
steadily in the months that followed. The Foreign Office experts were
not opposed to the idea of exploiting the situation in Spain to Germany's
advantage, but they were frightened by the possibility that a thoroughgoing commitment in Spain would sharpen the opposition of the Western
Powers and even involve Germany in a disastrous war.[86] Memoranda
prepared in the Wilhelmstrasse repeatedly stressed this idea and urged
the necessity of leaving open the way for retreat from support of the
Caudillo; as late as July 1937, the director of the Political Division was
writing: ". . . our goal should be rather the prevention of a general
conflict than the unconditional and complete victory of the Franco party
in the Spanish Civil War."[87] In this attitude, the Foreign Office was
strongly supported by the army high command, including War Minister
von Blomberg, General von Fritsch, the Commander in Chief, and the
Chief of General Staff Beck, all of whom regarded the military commitment in Spain as politically unwise and materially wasteful.[88] These
chance partners were always, however, uncertain of Hitler's real intentions and continually fearful of the influence upon the Fuehrer of other
groups and individuals who were seeking to direct Germany's Spanish
policy.

There were many of these: Johannes Bernhardt, German businessman
and director of the Economic Agency of the AO in Tetuán, who by virtue

[83] On this, see *The Nazi Conspiracy in Spain. By the Editor of the Brown Book of the
Hitler Terror* (London, 1937).

[84] *German Documents*, series D, III, 1-2.

[85] Weizsäcker, *Erinnerungen*, p. 129.

[86] *German Documents*, series D, III, 225-226.   [87] *ibid.*, p. 391.

[88] *ibid.*, pp. 50, 149, 168. For further details on the army's attitude, see Hossbach,
Zwischen Wehrmacht und Hitler, pp. 41-43, and Walter Görlitz, *Der deutsche General-
stab: Geschichte und Gestalt* (Frankfurt-am-Main, 1950), pp. 441-442.

of his transmission of Franco's letter to Hitler in July 1936 looked upon himself as "the Fuehrer's delegate to Franco" and who was instrumental in organizing the Spanish trading company *Hisma* and its German counterpart *Rowak* to facilitate the exchange of Germany military supplies for Spanish raw materials;[89] Colonel-General Hermann Goering, who also had an interest in *Hisma* and *Rowak* and who furthermore welcomed intervention in Spain as a means of testing the fighting qualities of the *Luftwaffe*; the Ministries of Economics and Propaganda and the *Dienststelle Ribbentrop*, which sought to exploit the Spanish situation for their own ends;[90] the shadowy figure of Admiral Canaris, head of the Counter Intelligence Section of the War Ministry, a personal friend and admirer of Franco and consequently much more cordial to the idea of an all-out commitment than Blomberg and Fritsch;[91] and even the newly accredited ambassador to the Burgos government, an ardent party member and retired general named Faupel who, far from sharing the doubts and hesitations of his nominal superiors in the Wilhelmstrasse, used his right of personal access to the Fuehrer to plead for a policy which would have involved the employment of as many as three German infantry divisions in the peninsula and the gradual assumption of direction over Franco's war effort by a German staff, presumably under his own leadership.[92]

With this welter of irresponsible agents wandering about in Spain, the pursuit of any clear-cut line of policy became well-nigh impossible. The continuation of the work of the Non-Intervention Committee in London, which was the best assurance against the outbreak of war among the Powers and which was participated in by Germany for that very reason, was constantly threatened by injudicious releases by the Propaganda Ministry[93] or experiments in brutality by Goering's air force. The policy of cooperation with Italy in Spain, which had the incidental advantage of diverting Mussolini's attention from the Danubian area by nailing his military forces down in the peninsula, was jeopardized by Faupel's rather obvious attempts to give Germany a stronger position in Franco's counsels than Italy.[94] Even the hope of winning solid economic advantage in return for the military aid sent to the Nationalists was weakened and eventually defeated by Bernhardt's clumsy attempts to blackmail the Burgos government into granting extensive mining concessions to Ger-

---

[89] *German Documents*, series D, III, 88, 111-114, 245-247.
[90] See, for instance, *ibid.*, p. 225.
[91] Karl Abshagen, *Canaris* (Bonn, 1949), pp. 161-164.
[92] *German Documents*, series D, III, 134, 137-139, 155-156, 159-162, 207, 236.
[93] See Weizsäcker's remarks on propaganda, *ibid.*, p. 429.   [94] *ibid.*, p. 219.

many.[95] All in all, Germany's Spanish adventure is a striking illustration of the confusion and lack of coordination which had come to characterize the administration of German foreign policy; and there is no more telling example of the extremes to which the Foreign Office had been reduced than the subterranean methods which it seems to have employed, in informal conspiracy with the army leaders, to discredit and unseat its own ambassador in Spain before his personal ambitions should produce a completely chaotic situation.[96]

It can nevertheless be noted, as one of the few victories won by the Foreign Office in this period, that the line of caution advocated by the Wilhelmstrasse and the Army Command was generally adhered to in the Spanish war, and that both military commitments and political risks were kept within careful limits by Hitler. In another field of policy, however, the Foreign Office and army partnership suffered a decisive defeat in this same period: namely, in the Far East.

Their antagonist here was Ribbentrop, whose appointment to London had neither put a stop to his interest in other aspects of Germany's foreign relations nor interrupted the activities of his Bureau. In the course of 1935, Ribbentrop, doubtless inspired by an expression of interest by the Fuehrer, had conceived the idea of effecting a closer relationship between Germany and Japan. While he himself had entered into conversations with Oshima, the Japanese military attaché in Berlin, his Bureau had made preliminary studies and drafts for a political treaty between the two countries, oriented against Russia although explicitly expressing only a common opposition to communism.[97] These studies and negotiations were kept strictly secret from the Foreign Office, and it was not until April 1936 that the officials there had any inkling of them.[98] Even after that date, they refused—as they had on other occasions—to be concerned; and the negotiations were permitted to continue until they eventuated in the Anti-Comintern Pact, which Ribbentrop returned from London to sign in November 1936.

The Pact was so innocuous in content that the Foreign Office attitude

[95] *ibid.*, chapter v, pp. 496-619 for details.

[96] *ibid.*, pp. 168, 423-424, 434. Faupel's recall came after Franco had requested it, but it seems clear from the German documents that the Foreign Office and its army allies helped effect this result.

[97] It was apparently Raumer of the *Büro Ribbentrop* who invented the term Anti-Comintern Pact, taking advantage of the frequently repeated claim of the Soviet government that it was not responsible for Comintern activities. See Poole in *Foreign Affairs*, XXV, 136.

[98] They learned of the negotiations for the first time from the ambassador in Tokyo, Dirksen, who had received hints from friends in the Japanese General Staff. Dirksen, *Moskau, Tokio, London*, p. 184.

seemed to have some justification. The treaty was, however, an earnest
of Ribbentrop's intention of effecting close cooperation with Japan in
world politics generally, and for this reason was worthy of more attention. Cooperation with Japan would, after all, involve taking her side in
her struggle with China, and this was in flat contradiction to the policy
of friendship with the Chinese National government which the Foreign
Office and the army had championed ever since the 1920's and which
had recently been strengthened by arrangements for military and economic aid to that government.[99] The issue was not clearly posed until
the outbreak of the China Incident in July 1937; but, after that time,
the Japanese government had no hesitation in demanding the cessation
of German aid to Chiang Kai-shek, basing their demands upon the spirit
of political collaboration which had been expressed in the Anti-Comintern
Pact.

The Foreign Office brusquely rejected the Japanese request, arguing
that Japan's military action was in itself inconsistent with the spirit of
the Anti-Comintern Pact, since it could only serve to drive China into
the arms of communism, and insisting further that Germany intended
to remain neutral in the Far Eastern conflict.[100] But this was a position
which it could not long maintain. Ribbentrop, disappointed in his earlier
hopes of obtaining a comprehensive agreement with Great Britain, had
now swung to the opposite extreme and had convinced himself that a
union of Germany, Italy, and Japan would assure his country of effective
control of continental affairs.[101] Throughout the fall of 1937 he was
working feverishly—and, characteristically, behind the Foreign Office's
back—to secure Italy's adhesion to the Anti-Comintern Pact, an objective
which he attained in November.[102] Simultaneously, he had accepted the
Japanese position completely and was making every effort to persuade
the Fuehrer that, since definitive Japanese victory in the Far East could
not be long delayed, it would be the part of political wisdom to yield to
Tokyo's desires.[103] The first intimation of his success came in October,
when Goering ordered the stoppage of military deliveries to China.[104]

[99] *German Documents*, series D, I, 852-853.   [100] *ibid.*, pp. 733-734.

[101] See, for instance, the confused, illogical, and often hopelessly inaccurate memorandum which he wrote in December 1937 and submitted to Hitler in January. *Ibid.*, pp. 162-
168.

[102] In the preliminary negotiations, the Foreign Office informed the Italian govern-
ment that Germany preferred a separate Italo-Japanese agreement. On the following day,
Raumer of the *Büro Ribbentrop* contradicted this, saying that Germany preferred Italian
adhesion to the Japanese-German treaty. *Ibid.*, pp. 15-18. See also Galeazzo Ciano,
L'Europa verso la catastrofe (Verona, 1948), pp. 212-226; Ciano, *1937-1938 Diario*
(Bologna, 1948), pp. 37-38; Kordt, *Nicht aus den Akten*, p. 169.

[103] *German Documents*, series D, I, 758-759.   [104] *ibid.*, pp. 767-769, 772.

The Foreign Office and the army command were able to have this order reversed; but this was a temporary victory and, in the spring of 1938—after a German attempt to mediate the eastern conflict was defeated by Japanese intransigence[105]—the last links with China were broken.[106]

By any measure, therefore, the period that stretched from the middle of 1936 to the end of 1937 was one of steady decline for the Foreign Office. Even in Spain, one area in which it could claim that its advice had not been wholly disregarded, a major part of its energies had been expended in seeking to discover and control the activities of other agencies which were trying to usurp its legitimate functions. Elsewhere, its consultative prerogatives had been ignored and its advice overruled, while it was frequently left in ignorance of pending agreements with other Powers or important changes in the direction of national policy. And now the professionals were to experience their crowning humiliation, for, in February 1938, in the major reorganization of the state administration which prefaced the opening of a new and aggressive phase of his foreign policy, Hitler dismissed Neurath and made Joachim von Ribbentrop Foreign Minister of the Reich.[107]

V

This was a shattering blow to a diplomatic corps which had persisted in believing that Ribbentrop would, sooner or later, overreach himself. Some attempts were made, of course, at self-reassurance. Ambassador Dirksen, who was to take over at London, comforted himself with the reflection that at least the ruinous competition between the Foreign Office and the Ribbentrop Bureau would now come to an end.[108] Ernst von Weizsäcker, head of the Political Department, who was now invited

---

[105] The documents bearing on the mediation attempt are in *ibid.*, pp. 787-825.

[106] For the further development of German-Japanese relations, see Chapter 20 below.

[107] The reasons for Hitler's action are by no means clear. At Nuremberg, Neurath claimed that he himself had taken the initiative; that he was so shocked by Hitler's revelation, in the famous conference with his generals on November 5, 1937, of his intention of proceeding against Austria and Czechoslovakia that he had a heart attack and subsequently submitted his resignation to Hitler; and that Hitler had accepted it reluctantly, saying, "But I will never make this Ribbentrop Foreign Minister!" *Conspiracy and Aggression*, Supplement B, pp. 969, 1491. Hossbach, who was present at the meeting of November 5, does not mention either objections or perturbation on the part of Neurath (*Zwischen Wehrmacht und Hitler*, pp. 217-220); and it is significant that Neurath did not resist his new appointment as head of the so-called Secret Cabinet or his subsequent elevation, after March 1939, to the position of Reich Protector of Bohemia and Moravia. On the other hand, Ribbentrop does not seem to have expected any change in his own position, as Erich Kordt tells us. (*Nicht aus den Akten*, p. 178.) It seems likely that Hitler believed that Ribbentrop's energy was more suited to the coming period of action than Neurath's lassitude and hesitations. See François-Poncet, *Souvenirs*, p. 290.

[108] Dirksen, *Moskau, Tokio, London*, p. 199.

to take Bülow's old post of Secretary of State,[109] also concluded that all might yet be for the best. In a mood which was reminiscent of that which pervaded the diplomatic corps at the time of Hitler's accession in 1933, he told himself that Ribbentrop, despite his "fantastic political imagination," could be influenced;[110] and that the Foreign Office might now regain its legitimate influence over the course of state policy.

There were, indeed, some aspects of Ribbentrop's activity which were immensely reassuring to the professionals of the Wilhelmstrasse. "He used to say," the chief of the Legal Division testified at Nuremberg, "that everything that the Foreign Office lost in the way of terrain under Neurath he wanted to win back and, with all his passion, he fought for this aim in a manner which can only be understood by somebody who actually saw it." "My main activity," the legal adviser added, "was nearly 90 per cent concerned with his competency conflicts.[111] The new Foreign Minister did what Neurath had never dared, or at least attempted, to do. He put up a strong defensive against the incursions of the AO, both within the Foreign Office itself and in the field missions, and gathered his strength for a successful offensive against Bohle's pretensions which was finally carried through in 1941. At the same time, he sought to regain the ground ceded earlier to the Propaganda Ministry and, by 1939, had persuaded Hitler to permit him to make known his "wishes and instructions" to Goebbels and to maintain liaison with the Propaganda Ministry. Against party comrades who sought to employ the tactics which he had himself used so successfully, Ribbentrop was a pitiless and effective antagonist; and his "paranoical battle to broaden (or at least defend) the jurisdictional sphere of the Foreign Office assured the latter of its institutional survival in a sea of competitors."[112]

It was essentially, however, a survival without meaning. In Ribbentrop's conception, the Foreign Office was meant to be a technical apparatus and nothing more. His most explicit definition of its functions was not made until the war years, when Steengracht von Moyland succeeded Weizsäcker as Secretary of State, but it may be taken as expressing his belief at the time of his entrance into the Foreign Office. "Your

[109] For other changes which took place at this time, see *Trials of War Criminals*, XII, 149. A complete list of officials as of December 1, 1937 will be found in *German Documents*, series D, I, 1187-1198, and a list as of June 1, 1938 in *ibid.*, II, 1031-1040.

[110] *Trials of War Criminals*, XII, 922. See also Weizsäcker, *Erinnerungen*, pp. 152-155.

[111] *Trials of War Criminals*, XII, 1190.

[112] Paul Seabury, "Ribbentrop and the German Foreign Office," *Political Science Quarterly*, LXVI (1951), 554. This article, from which some of the details in the paragraph above are taken, is the most intelligent treatment yet to appear of Ribbentrop's administration of the Foreign Office.

sphere of tasks," Ribbentrop said, "includes these points: you must handle routine contacts with diplomats in Berlin; you must maintain discipline in the Foreign Office; and you must protect the competencies of the Foreign Office towards all agencies with ruthless energy." Steengracht said modestly that he supposed that he would have a voice in policy matters also. Ribbentrop denied this absolutely. Policy, he said, "was exclusively the concern of Hitler and himself. The Foreign Office and myself [Steengracht] were just to carry out the orders we received."[113]

From the time of the *Anschluss*, which was effected before he had formally assumed charge at the Wilhelmstrasse, until the outbreak of the war and after, Ribbentrop directed the Foreign Office in this spirit. The virtue which he prized most highly in his subordinates was loyalty,[114] and he was fond of lining them up and gazing into their eyes, as if seeking to divine the extent of their devotion. But their advice on policy was not desired by a Foreign Minister who believed that his own chief function was to execute the Fuehrer's wishes and to protect Hitler from doubts and from the considerations which might instill them. It was for this reason that reports from Germany's embassies abroad which seemed to challenge the bases of the aggressive policy which Hitler was now following were carefully prevented from reaching the Fuehrer's eyes; the futility to which this reduced the ambassadorial function will be described in a later chapter.[115]

The Foreign Minister insulated himself and his master just as fully from the cautionary advices of his immediate aides. In August 1938, when Weizsäcker sought to convince the Foreign Minister that an attempt to solve the Czech problem by force of arms would almost certainly lead to war, Ribbentrop reminded him that it was not his duty to make comments of this nature. "Herr von Ribbentrop sought to represent the question of responsibility in such a way that I was responsible to him alone, he to the Fuehrer alone, and the Fuehrer solely to the German people, while I maintained that it was necessary to be deeply rooted in the theory of . . . policy in order to carry it out to the best advantage. Herr von Ribbentrop declared that the Fuehrer had never yet made a mistake; his most difficult decisions and acts (occupation of the Rhineland) already lay behind him. It was necessary to believe in his genius, just as he, R., did from long years of experience. If I had not yet reached the stage of blind belief . . . then he desired of me, in a

[113] *Trials of War Criminals*, XIII, 25.
[114] Kordt, *Nicht aus den Akten*, pp. 199-200.   [115] See Chapter 15 below.

friendly manner and urgently, too, that I should do so. I should certainly regret it later, if I did not succeed in doing so and the facts then contradicted me."[116]

In May 1939, as Germany began her preparations for the operation against Poland, Ribbentrop was more threatening in the advice which he gave to his permanent officials. Even if the Polish government elected to resist German claims and war came as a result, he is reported to have said, Poland would collapse within twenty-four hours and Britain would not dare to intervene; and, if he should hear a Foreign Office official expressing contrary views on this matter, he would personally shoot him and assume responsibility for this action before the Fuehrer.[117]

In the face of these admonitions, the Foreign Office became little more than a stenographic bureau. Even those officials who were dismayed by what was obviously a headlong rush toward war and the probable destruction of Germany were powerless to influence the course of policy. They were reduced to such methods as sending secret warnings of pending actions to friendly circles in foreign countries—warnings which were rarely understood or believed and never acted upon—and talking of conspiracies and putsches which never materialized until it was too late. Aside from this, they could only go about their customary dignified business of inditing notes and sealing diplomatic pouches, while they waited for the inevitable to happen.

[116] *German Documents*, series D, II, 593.
[117] Kordt, *Nicht aus den Akten*, p. 332.

14

Three Observers in Berlin:
Rumbold, Dodd, and François-Poncet

BY FRANKLIN L. FORD

THE position of the ambassador is one of the points where diplomatic history relates most clearly to the history of institutions, ideas, and social forms in general. For the envoy is the product of one society, transplanted into another which inevitably possesses certain unfamiliar characteristics. With the latter he must deal as best he can, combining the fullest possible comprehension and even sympathy with a steady awareness of the interests of his own nation. It is a balance more easily prescribed than achieved, and to analyze the performance of any given ambassador is to accept a challenge demanding the exploitation of every tool and every insight into human experience at the historian's disposal.

The above applies with particular acuteness to the case of foreign envoys to Germany in the 1930's, since the complexities of the ambassador's position are never greater than when the country to which he is sent is undergoing internal convulsions. In such a setting the foreign diplomat is no longer merely called upon to adjust to traditions and social forms differing in some degree from those of his own country, but not in themselves incomprehensible. Now he must describe, assess, even predict and recommend, in the light of changes that threaten his most comfortable assumptions about the state to which he is accredited.

Such was the situation confronting the three men, British, American, and French, respectively, with whom this chapter is concerned. Each of them served in Berlin during some portion of the decade preceding the second world war. Each brought with him some prior knowledge of and experience in Germany. Each had to decide what kind of a Germany was emerging under Nazi leadership. Would other nations be able to live with this Third Reich, and if so, on what terms? Ultimately the conclusions of each envoy were determined by his personal temperament and aspirations, by his conception of his country's vital interests, by his historically oriented judgment of the prospects, and finally—a point not easy to put succinctly—by his more or less conscient selection of those values in modern civilization which he felt must be defended. Obviously these separate elements differed from one man to the next, not only in specific content but also in their order of importance to the individual concerned. To appreciate the resulting variations of response, one need only refer to the body of diplomatic documents and personal memoirs now available for the period. Such records are by no means as yet complete, but already they offer a substantial basis for investigation.

I

On August 10, 1928, Sir Horace Rumbold, P.C., K.C.B., 9th Bt., presented his credentials to President Hindenburg. When Sir Horace took up his duties in the big embassy on the Wilhelmstrasse, just off Unter den Linden, Germany's Chancellor was a Social Democrat, Müller, and her Foreign Minister was Stresemann. In May 1933, when Sir Eric Phipps succeeded to the ambassadorship, Müller's party had just been suppressed and Stresemann's foreign policy was well on its way to oblivion. During a tenure of slightly under five years, Rumbold had seen Germany adhere to the Kellogg-Briand Pact in 1929, had seen Brüning advance to the Chancellorship in March 1930, and had seen economic disaster break upon central Europe in the spring of 1931. Then he had watched the procession of Chancellors, from Papen in May 1932, through Schleicher the following December, to Adolf Hitler in January 1933. When he left Berlin that spring, he had just witnessed the legalization of Nazi dictatorship in the Enabling Act of March 23.

Sir Horace, like his father and grandfather before him, was a professional, "the ideal diplomatist," Harold Nicolson was to call him.[1] Born in 1869 in St. Petersburg, he had passed his competence examination for the foreign service at the age of twenty-two. Between 1892 and the outbreak of the first world war he had served in Cairo under Lord Cromer, in Teheran, Vienna, Madrid, Tokyo, and finally, as counselor of embassy, in Berlin during the tense summer of 1914. Thereafter, he had been minister to Switzerland and to Poland, High Commissioner in Constantinople from 1920 to 1923, and ambassador to Spain until 1928. With this remarkable odyssey behind him he returned to Berlin after an absence of fourteen years.

He was now almost sixty, a heavy-set man possessed of impeccable manners, a certain wry wit, and very few discernible emotions. The

---

[1] In the dedication of *Diplomacy* (London, 1939).

personality which emerges from his dispatches and from his book on 1914[2] is that of an analyst who resists extreme views. Yet Rumbold was not easygoing. He could be stubborn, and intelligently so, as when he and General Sir Charles Harington refused in 1922 to deliver the British Cabinet's ultimatum to Turkey over Chanak, and subsequently received their government's thanks![3] For all his apparent blandness, he could become extremely upset and extremely angry; and in the long run the Nazis both upset and angered him. Speaking the careful, faintly archaic language of diplomacy, at times confused by false analogies drawn from a rich store of experience, at other times tripping over his own social and professional prejudices, he nonetheless won through to a strikingly prescient view of the dangers which appeared on the European horizon with the advent of Hitler.

Rumbold's judgment of the Nazi movement and its rise to political hegemony is, of course, the most significant aspect of his career in terms of the present chapter. It would be well, however, to pause long enough for a brief look at his methods and certain of his opinions regarding developments prior to Hitler's triumph. This is important, because the ambassador's performance in dealing with pre-1933 diplomats and politicians under relatively normal conditions in Berlin provides a background for his later comments on the pathology of Nazism.

Sir Horace was an assiduous reporter for his Foreign Office. His dispatches to London were frequent and detailed (in the second series of the British documents, there appear 303 messages from Rumbold sent between January 4, 1930 and March 25, 1933—and even these represent a selection). In return, he appears to have enjoyed the full confidence of his superiors in England. Nothing suggests that he was ever rebuked for indiscretions, as Nevile Henderson was to be later,[4] or that he ever felt that negotiations were by-passing him. In pursuance of his duties as an observer he used several sources of information, of which the easiest to identify was a definite circle of German officials chiefly notable for the moderation of both their views and their manners: Foreign Minister Curtius, Secretary of State Bülow of the Wilhelmstrasse, Secretary of State Weismann of the Prussian Ministry of Interior, Chief of the Presidential Chancellery Meissner, Secretary of State Planck of the Reich

---

[2] *The War Crisis in Berlin: July-August, 1914* (London, 1940).

[3] Harold Nicolson, *Curzon: The Last Phase* (Boston, New York, 1934), p. 275. In *Water under the Bridges* (London, 1945), Sir Nevile Henderson comments repeatedly and enthusiastically on Rumbold's firmness and intelligence during his period as High Commissioner in Turkey, at which time Henderson was himself a principal aide at Constantinople.

[4] See Chapter 17, § 1 below.

Chancellery, and others. His Majesty's representative had little personal contact with Germans who would have felt ill at ease in the deep arm-chairs of his own Travellers' Club in London.

In all fairness to Rumbold, however, it must be said that his assessment of events generally went well beyond anything suggested to him by highly placed Germans. Several explanations for this fact suggest themselves. For one thing, the embassy staff offered some variety of opinions. Further, although Sir Horace long retained a relative aloofness toward his fellow ambassadors, from time to time he mentions having compared notes with French, American, Dutch, or Italian colleagues, especially during his crowded final year in Berlin. Most important of all, he read the newspapers and periodicals. His spoken German was not fluent (he knew Arabic better and Japanese almost as well), but he conducted his own press survey day in and day out. Some of his shrewdest comments relate to items from *Der Tag*, the *Frankfurter Zeitung*, or *Vorwärts*.

As regards general outlook, many Western diplomats who were later to be far more conciliatory than Rumbold toward the Germany of Hitler were far harsher than he toward the Germany of Stresemann and Brüning. His tone was one of caution during the Weimar period and became one of unequivocal alarm with the proclamation of the Third Reich, but it cannot be said that he let degrees of German strength alone determine his attitude in speaking to or about the Germans themselves. There is in Rumbold's record none of that transition from arrogance to fawning which looms so unpleasantly in the case histories of some of his contemporaries.

Not that he could be called, by any stretching of the term, a Germano-phile. He never forgot the Kaiser or Tirpitz or Schlieffen, and he came to Berlin a convinced believer in Germany's war guilt of 1914. His book on the outbreak of the first world war makes no concessions on this point of history. Nor was he a partisan of any balance of power theory based on distrust of France and reliance on Germany. In the spring of 1930, he hoped that France would not delay its scheduled evacuation of the Rhine-land,[5] but added subsequently that Germany "has little to fear of French aggression."[6] Referring to reactions in Berlin after the French did leave the Rhineland, he wrote in July 1930: "It is an unattractive feature of the German character to display little gratitude for favours received, but when the receipt of favours is followed up by fresh demands, there are

[5] *British Documents*, 2nd series, I, 477. Rumbold to Henderson, May 2, 1930.
[6] *ibid.*, 563. Rumbold to Henderson, February 26, 1931.

grounds for feeling impatient."[7] While he reported in detail German complaints over the Versailles boundaries, he indulged in no expressions of sympathy for irredentist arguments.

Perhaps the fairest way to sum up Rumbold's attitude toward traditional nationalism in Germany is to say that he took it for granted. He seems to have assumed that the Weimar Republic would make certain claims and that men he admired, including Stresemann and later Brüning, would press their country's case, especially given the political pressure they themselves were under from the steadily growing mass chauvinism in the country. An old-fashioned kind of irredentism was something a seasoned diplomat could understand and presumably could parry. It had to be controlled by precautionary arrangements, might even have to be met head-on someday. Nevertheless, it was to be accepted as an inevitable product of returning German vitality.

Rumbold's treatment of three major issues of the pre-Hitler period, though none of them can be gone into in detail here, will at least illustrate his underlying assumptions. The first was the question of the German-Polish frontier. The ambassador was sure that, even under Weimar, this was the greatest point of danger in German foreign policy. In July 1930, he informed London of his concern over a talk he had had with Curtius, in the course of which the Foreign Minister had referred to Germany's eastern boundary as "absurd."[8] The following month he summarized a belligerent speech by Treviranus concerning the Polish Corridor and betrayed his own misgivings by saying that he *hoped* the flareup represented only an episode, not a developing trend.[9] Despite the official efforts in Berlin to play down the problem of *Ostpolitik*, Rumbold was still sure in February, 1931, that the Polish frontier dominated all other considerations in German thinking on foreign policy.[10] He never abandoned this conviction.

The second problem on which he spent much time and thought was that of Germany's armaments. Rumbold was sure that the Germans would rearm, especially in view of their hostility to Poland. In repeated dispatches he passed along reports of illegal activity. It should be stressed that he never argued for complacency toward these treaty violations, as did his military attaché on at least one occasion.[11] He did, however, in-

[7] *ibid.*, 485. Rumbold to Henderson, July 3, 1930.

[8] *ibid.*, 490. Rumbold to Henderson, July 3, 1930.

[9] *ibid.*, 491. Rumbold to Henderson, August 12, 1930.

[10] *ibid.*, 563. Rumbold to Henderson, February 26, 1931.

[11] *ibid.*, 11, Appendix IV. Colonel Marshall-Cornwall, in a report dated December 9, 1931, and forwarded by Rumbold to Simon, observed that there was much to be said for

sist that many German officials were going no further than nationalist agitation demanded, and he believed that left-wing opposition would keep rearmament within reasonable limits. The prevailing tone of his reports, on this point as on so many others prior to 1933, was a mixture of wariness and hope—wariness based on his fear of the potential violence of German nationalism, hope stemming from his belief in the essential moderation of the existing German government.

Third and last of these illustrative problems centered on the proposed German-Austrian Customs Union, the plan for which was communicated to the ambassador by Bülow in a talk on March 13, 1931. Rumbold's first move was to send London a factual account of the interview, attempting no analysis of its implications but giving full coverage to the Secretary of State's arguments, especially the plea that "the great point was to set the ball rolling and to revive trade."[12] Within ten days the British and French governments had been officially advised of the project by the accredited Austrian and German representatives, and the Western Powers' hostile reaction to the Union, as both a threatening preliminary to *Anschluss* and a discriminatory trade agreement, had begun to harden.[13] In Berlin, Rumbold carried out his instructions faithfully, representing to various officials his government's opposition to any special Austro-German arrangements. By July, in fact, he was able to report that his discreet urging had led influential members of the German Cabinet to accept the view that the plan should be withdrawn as soon as this could be done without a disastrous loss of face.[14]

This, however, was not the whole story from Rumbold's side. Equally important was the line he adopted toward his own Foreign Office in London. As early as March 26, less than a fortnight after learning of the proposed Union, the ambassador was emphasizing the dangers inherent in any public rebuff in Germany.[15] The next day he expanded this theme by conceding that the proposal had been badly presented but adding that Brüning "has to show the country some results" and that the Chancellor might be broken politically by a bullying reaction on the part of Britain and France.[16] Rumbold was particularly opposed to any move which would make the issue "devolve into a personal and public

---

the *Wehrgeist* as a defense against Bolshevism and added that "most decent Britons, were they Germans today, would be Stahlhelmers."

[12] *ibid.*, I, 587. Rumbold to Henderson, March 13, 1931.
[13] *ibid.*, II, 2-11. Vansittart to Rumbold, March 21 and 23, 1931.
[14] *ibid.*, 210. Rumbold to Henderson, July 17, 1931.
[15] *ibid.*, 16. Rumbold to Tyrrell (for Henderson), March 26, 1931.
[16] *ibid.*, 21. Rumbold to Henderson, March 27, 1931.

struggle between MM. Briand and Brüning."[17] One gets the impression that the ambassador was fully alive to the danger of a slide toward full *Anschluss* if the Union were effected, that he was willing to examine the economic technicalities involved and to press quietly for abandonment of the scheme, but that his attention remained riveted on the political aspects of alternative Franco-British attitudes and their repercussions in German domestic politics. There can be no doubt that he was relieved when other public questions appeared on the scene to divert attention from the Customs Union; but he could only deplore the damage already done by those elements of humiliation for Germany which remained to exacerbate rancorous nationalism and to endanger German leaders on whom he felt the West had no choice but to rely.

Rumbold had admired Stresemann greatly—perhaps more than the record would seem to warrant—and on the whole he maintained a kindly feeling toward the succeeding Foreign Minister, as he revealed when the latter left office in October 1931: "My principal colleagues and I regret Dr. Curtius' departure from the Ministry of Foreign Affairs. Although he had neither the imagination, the wide outlook, nor the political genius of his predecessor, he was a level-headed man, while his quiet and courteous manner made him pleasant to deal with."[18] His feeling toward Wilhelmstrasse officials was assuredly not one of uncritical confidence, as he had shown in his analysis of even Curtius' playing with fire on the Polish boundary issue,[19] and again in his reservations about the suave and amiable Bülow, "whom I suspect of Nationalist tendencies."[20] Nevertheless, the ambassador counted on such men for realism and a conservative resistance to chauvinistic gambles. At any rate, he had no difficulty in imagining much worse. His early admiration for Chancellor Brüning, whose "courageous frankness" in the face of economic depression and political agitation he pointed out to London early in 1931,[21] and his generally good opinion of President Hindenburg must be discussed in connection with the events of 1932 and 1933, since the latter modified in some respects his views concerning both men. The important point, however, is that, until Hitler came to power, Sir Horace never displayed any deep or consistent alarm with regard to

---

[17] *ibid.*, 24. Rumbold to Henderson, March 30, 1931.

[18] *ibid.*, 278. Rumbold to Reading, October 6, 1931.

[19] *ibid.*, I, 524. Rumbold to Henderson, October 27, 1930. "Whilst I am satisfied that he [Curtius] will not embark on a foreign policy of adventure, there are signs that he will, if I may use the expression, 'increase the *tempo*'."

[20] *ibid.*, II, 211. Rumbold to Tyrrell (for Henderson), July 18, 1931.

[21] *ibid.*, I, 573. Rumbold to Henderson, March 4, 1931.

German foreign policy. Hence, to understand how he arrived at the views which he was to expound on the eve of his departure from Berlin, it is necessary to examine his analysis of the overshadowing development in German domestic politics during his time there, to wit, the accession of the Nazis.

National Socialism began to figure prominently in the ambassador's dispatches only in the fall of 1930. Writing to London on September 7 of that year concerning the *Reichstag* election campaign, he noted the Nazis' intense activity as an exception to the general apathy and reported that some predictions gave this "new and vigorous movement" as many as 50 or 60 seats.[22] Actually it won 107 seats, as compared with its previous 12, in the voting a week later; but Herr Weismann hastened to dismiss the Nazis' success as ephemeral,[23] and Rumbold himself initially adopted the reassuring thesis that Hitler's party, unprepared for its sudden gains, would now have to quiet down and accept some parliamentary responsibility.[24] Though not inclined to take Nazism lightly, Sir Horace still felt in March 1931, that "a nation of such stout fibre, containing as it does unplumbed reserves of strength, especially in the business community, is not going to fail eventually to master its difficulties."[25]

An interesting aspect of the subsequent evolution in Rumbold's thinking was the change in his opinion as to where the Nazis should be placed in the political spectrum. On this point he originally accepted the view of his German informants that Nazism, like Communism and Social Democracy, was a proletarian movement. As late as December 1932, he called the NSDAP one of "the three great parties of the Left."[26] But he took due note of the Harzburg conference between Nazi and right-wing leaders in the fall of 1931;[27] and in a dispatch of June 28, 1932, he spoke of "those many better class people who regard the Nazi movement as a timely revival of nationalism which it will not be difficult for the right people to control and exploit."[28] The major change in Rumbold's thinking on this matter, however, came with the crisis in the Nazi high command at the end of 1932; for he felt that the defection of Gregor Strasser removed the last check on Hitler's own inclination to

[22] *ibid.*, 504. Rumbold to Henderson, September 7, 1930.
[23] *ibid.*, 510. Rumbold to Henderson, September 18, 1930.
[24] *ibid.*, 512. Rumbold to Henderson, September 25, 1930.
[25] *ibid.*, 573. Rumbold to Henderson, March 4, 1931.
[26] *ibid.*, IV, 92. Rumbold to Simon, December 7, 1932.
[27] *ibid.*, II, 295. Rumbold to Reading, October 14, 1931.
[28] *ibid.*, IV, 3. Rumbold to Simon, June 28, 1932.

join forces with big business.[29] The first dispatch following the selection of Hitler as Chancellor bluntly pairs him with Hugenberg as "reactionary and anti-parliamentary";[30] and a few days later Rumbold wrote that "the ship is definitely going to the starboard again."[31]

Concerning the Nazi leaders Rumbold had to sift widely differing judgments. He was told of Hitler's interest in fortune tellers,[32] heard him described by General Hammerstein as "a very mediocre personality,"[33] by General Groener as something worse than the "visionary but decent individual" he had at first appeared,[34] by Meissner as "quite reasonable and moderate" in private conversation, though apt to rave if excited.[35] Rumbold's first unequivocal assessment on his own authority was that "Hitler may be no statesman, but he is an uncommonly clever and audacious demagogue . . . fully alive to every popular instinct."[36] Of the other party chiefs Sir Horace generally spoke with contempt. The one exception was Strasser, whom he called "the ablest of the National Socialist leaders and a strong man."[37] Goebbels he considered "vulgar, unscrupulous and irresponsible";[38] Goering, a ruthless adventurer inclined to overplay his hand.[39] Before he left Germany, however, Rumbold had to concede that these "gangsters" had succeeded in their aim of "bringing to the surface the worst traits in the German character, i.e., a mean spirit of revenge, a tendency to brutality, and a noisy and irresponsible jingoism."[40]

As long as the issue in Germany was still in doubt, Rumbold placed his hopes in "that union of the bourgeois parties for which the situation seems to call."[41] He never sought to conceal his aversion to Communism; and he showed no particular warmth toward the Social Democrats until 1932, when they began to win his sympathy as victims of reactionary violence. Time and again it was the Center party to which he assigned the crucial role, pressing his hope that the moderate conservatives would rally to the support of Brüning. He neither expected

[29] *ibid.*, 385. Rumbold to Simon, January 11, 1933.
[30] *ibid.*, 398. Rumbold to Simon, January 30, 1933.
[31] *ibid.*, 409. Rumbold to Simon, February 7, 1933.
[32] *ibid.*, III, 99. Rumbold to Simon, February 17, 1932.
[33] *ibid.*, 101. Rumbold to Simon, March 1, 1932.
[34] *ibid.*, 113. Rumbold to Simon, April 13, 1932.
[35] *ibid.*, IV, 56. Rumbold to Simon, September 28, 1932.
[36] *ibid.*, 423. Rumbold to Simon, February 22, 1933.
[37] *ibid.*, 28. Rumbold to Simon, August 13, 1932.
[38] *ibid.*, 3. Rumbold to Simon, June 28, 1932.
[39] *ibid.*, 49. Rumbold to Simon, September 13, 1932.
[40] *ibid.*, 452. Rumbold to Simon, March 14, 1933.
[41] *ibid.*, II, 280. Rumbold to Reading, October 7, 1931.

nor thought desirable a restoration of the Hohenzollern monarchy, observing on one occasion that to ask a German if he were a monarchist would be like asking a drowning man how he felt about music and painting.[42]

It was to President Hindenburg that he looked for stability. Despite his awareness of Papen's hold over the old man and the influence of the President's Junker friends in blocking even timid reforms, Sir Horace long clung to his faith in Hindenburg's beneficent role. The fall of Brüning, whom he saw as an honest and moderate politician, disturbed him deeply. Nevertheless, in a dispatch written four months after that event, he conceded that Brüning's use of emergency decrees had helped to undermine the parliamentary system;[43] and he deplored the ex-Chancellor's efforts to reach an understanding with Hitler. As for Papen, the ambassador considered him a frivolous and cynical opportunist, whereas Schleicher impressed him as an intelligent political general who at least had stuck to his post after 1918.[44]

These few references will, I hope, have sufficed to reveal Rumbold as an observer of the German scene who was critical but until the Nazi coup d'état never blackly pessimistic. It is only against the background here sketched that one can appreciate the dramatic change in tone involved in his dispatches of late winter and spring 1933. Turning even on Hindenburg, he then wrote: "The Left parties are largely responsible for the President's re-election and are now compelled to witness the forces of reaction ruling this country with an irresponsibility and a frivolous disregard for all decent feeling which is without precedent in its history. There can be no other language to apply to the action of the present Government in ousting hundreds of Prussian and Reich officials from their posts for no other crime than the holding of political views to which they are constitutionally entitled."[45] This, be it remembered, was a seasoned professional diplomat and a baronet, speaking in defense of Germans, many of whom he disagreed with to the core of his political beliefs.

What could one expect of the "new Germany" in international affairs? Rumbold's valedictory, a dispatch sent on April 26, 1933, is explicit enough.[46] Reviewing the bellicose pronouncements in Hitler's speeches

[42] *ibid.*, IV, 83. Rumbold to Simon, November 24, 1932.

[43] *ibid.*, 54. Rumbold to Simon, September 21, 1932.

[44] *ibid.*, 92, 389. Rumbold to Simon, December 7, 1932, and January 25, 1933.

[45] *ibid.*, 423. Rumbold to Simon, February 22, 1933.

[46] This dispatch, which postdates those so far published in the *British Documents*, appears as an appendix to Rumbold's *War Crisis in Berlin*, 344-358. All quotations used here are from that text.

and in *Mein Kampf*, the ambassador concludes that "the outlook for Europe is far from peaceful. . . . It would be misleading to base any hopes on a return to sanity or a serious modification of the views of the Chancellor and his entourage. . . . I cannot help thinking that many of the measures taken by the new Government of recent weeks aim at the inculcation of that silence, or *Schweigsamkeit*, which Hitler declares in his memoirs to be essential to military preparations."

For Rumbold, the Germany of 1933, like that of 1905, was in transition. "The task of the present German Government is more complicated [than that of Admiral Tirpitz]. They have to rearm on land and . . . to lull their adversaries into such a state of coma that they will allow themselves to be engaged one by one." It was difficult to believe that a European government, after the experiences of the first world war, would embark on so dangerous a policy, "but the actions of the new Government have already shown the world that, like former German Governments, they are capable of almost any degree of self-deception." When Sir Horace went home to an exceedingly active retirement in May 1933, he expected the worst. When he died in May 1941, at his family home, Pythouse, in Wiltshire, his fears had long since passed into a terrible reality.

II

During those same spring weeks of 1933, while Rumbold was sending his final reports from Berlin, the United States government was hunting a replacement for Frederic M. Sackett, who in March retired as ambassador to Germany. The newly inaugurated President Roosevelt considered several possibilities for the post, including James M. Cox, Nicholas Murray Butler, and Newton D. Baker; but ultimately the choice fell on a professor of history at the University of Chicago, William E. Dodd. Roosevelt had never met Dodd; but the Secretary of Commerce, Daniel C. Roper, had known him since the campaign of 1916, when both had worked for Wilson, and the nomination had the support of the aging Colonel House, of Assistant Secretary of State R. Walton Moore, and of Secretaries Ickes and Swanson.[47] Roper recalls that he personally "believed that Dodd would be astute in handling diplomatic duties and, when conferences grew tense, he would turn the tide by quoting Jefferson."[48] Cordell Hull, though he knew and liked

[47] *Ambassador Dodd's Diary, 1933-1938*, ed. William E. Dodd, Jr. and Martha Dodd (New York, 1941), pp. 9-10.
[48] Daniel C. Roper, *Fifty Years of Public Life* (Durham, N.C., 1941), pp. 334-335.

Dodd, was less enthusiastic because of the latter's tendency to "run off on tangents every now and then, like our friend William Jennings Bryan."[49] The Secretary of State announced himself agreeable, however, and on June 8, 1933, the President telephoned his offer to Professor Dodd in Chicago. On the 10th the Senate confirmed his nomination.[50]

The ambassador-designate was an experienced teacher, a man of transparent integrity and a distinguished historian of America, especially of the South. Born sixty-three years before in Clayton, North Carolina, he had received his scholarly training at Virginia Polytechnic and at the University of Leipzig, where he took his Ph.D., with a thesis on Jefferson, in 1900. He had been on the faculty at Chicago since 1908. The long list of his published works included biographies of Nathaniel Macon and Jefferson Davis, *The Cotton Kingdom, Statesmen of the Old South, Lincoln or Lee, Woodrow Wilson and His Work,* in addition to the six volumes of Wilson's public papers which he edited with Ray Stannard Baker. Dodd's particular contribution to the historiography of the South had been a rare balance in treating the weaknesses and the virtues of southern society in the pre-Civil War era. For the rest, his writings reveal a devotion to Jeffersonianism at its most idealized, a Wilsonian faith in internationalism, and, in articles composed after Roosevelt's election in 1932, a lively enthusiasm for the New Deal as an antidote to the power of "big interests." Roosevelt's precise reasons for appointing him will probably never be known, but Dodd's belief that he was to go to Berlin as a living sermon on democracy seems to have reflected his early instructions honestly enough.

The President was also getting an envoy who would set forth with high hopes for German-American friendship. Through half a lifetime, Dodd had cherished the memories of his university life in the old empire. In addition, though only an irregular Baptist churchgoer, he looked with reverence upon the Lutheran Reformation and honored "this ancient realm of religious liberty."[51] He considered the Germans to be "by nature more democratic than any other great race in Europe,"[52] deplored the· harshness of Versailles and felt considerable hostility to-

---

[49] Cordell Hull, *Memoirs* (New York, 1948), I, 183.

[50] There has long been current a story, actually published by E. J. Flynn in *You're the Boss* (New York, 1947), p. 148, to the effect that the call to Dodd resulted from a confusion in names, since Roosevelt had decided to appoint Walter F. Dodd, a former law professor at Illinois and Yale, but by 1933 in private practice in Chicago. However, Flynn retracted the story almost immediately after the appearance of his book (*New York Times,* November 2, 1947). It is in any case flatly contradicted by Hull's and Roper's memoirs.

[51] *Ambassador Dodd's Diary,* p. 400.   [52] *ibid.,* p. 447.

ward French policy since 1918. As he boarded the *S.S. Washington* in New York on July 5, 1933, he issued the following statement: "The realities of the American past as well as the dilemma of the present reconcile me to the adventure I am about to undertake. Germany can hardly fail to realize the importance of friendly cooperation with the 120,000,000 people of the United States, and the United States can hardly fail to realize the value of economic and social cooperation with the land of Luther, Stein and Bismarck. Though difficulties lie ahead, one can hardly think that an honest, frank mission to Berlin can fail of good result."[53]

The Dodds, husband, wife and two grown children, docked at Hamburg on July 13 and went directly to Berlin, where after some delay they succeeded in renting a comfortable house on the Tiergartenstrasse. Dodd was insistent that the family should live within his salary of $17,500, since he had no extra funds of his own to spend.[54] Nevertheless, his daughter recalls that, at least during the first part of his ambassadorship, "our house was always full of people—young Germans, students, Foreign Office attachés, Government officials, newspapermen, and officers in the S.A., or S.S., or Reichswehr."[55] In addition to the American journalists, with whom he got along well on the whole, Dodd quickly acquired several confidants in the diplomatic corps, chief among whom were the Spanish ambassador, Zulueta (a former philosophy professor), and the aristocratic Dutch minister, Limburg-Stirum. Toward his other fellow diplomats he felt less cordial, though he liked Sir Eric Phipps better than he had expected to and enjoyed what he took to be passages of wit with François-Poncet at social functions or on strolls in the Tiergarten. One of François-Poncet's aides, young Armand Berard, came often to the house; and it was he who represented the real link between the French and American embassies, so far as Dodd was concerned.

A combination of nervous indigestion and boredom at formal affairs led the ambassador to keep his personal routine as simple as possible, given his position. On his occasional pleasure trips he studiously avoided luxury, and it was a point of pride with him that his modest habits made for closer contact with the German people than usual diplomatic be-

[53] *New York Times*, July 6, 1933.
[54] Not long after reaching Berlin, Dodd wrote to thank President Roosevelt for arranging to have the embassy salaries paid in gold, which action "prevented the necessity of resignation on my part." Franklin D. Roosevelt Library [hereafter cited as *R.L.*], P.P.F. (President's Personal File) 1043. Dodd to Roosevelt, October 28, 1933.
[55] Martha Dodd, *Through Embassy Eyes* (New York, 1939), p. 47.

havior would have permitted. He was careful to sidestep any honorary degrees under Nazi auspices, but he loved to visit the university towns. Only shrines of the Reformation attracted him as much. When in Berlin, he insisted on keeping up his scholarship, completing the first volume (and the only one to appear) of his *Old South* while still ambassador. I am told by one of his principal deputies in the embassy that, at least in 1936 and 1937, Dodd could frequently be found in his office thumbing through a card file containing genealogies of Virginia families. During his earlier, more optimistic and energetic period, however, he seems to have simply added his research and writing to the normal round of appointments and social appearances.

Dodd was ambassador to Germany for four and a half years. The period between his arrival and the Blood Purge of June 30-July 1, 1934, was a time of first impressions, of mounting indignation, but still of hope. In August, for example, he wrote to President Roosevelt, recommending that the U.S. government keep an open mind on the Nazis: "This is given not in defense of German armaments and anti-semitic attitudes (both contrary to all liberal philosophy), but to explain the tense situation and the possibility of worse things ahead. Fundamentally, I believe a people has a right to govern itself and that other peoples must exercise patience even when crudities and injustices are done. Give men a chance to try their schemes."[56]

His first interview with Hitler, on October 17, was not as alarming as he had expected it to be. Dodd's "final impression was of his belligerence and self-confidence," but the Chancellor promised to punish any Storm Troopers who subsequently attacked Americans and only ranted in a general way about the Treaty of Versailles.[57] At a second interview, the following March, Hitler was more truculent but still not wholly unconciliatory, declaring that "Germany wants peace and will do everything to keep the peace; but Germany demands and will have equality of rights in the matter of armaments."[58] In the interval between these two talks Dodd had written to Roosevelt that at least Hindenburg represented a moderate policy.[59]

All of this suggests, I think rightly, that well into 1934 the ambassador still believed in a wide range of future possibilities. Nevertheless, al-

[56] *R.L.*, O.F. (Official File) 523. Dodd to Roosevelt, August 12, 1933.
[57] *Foreign Relations*, 1933, II, 396-397. Dodd to Hull, October 17, 1933. Also *Ambassador Dodd's Diary*, p. 50.
[58] *Foreign Relations*, 1934, II, 220. Dodd memorandum, March 7, 1934.
[59] *R.L.*, P.S.F. (President's Secretary's File), Box 10, *Dodd* folder. Dodd to Roosevelt, February 8, 1934.

most from the day he arrived, he engaged in a campaign of admonition-by-analogy which left little doubt as to his feelings about the Nazi dictatorship. Speaking at the Columbus Day dinner of the American Chamber of Commerce in Berlin, just six weeks after having presented his credentials, he said in part: "There are not many forms of human association, though many new names have been invented from time to time. Half-educated statesmen of today swing violently away from the ideal purpose of Gracchus and think they find salvation for their troubled fellows in the arbitrary modes of the man who fell an easy victim to the cheap devices of the lewd Cleopatra. They forget that the Gracchus democracy failed upon the narrowest of margins and Caesar's succeeded only for a short moment as measured by the tests of history."[60] On the third day after this address, he wrote in his diary: "It is evident some dislike of me is arising here now in official circles. I believe it is simply Nazi opposition."[61]

Through the first months of 1934 Dodd maintained normal social contacts with leading Nazis—a *Bierabend* with Rosenberg, tea with Goebbels, a visit to Goering's hunting lodge, a chat with Ribbentrop. He had even invited S.A. leader Ernst Roehm to a dinner he was planning for July 6. Then came the Blood Purge—the execution of Roehm, Strasser, and scores of other party functionaries, the attack on Papen, the assassination of General Schleicher and his wife. So far as analysis was concerned, Dodd saw these measures as eliminating extremists, on both the Right and the Left, particularly the latter.[62] His emotional reaction, however, practically overpowered any effort at objectivity. Through the tense hours of the crisis, his daughter recalls, he was pale, excited, silent. On July 1, having learned that Papen was under house arrest, he made a point of stopping by to leave a card for the ex-Chancellor with the message, "I hope we may see you soon."[63] Of Hitler, Dodd wrote on July 13, "I have a sense of horror when I look at the man."[64] He never again had a private interview with the Fuehrer, though they met several times subsequently at large receptions for the entire diplomatic corps.

The next two and a half years, down to the end of 1936, constituted the second period of Dodd's service in Berlin, a period of worry over

[60] *New York Times*, October 13, 1933.
[61] *Ambassador Dodd's Diary*, p. 48.
[62] For Dodd's coverage of these events, see *Foreign Relations*, 1934, II, 229-243.
[63] *Ambassador Dodd's Diary*, p. 117; Martha Dodd, *Through Embassy Eyes*, pp. 148, 154-155.
[64] *Ambassador Dodd's Diary*, p. 126.

international conditions and of growing isolation from official life. He carried out his routine functions in the tedious and futile economic negotiations. He attended such social gatherings as he could not politely avoid. He had welcome trips to the United States in the winter of 1934-1935 and in the spring of 1936 (he had previously been home in the spring of 1934 for a rest). Back in Berlin, however, he remained hostile and despondent.

During those years Dodd never ceased to plead the cause of collective security. In August 1934, he urged Roper to sponsor more use of the League, especially after Russia's entry the following month, in order to restrain Germany and Japan.[65] In March 1935, the U.S. minister to Austria, Messersmith, noted Dodd's concurrence in a warning to Washington that no trust could be placed in Nazi promises and that Germany's aim was "unlimited territorial expansion."[66] The following October Dodd wrote to the President denouncing the Italian campaign in Ethiopia.[67] Germany's remilitarization of the Rhineland in March, 1936, he viewed as sending France into "a definite decline toward the position of Spain."[68]

The last year of Dodd's ambassadorship was, from his point of view, a near nightmare which included his involvement in the Supreme Court fight back in America, the Nuremberg Party Congress incident, and finally, his recall from Berlin. The first of these incidents can be briefly summarized. Dodd had never ceased to state his opinions on American political questions to anyone who would listen. Now, on May 11, 1937, the *Richmond Times-Dispatch* printed a letter written by Dodd to several United States Senators, and subsequently quoted by all leading papers, in which he urged support of Roosevelt's proposal for enlarging the Supreme Court, then went on to say: "There are individuals of great wealth who wish a dictatorship and are ready to help a Huey Long. There are politicians who think they may gain powers like those exercised in Europe. One man, I have been told by friends, who owns nearly a billion dollars, is ready to support such a program and, of course, control it."[69] Senator Borah promptly denounced Dodd as "an irresponsible scandalmonger" and "a disgrace to his country." Senators Van Nuys and King demanded his immediate recall. Senator

[65] *R.L.*, O.F. 523. Dodd to Roper, August 14, 1934.

[66] U.S. Department of State, *Peace and War: United States Foreign Policy, 1931-1941* (Washington, 1943), No. 44. Messersmith memorandum, March 22, 1935.

[67] *R.L.*, P.S.F., Box 10, *Dodd* folder. Dodd to Roosevelt, October 31, 1935.

[68] *ibid.*, Box 19, *Dodd* folder. Dodd to Roosevelt, April 1, 1936.

[69] *New York Times*, May 12, 1937.

Nye tried unsuccessfully to have him subpoenaed by Congress and forced to name his billionaire. The target of all this did not reveal the name, and he was not then recalled from Berlin. Nevertheless, there was no question that he was now *persona non grata* with influential groups in two capitals.

Dodd came home on leave for the fourth time in early August 1937, and did not return to Germany until the end of October. Just before leaving Berlin he had learned from François-Poncet that all or most of the diplomats accredited to the Reich would for the first time attend the Nazi Party Congress in a body that September. Dodd had curtly reiterated his view that ambassadors should not appear at party rallies.[70] This time, however, the State Department overruled him. American newspapers of September 4 not only discussed the appearance at Nuremberg of Prentiss Gilbert, our *chargé* in Germany during the ambassador's absence, but also printed sections of a confidential letter of protest which Dodd had written to Hull ten days before. Dodd was furious over the leak, which of course damaged still further his standing in Berlin, and over the public repudiation of his views. From Williamstown, Massachusetts, where he was attending a conference, he issued a statement calculated to suggest his possible resignation. The State Department for the moment sought only to terminate the incident as quickly and quietly as possible.[71]

Meanwhile, the question of the ambassador's position in Germany was becoming critical. On arriving in Norfolk on August 4, he had made a debarkation statement to the effect that "the basic objective of some powers in Europe is to frighten and even destroy democracies everywhere." The next day German Ambassador Dieckhoff cabled Berlin a report of his formal protest to Hull and Under-Secretary Sumner Welles; but he advised the Wilhelmstrasse to let the matter drop for the time being, so as "not to cool the inclination to recall Dodd from Berlin, which has existed in various quarters here for some time."[72] It is clear that Roosevelt found disquieting the reports concerning his envoy's health, emotional state, and general effectiveness. In early April 1937, the President notified the State Department that he would accept Dodd's resignation, effective September 1.[73] Under this plan the ambassador would not even have returned to Germany after his summer leave

[70] *Ambassador Dodd's Diary*, p. 425.

[71] *New York Times*, September 4-5, 1937; *Ambassador Dodd's Diary*, p. 427.

[72] *German Documents*, series D, I, 627. Dieckhoff to Neurath, August 5, 1937. See also pp. 627-630.

[73] R.L., P.S.F., Box 27, *Dodd* folder. Roosevelt to Moore, April 5, 1937.

of absence. By August, however, possibly because of his reluctance to have it appear that he was yielding to Nazi pressure, Roosevelt had changed his mind. When Dodd lunched with him a week after arriving in the country, the President remarked, "I wish you to return to Berlin for two to three months."[74] Dodd left his signed resignation for use at the discretion of the White House and the State Department when he started back to Germany, but his own suggestion was that he be retained until the following March.

There can be no doubt that he was startled and hurt when on November 23, less than a month after his return to Berlin, he received orders from Hull to present the name of Ambassador Hugh Gibson, then in Belgium, to the Foreign Office as his successor and to wind up his own affairs by December 31. Although the Secretary cabled that these were the President's wishes, Dodd was certain that it was Sumner Welles who had engineered his recall.[75] Gibson declined the appointment, but Hugh Wilson, our minister to Switzerland, was approved in time to maintain the indicated deadline. Dodd left Berlin on December 28, quietly and without prior notice to the German press. He arrived in New York on January 6, 1938, stating to American newsmen that he "doubted if any American envoy who held his ideals of democracy could represent his country successfully among the Germans at the present time."[76]

Almost immediately he began a series of speeches to anti-Nazi meetings, always on the threat of Axis aggression and the need for concerted action by the democracies. He joined the American Friends of Spanish Democracy out of sympathy for the Loyalists, correctly predicted the sequence of German moves against Austria, Czechoslovakia, and Poland, and urged strong resistance to Japan. Publicly Berlin deprecated "the retiring ambassador's habitual lack of comprehension of the new Germany";[77] and at Nuremberg in September, Goebbels reserved for Dodd some of his choicest invective. In secret, Dieckhoff tried vainly to shake Secretary Hull's disclaimer of responsibility for statements by the ex-ambassador, which the latter, as a private citizen once more, could not be prevented from making.[78]

By the end of 1938 Dodd was failing rapidly from a combination of nervous, respiratory, and abdominal ailments. In December he was arrested in Virginia on charges of hit-and-run driving; and his subsequent conviction, accompanied by temporary loss of his state citizenship, un-

[74] *Ambassador Dodd's Diary*, p. 426.   [75] *ibid.*, pp. 433-434.
[76] *New York Times*, January 7, 1938.   [77] *New York Times*, January 9, 1938.
[78] U.S. Department of State, *Peace and War*, No. 103. Hull memorandum, January 14, 1938.

questionably shook his fragile health still further. He was hospitalized in Washington in January 1939, and in July underwent an operation, complicated by bulbar palsy and bronchial pneumonia. He rallied briefly, but the following winter pneumonia struck again. On February 9, 1940, he died at Round Hill, Virginia, his family home, having lived just long enough to witness the beginning of the Nazis' war, which he had dreaded for so long.

I have thus far minimized references to Dodd's relations with Washington, in order that this aspect of his period as an ambassador might receive a few words of separate treatment. It is quite clear that so far as the State Department was concerned, he was never a key figure in the formulation of policy. The volume, *Peace and War*, which the Department published as a review of American foreign relations from 1931 to 1941, contains dispatches on the Third Reich sent by the U.S. ministers to Austria and Switzerland, the consul at Berlin and, our military attaché there; but not a single report by the ambassador himself was thought important enough to be included.

Secretary Hull, whose misgivings in 1933 have already been cited, clearly welcomed the retirement of a man whom he considered "sincere though impulsive and inexperienced."[79] During the summer of 1937 Dieckhoff informed his Foreign Office superiors that Hull had referred to the ambassador as "somewhat insane" on topics such as ideal Jeffersonian democracy and world peace.[80] It is impossible to be sure just whose words are being used in Dieckhoff's subsequent report to the effect that the Secretary of State had called Dodd "the sort of fool with whom one could not reason," but the tenor of the remarks was clearly unflattering.[81] Dodd himself never ceased to rely on Hull's good will and on that of his friend, Judge Moore, who in 1937 became Counselor of the Department. In addition, he felt some cordiality toward certain of his colleagues abroad, notably Messersmith in Vienna and Cudahy in Warsaw. However, he never dissembled the hostility he felt toward most career diplomats and businessmen in the Foreign Service. His diary bristles with remarks about "rich men," not only those in the Department or other missions, but certain of his own principal aides as well.

It was Sumner Welles who supplied the most consistent focus for Dodd's animosity. Even in 1934, on his first visit home, the ambassador had a rather tart interview with the then Assistant Secretary, whose

[79] Hull, *Memoirs*, I, 572.
[80] *German Documents*, series D, I, 627. Dieckhoff to Neurath, August 5, 1937.
[81] *ibid.*, 679. Dieckhoff to Neurath, January 14, 1938.

house in Washington irritated Dodd by its very size.[82] His later conviction that he knew precisely whom to blame for his recall finds partial
confirmation in the German documents. In September 1937, when Welles
met Dieckhoff aboard the *Europa* en route to New York, he reportedly
told Hitler's ambassador that Dodd seemed to him quite incomprehensible and that he would "take up the Dodd case immediately upon
his return."[83] A few days later, the Under-Secretary called Dieckhoff
in to inform him that Dodd's recall had now definitely been decided
upon.[84]

It would, however, be unfair to assume that Welles had to wage anything like a one-man campaign to oust the ambassador in Berlin. For
some months before the events just described there had been press reports of Dodd's impending resignation. The following, written by
Arthur Krock for the *New York Times* amid the uproar over the Supreme Court letter, is a representative sample: "[Mr. Dodd] has long
been one of the Department's worries. He has impressed his diplomatic
associates as a man who is inclined to forget his responsibilities as an envoy in his zeal as an historian and in his views as a contemporary observer of governing trends. For these impulses the Department is disposed to award Mr. Dodd full credit as a man. But it is no secret in those
generally discreet corridors that a change at Berlin has long been desired
and would be welcomed at any time."[85]

Not the least of the official grievances against Dodd was the personal
correspondence he was known to carry on with the President outside
regular departmental channels. Now that this correspondence is available
at Hyde Park,[86] it is possible to examine an interesting example of the
late President's personal diplomacy, marked by all the verve and charm
which he knew so well how to introduce into his relations with devoted
subordinates. I have already quoted from certain of these letters for
purposes of the general narrative; but they merit comment in their own
right.

The prevailing tone, on both sides, is one of confidence and cordiality.
"My dear Dodd," the President wrote in December, 1933, "that is an
exquisite pen picture of yours [of Hitler, Goebbels, and Goering]. It
confirms my impression. Merry Christmas! You are doing a grand

---

[82] *Ambassador Dodd's Diary*, p. 94.
[83] *German Documents*, series D, I, 630. Dieckhoff to Neurath, September 27, 1937.
[84] *ibid.*, 632. Dieckhoff to Neurath, October 1, 1937.
[85] *New York Times*, May 14, 1937.
[86] *R.L.*, O.F. 523; P.P.F. 1043; and P.S.F., Boxes 10, 19, and 27, *Dodd and Germany* folders.

job."[87] Even after the ambassador's position became more complicated, Roosevelt repeatedly sent words of encouragement and thanks for letters received. Dodd, on his part, wrote about whatever topic was uppermost in his mind: the Nazi leaders, collective security, personal finances, Japanese aggression, plans for selling the burned-out Blücher Palace (which was to have housed the U.S. embassy), predictions concerning German foreign policy, American history, and contemporary politics.

On only one point did the President introduce a distinctly official note into the correspondence. In March 1936, he asked Dodd to notify him "if in the days to come the absolutely unpredictable events should by chance get to the point where a gesture, an offer or a formal statement by me would, in your judgment, make for peace."[88] The following summer, he became more specific: "I should like to have your slant, in the utmost confidence, as to what would happen if Hitler were personally and secretly asked by me to outline the limit of German foreign objectives during, let us say, a ten-year period, and to state whether or not he would have any sympathy with a general limitation of armaments proposal."[89] Dodd carried out his assignment but had to report in October that his approaches to the Foreign Office had met with no success.[90] A few weeks later, Dieckhoff, then still Secretary of State in the Wilhelmstrasse, expressed to the ambassador his puzzlement as to "why people in America were so particularly worried" and admitted that Germany "would place no great hopes in a big disarmament conference."[91]

For the two years left to Dodd after his retirement, there are relatively few items in the Hyde Park collection. The correspondence really terminates with a birthday greeting which Dodd wrote, in a shaking longhand, in January 1939, from Georgetown University Hospital. After a pessimistic section—"What a world we live in!"—the old admiration comes through, now almost incoherent: "You are the greatest leader in the world and I hope you may be able to block things before too late. A master's job. Unequalled in history. Congratulations!"[92] The remaining messages from Dodd to the President offer pathetic evidence of their writer's desperate pessimism and declining mental, as well as physical, powers. The last is an expression of regret, written

---

[87] *R.L.*, O.F. 523. December 8, 1933.
[88] *ibid.*, P.P.F. 1043. March 16, 1936. Also printed in *F.D.R.: His Personal Letters, 1928-1945*, ed. Elliott Roosevelt (New York, 1950), I, 571.
[89] *R.L.*, P.S.F., Box 19, *Dodd* folder. August 5, 1936. Also printed in *F.D.R.: His Personal Letters*, I, 605-606.
[90] *R.L.*, P.S.F., Box 19, *Dodd* folder. October 19, 1936.
[91] *German Documents*, series D, III, 153. Dieckhoff memorandum, December 5, 1936.
[92] *R.L.*, O.F. 523. January 28, 1939.

three months before his death, that he could not attend the laying of the cornerstone for the very library where the letter, with all its predecessors, now reposes.[93]

It is not easy to dissociate one's sympathy for William E. Dodd as a sincere and humane individual, horrified by the vicious regime with which he was expected to deal, from one's judgment of him as a diplomat. Yet in this context the distinction must be made, even at the risk of dehumanizing diplomacy. Dodd's sense of defeat is apparent throughout his diary. In July 1934, he wrote, "Ought I to resign?"; in July 1935, after talking to Luther, the German ambassador to Washington, "I intimated that both of us ought to resign"; in December 1936, "I wait and watch for my time to retire"; in October 1937, "In Berlin once more. What can I do?"[94] Even his anger when finally recalled bespeaks reluctance to lay aside a piece of work while it still appeared a failure. But in what did this failure consist? To his way of thinking, it unquestionably lay in his inability to affect the course of German internal developments. His daughter has written (and his diary confirms) that he set off in 1933 thinking that "he could have some influence in moderating the policies of the Nazi regime," that there would be "a chance to bring them back to reason, to recall forcefully to them their recent democratic past."[95]

It is my own feeling that Dodd was ineffectual as an ambassador less because he failed to achieve his aim of changing the Third Reich by example and persuasion than because that was the aim he set himself. Once he discovered that he could not convert the Nazis, his despondency practically incapacitated him as a diplomatic representative. His general prophecies, it is true, proved accurate in their broad outlines; but one is struck, in reading the available reports from Dodd to Washington, by the comparative lack of concrete intelligence concerning *immediate* Nazi objectives and power. Finding the party chiefs unbearable, he fell back on contacts with German scholars, with aristocrats, and with men whom he considered "decent" officials: Neurath, Bülow, Dieckhoff, Schacht, even Papen. The result was that he could neither tell Washington as much as Rumbold had told London or Coulondre was to tell Paris about affairs within the Reich, nor present the American position to the German government with any hope of being taken seriously. Even if the latter task was frustrating—and would have been for any man—

[93] *ibid.*, P.P.F. 1043. November 10, 1939.
[94] *Ambassador Dodd's Diary*, pp. 123, 262, 375, 430.
[95] Martha Dodd, *Through Embassy Eyes*, pp. 15-16.

the ambassador's basic responsibility for close, accurate reporting still remained. Had Dodd made the most of his opportunities in that regard, he might conceivably then have demanded a hearing for whatever specific policy recommendations he cared to submit to his own government.

Viewed simply as a reporter, however, he suffered from several serious weaknesses. One was his lack of knowledge concerning modern German history. I make this statement fully aware of the frequency and scorn with which Dodd himself leveled the same charge against his contemporaries, but it is a conclusion which a study of his record makes inescapable. A case in point is the anachronistic standard he sought to apply. Nazi Germany was built on brutal fraud, and it was dangerous for the rest of the world. No honest man could—though many men did—try to make it appear otherwise. For Dodd, however, the alternative, the gauge to be used, was always a Germany that had once been, when it was not a Germany that had never been, save perhaps in "The Student Prince." Admiration for the land of Luther, Stein, and Bismarck offered few guideposts for setting a diplomatic course vis-à-vis the land of Hitler.

Even Dodd's Jeffersonianism, attractive enough in some connections, played him false in others. His individualistic orientation led him to see in Nazism nothing but the demonic work of certain evil leaders. Thus he poured his wrath upon Hitler and other prominent Nazis, while remaining singularly uncritical of groups which, if less blatantly murderous, were no less deeply implicated. "It all stems from Hitler himself," he wrote of anti-Semitism in a momentary surrender to the *Führerprinzip*.[96] This inability to appreciate the full significance of the Jewish question, here treated in terms simply of Hitler's personality, is a striking example of the ambassador's lack of historical perspective. He was horrified by physical cruelty to the Jews; and as a humane man he did what he could to help individual victims, while fulminating publicly against the moral lapse which such brutality represented. Yet he understood, to some extent he even shared, the older, subtler, admittedly nonviolent anti-Semitism of many members of the German professorial class. One may search in vain for any evidence that he appreciated how deep were the roots of German persecution of the Jews or how crucial was such persecution to the Nazis' hold on political power in Germany. History no more permits one to view anti-Semitism as incidental to Nazism than it permits him to view Nazism itself as an outburst which broke upon Germany as a result of some mistakes at Versailles and some

[96] William E. Dodd, "Germany Shocked Me," *The Nation*, August 20, 1938.

providential bad luck. Dodd talked much of history, but in the sense just noted, he applied it little. He could not fully understand the forces underlying Nazism because he could not think in terms of either the industrialized, urban society or the kind of farming community which had combined to produce the Third Reich. His nostalgia for a loosely organized polity of self-reliant freeholders, like his nostalgia for pre-1914 German university life, was profoundly misleading.

The alternative to a Dodd need not have been a morally neutral technician, smoothly rationalizing away what he saw in Germany. My critique presupposes no such model of diplomatic performance. George S. Messersmith, for example, distrusted the Nazis as much as did the ambassador, yet during the 1930's, both as consul-general in Berlin and then as minister to Austria, he managed to give far greater substance to his warnings. If Dodd could have retained his human values but served them more by cool assessment of the situation and less by self-conscious outpourings, if he could have buttressed his generally sound premonitions with evidence better calculated to impress Washington, he might have had less cause to look back on his record in Berlin as one of failure.

III

André François-Poncet came to Berlin as French ambassador a year and a half before Rumbold left and remained there until almost a year after Dodd's departure. It was on September 22, 1931, that he moved into the old embassy on the Pariserplatz, with Brüning still Chancellor and the Nazis, in the opinion of many observers, only an overrated band of swaggerers. He moved out, to become French ambassador to Italy, in October 1938, in the weeks just after the Munich Conference. Thus he supplies a sort of personal continuum for seven years of watching and maneuvering.

François-Poncet was born in Provins (Seine-et-Marne), the son of a Court of Appeals magistrate. He made a brilliant record at the Ecole Normale Supérieure, completing his thesis on Goethe's *Elective Affinities* in 1909, then accepting a professorship at the Lycée de Montpellier. The first world war, however, interrupted his promising career as a scholar and teacher. It also, by sending him to Switzerland for the French government and later to Washington as an adviser to the International Economic Mission, shifted his professional interests from academics to applied economics. Through his marriage he had acquired substantial holdings in the steel industry, and it was as a public defender of that industry, or more precisely of the powerful Comité des Forges, that he founded the Société d'Etudes et Informations Economiques at Paris in 1922. His connection with German affairs continued, however, at least during the Ruhr occupation, when he was economic adviser to the commanding general. He also entered politics as a member of that protean group, the Alliance Démocratique; and from 1924 until his departure for Berlin in 1931, he represented Paris (VIIᵉ) in the Chamber of Deputies. By the late 1920's he had distinguished himself as a skillful opponent of organized labor[97] and as one of French industry's cleverest parliamentary spokesmen. His rise in the government service began in 1930, when Tardieu made him Under-Secretary for Foreign Affairs; and at the time of his appointment to Berlin he was Laval's Under-Secretary to the Premier's Office.

He was forty-six when he went to Germany, a dapper, mustachioed, voluble man with a reputation for wit, flexibility, and an excellent command of German. For all his love of conversation, however, François-Poncet impressed those who knew him in Germany as rather inscrutable, except in the company of any of his eight children.[98] He and his strikingly handsome wife maintained a veritable court at the embassy, where on formal occasions liveried pages lined the big stairway in a setting reminiscent of Louis XIV with Napoleonic overtones.[99] The ambassador might relax over weekends at his villa on the Kleine Wannsee outside Berlin, but his working day was full enough. By eleven o'clock he had reviewed the daily press summary before it was telephoned to Paris, and then there were telegrams to be drafted and dispatches prepared for the courier pouch. The bound copies of his own reports, he tells us, eventually ran to forty volumes.[100]

Several circumstances complicate the study of François-Poncet's record during his period at the Pariserplatz. One is the intricacy of the narrative itself, seen from any point of view. Another is the extreme paucity of French documents available. The *Yellow Book* supplies a few, of course, for 1938-1939; and occasional French texts have found their way into other collections. For most of the 1930's, however, one must

---

[97] See his *Une formule nouvelle: le contrôle syndical* (Paris, 1921) and *La France et les huit heures* (Paris, 1922), both published by his Société d'Etudes.

[98] On his personality see Bella Fromm, *Blood and Banquets* (New York, 1942), pp. 28, 30-32, 37-38, 78, 118, 204; *Ambassador Dodd's Diary*, by index; Martha Dodd, *Through Embassy Eyes*, pp. 41-42, 150, 326-330; and scattered references in memoirs such as those of Henderson, Weizsäcker, and Paul Schmidt. See also the personal sketches from *Je Suis Partout* and *Marianne* in *The Living Age* (October 1931), 135-137, and (March 1937), 56-57.

[99] *Ambassador Dodd's Diary*, p. 54.

[100] André François-Poncet, *Souvenirs d'une ambassade à Berlin* (Paris, 1946), p. 6.

depend on German, British, and American official sources, supplemented by memoirs and occasional press reports of more than average value. A third difficulty arises from the nature of the ambassador's own account, in his *Souvenirs*. This volume contains several excellent descriptive passages and some interesting judgments of men and events. Nevertheless, it fails to mention a number of important aspects of its author's performance; and the latter's recollections of his own role, even where clearly set forth, differ sharply at several points from the versions to be found in other sources. All one can do is to cite these discrepancies where relevant.

The new French ambassador of 1931 had been identified with a policy of toughness toward Weimar Germany, because of his criticism of Briand in the Chamber and his known hostility toward the German-Austrian Customs Union of the preceding spring. He made no secret of the misgivings he felt about Brüning, who had just declined a French proposal for a ten-year truce on all boundary disputes. It appeared at first that François-Poncet might continue to espouse "hard" policies. In January 1932, for example, while on one of his frequent trips to Paris, he told the British ambassador there that he was apprehensive over German attempts to escape completely from further reparations;[101] and in the matter of armaments, he warned Sir Horace Rumbold against Germany's efforts to "force the pace in the question of equality of status"—admittedly an ambiguous statement.[102]

On one issue, however, François-Poncet could from the first be called conciliatory. This was the possibility of closer industrial ties between Germany and France. He recalls that his own government, having despaired of immediate progress in the political field, expected him now to explore the economic.[103] Even before his appointment to Berlin, while still an Under-Secretary in Paris, he had proposed a complex international cartel plan.[104] And in his initial press conference upon reaching the German capital he spoke with enthusiasm of an alliance between French and German industries, the former rich but technically inferior, the latter well-equipped but lacking capital.[105]

It is impossible, pending release of his actual dispatches, to reconstruct François-Poncet's coverage of the Nazi triumph inside Germany. The

[101] *British Documents*, 2d series, III, 23. Tyrrell to Simon, January 12, 1932.

[102] *ibid.*, IV, 178. Rumbold to Simon, September 19, 1932.

[103] *Souvenirs*, p. 23.

[104] *British Documents*, 2d series, II, 45. Rumbold to Henderson, May 6, 1931. Rumbold had learned of the scheme from Bülow at the German Foreign Office.

[105] Bella Fromm, *Blood and Banquets*, pp. 30-32.

discussion in his *Souvenirs* is an historical essay, not a portrayal of his on-the-spot reactions. At times he seems to have entertained hopes that Papen, or if not he then Schleicher, could hold together a conservative regime resting on the authority of Hindenburg. At other times, unlike Rumbold, the ambassador toyed with the prospect of a monarchist restoration. In the summer of 1932 a Paris weekly quoted him as saying, "Before spring comes a Hohenzollern, if not William II himself, will be seated again on the throne of his fathers. . . . A Hohenzollern would be a guarantee of at least ten years of peace."[106] So far as the Nazis were concerned, he states that during the year before January 1933, he never had any contact with their leaders.[107]

For the first eighteen months after Hitler became Reich Chancellor, the French envoy moved suavely through the social and official life of Berlin in his normal fashion. He continued to negotiate with the Foreign Office over the German demands for equality of armaments. He began to form personal impressions of the energetic new masters of Germany, including especially Hitler, whom he saw on official business about once a month. But he also saw Papen and many other gentlemen of the *Herrenklub*, remained the personal friend of Schleicher and had at least social contacts with Roehm and his circle. Hence, when the Blood Purge struck, he experienced several days of near panic. "It is popularly supposed [Dodd cabled Washington on July 2, 1934] that France was the foreign power with which, according to official version, Roehm was dealing. This allegation would find certain confirmation in known desire of French Ambassador for reform in German Government such as would be conducive to less *intransigeance* in international politics."[108] Although the official version here referred to was restated by Hitler before the Reichstag on July 13, and although François-Poncet had certainly followed closely the feuds within the Nazi party during the preceding months, there is no evidence to contradict his assertion that he never offered the support of his government to any dissident group. The Nazi chiefs, including Hitler, were apparently convinced within a few weeks that the French embassy was not a danger spot after all.[109]

François-Poncet was at this time engaged in revising his own views in a direction which made for easier personal relations with German leaders. By early 1934 he was convinced, he tells us, that the only hope lay in permitting the Reich to rearm under international surveillance, since a

[106] *New York Times*, August 30, 1932.   [107] *Souvenirs*, p. 142.
[108] *Foreign Relations*, 1934, II, 230-231. Dodd to Hull, July 2, 1934.
[109] *Souvenirs*, pp. 9 and 194.

formal convention might retard the German pace and would, at the very least, establish some limits, the infraction of which would alert the democracies to their danger.[110] Here he began to sound a note that was to recur over and over again in his subsequent arguments, a note of pessimism concerning the chances of blocking Hitler by frontal resistance, but also of hope that a policy of accommodation might leave the Allies with some measure of control still in their hands.

There remained one alternative which he was prepared to advocate: a close alliance of the Western democracies with Italy. Only with the aid of Mussolini could he envisage the resumption of a hard policy. For François-Poncet, the Stresa Conference of April 1935, after Hitler had announced full rearmament, represented the high point in European solidarity. Mussolini's Ethiopian venture, however, destroyed the "Stresa Front" before it had even begun to affect international relationships; and in Berlin the French ambassador resumed his advocacy of what was coming to be regularly referred to as "business pacifism." By November 1935, questions were being raised in the French press concerning Laval's efforts at Franco-German rapprochement, with François-Poncet identified as the go-between. Although Laval, in the Chamber of Deputies, flatly denied any secret intentions, the uneasiness in Paris continued, fed, as one American analyst has put it, by "the known enthusiasm of the Ambassador for the National Socialist system and the suspicion of proposals made behind closed doors."[111]

Whatever Laval might tell the Chamber, there were such proposals. As early as November 1935, François-Poncet recommended to the Quai d'Orsay that a conference with Germany be held at once on the question of the Rhineland, in order to anticipate Hitler's remilitarization of the area and to limit him to light forces.[112] When the Spanish civil war broke out in mid-1936, the ambassador began a long series of talks with Neurath and Dieckhoff, in which he made clear his lack of sympathy for the Spanish government but urged the Germans not to precipitate a crisis through too open support of Franco.[113] In his memoirs François-Poncet cites only his desire that the fighting in Spain, regardless of its outcome, should remain localized. While the civil war was in progress, however, he was much more explicit about his sentiments, on one occasion complaining to the German ambassador in Rome that Bonnet had

[110] *ibid.*, pp. 174-179.
[111] Elizabeth R. Cameron, *Prologue to Appeasement* (Washington, 1942), p. 177.
[112] *Souvenirs*, p. 248.
[113] *German Documents*, series D, III, Doc. Nos. 29, 32, 37, 45, 46, 54, 66, 166, 177, 195, 270, 371, 427, 430.

made a blunder in not recognizing Franco in the general confusion after Munich and thus having done with the Spanish government, "this last stronghold of the Popular Front."[114]

Meanwhile the ambassador was seeking to convince the German Foreign Office that friendship between Berlin and Paris was both desirable and attainable. With this end in view, he had to make clear his own dislike for the Franco-Soviet pact of 1935. In September, 1936 he asked Secretary of State Dieckhoff whether Germany was interested in negotiating a Western agreement or would demand first that France renounce its Russian alliance. "If Germany followed the first course," Dieckhoff records, "he [François-Poncet] believed he could say that the Franco-Russian ties would gradually cool, particularly since they had never been popular with a large sector of the French people."[115] More than a year later, after Flandin's visit to Berlin had failed to produce any explicit pledges from the Germans, Papen, home on leave from Vienna in December 1937, found the French ambassador dejected over the slow pace of negotiations. "Flandin, as is well known," Papen added, "is very close to François-Poncet politically."[116]

The year 1938, which was to witness his greatest personal triumphs, began unpleasantly for François-Poncet, with a cold rebuff from Ribbentrop on the subject of what the new Foreign Minister was pleased to call the "family affair" in Austria.[117] When, on March 11, Seyss-Inquart invited German troops to enter Austria, it was the duty of the ambassador, who in his memoirs has almost nothing to say about the *Anschluss*, to deliver the sharp French note of protest.[118] Affronts such as this were damaging to the policy of accommodation, especially given the manner in which they were perpetrated. The French envoy's argument, as he now repeats it, however, was still that since France had been timid while Germany was weak, she could scarcely become intransigent as the Reich grew stronger.

It was the Czech crisis which gave François-Poncet a chance to influence directly the course of Franco-German negotiations. In May 1938, when the first Sudeten scare was brewing, he suggested to the sympathetic Sir Nevile Henderson the possibility of Germany's accepting the good offices of the Western Powers in its dispute with Czechoslovakia.[119] "It

[114] *ibid.*, IV, 460. Mackensen to Ribbentrop, November 22, 1938.
[115] *ibid.*, III, 66. Dieckhoff memorandum, September 1, 1936.
[116] *ibid.*, I, 129. Papen to Weizsäcker, December 16, 1937.
[117] *ibid.*, 529. Ribbentrop memorandum, February 17, 1938.
[118] *ibid.*, 578. François-Poncet to Neurath, March 11, 1938.
[119] *British Documents*, 3rd series, I, 238, 286. Henderson to Halifax, May 3 and 12, 1938.

is time," he told Henderson, "that Europe revised its opinion of M. Benes."[120] Back in Paris, early in June, he made clear to his old colleague, Sir Eric Phipps, now ambassador to France, that he did not trust Benes and that the Allies should offer Hitler a deal on the Sudeten question.[121] By the end of that month he and Henderson were agreed that "allied to Russia, [Czechoslovakia] constitutes a perpetual menace to Germany."[122]

Toward the Germans, he was simultaneously holding out hopes of conciliation, expressing his anxiety to Ribbentrop in mid-May,[123] by late June urging the possibility of a Great Power settlement and "evolutionary changes" in existing alliances,[124] a month later assuring Weizsäcker of British and French sincerity in urging Prague to be reasonable.[125] Throughout this busy summer he asked only that the Reich avoid injuring French dignity and do what it could to minimize the general tension.

Reducing tension, however, scarcely fitted into Hitler's scheme of things, and the Fuehrer's blustering at Nuremberg in early September seemed to spell the doom of any settlement by negotiation. François-Poncet seems to have lapsed into despondent inactivity even before the Party Congress (his nervous state has been described by the diplomatic correspondent, Bella Fromm, who called on him at the Wannsee villa late in August).[126] Or perhaps he had been temporarily restrained from further advances by instructions from Paris. In any event, as late as September 27, when Chamberlain's Berchtesgaden and Godesberg visits seemed to have come to naught, the Polish ambassador to Germany was told by Weizsäcker that "François-Poncet had not set foot in the Foreign Office for nearly a fortnight."[127]

Actually, however, the French envoy was about to take the center of the stage. During the night of September 27-28, he received orders from Bonnet to see Hitler and to reopen with him the discussion of possibilities for a peaceful solution. By eleven o'clock the next morning he was at the Chancellery. Once in the presence of the Fuehrer, Ribbentrop, and the chief translator Paul Schmidt, he spread out a map showing the phases for a Czech evacuation of the disputed borderlands and then launched

---

[120] *ibid.*, 273. Henderson to Halifax, May 10, 1938.
[121] *ibid.*, 452. Phipps to Halifax, June 8, 1938. See also p. 460.
[122] *ibid.*, 534. Henderson to Halifax, July 1, 1938.
[123] *German Documents*, series D, II, 284. Ribbentrop memorandum, May 17, 1938.
[124] *ibid.*, 428. Ribbentrop memorandum for Hitler, June 23, 1938.
[125] *ibid.*, 515. Weizsäcker memorandum for Ribbentrop, July 26, 1938.
[126] *Blood and Banquets*, p. 280.
[127] *Documents and Materials*, p. 230. Lipski to Beck, September 27, 1938.

THREE OBSERVERS IN BERLIN

into an address on the horrors of the war which threatened.[128] "You are naturally confident of winning the war, just as we believe that we can defeat you," Dr. Schmidt quotes him as saying to Hitler, "but why should you take this risk when your essential demands can be met without war?"[129] It was while this discussion was in progress that Hitler was called out of the room to speak to the Italian ambassador Attolico, bearer of Mussolini's offer to propose an immediate four Power parley.

Hitler's acceptance of the Duce's initiative and what followed from that acceptance are too well known to require recapitulation here. François-Poncet went down to Munich for the conference, was in fact present at the second session; but his real contribution had occurred in Berlin on the 28th. Recalls Paul Schmidt, "The Munich Conference was regarded at the time as the decisive turning point in the Sudeten crisis. Actually this had occurred the day before, in Hitler's talk with Attolico, after the vital preparatory work carried out by François-Poncet."[130] The ambassador's memoirs tend to minimize his own importance in this instance, stressing instead the decisive role of British policy throughout the crisis.[131] He is content to argue that the deal on Czechoslovakia bought the Allies a precious year for further arming before war broke out and that the British air victories of 1940 were in effect won at Munich. He is not impressed by the counterargument that the same year saw an even more rapid increase in Germany military power, the absorption of the Skoda works into the Reich's industry, the liquidation of Czechoslovakia's strategic value (even if only nuisance value) in a two-front war, and the neutralization of Russia.

The remaining month of François-Poncet's ambassadorship in Germany was an active one for him. For one thing, as a member of the International Commission which met in Berlin to supervise the transfer of the Sudeten areas, he made some short-lived attempts to maintain the appearance of a negotiated solution. His own Foreign Office failed to support him, he complains, and it was only a few days before the German interpretation prevailed on every important point.[132] The other

---

[128] *Souvenirs*, p. 328.

[129] Paul Schmidt, *Statist auf diplomatischer Bühne* (Bonn, 1949). The translation here quoted is from the American edition, *Hitler's Interpreter* (New York, 1951), p. 106. François-Poncet's command of German left Schmidt no function save that of recording the discussion.

[130] *ibid.* (American edition), p. 108.

[131] *Souvenirs*, p. 328. Hitler, on the other hand, is reported to have said later on several occasions, "François-Poncet was the only one who made a sensible proposal." Schmidt, *Hitler's Interpreter*, p. 107.

[132] *Souvenirs*, pp. 334-335. See also *German Documents*, series D, IV, 12, Minutes of

development of that October was François-Poncet's culminating effort to achieve better relations between Paris and Berlin. To his own Foreign Office he wrote that no effort should be spared to strengthen French powers of resistance and that the Nazis would bear watching, even during this breathing spell, but that France must not let any show of intransigence on her part cost her the moral advantage in world opinion. The Fuehrer, though dangerously mercurial, was capable of astounding changes of front; and should he, for any reason, try the road to peace, "it is possible that he will end by not being able to turn back again, even if he wished."[133]

To the German Foreign Office, on October 13, he suggested a non-aggression pact, to be signed on the occasion of Ribbentrop's projected visit to Paris. "Such an agreement," noted Weizsäcker, "would fulfill an idea which he, Poncet, had already urged for a long time."[134] Five days later occurred the final visit with Hitler in the Berchtesgaden "eagle's nest," so eloquently described by the ambassador.[135] It was a long discussion, for the last hour of which the two principals were alone. In the course of a review of the entire European situation, the Fuehrer complained of his disappointment over the continuing international tension and burst forth once or twice against Great Britain. In general, however, it was a cordial talk. François-Poncet declared that Munich had proved the value of Great Power collaboration; and before he left, he had Hitler's assurance of interest in a Franco-German friendship pact. Back in Berlin, the ambassador was able to report to Weizsäcker and to Goering that Paris accepted in principle the ideas discussed at Berchtesgaden on the 18th.[136] In his interview with the former, he mentioned that Britain, Italy, even Belgium should be kept informed and later drawn into the arrangement. "It would, however, be a mistake," he went on, "not to strike while the iron was hot in the matter of purely Franco-German relations."[137] The Ribbentrop-Bonnet declaration of friendship, mutual acceptance of common boundaries, and determination to remain in contact on all questions was actually signed in Paris on

---

the International Commission, October 1, 1938; and II, 53, Weizsäcker memorandum, October 10, 1938.

[133] *The French Yellow Book*, published by authority of the French government (New York, 1940), Doc. No. 18. François-Poncet to Bonnet, October 20, 1938. See also Doc. No. 16 for François-Poncet's dispatch of October 4.

[134] *German Documents*, series D, IV, 436. Weizsäcker memorandum, October 13, 1938.

[135] *French Yellow Book*, Doc. No. 18. François-Poncet to Bonnet, October 20, 1938.

[136] *ibid.*, Doc. Nos. 19-21. Bonnet to François-Poncet, October 21, 1938, and François-Poncet to Bonnet, October 22 and 24, 1938.

[137] *German Documents*, series D, IV, 438. Weizsäcker memorandum, October 22, 1938.

December 6. Six weeks earlier, its most ardent sponsor had left Berlin to take up his duties in Rome, where he remarked to the German ambassador that it had been time for him to leave the Reich: "You should stop while it tastes best."[188]

François-Poncet's activities in Italy during the next year and a half can here be treated only as they relate to his views of the Axis problem in general. He had long admired Mussolini and as recently as Munich had reaffirmed his conviction that the Duce offered the best hope of restraining Hitler.[139] Hence, though he insisted that France would yield not an inch of territory, he was willing to swallow the insults he received in Rome and to keep at the task of securing an Italo-French rapprochement to fortify the Franco-German. In his first talk with Mussolini, according to the version he gave his British colleague, he announced that "he had come to develop the policy of the Munich Agreement" by converting into reality the dream of a four Power system.[140] In a public address on New Year's Day, 1939, he further elaborated his view of the "Munich Spirit" which was to bring France, Italy, Germany, and Britain into closer association. The onrushing events in the north, however, paid little heed to this vision. When war came the following September 1, the ambassador could only support Mussolini's unsuccessful effort to mediate once again, as he had done over Czechoslovakia.[141] All was to no avail. On June 10, 1940, when Ciano called him in to receive the Italian declaration of war, he managed a sarcastic reply, then shook the Foreign Minister's hand and said, "Don't get yourself killed."[142]

Back in France, after the defeat, he served under the Vichy government as a member of the National Council and as Controller-General of the Press, only to be arrested by the Germans in August 1943 (having been incriminated in their eyes, he believes, by captured documents) and held in confinement in the Austrian Tyrol until his liberation in May 1945. In 1948, he was appointed adviser to the Military Governor of French-occupied Germany and a year later became French High Commissioner in the former Reich.

Concerning François-Poncet's feelings toward the Nazis there will probably always remain some disagreement, though the external aspects of his relations with them are clear enough. He was generally conceded

---

[138] *ibid.*, 460. Mackensen to Ribbentrop, November 22, 1938.

[139] *Souvenirs*, p. 307.

[140] *British Documents*, 3d series, III, 461. Perth to Halifax, November 29, 1938.

[141] *French Yellow Book*, Doc. Nos. 306, 332, 360 and 363. François-Poncet to Bonnet, August 31–September 2, 1939.

[142] Galeazzo Ciano, *Diario* (Milan, 1948), I, 278.

to be the Fuehrer's favorite ambassador, once the suspicions of the Blood Purge period had disappeared. François-Poncet, on his part, adopted a tone of easy familiarity with Hitler. Sometimes he was jocular, as when he arrived for the historic interview on the day before Munich exclaiming cheerfully, "You know, Mr. Chancellor, I have always been your good star."[143] Sometimes he was more acid, as during the 1937 Party Congress when, referring to a recent speech by Goebbels, he remarked, "You see, Herr Reich Chancellor, the 'stupid cow nations' did not hesitate to come to Nuremberg."[144] The recently published collection of the Fuehrer's "table talks" confirms the warmth of Hitler's feelings for an ambassador who was so broad in his European views and so generous with chocolates specially shipped from Paris.[145]

The discrepancy in interpretation arises only over the question of François-Poncet's true sentiments. Ambassador Dodd classified him as "not far from being a fascist,"[146] sections of the French press spoke bluntly of his high regard for Nazism,[147] and the German newspaperwoman, Bella Fromm, described him as "hypnotized by Hitler."[148] Judgments such as these, according to François-Poncet, are just so many tributes to his success in playing a part. "National Socialism I had always found revolting, for I was brought up as a liberal and a humanist. The spectacle of tyranny trampling human values, exalting brutality and glorying in savagery, I found odious. The earliest manifestations of Nazi rule filled me with an enduring aversion. . . . I did not display my feelings, but I did not seek to conceal them. Usually I gave vent to them in the ironic mode, in a form that would not offend. Most of the epigrams circulating in Berlin about the Nazis were attributed to me; but since I also showed my interest in Nazi ideology and in the reforms the Nazis introduced in every field, instead of holding these sallies against me, they found them amusing. My relations with the Nazis were not bad, or, to be more exact, I ended by being on fairly good terms with some of them."[149]

I have seen no evidence that the ambassador was an uncritical admirer of the government to which he was accredited. If he liked Goering and was impressed by Hitler and Goebbels, he certainly was not attracted to

[143] Ernst von Weizsäcker, *Erinnerungen* (Munich, 1950), p. 210.
[144] *New York Times*, September 12, 1937.
[145] Henry Picker, *Hitlers Tischgespräche im Führerhauptquartier, 1941-42* (Bonn, 1951), pp. 105-106.
[146] *Ambassador Dodd's Diary*, p. 347.   [147] See above, at note 111.
[148] *Blood and Banquets*, p. 280.
[149] *Souvenirs*, p. 8. The translation quoted here is from the American edition, *The Fateful Years*, tr. Jacques LeClercq (New York, 1949), x-xi.

Rosenberg and, like most other diplomats, loathed Ribbentrop. If he approved the social and political discipline enforced by the regime, he did not approve its tawdry racism or its risky foreign policy. About all that can be said with confidence is that nothing about Nazism so repelled him as to inhibit his efforts to arrange an understanding between the French government and French industry, on the one hand, and Hitler's Reich, on the other.

François-Poncet put little stock in a violent overthrow of the Nazis, at least after 1934. In his memoirs he insists that even had the French army resisted the reoccupation of the Rhineland in 1936, no German group could have ousted Hitler.[150] It is worth noting that in his dispatches of autumn 1938, he remained unimpressed by General Beck's efforts to organize a military coup the previous summer and spoke of future changes only in terms of the Fuehrer's own personality. The strange concept of Hitler's possibly going so far along the road to peace that he could not turn back presumably grew out of François-Poncet's hopes that an eventual increase in the influence of traditional conservatives would modify the ambitions of the Nazi leaders.

One final topic, concerning which it is necessary to compare carefully the ambassador's account and the evidence from other sources, is the part he played in formulating French policy during the decade before 1940. Of his indirect influence, as an assiduous observer and analyst, there can be no doubt. As he himself remarks, the political atmosphere of Berlin lent itself to clever exploitation for purposes of gathering information.[151] Not only was he in touch with a wide variety of leading Germans, he also, at least during the first years of his mission, had informal monthly dinners with his foreign colleagues.[152] His successor at the Pariserplatz was duly impressed by the intelligence operation which François-Poncet had organized.[153]

What did he do with all the information he assembled? Some of it he communicated directly to the French General Staff through his personal liaison officer. The rest, he tells us, simply disappeared into the labyrinth of the Quai d'Orsay: "What I thought personally mattered little. I gave my opinion of my own accord. I was never asked for it."[154] Ambassadors of the Third Republic he describes as nothing but "prefects abroad—préfets de l'extérieure," rigidly subordinated to the centralized control of their government.[155]

[150] *Souvenirs*, p. 256.   [151] *ibid.*, p. 212.   [152] *ibid.*, pp. 161-164.
[153] Robert Coulondre, *De Staline à Hitler* (Paris, 1950), p. 204.
[154] *Souvenirs*, p. 12.   [155] *ibid.*, p. 13.

The British and German documents, however, give a strikingly different picture. We have, for example, Rumbold's and Campbell's references to François-Poncet's initiative in negotiations for a truce on boundary disputes in 1932,[156] as well as German records of his overtures from 1935 to 1937 (at least partly self-motivated, it would appear).[157] It is for 1938 that evidence of his personal influence is most abundant. His sympathy for German grievances and how he expounded his views in Paris and Berlin have already been mentioned.[158] There is a further hint of his pre-Munich role in a note which Bonnet handed to Sir Eric Phipps summarizing the September 28 interview between Hitler and François-Poncet. The latter, according to this document, had advised Paris that "it seemed to him that the business had been badly joined, under imprecise conditions, and that if it were possible to have some more precise proposals and especially to answer the essential objection made by Hitler on the subject of protection for the Sudetenlanders, it would not be impossible to arrive at an agreement."[159] Yet, in speaking of Munich François-Poncet's memoirs portray their author as "only an informant, an intermediary, an assistant, an executor, who was never consulted when the major decisions were made."[160]

Certainly not even he would deny his contribution to the Franco-German rapprochement following the Sudeten crisis. Beginning with remarks to Weizsäcker, reaching a decisive point in the farewell visit to Berchtesgaden, continuing in Berlin and then back in Paris, the ambassador's efforts to secure a treaty of friendship overshadowed all other aspects of relations between the two Powers that autumn. "M. A. François-Poncet had caught the ball on the rebound in inaugurating this negotiation," writes his successor, Robert Coulondre, "and the French Government was logical with itself in pursuing it."[161] From Paris the German envoy informed his government: "Yesterday François-Poncet called on me and gave me, quite spontaneously, details of his conversation with the Fuehrer. According to his account, the initiative in the matter of continuing the Munich conversations with a view to a settlement of and improvement in Franco-German relations had come from him—François-Poncet."[162]

---

[156] *British Documents*, 2d series, III, 135, 137. Rumbold to Sargent, May 4, 1932; Campbell to Sargent, May 13, 1932.
[157] See above, notes 113, 115.   [158] See above, notes 119-121.
[159] *British Documents*, 3d series, II, 607. Bonnet note, transmitted by Phipps to Halifax, September 29, 1938.
[160] *Souvenirs*, p. 314.   [161] *De Staline à Hitler*, p. 195.
[162] *German Documents*, series D, IV, 444. Welczeck to Weizsäcker, November 1, 1938.

The policy for which François-Poncet was agitating, once identified beneath the disavowals that burden his *Souvenirs*, is not in itself very surprising, certainly not unique. It was, in fact, the common property of a substantial section of the French Right. Fear of the Russia of Stalin, indifference toward the Czechoslovakia of Benes, reliance on the Poland of Beck, admiration for the Italy of Mussolini, all were implicit in the ambassador's attitude, as they were explicit in the speeches of Fabre-Luce or Louis Rollin and the articles of d'Ormesson or Pierre Gaxotte. But the argument inevitably centered on Germany. François-Poncet had been tough toward the Weimar Republic, as had his political intimates in Paris. Concerning the formidable Third Reich, however, he argued, as did they, that given Anglo-French pacifism, all that could be done was to put obstacles in Hitler's way, hamper him with public agreements, and thus either divert him from warlike undertakings or, if he could not be diverted, leave him exposed as a perjurer and an aggressor.[163]

A natural question arises as to François-Poncet's basic attitude toward the Reich, judged by his performance over the whole decade of the 1930's. Was the underlying reason for his seeking to conciliate Hitler a fatalistic sense of Germany's irresistible strength? Or did his early interest in Franco-German cartel arrangements assert itself ever more strongly as an independent factor in his calculations? The answer is necessarily a matter of guesswork, and an "either-or" formulation should probably be avoided. On his record, the ambassador would appear to have favored close industrial cooperation under the dominance of France. Even after the change in Germany's power position destroyed all hope of realizing this dream in its original form, the dream remained—modified to allow, if necessary, for German leadership, but a consolation still. So long as there remained a chance for wealthy Frenchmen to have a share in the prosperity of the New Order, one might reconcile himself to the changed balance of forces in European diplomacy.

The all-important thing, François-Poncet had maintained in a little book published in the mid-1920's, just after his election to the Chamber, was to look facts in the face. Speaking for his parliamentary group, he wrote: "We belong to the school of contingencies. Politics appears to us as essentially the art of the real and the possible. . . . For 'realists' truth is never finished or closed. By definition it cannot be, for truth is a perpetual becoming. . . . They [the realists] are steeped in reality, opposed to abstractions and utopias, liberal and conciliatory but not, for

---

[163] *Souvenirs*, p. 12. On this general subject, see C. A. Micaud, *The French Right and Nazi Germany, 1933-1939* (Durham, N.C., 1943).

all that, skeptical; because they install themselves in that which is; they accept it, they wish to live with it; their dominant concern is to organize it, ameliorate it, get the best out of it."[164] Now, in the 1930's, realism demanded that a Frenchman identify correctly the posture of affairs and the locus of his own and his country's interests therein. Having Germany strong was not in itself a welcome circumstance. The fact that Germany had become strong, however, had to be accepted. If Hitler was amenable to reason, a deal could be arranged. If he was not, one might then still claim credit for having sought to save the peace.

IV

Between Sir Horace Rumbold's introduction to Hindenburg in 1928 and André François-Poncet's farewell to Hitler in 1938 lay a decade surpassed in violence but not in complexity of action by that which followed. An essay of the present length, even using the vicarious vantage point of Berlin, can recreate those ten years only in the broadest outlines or in selected vignettes of greater detail but tiny scope. It would be possible, with the wisdom of hindsight, to erect a sort of scoreboard for tallying the accuracy of any man's detailed predictions and the soundness of his advice during the period in question; but it would be neither very fair nor particularly useful. The main question here is simpler and at the same time larger: when all was said and done, how did these three observers see Nazi Germany?

Rumbold, cool, tolerant, rather skeptical of the reality of supposedly new departures, not easily hurried or readily flustered, ended by lashing Nazi behavior with measured strokes and by warning London to stand by for trouble. Drawing to the close of a long career, he could speak with detachment of his nation's stake in the struggle ahead. Not unnaturally, he saw that struggle in relation to his own experience with the Germany of 1914. It was to recollections of the Kaiser and Tirpitz and Schlieffen that he turned for illustrations and insights. Britain must assume that this Third Reich, to whatever extent it surpassed the Second in power and insatiability, would to that extent be more dangerous.

Beyond the realm of purely national interests, however, Rumbold perceived some other issues. He sensed, in his undramatic fashion, that Western man could no longer relax comfortably with a hodgepodge of half-formulated, frequently conflicting values. It might soon be necessary to distinguish between those features of our civilization without which the word itself would become meaningless and those which could, if

[164] A. François-Poncet, *Réfléxions d'un républicain moderne* (Paris, 1925), pp. 16, 27-28.

necessary, be modified. When Rumbold came to the defense of the German Social Democrats' constitutional right to their views, he was in effect saying that if he *had* to choose, at least for Germany, he would uphold civil liberty, even at some risk to private property. Since he personally felt not the slightest aversion to the latter, this was, I submit, a value choice of some moment.

For Dodd also, the threat of Hitler's Germany and the need to resist were starkly apparent. Like Rumbold, he spoke at the end of a long career; like Rumbold, he employed an historical frame dominated by comparisons with the old Empire. But here the similarities end. Nervous, self-conscious, loving the startling analogy, the sharply drawn distinction, the categorical prophecy, Dodd combined the didactic techniques of the professor with those of the preacher. When he referred to pre-1914 Germany, it was to evoke the picture of a genial, sturdy, intellectual nation and to despair of this new race which seemed to have forgotten all that he recalled.

America must be prepared, he felt, to defend its democracy against foreign as well as domestic enemies, and he had not the slightest doubt that the developing threats at home and abroad were related. His chosen value *sine qua non* was individual freedom. Without that golden talent, western civilization could not survive as he knew it. Forced to its conclusion, his plea set resistance to Hitler, even at the cost of war, above the value of peace, if the latter could be bought only at the price of acquiescence in tyranny.

François-Poncet, still in mid-career, ambitious, supple, highly resistant to any lasting despair, simply kept adjusting his definition of realistic optimism to fit changing conditions. In one respect, he was less bound by history than were the preceding two men. That is, he was inclined to view Nazism as an unprecedented phenomenon and hence to sustain the hope that it might evolve in an acceptable manner. Hitler's regime was obviously capable of breathtaking abruptness in its formulation of demands. Might it not also, unlike the deep-keeled state of the turn of the century, be capable of an equally rapid change of course toward peaceful development of its resources? In another respect, however, he too was the captive of history. The problem was for him definable, and hence soluble, in terms of traditional European power relationships. The possibility that the great non-European nations, America and Russia, might hold some high cards, might in fact play the final cards, entered into his calculations almost not at all.

The accommodation for which François-Poncet was working would promise little to victims of Hitler's internal policies and scarcely more to the small states in Germany's sphere of influence. It would, however, keep Europe's industrial output high and its economic organization stable. This made some sense if one assumed that the basis of our civilization is its material productivity and its existing social structure. The French ambassador might add that his distaste for Nazi crudities implied a lingering respect for certain aesthetic values in Western culture.

After all, François-Poncet seems to have asked himself, what does the new Reich represent? An industrial giant, to be sure, one with which French business could either compete, at grave risk, or cooperate, to its own profit. A potential threat to international peace, unquestionably, but surely not a Power capable of defying a judiciously constructed Anglo-French-Italian entente. A state directed by some dangerously changeable adventurers, but also by some sensible conservatives whose influence might increase with time. For the rest, a mighty bulwark against Communism and a not unwelcome model of social discipline in an otherwise disturbingly clamorous age.

The three ambassadors here discussed influenced the policies of their respective governments in different ways and to varying degrees. Rumbold's dispatches must have been buried in the files so far as Chamberlain was concerned, but their impact was not spent so long as a Vansittart or an Eden had any influence in London. Dodd was important primarily for whatever part his views may have played in strengthening the personal forebodings of Roosevelt. Of the three, François-Poncet had the most easily discernible influence, in that he fortified the Laval-Flandin-Bonnet line in French thinking on foreign policy questions. Even he, however, could not overcome the distrust of Mussolini and Franco felt by many at the Quai d'Orsay, nor prevent recurrences of interest in reliance on Russia.

It would be a mistake to think of any of the three envoys as personifying his own nation's reactions to Hitler. In the late 1930's, it was a Frenchman, Coulondre, who represented a continuation of Rumbold's attitude more clearly than did leading British policymakers. By the same token, it was Sir Nevile Henderson who clung most tenaciously to the hope of a deal with Hitler after François-Poncet left Berlin. Needless to say, there were American diplomats of all persuasions, ready to echo the voices of one or another of the men here discussed. Thus the records of these three serve not to illumine national differences of outlook but to exemplify emotional and intellectual crosscurrents simultaneously operative in London, Paris, and Washington during those tormented years when the West sought a way out, between war and capitulation.

15

Two German Ambassadors: Dirksen and Schulenburg

BY CARL E. SCHORSKE

IN THE RAPIDLY SHIFTING INTERNATIONAL SCENE of 1938 and 1939, no positions in the German foreign service had greater importance than the ambassadorships to London and Moscow. The men who held these crucial posts were both diplomats of the old school, men who sought to exploit the possibilities afforded by their positions to promote Germany's revisionist aims without jeopardizing its national existence. Each saw the key to this objective in the development of close ties between Germany and the country to which he was accredited. Each developed his own variation on one of the two traditional themes which have always been heard at the Wilhelmstrasse: those of eastern and western orientation of Germany's foreign policy. During the period from the Munich Conference to the signing of the Nazi-Soviet Pact, the themes played by Dirksen in London and Schulenburg in Moscow formed a kind of diplomatic counterpoint, which could be heard in full clarity by neither of the two players but only by the music-masters in Berlin. In this contrapuntal relationship between Dirksen and Schulenburg one can study in microcosm the formation of Nazi foreign policy in the final prewar years and the ironic, almost bizarre fate of those career diplomats whose loyalty to that great abstraction, *der Staat*, led them into the attempt to serve the Nazi Foreign Office as they had served its predecessor.

Before Munich, the work of the two ambassadors was not on the same level of importance. A totally negative policy toward the USSR was not only ideologically congenial to Hitler but essential to his policy of softening up the ruling classes of Western Europe. While Dirksen led an active, often hectic diplomatic life in the heyday of appeasement in London, Schulenburg sat quietly in Moscow as a mere observer, too well aware of the realities in the Kremlin and the *Reichskanzlei* to indulge in

[477]

idle talk of a Russo-German *détente*. After Munich, which unraveled the tenuous cords that bound the Soviet Union to the Western Powers, new diplomatic possibilities opened up in Moscow. The November pogroms depressed Anglo-German relations to a point where Dirksen was obliged to operate on the same level as his Moscow colleague. Thenceforth until August 1939, the two ambassadors were engaged in a kind of unwitting competition, each trying in his way to save his country from the catastrophe of a two-front war if not from war itself. As Germany's leaders took the decisions which led to war, the field of diplomatic possibilities progressively narrowed and the lines pursued by Dirksen and Schulenburg became increasingly conflicting and incompatible. In order to realize its aims against Poland, Germany could, in late July and early August, choose either London or Moscow, not both. In a nightmarish kind of way, the diplomatic counterpoint of the two ambassadors became transformed into a game of musical chairs, in which Hitler and Ribbentrop would decide when to stop the music and who—Dirksen or Schulenburg —would sit on the last remaining chair.

I

Of the two ambassadors, Herbert von Dirksen was the more complex in temperament and character—and the closer to the Nazis. He came from a line of hard-working bourgeois civil servants, whose generations of labor for the Prussian state were rewarded with a patent of nobility granted by the emperor to the ambassador's father, Willibald, in 1887. Willibald Dirksen was a typical parvenu aristocrat of the Wilhelmian era. He passed through the classic school in which the sons of prominent burghers acquired Junker values: the reserve cavalry. Through his marriage to a wealthy banker's daughter, he acquired the funds to purchase a vast, "representative" holding in Silesia. After his retirement from the Foreign Office, he stood for the *Reichstag* on the ticket of the conservative, nationalist, and rather anti-Semitic *Reichspartei*. He was a fanatical admirer of Kaiser Wilhelm II, whom he loyally visited at Doorn after the abdication.[1]

Like many another Junkerized bourgeois, Dirksen's father, psychologically insecure on his newly-reached social pinnacle, tried to force his children into the role of perfect aristocrats. From an early age their free development was stifled in a strict regimen designed to produce "exem-

---

[1] *Genealogisches Taschenbuch der briefadeligen Häuser, 1908* (Gotha, 1908), p. 215; Herbert von Dirksen, *Moskau, Tokio, London. Erinnerungen und Betrachtungen zu 20 Jahren deutscher Aussenpolitik, 1919-1939* (Stuttgart, 1950), pp. 9-10.

plary bearing." Herbert, who wished to prepare himself for a diplomatic career, was forced by his father into the domestic civil service in order that the son might, after the father's death, be technically qualified to manage the great estate to which he would fall heir. After completing his education at Heidelberg, where he had joined the most aristocratic fraternity, Herbert was enrolled in the fashionable Third Guard Ulan regiment at Potsdam.[2]

In all externals, Herbert von Dirksen became what his father wished him to be: a correct and proper aristocrat with all the right connections. But, unlike the true aristocrat, he had an uncommon respect for and fear of those who held authority and wielded power in the modern world. It was this characteristic, so relentlessly hammered into him by his father in another era, which separated Dirksen from the aristocrats of more ancient lineage such as Schulenburg and Welczek. It was this too which made him more than a loyal civil servant to the Nazis—a true if not ardent believer in Hitler. Finally, it was this quality which made it morally impossible for Dirksen, even after his disillusionment, to join in the resistance against Hitler in which his Moscow colleague met his death.

The attention of Ribbentrop was first drawn to Dirksen when the latter was ambassador to Japan. During the years 1935 to 1937, German policy in the Far East was one of the major issues over which the unseen struggle between the Nazi party and the older Foreign Office and military bureaucracy was fought out. The Foreign Office had traditionally based its Far Eastern policy on China, with which Germany had close commercial and military ties. The development of antagonism between Germany and Russia in the first years of the Nazi regime made it seem doubly important to keep good relations with China lest that country be driven by Japanese aggression into the arms of the Russians. To that end Germany established a group of military advisors with the Chinese government in 1934 and shipped it substantial quantities of arms. The German Foreign Office frowned on Japanese expansion in China, not merely because of its effect on Russo-Chinese relations, but also because it might mire the anti-Soviet potential of Japan in the quicksands of China. The Nazi party, on the other hand, early developed a policy of giving Japan a free hand in China in order to win the Far East's most powerful state as an ally of Germany. Ribbentrop was the architect of this policy long before he emerged from his paradiplomatic *Dienststelle* in the regalia of a Foreign Minister. Its visible expression—a great

[2] Dirksen, *Moskau, Tokio, London*, pp. 10-12.

personal triumph for Ribbentrop over the Foreign Office—was the Anti-Comintern Pact of November 1936.

During the development of this internecine feud, Dirksen maintained an ambivalent position. Out of a deeply felt affinity for the moderate expansionists of Japan, and with an ambassador's natural penchant for promoting good relations with the country of his accreditation, Dirksen favored the substance of Ribbentrop's policy. But he favored the Foreign Office in form; the Foreign Office alone should be the executor of foreign policy. When Dirksen learned (from a Japanese source) of the negotiations for the Anti-Comintern Pact, he went home to Germany, interviewed Ribbentrop, and transmitted his information to the ill-informed Foreign Minister, von Neurath.[3]

With the outbreak of the "China incident" in July 1937, the conflict between party and Foreign Office over Far Eastern policy reached a new fury. The Foreign Office enjoined strict neutrality in the conflict,[4] but maintained its military aid to China; while the party wheels—Goering, Ribbentrop, and Goebbels—all pressed for a pro-Japanese policy.[5] Dirksen took the Nazi line, urging that "the surest way of avoiding . . . conflicts with Japan would be to recall our military advisors from Nanking." Well aware that this suggestion would be unacceptable to the Foreign Office and army, however, he suggested further that his superiors consider German mediation in the Sino-Japanese conflict as a means to "extricate us from the difficulties of neutrality."[6] The difficulties, be it noted, were not merely international, but also domestic. Dirksen, occupying a position halfway between the Nazis and the old bureaucracy, was proposing to solve on the international plane a domestic struggle for control over foreign policy.

Thanks to the decision of the Western Powers to try to settle the conflict through the Brussels Conference, the German leaders accepted Dirksen's proposal. From October 1937, to January 1938, the negotiations dragged on, only to end in failure.[7] With the collapse of the mediation effort Dirksen drafted a dispatch in which he recommended a basic reorientation of Germany's Far Eastern policy toward Japan: the cessation of arms shipments to China, the withdrawal of military advisors, and the recognition of Manchukuo.[8] By the time this policy memorandum reached Berlin, Ribbentrop had become Foreign Minister (February 4, 1938). The new incumbent placed Dirksen's recommendations before

---

[3] Dirksen, *Moskau, Tokio, London*, pp. 184-185. See also Chapter 13, §IV above.
[4] *German Documents*, series D, I, 733-734.
[5] *ibid.*, pp. 752-754, 767-769, 772.
[6] *ibid.*, pp. 754-755.
[7] *ibid.*, pp. 771-825, *passim*.
[8] *ibid.*, pp. 826-831.

Hitler.[9] On February 20, the Fuehrer announced Germany's recognition of Manchukuo.

While Dirksen was en route home for a holiday in Germany, news reached him of his appointment to London. In the great February overturn of Foreign Office and army, Dirksen had emerged with the signal honor of succeeding the Nazi Foreign Minister in Germany's most important diplomatic post. Ribbentrop's selection is easy to understand: Dirksen had supported his pro-Japanese line throughout. He had gotten on well with the principal agent of the *Dienststelle Ribbentrop* in Japan.[10] He had joined the party in 1936 and was genuinely impressed with its economic and political achievements.[11] All these factors would have recommended Dirksen to Ribbentrop. True, Dirksen was a career foreign servant, and for this reason Ribbentrop could never wholly trust him. During neither his Japanese nor his British assignments was Dirksen made privy to the party's plans in foreign affairs. Yet the very fact that Dirksen was on good terms with the old school professionals might have its uses for the Nazi Foreign Minister as long as Dirksen remained loyal to the party line.

Dirksen too had some ambivalence about serving under a Foreign Minister whose unorthodox ways offended his bureaucratic sensibilities. "But as the poacher made forester often becomes quite a useful member of society, I thought, so Ribbentrop too, having attained the object of his vain desire, would be amenable to reason and good counsel. Besides, the competition between the Foreign Office and the Ribbentrop Bureau would now have to cease."[12] Yes, there would henceforth be but one authority over Germany's foreign policy. By that very fact the half-Nazi, half-aristocratic Dirksen was already obsolescent as a political person. Dirksen did not realize that the supremacy of the party in the Wilhelmstrasse would deprive him of the latitude which domestic rivalries had afforded him in Japan. Nor could he grasp the fact that his rigid bureaucratic ethic would prove a handicap in pursuing his own concept of the national interest when Ribbentrop's policies ran counter to it.

II

Dirksen prepared for his new mission in a mood of high optimism. His belief that Hitler desired good relations with Great Britain and wished to build further upon the foundations laid in the Anglo-German Naval Agreement of 1935 was confirmed by the somewhat vague in-

[9] *ibid.*, pp. 839-840.
[11] *ibid.*, pp. 182-187.
[10] Dirksen, *Moskau, Tokio, London*, p. 160.
[12] *ibid.*, p. 199.

structions of the Foreign Minister. Although Hitler angrily complained to Dirksen of Britain's lack of understanding for Germany's demands, the ambassador saw nothing permanent in the Fuehrer's negative attitude.[13]

On taking up his post in London on May 3, 1938, Dirksen at once sought to exploit to the utmost such powers as his ambassadorial position gave him to promote cordial relations between the two countries. At his initial call on Lord Halifax, a general conversation developed on the Sudeten question, just then emerging into dangerous prominence. Dirksen told the Foreign Secretary that the Germans "were very anxious to keep things quiet in Czechoslovakia"—a statement which could not have emanated from his home government, and which he did not report to it.[14] The ambassador quoted Halifax as entertaining the idea "that the Reich Government could perhaps make a contribution to the solution of the [Sudeten] question by formulating in writing their desires in this respect."[15] No mention of this suggestion appears in Halifax's record of the conversation. Thus in his first significant dispatch from London, Dirksen appears to have been trying to push his government toward negotiations on the Czech question faster than the British themselves wished to go. A few weeks later (June 8), in his effort to win the confidence of the British, Dirksen went so far as to be "frankly outspoken" with Halifax on the subject of Ribbentrop. He told the Foreign Secretary—frankly but falsely—that Ribbentrop recognized that his mission to England had been a failure because "he had always felt obliged to keep one eye so much on the German end. . . . None the less, he [Ribbentrop] still wished to establish closer relations between our two countries."[16] From some rather general remarks of Halifax on improving Anglo-German relations, the ambassador extrapolated for Wilhelmstrasse consumption the Foreign Secretary's "clearly discernible . . . intention of making an approach to the German Government again, with a view to resuming within measurable time the negotiations" interrupted by the rape of Austria.[17] By a little exaggeration of the will to improved relations in both capitals, Dirksen sought to pave the way for a *détente*.

The first month of Dirksen's mission was not an easy one. The so-called "week-end crisis" of May 21, when the Czechs mobilized in the mistaken

[13] Dirksen, *Moskau, Tokio, London*, pp. 209-210.

[14] *British Documents*, 3rd series, 1, 240; cf. *German Documents*, series D, II, 255-256.

[15] *German Documents*, series D, II, 255.

[16] *British Documents*, 3rd series 1, 455; cf. Dirksen, *Moskau, Tokio, London*, p. 209, where he states that Ribbentrop avoided any discussion of the failure of his London mission.

[17] *German Documents*, series D, II, 398; cf. *British Documents*, 3rd series, I, 454-455.

belief that the Germans were massing troops on their borders, provided a poor atmosphere for inaugurating a new phase in Anglo-German relations. In that crisis, Dirksen formed the impressions of both the Chamberlain government and of British public opinion which governed his thinking until the end of his mission. He was convinced that the ruling circles in Great Britain would do anything to avoid war, but would fight if Germany should resort to force. "Most brutal, but also most characteristic [wrote Dirksen in his report on the May crisis], is the advice given to a German acquaintance by an influential Englishman: 'Don't shoot Czechoslovakia, strangle her.' Or in other words: Anything which can be got without a shot being fired can count upon the agreement of the British."[18] Chamberlain, because he realizes clearly "that the social structure of Britain, even the conception of the British Empire, would not survive the chaos of even a victorious war . . . is committed to the idea of European settlement with all the obstinacy which is characteristic of his family. He knows very well that Anglo-German agreement is the keystone of such a European settlement."[19] Chamberlain's was "the first postwar Cabinet which has made agreement with Germany one of the major points of its program." It displayed maximum understanding of German demands, not only in the Czech question, but also "with respect to excluding the Soviet Union from the decision of the destinies of Europe, the League of Nations likewise, and the advisability of bilateral treaties and negotiations."[20]

While Dirksen stressed British willingness to accommodate to Germany's demands, he also pointed out the limits of British tolerance. British public opinion, he felt, had been revolutionized by the German action in Austria. In the May crisis, Dirksen wrote on June 8, "the feeling . . . of being made a fool of in that affair, grew up again, together with the determination not to allow unchallenged further alterations in the balance of power in Europe. . . . The attitude of the British people to the possibility of war has changed entirely since 1936. They are ready to fight should their government show them that this is necessary in order to put an end to a state of subjectively experienced threats and uncertainty. . . ."[21] The Chamberlain-Halifax government could well be unseated by a "psychotic" public opinion aroused by another German *fait accompli*. "To regard the excitement of the last weeks as mere bluff might .

[18] *German Documents*, series D, II, 393.

[19] *ibid.*, 473.

[20] *Dirksen Papers*, p. 34; for Dirksen's reports on the British attitude toward the USSR, see also *German Documents*, series D, II, 434, 486.

[21] *German Documents*, series D, II, 323, 394-395.

turn out to be a fatal error." Alternatively, the Chamberlain government itself would, "without the slightest doubt," go to war if Germany resorts to war to achieve its ends. The willingness of the British government to make sacrifices to meet Germany's demands was limited by "the *one* condition, that Germany would endeavor to achieve these ends by peaceful means."[22]

Dirksen's evaluation of the British situation was realistic and his advice to the Wilhelmstrasse, within the framework of the German aim of hegemony in Eastern Europe, thoroughly sound: Chamberlain's government, he said in effect, is Germany's greatest political asset. But to realize its value, you must go slow, you must proceed by diplomatic blackmail, not by overt military force. As in the early days of his mission to Tokyo, Dirksen differed not with the stated aims of the Nazis but with their pace and method.

Did Dirksen's policy recommendations have any influence in Berlin? Certainly not at the level of grand strategy. On May 30, Hitler had issued his new directive for Operation Green, with its "unalterable decision to smash Czechoslovakia by military action in the near future." No mention was made of British intervention in this document. In a supplementary directive, dated July 7, French and British intervention during the execution of Operation Green was stated, in flat contradiction of Dirksen's expressed judgment, to be "contrary to our expectations."[23]

In the Wilhelmstrasse, opinion seems to have been divided. Weizsäcker, in early June, felt that the avoidance of Franco-British intervention must be "the first care" of German policy toward Czechoslovakia. "Germany is not free to choose the moment when this fruit may be plucked without too great a risk. She is only in a position to organize the desired development around the slogan emanating at this moment from Britain, 'Self-determination for the Sudetenland.' "[24] As opposed to the use of force, Weizsäcker advocated a "chemical process of disruption" which would take into account the kind of dangers pointed out by Dirksen. Ribbentrop seems to have largely ignored the question as to whether Britain's ultimate attitude should be taken into account. In his diplomacy from May to July his primary concern was to elicit, in the bluntest conceivable way, a British denial that the United Kingdom would support Franco-Czech military resistance if war should break out. He wished the British to make this denial in public form if possible, in order to weaken

[22] *ibid.*, p. 395; *Dirksen Papers*, p. 34.
[23] Royal Institute of International Affairs, *Survey of International Affairs, 1938* (London, 1951), II, 140-146; *German Documents*, series D, II, 475.
[24] *German Documents*, series D, II, 420-422.

Czech resistance to the "chemical process."[25] What the Foreign Minister must have thought of Dirksen's warnings of Britain's willingness to fight may be inferred from a marginal notation he wrote in English on a similar warning from another source: "Secret Service Propaganda!"[26] But even if the Western Powers would intervene, so be it. On July 21, Ribbentrop told Weizsäcker that Germany was prepared to fight on the Czech question and to win—to which Weizsäcker replied that "even if it was our business to fool foreign countries, it was nevertheless our duty not to dupe one another."[27]

Of Hitler's and Ribbentrop's full intentions Ambassador Dirksen knew nothing during the spring and early summer of 1938. Where Britain was fooled, Dirksen was duped. Both pinned their hopes not so much on Ribbentrop as on Hitler's good sense and the power of the restraining elements in his entourage.

When the sky grew darkest, there always seemed to be a ray of hope at hand. In July 1938, the Sudeten issue was seething again. Suddenly Captain Wiedemann, Hitler's personal adjutant, appeared in London on a highly secret mission to extend the olive branch to Britain. Of course Dirksen warmly welcomed Wiedemann, whose task was to sound out the British government on the possibility of a visit by Goering to Britain to discuss the improvement of Anglo-German relations. Wiedemann's purpose was entirely congenial to Dirksen. But the form of this approach created difficulties for the ambassador, difficulties which revealed the deliberate ambiguity in the line of responsibility in Hitler's administrative system. Wiedemann's mission had been undertaken under Goering's auspices and with Hitler's consent, but without the knowledge of Foreign Minister von Ribbentrop.[28] Although Wiedemann wished to keep Ribbentrop in the dark concerning his visit, Dirksen persuaded him to report to the Foreign Minister on the content of his conversation.[29] Dirksen was still trying, as in Tokyo, to keep the lines clear. But where in Tokyo he had to maneuver between the party and the old bureaucracy, he now had to contend with two wings of the party. The more aggressive of these, with whose aims he no longer sympathized, firmly controlled the Foreign Office to which he felt a primary bureaucratic allegiance. Throughout, Hitler seems to have given both groups some latitude—either because he had not made up his mind or because

[25] Cf. e.g., *German Documents*, series D, II, 377, 409-411; also Royal Institute of International Affairs, *Survey, 1938*, II, 137, note 1.
[26] *German Documents*, series D, II, 440.   [27] *ibid.*, p. 504.
[28] *British Documents*, 3rd series, I, 587.
[29] Dirksen, *Moskau, Tokio, London*, pp. 216-217.

he wished to confuse his potential adversaries with the open-ended character of his policies.

The Wiedemann mission greatly encouraged Dirksen. When he made his farewell call on Sir Horace Wilson before taking home leave (July 22), Sir Horace quite unexpectedly ushered him in to the Prime Minister, who expressed his gratification at Wiedemann's message and asked Dirksen to convey his views to Hitler if he saw fit. Dirksen was delighted with Wiedemann's assurance to Chamberlain that Hitler "would wish to get negotiations [between the Sudeten German party and the Czech government] resumed" if they should break down.[30]

How impossible it was to place any reliance on gestures of friendship from Ribbentrop's rivals was clearly shown in the ill-fated attempt of Halifax and Dirksen to win the support of Germany for the Runciman mission. Ribbentrop brusquely rejected Halifax's first request for support of the Runciman mission (July 26) as a "purely British affair."[31] On July 28, Halifax wrote a personal letter to Ribbentrop deploring the indifference of the German government to the mediation effort and again urgently requesting its support. Fearing that "in his present temper there was a real danger" that Ribbentrop "might not show it [Halifax's letter] to Hitler at all," the British took two further steps to reach "the sole arbiter of Germany's fate."[32] Chamberlain wrote a private letter to Dirksen in Germany, asking him to request Hitler "to give full consideration to the contents of the personal letter that Lord Halifax recently addressed to Herr von Ribbentrop in regard to Lord Runciman's Mission."[33] Correct as ever in his bureaucratic procedure, Dirksen submitted Chamberlain's letter and a draft reply to the Under-Secretary of State. The Under-Secretary, also taking account of von Ribbentrop's "present temper," excised from Dirksen's draft reply both a reference to German public sympathy for Runciman's mission and a promise to mention the Halifax letter to Hitler.[34]

Dirksen's chances of an interview with Hitler, slim at best, were surely not improved by submitting the Chamberlain letter to the Foreign Office. They became still weaker when Lord Halifax took a second step to circumvent Ribbentrop and to communicate directly with the Fuehrer. With Ribbentrop thoroughly outraged and with Hitler resolved neither

[30] *British Documents*, 3rd series, I, 618-620; *German Documents*, series D, II, 509-510.

[31] *German Documents*, series D, II, 517; *British Documents*, 3rd series, II, 13.

[32] *British Documents*, 3rd series, II, 41, note 1; I, 603.

[33] *ibid.*, II, 41.

[34] Cf. *German Documents*, series D, II, 542-543, with *British Documents*, 3rd series, II, 60.

to support the Runciman mission nor to retard his plan to force a military showdown,[35] Dirksen's hopes of laying Chamberlain's position before the Fuehrer evaporated. His application for an audience through the Foreign Office brought no results. He visited several high Nazis (Bohle and Hess) who might carry his message to Hitler indirectly. He tried again to get an interview with Hitler through an influential friend in the Fuehrer's Berchtesgaden entourage—to no avail. Not until the Nuremberg Congress in the second week of September was Dirksen finally granted an audience with his chief of state. The conversation lasted only seven minutes, during which Hitler maintained a completely closed attitude toward Chamberlain's plea and rejected any consideration of support for that "rabid democrat" Lord Runciman.[36]

With this interview ended the first phase of Dirksen's illusory efforts to achieve an Anglo-German *détente*. At Nuremberg, the ambassador was told that, in view of the acuteness of Anglo-German tension, he should not for the present return to his post. In the Munich crisis, Dirksen played no direct part. But his work in London had helped to prepare the ground for Hitler's most successful blackmail operation. Incapable of understanding the connection between the Nazi aims with which he sympathized and the Nazi methods which he disliked, he had, by his sympathetic discharge of his London mission, done his best to help encourage in the British statesmen the belief that moderate, conservative Germany still participated in the formulation of Hitler's policies.

After five months of labor, Dirksen had become little more than a voice of the British appeasers in the Nazi Foreign Office. In this respect, his position was not unlike that of his British opposite number, Sir Nevile Henderson—with the unfortunate exception that Henderson's voice was listened to in London, while Dirksen's was ignored in Berlin.

III

During the years of Dirksen's labors to further Nazi aims in the Far East and to mitigate the effects of Nazi policy in pre-Munich London, Count Werner Friedrich von der Schulenburg represented Germany in Moscow. A cool, somewhat skeptical nobleman of ancient family, Schulenburg showed none of the emotional instability or personal *Geltungsdrang* of his parvenu-aristocratic colleague. Where Dirksen was always

---

[35] *German Documents,* series D, II, 576-577, 593. Cf. also Ribbentrop's answer, August 21, to Halifax's personal message of July 28, *ibid.,* 599-600.

[36] Dirksen, *Moskau, Tokio, London,* pp. 229-231; *Dirksen Papers,* pp. 157-158.

on the lookout for opportunities to act or to make policy recommendations, Schulenburg was the patient, impersonal, and disengaged spectator of the passing show. His reports from Moscow contain policy suggestions only on the rarest occasions; and if, like all western diplomats in the Soviet capital, he perforce engaged in speculation, he did so less frequently and more soberly than most.

Schulenburg began his mission to Moscow in October 1936. His predecessor, Nadolny, a man of unalterable Eastern orientation, had resigned his post in protest against Hitler's total rejection of the Rapallo policy. Schulenburg was by temperament admirably suited to head an embassy which, with Russo-German relations at their nadir, could be little more than a highly important listening post during the next three years. His published dispatches for the years from 1936 to 1938 reveal nothing of that Eastern orientation for which he became famous through the pact negotiations and the later resistance movement against Hitler.

Schulenburg's political analysis was clearheaded and somewhat old-fashioned. In his evaluation of the USSR, he consistently played down the Marxist revolutionary component in the Soviet leaders' policies. The idea of *Staatsräson* dominated his thinking about Russia as about Germany.[37] At the root of all political activity in the Soviet Union, he said in November 1937, were two convictions: The first was "that Imperial Russia owed her defeat in the World War to the *lack of an adequate war industry*"; the second, "born partly of respect, partly of fear ... that of the *fearful strength of the German people*." The second conviction had gained impetus through the rise of Hitler and German rearmament, which "led to the Soviet-French and Soviet-Czech mutual assistance pacts," to "the enormous increase in Soviet armament expenditures," and to the cultivation of Soviet patriotism, "a measure to strengthen the defensive spirit of the nation."[38] On the relationship of the purges then in progress to the basic convictions which he believed to motivate Soviet policy, Schulenburg felt unclear. He inclined to the current view that the purges were connected with Soviet isolationism, and was certain that the wave of persecution had "gravely shaken the organism of the Soviet State. . . . But [he added] it would be unwise to assume that this downward development *must* be permanent. . . . As for what may come tomorrow, we must wait and see."[39]

During the development of the Czech crisis, Schulenburg seems not

[37] Cf. Peter Kleist, *Zwischen Stalin und Hitler* (Bonn, 1950), pp. 34-35.
[38] From an address before the German Wehrmacht Academy, November 25, 1937. *German Documents*, series D, I, 899.
[39] *ibid.*, 899-900.

[488]

to have been fearful of a rapprochement between the Soviet Union and the West. Internal instability and fear of war on two fronts would, he thought, militate against any serious Russian intervention on behalf of Czechoslovakia, although minimum aid was not to be excluded. "The Soviet Union will intervene [Schulenburg wrote after the May crisis] only if she herself is attacked, or if it becomes manifest that the outcome will be favorable to the side hostile to Germany."[40] The core of Russia's policy, he insisted, was isolationist: to build up military strength and hold aloof from any potential conflict. How was this evaluation to be squared with Russia's repeated declarations of support for collective security in general and Czechoslovakia in particular? Schulenburg believed that it was Litvinov's basic aim to stiffen the resistance of the Western Powers to Germany by every means, whether promises or taunts. In this framework, Schulenburg interpreted a suggestion of a Soviet approach to Germany in June 1938. Not to be taken at face value, it merely gave the USSR "the opportunity once more to hold up before the French ally the specter of a German-Soviet understanding."[41]

With his premise that Russian policy was based on *Realpolitik*-from-weakness, Schulenburg was of course alert to any changes in the Soviet line which might offer opportunities for Germany. Reporting on a speech of Litvinov after the May crisis (June 23), he took seriously Litvinov's disappointment with the democracies' "compliant attitude" toward the aggressors. "Litvinov indicates that Soviet policy, whose aim it was only a few years ago to collaborate as closely as possible with the democratic great powers and to be admitted to the circle of these states itself, will henceforth—without abandoning the principle of collective security—break with the policy of the western powers and decide in each case whether its own interests require cooperation with England and France."[42]

A point of particular importance to Schulenburg was Litvinov's clear indication that the Soviet Union was no defender of Versailles. "If the Soviet Union has sided with the democracies and the League of Nations during the last few years, it has done so because Germany aims not merely at the restoration of her pre-war boundaries and the rights denied her by Versailles, but also pursues an open and 'mad' anti-Soviet policy and a policy of unlimited aggression."[43]

[40] *German Documents*, series D, II, 363-364, 423-426. Schulenburg's military attaché, General Köstring, freely communicated his estimates of Soviet military weakness and isolationism to his British opposite number. See *British Documents*, 3rd series, I, 418-424.
[41] *German Documents*, series D, I, 921. [42] *German Documents*, series D, I, 929.
[43] *ibid.*, 928.

The ambassador drew no explicit conclusions for German policy from Litvinov's address. He merely pointed out that Russia was again reserving freedom of action, and that "the attempt to arrive at an objective attitude toward the Third Reich is striking."[44] Yet from his dispatch two implications emerge for the German Foreign Office: (1) that the Western orientation of the USSR was artificially induced by Hitler's "mad" anti-Soviet policy; and (2) that the USSR, if Germany were to assume a more friendly attitude, might well lend diplomatic support for the recovery of Germany's pre-world war I boundaries. Like Dirksen in London at the same time (June 1938), Schulenburg was informing his superiors that, in the government to which he was accredited, there was understanding for Germany's aims but not for Hitler's methods.

On the whole, Schulenburg's reports during the first nine months of 1938 could only reassure Hitler that he need have no immediate fears of Russia as long as he made no direct assault upon her. "Whereas the Soviet Union is attempting to force France and Great Britain to take the initiative against Germany, she herself will hold back." On August 26, 1938, when the Czech crisis was approaching its climax, Schulenburg stuck resolutely to this line, in the face of Litvinov's explicit statement to him that "the Soviet Union had promised Czechoslovakia her support; she would keep her word and do her best." He noted that Litvinov repeatedly attacked British policy, and that he avoided answering the question as to the form which Soviet help to Czechoslovakia would take. The German embassy estimated that Soviet aid would probably be confined to the shipment of war materials. "The sending of troops is . . . not in the interests of the Soviet Union."[45]

Such were Schulenburg's honest evaluations of Soviet intentions and capabilities, and they could only have heartened Hitler on his road to war with Czechoslovakia and the West. Yet the ambassador was not happy to provide this encouragement to the framers of Germany's adventurous policies, and did what he could to offset his professional analysis of Soviet policy. During August and September 1938, he reported fully and frequently opinions of the Moscow diplomatic corps to the effect that France and Britain would fight.[46] He cited the universal opinion that the Soviet Union would be "the only one to gain" from a European war. In two dispatches he quoted the words spoken to him by M. Coulondre, the French ambassador, words which doubtless expressed his own feelings: "I hope with all my heart that it will not

[44] *ibid.*, 923-924.   [45] *German Documents*, series D, II, 630-631.
[46] *ibid.*, 602, 605, 631, 655-657, 666-667.

come to a French-German conflict. You know as well as I do for whom we are working if we come to blows."[47]

With his reporting on Western intentions, Schulenburg joined his warning voice to that of Dirksen. There is evidence to suggest that he took a more drastic step to avoid the catastrophe: a *sub rosa* approach to the British. On August 22, Herwarth von Bittenfeld, a member of the German embassy staff who was close to Schulenburg, appealed to the third secretary of the British embassy for a clearer declaration by his government of its willingness to fight. Herwarth showed himself familiar with the substance of Dirksen's warnings and informed his interlocutor that "little attention was paid in Berlin to Dircksen's [*sic*] reports, or, for that matter, to those from other missions abroad."[48]

He went on to reveal that the dispatches and instructions from the Wilhelmstrasse reflected Hitler's and Ribbentrop's confidence ". . . that Germany would be able to invade Czechoslovakia with impunity. This, our informant said, was very disturbing to professional diplomats like his ambassador, who saw their country about to involve herself in a war in which the odds would in their opinion be heavily against her. . . . The blame, they felt, would lie to a certain extent with His Majesty's Government, who, as in 1914, had failed to make their position sufficiently clear. *The only* hope in their opinion would be for a representative of His Majesty's Government to inform the Führer himself quite categorically that in certain circumstances Great Britain would quite certainly go to war in defence of Czechoslovakia."[49]

It cannot be proved that Schulenburg prompted Herwarth's appeal against British appeasement, but the secretary's references to his chief's views suggest that the ambassador stood behind him on his bold mission. Schulenburg's initiative in the affair would have been quite consistent with the strength of character he revealed in the later conspiracy against Hitler.

None of the foregoing evidence of Schulenburg's attitudes should be construed as indications of a Western orientation on his part. If he did what little he could to avoid a struggle with the West, it was out of cool consideration for his country's interest. If in his published dispatches of the pre-Munich years he showed no disposition to advocate an Eastern orientation, it was because the policies of his government were hopelessly unreceptive to any rapprochement with the Soviet

[47] *ibid.*, 602, 631.
[48] *British Documents*, 3rd series, II, 141.
[49] *ibid.*

Union.[50] A *Realpolitiker* of the old school, Schulenburg reported what he saw, acted when he could in his country's interest as he construed it, and bided his time.

IV

The Munich Pact sent a feeling of triumphant relief through the German Diplomatic Service. The Moscow mission was no exception. "At the Embassy [wrote the Counselor of Embassy] there prevails great jubilation over the enormous, unimaginable success which the Führer has won for Germany. . . . That the policy of Litvinov has suffered a complete fiasco, that the war, from which chaos and the weakening of Germany was expected, has not broken out, that the policy of pacts and alliances has failed, that the collective idea has collapsed, and that the League of Nations has disappointed the hopes reposed in it, can in my opinion not remain without consequences for Soviet policy. . . . As regards ourselves, a more positive attitude on the part of the Soviet Union might be possible."[51] Dirksen records the "great joy" he felt at the signature of the Anglo-German protocol, which he hoped "would open a new and happier chapter in the relations of the two countries."[52]

Both ambassadors assumed that Hitler, having achieved his aim in disrupting Czechoslovakia and the post-Versailles security system, must be ready to normalize relations with the capitals to which they were accredited. They now entered into a kind of unwitting competition with each other which culminated ten months later in a technical victory for Schulenburg with the conclusion of the Nazi-Soviet Pact.

Dirksen was well aware of the riven condition of British official and governmental opinion, but he was rightly convinced that Chamberlain and his closest followers were determined to do everything in their power to develop the cordial Anglo-German relations promised by the Munich protocol.[53] The important thing now, as Dirksen saw it, was for the German government to avoid all provocative utterance which might feed ammunition to the Conservative and Labor opposition. Thus the way could be smoothed for constructive diplomatic work.

Hitler at once crossed Dirksen's suggestions by a sharp public attack on the British opposition and British rearmament (Saarbrücken speech, October 9). In response to an inquiry by Lord Halifax concerning the

[50] The British ambassador Viscount Chilston was aware of Schulenburg's dilemma. Cf. *ibid.*, 141, note 1.

[51] *German Documents*, series D, IV, 602. See also Chapter II, §III above.

[52] Dirksen, *Moskau, Tokio, London*, p. 235.

[53] *German Documents*, series D, IV, 310.

treatment of non-Nazi Sudeten Germans, Hitler answered in his speech:
"We cannot any longer tolerate the tutelage of British governesses.
Inquiries of British politicians concerning the fate of Germans within
the frontiers of the Reich—or of others belonging to the Reich—are
not in place."[54] Dirksen wrote personally to Weizsäcker to persuade him
that such outbursts could only give a new lease on life to the Churchill-
Eden group.[55] This was but the first of a series of efforts by Dirksen to
instruct Hitler and Ribbentrop on the best way to strengthen the hand
of Germany's friend, Chamberlain. He advised that they avoid attacks
on Churchill's group and on British rearmament; that they emphasize
the line of the Anglo-German protocol: "Never again war between Britain
and Germany"; and that they take the initiative in launching disarmament talks and respond with positive proposals to British feelers for a
détente.[56] Dirksen urged bilateral disarmament discussions, which he felt,
would strengthen Chamberlain's position to the point where a colonial
settlement could be approached with every prospect of success. Dirksen's
recommendations were not products of his imagination, but based on conversations with British Cabinet ministers and other intimates of the Prime
Minister.

It soon became clear that Berlin was firmly resolved to ignore Dirksen's "do's" and "don'ts." Weizsäcker informed the ambassador that
the German press campaign against British rearmament "was instigated
on the direct instructions of the Foreign Minister." He advised Dirksen
against forwarding to Ribbentrop a report by Dr. Hesse, head of Ribbentrop's own London *Dienststelle*, because Hesse's arguments "tend too
strongly in a direction which, as things are now, is not the same as that
taken here." It was only three weeks after Munich when the Secretary of
State wrote to Dirksen: "Things here are moving rapidly but not in the
direction of a German-British rapprochement at present."[57] Which way
they were moving, the ambassador was of course not told. It is striking
that Dirksen's October recommendations for future negotiations referred
only to those questions which the British wished to discuss—disarmament and colonies—while the issues on which Hitler was preparing to
act—rump Czechoslovakia, Memel, Danzig, and Poland—were almost
wholly ignored.

With the shock of November pogroms, Dirksen had to suspend his
efforts to prepare the ground for a *détente*. When in mid-December

[54] *ibid.*, 302-303.　　　　　　　[55] *ibid.*, 303-305.
[56] *German Documents*, series D, IV, 305-311, 319-323; also *Dirksen Papers*, pp. 160-
161.
[57] *German Documents*, series D, IV, 311-312; cf. also p. 327.

he resumed them, he went to work on a more modest plane: that of economic relations. A new sense of urgency informed the ambassador's recommendation for pursuing an accord in the economic field. On December 16, 1938 he wrote to Weizsäcker: "How long Chamberlain can keep his place . . . is a question about which I am by no means so confident as I was a month or two ago. If therefore there should be any wish on our side for a certain degree of *rapprochement*, I should be in favor of not waiting too long."[58]

During January and February Dirksen had some grounds for optimism. Negotiations of an Anglo-German coal agreement were proceeding smoothly, and other industry conferences between the two countries were successfully initiated. Hitler himself made an unusually conciliatory speech on January 30. Although Dirksen failed to win his government's assent to a British request that Funk, the German Minister of Economics, pay a visit to England, he arranged for the issuance of an invitation to visit Germany to Sir Oliver Stanley, President of the Board of Trade.[59] Perhaps most encouraging to the ambassador was the fact that, at the end of February, Ribbentrop commissioned Dr. Hesse to approach Chamberlain through his personal press secretary with a view to a really broad rapprochement, to be crowned by an Anglo-German nonaggression treaty. Ribbentrop indicated his willingness to come to London to sign such a treaty.[60]

These promising beginnings of improved Anglo-German relations were once more crushed by the march into Prague. Germany's gestures of accommodation during the preceding two months were revealed as a mere decoy to distract the attention of the British from Hitler's next undertaking. The Hesse mission performed the same function in the second Czech crisis as the Wiedemann mission had in the first. Dirksen, with his unlimited will to believe in Hitler's good intentions, was equally fooled by both, and participated with innocent eagerness in the work of building decoys for the British.

If most of Dirksen's labors, during the period from October 1938 to March 1939, were conducted in ignorance of Hitler's precise intentions, he was privately informed of the impending march on Prague a week or more before the event when in Berlin on a short leave.[61]

---

[58] *German Documents*, series D, IV, 354.

[59] *German Documents*, series D, IV, 389ff.; cf. also *British Documents*, 3rd series, IV, 138, note 1. The Stanley visit was called off by the British after the march into Prague.

[60] *Dirksen Papers*, pp. 165-166; Dirksen, *Moskau, Tokio, London*, pp. 238-239.

[61] Dirksen, *Moskau, Tokio, London*, p. 240; cf. *Dirksen Papers*, p. 166.

Returning to England on March 9, Dirksen found "the same optimistic mood as had prevailed in February. Stanley's visit to Berlin was to take place soon—on March 17—and it was obvious that the British Government attached great importance to it."[62] The ambassador, loyal as ever to his government, did nothing to disturb the optimistic mood of the British, breathed no word of the impending coup in Prague. Before his recall to Berlin on March 18, Dirksen had two stormy conversations with the irate Lord Halifax. Despite the ambassador's attempt at a bold front, in which he drew once more upon his own hatred of Versailles, Halifax observed that "his demeanour was one that suggested that he felt considerable difficulty himself in defending the action taken by his government."[63] Dirksen's house of cards had collapsed no less than Halifax's. But Dirksen still drew no personal consequences from the fact. To justify his government's policy may have been difficult for Dirksen; to cease to serve that policy was still unthinkable. With Ribbentrop unwilling to receive or hear him on his return to Germany, Dirksen sulkily withdrew to his beloved Gröditzberg to wait for two months until his master should give the signal for his next jump through the hoop.

V

With the signing of the Munich Pact, Germany incidentally achieved one of the major aims of its foreign policy: the exclusion of the Soviet Union from the European international community. The German embassy in Moscow, on the morrow of Munich, expected the early dismissal of Litvinov, whose efforts to bolster the European security system had proved a "complete fiasco."[64] Although this event did not take place with the anticipated speed, the embassy felt that circumstances were favorable for an approach toward normalizing relations with the USSR. Schulenburg abandoned his previous reserve. Believing that the Soviets, in their isolation, would feel an increased need for foreign goods to support accelerated war production, Schulenburg authorized a proposal to the Foreign Office that it seize the occasion to negotiate a new economic agreement with the Soviet Union (October 10, 1938).[65] Little more than a fortnight later, Schulenburg was turning over a broader program in his mind: "It is my intention in the immediate future to approach

[62] *Dirksen Papers*, pp. 166-167; cf. L. B. Namier, *Diplomatic Prelude* (London, 1948), pp. 65-66.
[63] *German Documents*, series D, IV, 281-282; *British Documents*, 3rd series, IV, 270-272.
[64] *German Documents*, series D, IV, 602-603.   [65] *ibid.*, 603.

Molotov, the Chairman of the Council of People's Commissars, in an attempt to reach a favorable settlement of the questions disturbing German-Soviet relations. The most favorable opportunity for this step would be the beginning of the negotiations on the 1939 German-Soviet agreement on trade and payments and the larger credit on goods to the Soviet Union." This agreement would provide the basis for discussions of a long list of issues outstanding between the two countries: disputes arising out of the transport of German goods through the USSR to Iran, unfavorable treatment of applications for entry permits for German businessmen, failure to release from Soviet citizenship wives of German citizens who had left or been expelled from the USSR, etc.[66] It is striking that Schulenburg should have contemplated so complete a circumvention of Litvinov in favor of a direct approach to Molotov. There is, however, no indication that he carried out this plan.

This program of diplomatic action, broad as it was compared to anything which might have been contemplated before Munich, manifests no intention to produce a diplomatic revolution. In his sober fashion, Schulenburg drew—at least for his government—none of the radical conclusions entertained by his French colleague, Coulondre: that Munich would throw the Soviet Union into the arms of Germany.[67] The Polish question—the traditional hinge of Russo-German relations—is scarcely touched upon in the published diplomatic dispatches for the six months after Munich. The Soviet warning to Poland that the USSR would denounce the Soviet-Polish nonaggression pact if Poland marched on Czechoslovakia was interpreted by the German embassy as a "meaningless action," a wordy gesture born of Soviet weakness and isolation.[68] By November 18, Schulenburg had reached the conclusion that Soviet policy had undergone no major change since Munich. The Soviets had not given up "the hope that yesterday's methods (League of Nations, Popular Front) may once more be put to use."[69] Meanwhile, oppressed by the danger of encirclement, the Soviet government would do everything possible to strengthen its armed forces and their industrial base.[70] Herein Schulenburg saw Germany's opportunity for a short-run *détente* based on an economic accord.

Where Dirksen presented his short-range diplomatic proposals in terms of his grandiose objective of a reorganization of international

---

[66] *German Documents*, series D, IV, 607-608. It is not certain that Schulenburg forwarded this memorandum to Berlin at the time.

[67] Robert Coulondre, *De Staline à Hitler* (Paris, 1950), pp. 160-171.

[68] *German Documents*, series D, IV, 606. [69] *ibid.*, 612.

[70] *ibid.*, 610-611, 613.

relations on the basis of an Anglo-German bloc, Schulenburg contented himself with exploiting an unexpected opportunity to strive for a modest *détente* of uncertain duration. Both ambassadors, at the turn of the year, concentrated their diplomatic efforts at the level of economic agreements, the bedrock of international relations. Dirksen had been pushed down to this level as a result of the deterioration of Anglo-German relations in October and November 1938. Schulenburg had climbed up to it out of the poisonous calm of the pre-Munich years.

Schulenburg's modest proposal for economic negotiations met with a reasonably warm response in Berlin. No broad political considerations were involved here. A memorandum by the Director of the Economic Policy Department of the Foreign Office explains the motivation for the discussions, in which Goering's hand is plain to see: "Germany's raw materials situation . . . is such that the emphatic demand has been raised by Field Marshal Göring's office and other interested agencies at least to try to reactivate our Russian trade especially insofar as imports of Russian raw materials are concerned."[71]

In December, preparations for negotiations were begun in Berlin with the deputy Soviet trade representative. The Soviets asked Germany to send a full trade delegation to Moscow for the talks. The Soviet ambassador explained that the invitation was an expression of his country's desire "to begin a new era in German-Soviet economic relations."[72] In the Wilhelmstrasse, counsels were divided. The Director of the Economic Policy Department recommended acceptance of the Soviet invitation. He recognized that "the Soviet government would like to demonstrate to the outside world the value placed . . . by the Third Reich on the continuance of economic relations," and that Germany had no political interest in such a demonstration. But, he advised the Foreign Minister, Germany's need for Soviet raw materials was so great "that it does not appear expedient to frustrate the negotiations in any way."[73]

It was difficult for Ribbentrop to oppose any policy connected with the strengthening of Germany's war economy, but he found the whole prospect of Soviet-German talks uncongenial and untimely. During the month of January, Hitler's and Ribbentrop's East European political interest centered on Poland. Hitler had made his proposals on the questions of Danzig and the Polish corridor to M. Beck on January 5. Ribbentrop was pursuing a scheme for attaining simultaneously Polish

[71] *German Documents*, series D, IV, 608; cf. also a later statement on the origin of the negotiations "on instructions from Field Marshal Goering," *ibid.*, 624.
[72] *ibid.*, 620.　　　　　　　　　　[73] *ibid.*, 621.

acceptance of Hitler's proposals and Polish adherence to the Anti-Comintern Pact. He calculated that Polish national feeling over the loss of Danzig could find outlet in a firm anti-Russian combination with Germany.[74]

At the very time when Goering and the Ministry of Economics were urgently pressing for a Soviet-German economic agreement, Ribbentrop was preparing for a state visit to Warsaw to put the capstone on his anti-Soviet Polish-German combination. Eager to preserve all appearances of Soviet-German antagonism, he refused the Russian request to dispatch a trade mission to the Russian capital. It must have been with great reluctance that Ribbentrop approved, as a compromise arrangement, a visit to Moscow by Julius Schnurre, head of the East European section of the Foreign Office's Economic Policy Department.[75]

To quiet any possible Polish suspicions, Schnurre was to proceed first to Warsaw for economic talks, and to leave for Moscow only on January 30 after Ribbentrop's visit.[76]

On the 26th, Ribbentrop arrived in the Polish capital, where his reception was noticeably cool. Before he had begun serious talks with the Polish leaders, the *Daily Mail* and several French papers published the sensational news that Schnurre was en route to Moscow with a delegation of more than thirty prominent German economic leaders to develop a comprehensive plan for Russo-German economic collaboration.[77] Ribbentrop exploded in a fashion worthy of his Fuehrer. "At the moment when I want to achieve basic collaboration between Germany and Poland against the Soviet Union, they knife me in the back with this scandalous, disruptive report. Schnurre should return to Berlin at once!"[78]

Schnurre did return to Berlin at once and a monkey wrench was thrown into Schulenburg's machinery. So furious was the Foreign Minister over the failure of his Polish plan that he seriously contemplated a rupture of diplomatic relations with the USSR.[79] For once Schulenburg too lost his reserve and gave vent to his irritation at the recall of Schnurre. In a letter to Weizsäcker, he castigated those "to whom the maintenance of Russo-German antagonism is a matter of interest and

[74] Kleist, *Zwischen Hitler und Stalin*, pp. 17-18. As early as August 1937, Ribbentrop had tried to enlist Japanese support to win Polish adherence to the Anti-Comintern Pact. Cf. *German Documents*, series D, I, 750-752.

[75] *German Documents*, series D, I, 621.

[76] *ibid.*, 621-622.

[77] Kleist, *Zwischen Hitler und Stalin*, p. 20.

[78] *ibid.*, pp. 21-22. Cf. also *German Documents*, series D, IV, 622.

[79] Cf. *German Documents*, series D, I, 624-625.

who see something 'suspicious' if we import so much as a little timber, manganese and petroleum from the Soviet Union."[80] He suggested that the Poles were at the bottom of the business—a natural suspicion for a German concerned with Russo-German relations.

Despite the Schnurre incident and Ribbentrop's basically negative attitude toward a *détente* with the USSR, Schulenburg was permitted to pursue economic talks in Moscow until the eve of the march on Prague. The failure of Germany to win Polish assent to its plans no doubt contributed toward keeping the door to Russia ajar, but the decisive factor would seem to have been the insistence of Goering and other economic officials on the need for Russia's raw materials. It was only when the latter withdrew their support that Schulenburg's work was suspended.

On March 8, Schulenburg learned that Berlin was no longer willing to continue serious negotiations. This time it was the Ministry of Economics which spoke the decisive word:

"The pending negotiations . . . must be brought to a stand-still in a suitable way because [the] German economy, on account of its preoccupation with certain domestic tasks, is not in a position to make the necessary deliveries. . . . This deterioration of the production situation arose only recently as a result of newly issued instructions.

"It is generally agreed that the rupture of credit negotiations is regrettable in view of Germany's raw materials position. . . ."[81]

The "domestic tasks" with which the German economy was to be preoccupied can only refer to a vast increase in armaments production. As the needs of Germany's war economy had motivated the economic overtures to the Soviet Union, the acceleration of its production of direct armaments items on the eve of the second Czech crisis brought the negotiations to a halt. Whatever Schulenburg's personal attitudes, the German government had been motivated primarily by military-economic, not by political, considerations, and these no longer demanded a Russo-German economic accord. *Mutatis mutandis*, Schulenburg's situation was not dissimilar to Dirksen's in March 1939. The "constructive" diplomatic labors of both ambassadors after Munich had been disrupted by their government which, for the time being, had lost all interest in diplomacy as an instrument of international policy.

VI

Not until May 1939 was Dirksen informed that he should return to his London post. This time he refused to go unless Ribbentrop would

[80] *ibid.*, 623.   [81] *German Documents*, series D, IV, 630-631.

receive him first.[82] A strange Foreign Office, where an ambassador could gain access to his minister only by threatening to withhold his service.

Ribbentrop's instructions were clear and scarcely promising: ". . . We did not want war with Britain, but . . . were prepared for all eventualities. If Poland started anything with Germany, she would be smashed. We were prepared for a ten years', even for a twenty years' war. The British should stop supporting Poland."[83]

Given the nature of these instructions, and the concentration of British policy on somehow reconstructing the shattered security system against Germany, Dirksen decided to make no formal contact with the British until some approach should be forthcoming from their side. He felt he had to avoid any further weakening of his position in Berlin, and hence abandoned his pre-Prague "eager beaver" style for one of correctness and cautious informal probing.[84]

We have little documentary evidence for Dirksen's activity during May and June of 1939. His later account of his conception of his assignment at that time is consistent with what we know of his behavior. He saw his task as a threefold one: to warn his superiors of the determination of Great Britain to resist further aggression; to warn the British of the consequences of their "encirclement policy"; and to be alert to any possibilities for a *détente*.[85]

The execution of the second of these tasks was not uncongenial to Dirksen. He firmly believed in the justice of Hitler's anti-Polish policy. Like most German nationalists, he held the Poles in complete contempt, a contempt fortified in his case by service in Warsaw and Danzig in younger years. "Britain, by her guarantee to Poland, had placed the peace of the world in the hands of minor Polish officials and military men," Dirksen argued. In informal conversations, he regaled Halifax and others with examples of Polish adventurism and turpitude.[86] He wanted, he tells us in his final report, "to enlighten the English, who are unsophisticated in continental, and especially in East European, affairs, on the nature of the Polish State, and on our claims to Danzig and the Corridor."[87] He likewise left his British interlocutors in no doubt that the German people "were unanimously determined to parry this danger of encirclement and not to tolerate a repetition of 1914."[88] Tirelessly as ever, Dirksen labored to create understanding of Germany's stated aims.

[82] *Dirksen Papers*, p. 172.   [83] *ibid.*
[84] Dirksen, *Moskau, Tokio, London*, p. 247; *Dirksen Papers*, pp. 173-177.
[85] Dirksen, *Moskau, Tokio, London*, p. 247.   [86] *ibid.*, pp. 247-248.
[87] *Dirksen Papers*, p. 177.   [88] *ibid.*

Dirksen's will to believe in the power of the British appeasers was as unshakable as his faith in the ultimate reasonableness of Hitler, and both added up to the conviction that war could still be avoided. After the great wave of British indignation over Danzig in early July, Dirksen reported soberly that the British people would "not tolerate any more nonsense," were ready to fight, and had "taken over the initiative from the Government," and were "spurring the Cabinet on." Yet he closed his dispatch with a cheerful note: "The wave of excitement will ebb just as it rose, as soon as the proper conditions exist. The most important condition is a quieter atmosphere in England which would permit a more unprejudiced assessment of the German viewpoint. The germs of this already exist. Within the Cabinet and a small but influential group of politicians, a desire is manifested to pass from the negativity of the encirclement front to a constructive policy toward Germany. And however strong the counter-forces trying to stifle this tender plant may be— Chamberlain's personality is a certain guarantee that British policy will not be placed in the hands of unscrupulous adventurers [i.e., Churchill, Eden, etc.]."[89]

Was Dirksen too starry-eyed in his belief that something might yet be gained from the appeasers? He saw the "growing disillusionment" with Poland and Russia during the early summer. He knew well the reluctance of the Cabinet to enter the partnership with Bolshevism which public and Parliament were forcing upon it. In Chamberlain's and Halifax's speeches he read signs of a "dual policy": "England wants by means of armament and the acquisition of allies to make herself strong and equal to the Axis, but at the same time she wants by means of negotiations to seek an adjustment with Germany, and is prepared to make sacrifices for it: on the questions of the colonies, raw materials supplies, *Lebensraum*, and spheres of economic influence."[90]

How should Dirksen exploit this weakness in the encirclement front? Through Ribbentrop there was of course no hope. His mind turned to the selection of some Britisher who could talk directly to Hitler—"a person whom the Fuehrer would find congenial, that is, a straightforward, blunt and soldierly fellow who at the same time spoke German."[91] Dirksen's faith in Hitler is revealed in his explanation of the motivation of this approach to a *détente*: it was a remembered remark of Hitler, that "it would be easier to remove all difficulties with England

[89] *Dirksen Papers*, pp. 65-66.   [90] *ibid.*, p. 176.
[91] *ibid.*, p. 178.

if he could converse in German for two hours with a reasonable Englishman."[92]

Before the ambassador and his British friends had hit upon the proper
person to approach the source of all power, Chamberlain and his good
man Friday, Sir Horace Wilson, took the matter into their own hands.
In mid-July, even as the British negotiations in Moscow were approaching the critical stage, the government made its final effort to make those
broad concessions to Hitler which might enable the Cabinet to restore
its foreign policy to a German axis. Before examining the content of
the Wilson-Wohltat conversations in which the British made their
final offer, we must briefly review the activities of Count Schulenburg
in Moscow; for upon them the last efforts of Dirksen and the British
to rebuild the collapsed structure of Munich were about to founder.

Ambassador Schulenburg's situation in the two months following
the seizure of Prague could hardly have seemed to him more promising
than Anglo-German relations did to Dirksen. His own government had
called off the economic negotiations which had finally been inaugurated
after so many difficulties. If the deterioration of Polish-German relations and Britain's extension of a guarantee to Poland created the objective basis for a Soviet-German accord, neither the Germans nor the
Russians were in any hurry to reconstruct their policies on this foundation. Though the documentary evidence is sparse, there seems little
evidence to support the contention, based on the testimony of Ribbentrop and Molotov in August and September 1939, that Stalin's speech
to the Eighteenth Communist Party Congress "brought about the reversal in political relations" between the two countries.[93] By mid-April,
Britain, France, and Russia had resumed their tentative exchanges looking toward the formation of a united front against the aggressor.

It must have been amply clear to the ambassador that, with the collapse of the Locarno-Munich system at Prague, the USSR controlled the
balance of power in Europe, and that his task, even as Dirksen's, must
be to forestall the encirclement of Germany by every means at his command. But there is no evidence that his superiors gave him any specific
instructions to pursue this objective. Nor did Russia go beyond the
hint of Ambassador Merekalov to Weizsäcker (April 17, 1939) that

[92] Dirksen, *Moskau, Tokio, London*, p. 249.
[93] A. Rossi, *The Russo-German Alliance* (London, 1950), pp. 7-10; for a sounder
analysis, see Royal Institute of International Affairs, *Survey of International Affairs,
1939-1946: The World in March 1939* (London, New York, Toronto, 1952), pp.
530-531.

"there was no reason why she should not live with us [Germans] on a normal footing."[94]

Even Molotov's appointment as Foreign Commissar was not heralded by the German mission as the dawn of a new era, although Tippelskirch, Schulenburg's counselor of embassy, cautiously observed that the appointment was apparently connected with "differences of opinion in the Kremlin on Litvinov's negotiations" and Stalin's "caution lest the Soviet Union be drawn into conflicts."[95] In the succeeding weeks, however, the Soviet chargé in Berlin indicated in several quarters that his government desired better relations with Germany.[96] For a month, there had been discussions in Berlin about a political approach to the USSR.[97] This time Ribbentrop decided to put out a feeler in his turn, and instructed Schulenburg to suggest to Molotov the resumption of economic negotiations. These would be carried on in Moscow by the same Herr Schnurre whose visit had been so abruptly canceled in January.

In Schulenburg's conversation with Molotov on May 20, the Foreign Commissar was friendly, but scarcely open. He stated that the Soviet government had got the impression from the course of the previous economic discussions that the Germans "had only played at negotiating for political reasons. . . . The Soviet Government could only agree to a resumption of negotiations if the necessary 'political basis' for them had been constructed."[98] Schulenburg pressed Molotov in vain for a definition of his idea of the "necessary political basis." In reporting to Weizsäcker, the ambassador interpreted Molotov's position as an invitation to "more extensive proposals of a political nature" from the German side, which it certainly was. Schulenburg, more than usually bearish, offered no suggestions as to what Germany might propose. Just as Molotov feared that the Germans might use new talks merely to impede the Anglo-Russian negotiations, Schulenburg urged "extreme caution" in advancing political proposals "as long as it is not certain that . . . they will not be used by the Kremlin only to exert pressure on England and France. On the other hand, if we want to accomplish something here, it

[94] *Nazi-Soviet Relations*, p. 2. According to Peter Kleist (*Zwischen Hitler und Stalin*, pp. 26-29), the Soviet chargé informally expressed to him Russia's willingness for such a far-reaching agreement with Germany but Hitler and Ribbentrop were "frightened off" by it.

[95] *Nazi-Soviet Relations*, pp. 2-3. For an excellent statement of the significance of Molotov's appointment for Soviet policy, see W. L. Langer and S. E. Gleason, *The Challenge to Isolation, 1937-1940* (New York, 1952), pp. 105-107.

[96] *Nazi-Soviet Relations*, pp. 3-5.

[97] Kleist, *Zwischen Hitler und Stalin*, pp. 30-38.

[98] *Nazi-Soviet Relations*, pp. 5-7.

is unavoidable that we sooner or later take some action."[99] The ambassador saw the dilemma, but offered no way out of it. On May 21, Weizsäcker informed Schulenburg that Germany "would now sit tight and wait to see if the Russians would speak more openly," and "to see how deeply Moscow on the one hand and Paris-London on the other are willing to commit themselves."[100]

Scarcely had the order to sit tight been given when two new factors suddenly increased the importance of Russia to Germany, both positively and negatively. On May 23, Hitler announced to his intimate advisers his intention "to attack Poland at the first opportunity." On May 24, Chamberlain reported to the House of Commons that the Anglo-Russian conversations had produced agreement on essentials.[101] On May 30, Schulenburg was informed by Weizsäcker of a change in line: "Contrary to the policy previously planned, we have now decided to undertake definite negotiations with Moscow."[102]

During June and July, most of the initiative was on the German side, but the negotiations proceeded slowly. The Russians took every advantage of the fact that they were being wooed by both the Western Powers and the Reich, and maintained a frigid reserve. To both sides, to be sure, they gave occasional encouragement. Thus on June 14, the Soviet chargé in Berlin told the Bulgarian minister—clearly for Wilhelmstrasse consumption: "If Germany would declare that she would not attack the Soviet Union or that she would conclude a non-aggression pact with her, the Soviet Union would probably refrain from concluding a treaty with England."[103]

While the Germans kept hinting at possible areas of mutual interest—Poland, the Baltic states, the Berlin Treaty—the Russians responded by raising doubts as to Germany's intentions. Mikoyan, Commissar of Foreign Trade, proved a particularly sticky negotiator in the economic talks.[104]

By the end of June, Berlin was getting distinctly fed up, and Schulenburg knew it. He tried to describe progress where little was to be recorded.[105] On June 29, Hitler very nearly called off the entire negotiations,[106] while Ribbentrop decided that Schulenburg should say nothing more in the political field until further notice.[107] In the first weeks of

[99] *ibid.*, pp. 8-9.   [100] *ibid.*, pp. 7, 9.
[101] E. H. Carr, *German-Soviet Relations between the Two World Wars* (Baltimore, 1951), pp. 130-131.
[102] *Nazi-Soviet Relations*, p. 15.   [103] *ibid.*, p. 21.
[104] Cf. e.g. *Nazi-Soviet Relations*, pp. 21-25.
[105] Cf. his interpretation of his interview with Molotov on June 29, *ibid.*, p. 27.
[106] *ibid.*, pp. 25-26.   [107] *ibid.*, pp. 27-28.

July, Schulenburg seems to have feared that he would be reassigned, and asked his counselor of embassy to intercede with the personnel division to keep him at his post.[108] Tippelskirch tried to reassure the Foreign Office that "the Embassy and particularly . . . [Schulenburg] had done everything possible, but he could not drag Molotov and Mikoyan through the Brandenburger Tor."[109]

From June 29 to July 21, the economic negotiations seem to have been deadlocked. Then on July 22, the Soviets suddenly announced their resumption.[110] It seems to have been the Russians who broke the deadlock with a concession: to resume the economic negotiations, previously conducted in Moscow, in Berlin. Schulenburg had suggested such a course to the Wilhelmstrasse as a way of circumventing the thorny Mr. Mikoyan.[111] Just when the Germans proposed this solution to the Soviets does not emerge from the documents; on the basis of previous Russian sensitivity concerning the site of the discussions, however, one can only assume that the Russians finally accepted the German proposal in order to get the negotiations resumed. On July 24, only two days after the Russian overture to the Germans, Molotov made a concession to the West to break a deadlock of several weeks duration in the negotiations with Britain and France.[112] The Russian game of pitting its suitors against each other began to be played in earnest.

In the meantime, Prime Minister Chamberlain, who had been forced into the talks with the Soviet Union against all his instincts, developed a double game of his own. On or about July 20—two days before the Russian overture to Germany and four before Molotov's to Britain—Chamberlain tried to return to his appeasement policy with an offer of a "world-political partnership" between Britain and Germany. The recipient of this proposal was Goering's special assistant, Dr. Wohltat, who was attending the International Whaling Conference in London. Secretary Hudson of the British Ministry of Overseas Trade approached Wohltat on July 20 with plans for joint Anglo-German exploitation of world markets, notably those of the British Empire, China, and the USSR. Like a voice from the 1890's, Hudson spoke of delineating spheres of economic interest between the two Powers in order to avoid competi-

---

[108] *ibid.*, p. 31.   [109] *ibid.*
[110] *ibid.*, p. 25. The month-long deadlock is deduced from the absence of any documents in the collection.
[111] *ibid.*, p. 27.
[112] The full story of these negotiations has yet to be told. The most comprehensive, though often conflicting, accounts are to be found in Namier, *Diplomatic Prelude*, pp. 143-210 and Langer and Gleason, *Challenge to Isolation*, pp. 115-121.

tion.[113] Sir Horace Wilson supplemented Hudson's proposals in two conversations with Wohltat, in which he set forth in broad outline an agreement on political, military, and economic matters.[114] Wilson spoke from a prepared paper, and invited Wohltat to confirm Chamberlain's support of its contents by a personal interview with the Prime Minister, which the German declined. The conclusion of a nonaggression pact was the heart of Wilson's program—not "the customary pacts of nonaggression which Germany had concluded with other powers," but one which would involve "renunciation of aggression in principle."[115] According to Dirksen's memorandum on the second conversation, "Sir Horace Wilson definitely told Herr Wohltat that the conclusion of a nonaggression pact would enable Britain to rid herself of her commitments vis-à-vis Poland." The two nations were also to conclude a pact of nonintervention which was to embrace a "delimitation of spheres (*Grossräume*) of the Great Powers, in particular as between Britain and Germany." Some kind of international scheme for the governance of Africa was adumbrated to meet Germany's colonial demands. Finally, Sir Horace added that the British government would agree to the Germans adding any other questions to the agenda: "The Fuehrer had only to take a sheet of paper and jot down his points; the British Government would be prepared to discuss them." The decisive thing, Sir Horace said, was that the Fuehrer designate someone to discuss the program. Once this step were taken, "it was immaterial to the British how the further negotiations were conducted." Dr. Wohltat agreed to try to find out "whether the Fuehrer considered that the moment had now come to start such discussions."

Ambassador Dirksen was, of course, only on the periphery of these discussions. Nevertheless, he leapt at them as a proof of his earlier contention (June 24) that the British government was moving away from encirclement and toward a more "constructive" policy. Moreover, the strange amalgam of fin-de-siècle imperialism and Kellogg-Briand utopianism reflected in the proposals, if most ill-suited to Hitler's temperament, was quite congenial to Dirksen's. While the primary responsibility for reporting them lay with Wohltat, Dirksen, in a dispatch of July 24, outlined the principal points of Wilson's proposals, and emphasized that Germany must make the next move—and that soon—if "Churchill and the other incendiaries" were to be thwarted.[116]

[113] *Dirksen Papers*, pp. 67-68. See also *Documenti Italiani*, 8th series, XII, 511-512.
[114] *Dirksen Papers*, pp. 67-68. [115] *ibid.*, pp. 68-72.
[116] *ibid.*, pp. 73-76.

We do not know when the pouch bearing Dirksen's significant dispatch of July 24 reached Berlin. By the 31st, neither Ribbentrop nor Weizsäcker had seen it.[117] Their first knowledge of the full scope of the British proposals came in the form of Wohltat's written report which was transmitted to the Foreign Minister by Field Marshal Goering.[118] On July 31, Ribbentrop sent Dirksen a heated telegram requesting an immediate report on Wohltat's negotiations—"especially a report on Wohltat's conversations with you, since he states that the political negotiations were conducted in agreement with the Ambassador."[119]

Goering had, no doubt, sent a copy of Wohltat's report to the Fuehrer. But more was at stake now than the rivalry between two high Nazi courtiers. On July 25, it became known that France and Britain were sending military missions to Moscow. Ribbentrop decided to press the Russian negotiations on the broadest possible basis and "at an unheard-of tempo."[120] On July 26, on Ribbentrop's instructions, Schnurre had really put the German cards on the table in an informal evening of conversation with the Soviet chargé and the chief of the trade mission. He had proposed the establishment of really good relations in a series of stages, of which the last would remove all conflicts of interest from the Baltic to the Black Sea. German policy, said Schnurre, was aimed primarily against England. "What could England offer Russia? At best, participation in a European war and the hostility of Germany, but not a single desirable end for Russia. What could we offer on the other hand? Neutrality and staying out of a European conflict and, if Moscow wished, a German-Russian understanding which, just as in former times, would work out to the interests of both countries."[121] But, he argued against the Russians, agreement must be reached quickly. If Russia should come to an accord with Britain, it would be too late.

On July 29, Weizsäcker drafted instructions to Schulenburg to sound out Molotov for his reaction to Schnurre's overtures. If Molotov abandoned his previous reserve, Schulenburg was to "advance another step": to introduce the Polish question and to express Germany's readiness for an understanding with the Soviets on Poland against the possibility of war.[122] Thus when Wohltat's report of the British overture reached the Wilhelmstrasse, Germany was sailing full steam ahead toward the east.

[117] *Dirksen Papers*, pp. 88, 91-92.   [118] *ibid.*, p. 91.
[119] *ibid.*, p. 88.
[120] Kleist, *Zwischen Hitler und Stalin*, p. 46.
[121] *Nazi-Soviet Relations*, p. 34; for the entire discussion, see pp. 32-36.
[122] *ibid.*, p. 36.

The Chamberlain-Wilson offer must have thrown open once more the whole question of Germany's foreign policy, if only for a moment. Germany had been competing with Britain for the favor of Russia on the assumption that she could not realize her aims in Eastern Europe without Britain resorting to arms. Now Germany, the aggressor, was herself being courted by Britain with an offer which would "enable Britain to rid herself of her commitments *vis-à-vis* Poland." In the extraordinary triangle of European power politics, Germany was now the wooed. How should she choose?

In working out an answer, Weizsäcker called on Dirksen. Nine hours after Ribbentrop had dispatched his peremptory telegram, Weizsäcker sent another, asking the ambassador "whether these British overtures presume at the same time the abandonment of the encirclement policy negotiations, in particular with Moscow."[123] Dirksen answered with a vigorous affirmative: "leading persons" in London regarded an adjustment with Germany as obviously incompatible with the prosecution of the encirclement policy. "The continuation of the negotiations for a pact with Russia, in spite of—or rather, just because of—the dispatch of a military mission is regarded here with skepticism. This is borne out by the composition of the British military mission: the admiral, until now Commandant of Portsmouth, is practically in retirement, and was never on the staff of the Admiralty; the general is likewise purely a combatant officer; the air general is an outstanding aviator and air instructor, but not a strategist. This indicates that the object of the military mission is more to ascertain the fighting value of the Soviet Army than to make operational arrangements."[124]

Poor Dirksen! He thought that this information could only heighten the Foreign Minister's receptivity to the British overtures. Instead it had the opposite effect. The ambassador confirmed what was implied by Chamberlain's overtures: that the Anglo-Russian military negotiations would come to naught, for, whatever the Soviet attitude, the British were not really interested. Dirksen's belief that his masters would under these circumstances be interested in an adjustment with Britain that would "chemically dissolve the Danzig problem" was superannuated, to say the least.

On the evening of August 2, the day when Dirksen's answer to

[123] *Dirksen Papers*, pp. 91-92.
[124] *Dirksen Papers*, p. 103. This statement throws some incidental light on the veracity of Weizsäcker, who tells us in his *Erinnerungen* (Munich, 1950), (p. 246) that he was certain from the reports of the ambassador in London of the successful prosecution of Russo-French-British negotiations.

Weizsäcker had probably arrived in Berlin,[125] Ribbentrop summoned the Russian chargé. He resumed the line taken by Schnurre on July 26, but with a new air of assurance. There was no longer any talk of speedy solutions. Ribbentrop stated that "our policy was a direct and long-range one; we were in no hurry. . . . We were making no fuss about it; the choice lay . . . in Moscow."[126] The Foreign Minister, with a new sense of security, was enjoying his work. On August 3 he reversed previous instructions for Schulenburg to carry on the conversations in Moscow: "We are anxious to continue . . . the clarification . . . *in Berlin*."[127]

The tragi-comedy of the two ambassadors was nearing its end. Neither Dirksen nor Schulenburg were quite irrational enough to be realistic in evaluating the strange diplomatic world of August 1939. Dirksen pursued the will-o'-the-wisp of an Anglo-German world-political partnership which would solve the Danzig problem without war. In a two-hour conversation with Sir Horace Wilson on August 3, Dirksen convinced himself that a German reply to the British feeler could save the day.[128] He resolved to go to Berlin to throw his weight behind earnest consideration of the British proposition—"perhaps in collaboration with Wohltat." Arriving on August 14 after a departure oddly leisurely, Dirksen found the city alive with rumors of the impending blow against Poland. When he asked Weizsäcker how his reports on the British proposals had been received, the Secretary of State "shrugged his shoulders and made a gesture as though he were brushing something off the table." Dirksen learned that his reports of the Wilson conversations had been interpreted as a further sign of British weakness.[129] He learned too that Germany's masters did not believe that the British would intervene in the German-Polish war. The ambassador who had come home to preach one illusion now had to devote himself to dispelling another. But he could find no audience for his warnings. Ribbentrop scolded him from afar for his defeatist utterances, but would not receive him.

Dirksen's experience in the last weeks before the war reads like that of the protagonist of Kafka's *The Castle*: the same hopeless attempt to reach the masters who neither wanted nor released him, the same incapacity to grasp the nonrational rules by which the Castle operated, the same ambiguous treatment by the lower officials, and the same blind effort to serve rather than merely to obey. It was a fitting if psychologi-

---

[125] Dirksen's briefer telegram of July 31 had certainly been received by that time. Cf. *Dirksen Papers*, pp. 89-90.
[126] *Nazi-Soviet Relations*, p. 38.   [127] *ibid.*, p. 37. Italics mine.
[128] *Dirksen Papers*, pp. 117-125.
[129] Dirksen, *Moskau, Tokio, London*, pp. 255-256.

cally gruesome climax to Dirksen's career under the Nazis. Equally fitting was the fact that he neither resigned nor was fired. He simply withdrew to his Gröditzberg estates on indefinite leave, to remain there until the Russians drove him out.

Was Count Schulenburg better able to understand the world of August 1939 than his London colleague? His task was easier, he was riding the wave. But down to the last ten days of the Russo-German negotiations, his analyses would hardly have justified confidence in the early conclusion of the pact. His belief in Soviet mistrust of Germany was too well grounded by his long experience. On August 4, he wrote after an interview with Molotov: "My overall impression is that the Soviet Government is at present determined to sign with England and France if they fulfill all Soviet wishes. I believe that my statements made an impression on M.; it will nevertheless take considerable effort on our part to cause the Soviet Government to swing about."[130] Perhaps Schulenburg was right in principle; what he lacked was the knowledge which Ribbentrop had just received from Dirksen: that England had no intention whatever of "fulfilling all Soviet wishes." On August 10, the Soviet chargé in Berlin, while indicating that Russia's negotiations with England "had been entered upon without much enthusiasm," felt that his government, even though the conversations with Germany were well under way, still could not "break off something which had been begun after mature consideration."[131] A few days later, Schulenburg wrote to Weizsäcker: "I am still of the opinion that any hasty measure in the matter of our relations with the Soviet Union should be avoided; it will almost always be harmful. . . . The British and French military missions have been in Moscow for three days now. . . . I assume that the negotiations will last a long time."[132] While Schulenburg was committing these restrained notions to paper (August 14), Ribbentrop was drafting his dramatic proposal for a personal visit to Stalin to "clear up jointly the territorial problems of Eastern Europe." Less than ten days later, the Nazi-Soviet Pact was signed, the diplomatic revolution accomplished.

However responsible Schulenburg may have been for the groundwork of the Russo-German alliance, he neither advised Ribbentrop's lightning courtship of Stalin nor anticipated its astonishing success. Like Dirksen, Schulenburg moved in a political world he could not fully understand. But where Dirksen erred on the plus side in his evaluation of diplomatic possibilities, Schulenburg erred on the minus side. The Moscow ambassa-

---

[130] *Nazi-Soviet Relations*, p. 41.   [131] *ibid.*, p. 46.
[132] *ibid.*, p. 41.

dor shared few of the illusions about Nazi Germany which captured the imagination of Dirksen and his idol, Neville Chamberlain. For all his sustained skeptical realism, Schulenburg permitted himself to overestimate the rationality of the Nazis on one fateful point: that they would not jettison an achievement of such obvious value to the German national interest as the Russo-German Pact in favor of a suicidal two-front war. Less than two years after the victory of the eastern orientation which ended Dirksen's career, Schulenburg found himself recapitulating Dirksen's experience of August 1939, vainly trying to dissuade his superiors from launching an unnecessary war on false political assumptions. Thus for all their differences in temperament and character, Schulenburg and Dirksen saw their intertwined but polaric diplomatic achievements united in destruction. Both had to learn the hard way that the time-honored principles of *Realpolitik* could not be made to govern the political behavior of Nazi Germany.

Though their diplomatic labors met a common fate, the two men drew different consequences from it, each according to his character and social tradition. Dirksen, who could not contemplate a revolt against constituted authority, whatever its nature, withdrew from politics into the spurious but satisfyingly aristocratic isolation of a Silesian *Rittergutsbesitzer*. It was the role his father had cut out for him many years before. Schulenburg, heritor of an older and more autonomous aristocratic tradition, stayed in the civil service but entered the resistance movement. In doing so, he was motivated still by his loyalty to the German state. The same allegiance to an abstraction which had enabled him to justify his service to the Nazis for a decade led to him to rebel against them. For his conception of *Staatsräson* permitted him, however belatedly, to distinguish, in Germany as in Russia, between the state and those who held power in it. His realism told him when to break from the latter in the interest of the former. Had the plot against Hitler succeeded, Schulenburg might have become the Foreign Minister of the state he hoped to save from destruction. Instead, with other aristocrats of the old school, he met his death in the attempt.

16

Ciano and his Ambassadors

BY FELIX GILBERT

"IN ITALY, the most Fascist ministry is that of Foreign Affairs," Galeazzo Ciano said proudly to a German visitor in October 1937.[1] The Fascist penetration of the Italian Foreign Office appeared to him a remarkable achievement, the result of a slow and difficult process; it is clear, moreover, that he believed that he deserved the credit for having accomplished it. "In Italy," he confided to his Diary, "fifteen years were needed to conquer the Palazzo Chigi."[2] The time span mentioned is significant. Ciano himself had become Foreign Minister in 1936, just as the fifteenth year of the Fascist regime was dawning; and there is no doubt that he believed that his arrival at the Palazzo Chigi was the decisive event through which Italian foreign policy became fully Fascist.

Ciano's Diary is full of sudden ideas without practical consequences, of fleeting thoughts which disappeared as soon as they had been put down in black and white. As a source for the history of Italian diplomacy, the Diary must be used with caution.[3] But Ciano returned so frequently and insistently to the claim that, under his direction, Italian foreign policy had become a malleable instrument of the regime, that this view must be accepted as a true expression of his mind, as one of his basic ideas.

But what does Ciano actually mean by the assertion that he had imposed a Fascist pattern on Italian foreign policy? Did his arrival in the Palazzo Chigi imply a change in Italian diplomacy? Was a tradition— the tradition of professional diplomacy which worked within the rules of the game and on the foundation of historically tested experience— thrown overboard and replaced by a new Fascist diplomacy with different methods and new aims? Was there any reality behind Ciano's airy claim of having introduced a truly Fascist diplomacy?

[1] Galeazzo Ciano, *1937-1938 Diario* (Bologna, 1948), p. 40.
[2] *ibid.*, p. 55.
[3] On the authenticity of Ciano's Diary and on the value of its various editions, see Mario Toscano, "Fonti documentarie e memorialistiche per la storia diplomatica della seconda guerra mondiale," *Rivista Storica Italiana*, LX (1948), 106-108.

The most obvious explanation is that Ciano believed he was the first real Fascist installed at the head of the Palazzo Chigi. A closer examination of this statement is interesting because of the light it sheds on the view which Ciano held about his own role in the Fascist regime. Insofar as it testifies to the influence which diplomatic tradition and professional diplomats had exerted in the first decade of the Fascist regime, the statement contains an element of truth. As it was shown in a previous chapter,[4] even the appointment of such a zealous Fascist as Dino Grandi had not broken the strength of this tradition. On the contrary the professionals had tamed the young radical and made him an advocate, among the party hierarchy, for the maintenance of the traditional course. Grandi's dismissal in 1932 was the result of Mussolini's dissatisfaction with the docility with which his Foreign Minister had absorbed the atmosphere of professional diplomacy. According to Mussolini, Grandi "had permitted himself to become prisoner of the League of Nations, had conducted a pacific and internationalist policy, had acted the ultra-democrat and League of Nations man; he had made Italian policy deviate from the straight course of egoism and realism and compromised the aspirations of a new generation."[5]

But when, after Grandi's departure, Mussolini took over the Foreign Ministry, changes were less radical and thorough than one would have expected. For this there were various reasons. Being not only Foreign Minister but also head of the government, Mussolini was unable to exert a detailed control and supervision over the Palazzo Chigi from the Palazzo Venezia. The new situation created by the rise of Nazism demanded experience and caution. Because of the widening gap between the Western Powers and Germany, and because of the Nazi pressure on Austria, Italian foreign policy was not only offered new opportunities but it was also faced with new dangers. There was no fundamental conflict between Mussolini and the professionals about the evaluation of this new situation. The career diplomats shared Mussolini's view that the rift among the Great Powers offered a unique chance for the realization of Italy's African aspirations, and the Palazzo Chigi took an active part in preparing the developments which led to the Abyssinian War.[6] In the course of the Abyssinian crisis, however, a divergence of views emerged. The professionals were concerned with making the Abyssinian enterprise

[4] See Chapter 7, §III above.

[5] Roberto Cantalupo, *Fu la Spagna. Ambasciata presso Franco Febbraio-Aprile 1937* (Verona, 1948), p. 42.

[6] See Raffaele Guariglia, *Ricordi 1922-1946* (Napoli, 1949), pp. 212ff.

an episode rather than a new departure and with preventing a development which would constitute a definite and final break with the traditional system of Italian foreign policy. They looked with skepticism upon
the Fascist claim that through the conquest of the African empire, Italy
had been raised to the status of a Great Power of the first rank; thereby
they laid themselves open to the accusation of diplomatic pusillanimity
and betrayal of the heroic spirit of the regime. A press campaign making
such charges was promoted by the Ministry of Press and Propaganda
over which Ciano then presided, and this served to prepare his entry
into the Palazzo Chigi.[7] Thus Ciano took over as the representative of
the Fascist outlook.

Even if there is some basis for the claim that, before 1936, the Italian
Foreign Office had not been much affected by party enthusiasm and had
preserved a traditional outlook in foreign affairs, few people in Italy
would have considered Galeazzo Ciano as particularly suited for the task
of accomplishing the Fascization of the Palazzo Chigi, for he was far
from being a typical representative of the Fascist party. Ciano's unique
position in the Fascist hierarchy is sharply outlined in a story told by
Gafencu.[8] The Rumanian statesman was present when an official delegation arrived for a reception with the Italian king. The Duce was march-
ing at the head, clad in his black shirt; his glance was imperious, his gait
exaggerated, the dignitaries followed in serried ranks; in front of them,
but behind the Duce, walked Count Ciano, sprightly and carefree, waving
joyously whenever he saw an acquaintance.

Ciano stood out from the bulk of Fascist hierarchs. In party circles he
was a most unpopular figure. The older leaders of the party—men like
De Bono and Volpi who had been well known when they had joined
Mussolini's movement after the first world war—considered Ciano as a
spoiled child of fortune, raised to prominence because he was the son of
one of Mussolini's chief assistants and the Duce's son-in-law. Ciano fully
reciprocated these feelings; his Diary indicates that he considered these
older leaders as unbearably dull and loquacious fools;[9] it seems most
unlikely that in his behavior he succeeded entirely in concealing the contempt he felt for them. The widely held belief that Ciano was groomed
by Mussolini to become his successor must have been resented by the
men of the middle generation like Grandi and Balbo whose chances for
succession were ruined by the arrival of this youngster. The glee with

[7] *ibid.*, pp. 213, 328.

[8] Grigore Gafencu, *The Last Days of Europe* (London, 1947), p. 136.

[9] For instance, Ciano, *1937-1938 Diario*, pp. 34, 125.

which, in his Diary, Ciano sets down every unfriendly thing he hears about them reflects the feelings of rivalry and competition which existed between Ciano and these men. Even before foreigners he gave free vent to such feelings; Grandi, he said to Serrano Suñer, was not worth knowing: "He is quite uninteresting and has the intelligence of a mosquito."[10]

Born in 1903, Ciano was a schoolboy at the time of the march on Rome. While most of the others who had reached prominent positions in the 1930's could claim to have joined the Fascist party when this action involved risks or commitments, Ciano had arrived, after the battle was over, to enjoy the victory and to participate in the loot. His claims to this privilege were supported by good looks and a nimble mind, but certainly more by the influence of a father who had been a national hero of the first world war and subsequently one of Mussolini's most valued collaborators.[11] His alliance by marriage with the family of the Duce was doubtless also useful. In any event, he had no difficulty in advancing rapidly from one interesting job to another—diplomat in Argentina and China, Under-Secretary and Minister of Press and Propaganda—until, at the age of thirty-two, he had become Italy's Foreign Minister and the most important political figure after the Duce. The party hierarchs must have resented the preferment of a man who came to reap the fruits of work performed by others.

It is characteristic of Ciano that he seems to have been quite unconcerned about these chinks in his Fascist armor. He was proud of his youth and gloried in being the representative of a new generation. Institutional questions, like the corporate state—central issues of Fascist belief to a man like Bottai[12]—did not interest Ciano. One is tempted to conclude that he regarded concern over questions of political organization and political principles as something obsolete, as a sign that those who bothered about them had not yet freed themselves from the egg-shells of the pre-Fascist period. Ciano had no doubt that he was a true representative and embodiment of Fascism, but the precise ideas which he associated with this concept are difficult to discover. Perhaps one comes closest to an explanation if one says that Ciano considered Fascism chiefly as a new "style of life"; he regarded himself as a perfect Fascist specimen because only the new generation which had grown up in an atmosphere entirely unencumbered by the heritage of the past could

---

[10] Ramon Serrano Suñer, *Entre Hendaya y Gibraltar* (Mexico, 1947), p. 325.

[11] It should perhaps be noted that, while Ciano's noble title was not of Fascist creation, its origins were very recent. His father had been made Count as a reward for his naval exploits in the war.

[12] Giuseppe Bottai, *Vent'Anni e un Giorno* (Editore Garzanti, 1949).

fully "live" the new attitude. In a passage of his Diary, Ciano gave expression to his admiration for D'Annunzio;[13] it seems likely that in Ciano's rather immature mind Fascism had become identified with the amoral belief in living life to its fullest that one finds in the hero of a D'Annunzio novel. Certainly there is a D'Annunzian flavor to his confession to Serrano Suñer: "Life is always good and pleasant. When I am eighty I shall stroll along here swinging my cane and enjoying the lovely sun. I want to die here in Leghorn after I have seen all my enemies passing before me on their way to death."[14]

But the doubts which could be raised against Ciano from the point of view of Fascist orthodoxy cannot have given much reassurance to the professional diplomats; they had every reason to regard the advent, at the Palazzo Chigi, of this self-styled leader of the young Fascist generation with suspicion and displeasure.

When Ciano spoke of the Fascist outlook which Italian diplomacy acquired in the 1930's was he thinking principally of his influence on foreign policy or could he point also to changes in personnel and organization? In the years preceding Ciano's assumption of office, Fascism had made hardly any inroads in the Diplomatic Service. It is true that in 1928, in order to permeate diplomacy with a new spirit, a number of Fascist party members without special professional training had been taken into the Diplomatic Service, but the power of the professional diplomats had been strong enough to restrict sharply the number of new admissions and to keep the "men of '28," the "*ventottisti*" as they were called by the career diplomats, in subordinate positions.[15] At the first glance it would seem that in Ciano's time also the diplomatic bureaucracy was able to continue its successful resistance against the penetration of outsiders and to preserve its professional and career character.[16] At least during the years before the war, all the great embassies were headed by career diplomats. The key position in Berlin was held by Bernardo Attolico. He had been a member of the Italian delegation at the Paris Peace Conference and, for five years, from 1922 to 1927, had directed the Communications Section in the League of Nations Secretariat at Geneva; he had also served as ambassador in Rio de Janeiro and Moscow before he came to Berlin in 1935. When Ciano became Foreign Minister,

---

[13] Ciano, *1937-1938 Diario*, p. 221, also p. 124.

[14] Serrano Suñer, *Entre Hendaya y Gibraltar*, p. 316.

[15] Mario Donosti, *Mussolini e l'Europa* (Roma, 1945), p. 15.

[16] For a list of the Italian diplomatic corps as of January 23, 1939 and the officials of the Italian Foreign Office as of October 12, 1938, see *Documenti Italiani*, 8th series, XII, 633-645.

Vittorio Cerruti, who had started his diplomatic career at the Italian embassy in the Vienna of the Emperor Francis Joseph, was ambassador in Paris; in 1938 he was replaced by Raffaele Guariglia whose "professionalism" is perhaps best attested by the fact that he became Italian Foreign Minister in 1943 when, after the fall of Mussolini, Badoglio formed his cabinet of technical experts. Also Augusto Rosso, the ambassador in Moscow, had started his service in Italian diplomacy in the prewar era. The only prominent Fascist who directed one of the great European embassies was Dino Grandi, who was in London from 1932 to 1939, but since Mussolini had moved him from Rome to London for being too much inclined to adopt the Foreign Office point of view, Grandi can hardly have been regarded as an alien and hostile element by the professionals.

Representatives abroad had no policy-making function: the policy makers were at Rome, in the Palazzo Chigi. But here too, career diplomats were in charge. Work at the Italian Foreign Office was distributed among three political divisions, that of General Affairs, of European and Mediterranean Affairs, and of Overseas Affairs. Each of these divisions was headed by a director and throughout the 1930's these positions were held by professionals: Leonardo Vitetti, Gino Buti and Emanuele Grazzi. Thus from the point of view of personnel there seems to be little substance to Ciano's claim of having conquered the Palazzo Chigi for Fascism.

But the impression of a continued dominance of the professional tradition in Italian diplomacy is deceiving. A report by Roberto Cantalupo gives insight into the strange situation at the Palazzo Chigi soon after Ciano had taken over.[17] Cantalupo, who was Italian ambassador in Brazil, had returned to Rome after several years of absence from Italy. He found at the same desks the same faces he had known before, but something had changed in the atmosphere. Cantalupo says he felt that "the clockwork was broken." The functionaries were like shadows, moving around in the usual way but without purpose. He was told that the officials did not know what was going on because all important work was done by the Gabinetto. And so he heard for the first time of the growth of that organization which became Ciano's chief instrument for directing the course of Italian foreign policy, and which, in relatively short time, reduced the traditional apparatus to an empty shell.

In the past the Gabinetto had been nothing more than the personal

[17] Cantalupo, *Fu la Spagna*, pp. 67-68.

secretariat of the Foreign Minister. Under Ciano it grew rapidly.[18] He filled it with young men who shared his general attitude towards life and looked up to him admiringly as future leader. "The officials of the Gabinetto 'spoke seldom, but all their words were tuneful sweet,' like those of the great souls banned by Dante into the Limbo, and they treated their colleagues in the other offices with an icy, smiling and contemptuous politeness, typical of a great lord who has dealings with people who don't belong to his class."[19] Among the officials of the Gabinetto, the most influential and probably the most intelligent was Ciano's contemporary and long-standing friend, Filippo Anfuso, who in the later years of Ciano's foreign ministry became head of the Gabinetto.[20] A chief function assumed by the Gabinetto—and the function about which the professional diplomats complained most bitterly—was control over the distribution of incoming information. The officials of the Gabinetto determined whether reports should be handed over to the political desks of the Palazzo Chigi or whether they would be kept in the Gabinetto for the use of the Minister. Thus the Gabinetto developed into a center where all the most important information and reports of special significance were handled.

The memoirs of Italian career diplomats are filled with stories describing the confusion and errors caused by the arbitrary proceedings of the functionaries in the Gabinetto. Newly appointed ambassadors who wanted to read the relevant diplomatic correspondence before leaving for their posts were told by division heads that the most important interchanges were kept in the Gabinetto, that they had not seen them, and that complete files did not exist. A serious mistake occurred in the critical summer of 1939, when the Italian ambassador in Moscow received detailed information about the progress of the German-Russian negotiations from his German colleague in Moscow and forwarded it to Rome. Since Soviet Russia seemed only on the periphery of decisive events, the Gabinetto simply handed the reports from Moscow on to the political desks as of no particular significance. Thus, when the news of the German-Russian agreement arrived, Mussolini and Ciano were more surprised than they should have been, in view of the fact that the Palazzo Chigi was in pos-

---

[18] On the role of the Gabinetto, see—aside from Cantalupo—Emanuele Grazzi, *Il Principio della Fine* (Roma, 1945), pp. 8-11, and in general, Donosti, *Mussolini e l'Europa*, pp. 12-20. See also the introduction to *Documenti Italiani*, 8th series, XII, ix-x.

[19] Grazzi, *Il Principio della Fine*, p. 10.

[20] He has written very revealing memoirs: Filippo Anfuso, *Roma Berlino Salò (1936-1945)* (Editore Garzanti, 1950). He remained loyal to Mussolini till the end.

session of the most relevant facts.[21] This lack of coordination was characteristic of Ciano's reformed Foreign Office and was the result of a development which was of central importance for the conduct of Italian diplomacy: the decline in the importance of the regular political divisions and of the professional diplomats who staffed them.

The key importance which the Gabinetto gained in Ciano's time explains the apparent contrast between his claim to have achieved a Fascization of Italian diplomacy on the one hand and his continued irritation against his professional diplomats and his complaints about their cautiousness, timidity, and lack of true dignity in the face of foreigners on the other.[22] When Ciano spoke of a Fascization of Italian diplomacy he did not mean that he had transformed diplomacy by infiltrating new men, Fascists, into the existing diplomatic bureaucracy. What he could rightly claim was that he had restricted the sphere of action of the professional diplomats. The diplomats were not asked to give advice or make recommendations. Decisions were made from above, perhaps prepared and discussed by the young men whom Ciano had assembled in the Gabinetto. In Ciano's time, Cantalupo remarks, "the Ministry existed only to obey."[23]

The low estimation of the role of professional diplomacy permeated the routine business of diplomacy. There was a kind of silent war, between Ciano and his young men on the one side and the professional diplomats on the other. Ciano wanted to keep all the threads in his own hands, perhaps because he was afraid that the professionals might take concerted action against him. He discouraged direct contacts and exchange of information among the Italian ambassadors. Neither information about the general political situation nor news of developments with which they were specifically concerned were regularly transmitted to the Italian representatives abroad.[24] Ambassadors had to leave for new destinations without thorough briefing; when they wanted to see Ciano before their departure he had nothing to say to them and often no time to receive them.[25] This happened so frequently that it cannot have been entirely by accident, although occasionally Ciano's lack of time may have been caused by his passionate devotion to the pleasures of Roman society.

[21] Mario Toscano, *L'Italia e gli Accordi Tedesco-Sovietici dell' Agosto 1939* (Firenze, 1952), p. 38.

[22] Ciano, *1937-1938 Diario*, pp. 75-76, or *Diario* (Milano, 1948), I, 17.

[23] Cantalupo, *Fu la Spagna*, p. 67.

[24] Guariglia, *Ricordi*, pp. 357-358; Grazzi, *Il Principio della Fine*, p. 123.

[25] Guariglia, *Ricordi*, p. 357; Grazzi, *Il Principio della Fine*, p. 18; Dino Alfieri, *Due Dittatori di fronte* (Milano, 1948), p. 23.

Because of the distrust with which the Gabinetto regarded the professional diplomats, its young men placed little reliance on the heads of missions for collection and evaluation of information, but tried to develop an information service of their own, sometimes with grotesque results. When, after the outbreak of the second world war, the Italian ambassador in Athens maintained that the British had no intentions of landing in Greece, the Gabinetto refused to accept this view and turned directly to the various Italian consuls. It is reported that even Ciano's young men were startled when in reply they received from one of the consuls the following telegram: "The hairdresser of my wife told her this morning that a British landing is expected within a week."[26]

Quite in accordance with this contempt for professional diplomats, Ciano liked to work outside the regular diplomatic channels. At important embassies he had confidants, through whom he acted behind the back of the ambassador. Particularly important contacts were established and maintained through special emissaries. One of them was Anfuso; he was sent to Franco in the early months of the Spanish civil war, and, in a secret mission to Hitler in 1936, it was he who prepared the terrain for Ciano's visit of October of that year, which marked the beginning of the close cooperation between Italy and Germany.[27] Ciano cultivated the method of direct meetings with foreign statesmen; he was frequently away from Rome, traveling to Germany and to the capitals of Eastern and Southern Europe.

As Ciano was quite uninhibited by the traditions of the diplomatic profession, the range of his activities went far beyond what is customarily considered to be the sphere of action of a Foreign Minister. He himself established contact with revolutionary forces of other countries when they could be used in favor of Fascist Italy, and he extended his interference into the military sphere when the aims of his foreign policy could be promoted by direct military action.[28] Cantalupo had a typical experience of the subordinate role which the professional diplomat held in Ciano's strategy of foreign policy.[29] Ciano had appointed him in 1936 to be the first Italian ambassador in Franco Spain. Cantalupo was most anxious to hear the views of the newly appointed Foreign Minister on the Spanish problem, the first great political issue with which Ciano was concerned. When the civil war broke out the Western Powers were trying to bury the sanctions issue and to build golden bridges for Italy's

[26] Grazzi, *Il Principio della Fine*, p. 104.   [27] Anfuso, *Roma Berlino Salò*, pp. 20-26.
[28] See below, note 43.
[29] For the following see Cantalupo, *Fu la Spagna*, pp. 62-67, 75-78, 244-250.

return to Geneva. Thus, the handling of the Spanish crisis would reveal whether the Abyssinian Affair was intended to become a soon forgotten episode, permitting Italy to return to its traditional system and friendships, or whether the masters of Italy would try to embark on an entirely new course. Cantalupo found the manner in which Ciano explained the Spanish issue to him most reassuring and satisfactory. Ciano indicated that Mussolini had only very hesitantly agreed to lend Franco military support. Italy had no territorial ambitions in Spain. Aside from the fact that the establishment of Bolshevism there must be prevented, Italy was not concerned with ideological issues, and had no special interest in promoting a totalitarian regime in Spain; Franco should be advised to take a reconciliatory attitude towards other parties. Thus the Spanish conflict should not widen the gap between Italy and the Western Powers and, as soon as the Spanish affair was composed, Ciano added, he hoped to make a visit to Paris.

As satisfactory as Ciano's exposition of the Spanish situation sounded to Cantalupo, he noticed some things which disquieted him. Before he left Ciano's office, Ciano explained to him the military situation in Spain. A big map was spread out on the table, with little flags indicating the position of the various military units, and soon Ciano and Anfuso began to move them around, like enthusiastic schoolboys, becoming engrossed in planning Franco's campaign. Furthermore, Cantalupo soon learned that Ciano had established at the Palazzo Chigi a special office for Spanish affairs which was concerned with the military aspects of the enterprise. Finally, when, immediately before his departure, Cantalupo saw Ciano again for a farewell visit, the Foreign Minister told him that the Italian Fascist party was exerting strong pressure on him to take a radical ideological line in the Spanish issue, and that he was forced to make some concession; Farinacci, the old party wheelhorse, would therefore go to Spain on a special mission as representative of the party. Ciano assured Cantalupo that he did not need to worry about this. Actually Farinacci's presence in Spain ruined any chances Cantalupo's embassy may have had. He refused to have any contact with Cantalupo; he himself soon came to be considered as the true mouthpiece of the Italian leader in Spain; and Cantalupo could make no headway with his more conciliatory recommendations. Moreover, after he returned to Rome, Farinacci began a systematic campaign against Cantalupo's "defeatism," and the ambassador was recalled after two months. Upon his return he soon realized that he had fallen into disgrace; people studiously avoided him, and the police kept checking on all his movements and contacts. When he was finally admitted to Ciano, he found a different man, cool and distant; Ciano was unwilling to permit Cantalupo to present his views to Mussolini and showed himself entirely uninterested in what Cantalupo had to report. Cantalupo's diplomatic career had ended.

It is possible that when Cantalupo was appointed ambassador to Franco the course to be followed by Italy in the Spanish civil war had not yet been definitely set. The Italian-Spanish Agreement of November 28, 1936,[30] which preceded Cantalupo's mission, guaranteed the inviolability of Spanish territorial possessions and provided for close cooperation between the two countries. The common outlook between the Fascist regime and the Spanish Nationalist government was emphasized though the wording of the treaty was not incompatible with what Ciano had told Cantalupo about Italian policy in the Mediterranean. After the defeat of the Italians in the battle of Guadalajara, which took place while Cantalupo was in Spain, an intransigent and radical line may have seemed necessary in order to restore Italian prestige. But it is equally possible that, from the outset, Ciano had higher aims than gaining a friend for Italy in the Western Mediterranean and that he was working for the establishment of a regime identified with Fascist Italy also in internal structure. If this is the case, he used Cantalupo's mission as a cover behind which he hid his true intentions and simultaneously kept open a line of retreat in case his maximum aims could not be obtained. In any case Cantalupo's mission to Franco is a striking example of the variety of instruments on which Ciano relied in the conduct of foreign policy. Among these instruments, the professional diplomat was only a very minor and not a very highly esteemed factor.

II

As has been noted, the Spanish civil war was the first great issue with which Ciano had to deal as Foreign Minister. In referring to this event we have touched upon the central problem of our study. To what extent did Ciano's diplomatic methods, his Fascization of diplomacy, change Italy's attitude to the outside Powers and vary or deviate from the traditional course of Italian foreign policy?

Ciano indicated frequently that the traditional diplomats had failed to give foreigners the right impression of Italy's newly acquired strength. Now the diplomats were supposed to show a stern and imperious face to the outside world, they were expected to employ a *tono fascista*.[31] In

---

[30] For the text see Galeazzo Ciano, *L'Europa verso la Catastrofe* (Verona, 1948), pp. 120-121.

[31] Guariglia, *Ricordi*, p. 193.

his Diary, Ciano notes with evident contempt occasions when foreign statesmen or diplomats showed signs of emotion when they were worried or perturbed, or became pale or had tears in their eyes. He evidently expected that Italy's representatives would show none of these weaknesses, and his diplomats were well aware of how they were supposed to behave. The reports which they sent home sound frequently more like the descriptions of military encounters than the résumés of polite diplomatic interviews.[32] It is reported that Grandi during the Abyssinian crisis delivered a conciliatory speech in England. The conciliatory passages were carefully deleted from the text which he sent to the Palazzo Chigi.[33] When Guariglia was appointed ambassador in Paris, he showed Ciano the draft of a speech which he wanted to deliver in presenting his credentials to the President of the French Republic. This draft contained the customary allusions to the common European heritage and the historical bonds between the Italian and French people, but when Ciano returned the draft these innocuous expressions of diplomatic politeness had been cut out.[34] Ciano modeled his own conduct upon the precepts he gave to his ambassadors. When a report had arrived that the Greek military attaché in Budapest had made some disparaging remarks about the military qualities of the Italian army, Ciano threatened to break off diplomatic relations between Italy and Greece, and serious consequences were avoided only because the Greek government agreed to retire the talkative officer.[35]

The same brutal disregard of custom was shown also in the use of intercepted messages.[36] The Italian government had a particularly well-functioning secret service which provided the Palazzo Chigi with complete information about the interchanges between the British ambassador in Rome and the London Foreign Office, and also with the diplomatic correspondence of many other countries. Ciano was not satisfied with

[32] As an example see Grandi's report on his interview with Chamberlain and Eden in February 1938, shortly before Eden's dismissal, in Ciano, *L'Europa verso la Catastrofe*, pp. 249-278. For further examples of the approved *tono fascista*, see *Documenti Italiani*, 8th series, XII, 82-83, 120-125, 157-158, 507, 610.

[33] Guariglia, *Ricordi*, p. 743.

[34] *ibid.*, pp. 355-357, where Guariglia's original draft and Ciano's revised text are both printed.

[35] Grazzi, *Il Principio della Fine*, pp. 12-13.

[36] "The brazen and extensive use made of material thus acquired" is discussed by Namier in his review of "Ciano's Early Diary," printed in L. B. Namier, *Europe in Decay* (London, 1950), pp. 112-115, where most of the facts mentioned above are discussed. The article by Mario Toscano, "Problemi Particolari della Storia della Seconda Guerra Mondiale," *Rivista di Studi Politici Internazionali*, XVII (1950), 388-398, deals with the interesting question of the influence which these interceptions had on the course of Italian foreign policy.

using the secret information for the planning of his diplomatic moves; he was eager to impress other statesmen with Italian omniscience and he used the material as a means of increasing tension. On a famous occasion, a dossier of English reports about Germany was prepared and shown to Hitler with the desired effect of inciting him against the British; on another, Schuschnigg of Austria was harassed with some incautious remarks which the Austrian Foreign Minister had uttered when he was dining at Geneva with Vansittart.

The *tono fascista* of Italian diplomacy in itself did not represent a new course of action but it was important in determining and restricting the framework within which Italian policy could and would take action. Slow proceedings and cautious legal formulas were considered as contradictory to the emphasis on decisive action which was supposed to be characteristic of Fascism and to animate its diplomacy. Collective agreements and multilateral treaties were condemned;[37] preference was given to those countries where an individual had the full power of decision, where concern for parliamentary bodies was unnecessary, and where agreements could be reached in personal meetings. Ciano was much influenced by his personal impressions of foreign statesmen; he preferred to deal with those who corresponded to the "new fascist type." The development of the relations between Yugoslavia and Italy offers a characteristic example. In March 1937, an agreement was signed between these two countries who had been bitter opponents. From the Italian point of view the agreement represented an attempt to undermine the Little Entente and thereby to weaken the French influence in the Balkans; at the same time, it was meant to block the expansion of Germany which was beginning to draw Austria more and more into her orbit. Ciano was particularly proud of this agreement, in which he saw a first fruit of his own activities as Foreign Minister, but his "new course" was based entirely upon his estimate of the personality of the Yugoslav Premier Stojadinovic, whom he regarded as a man of the new type. When in 1939, the future Yugoslav dictator was thrown out of power like any weak parliamentary Prime Minister, Ciano took this almost as a personal affront and immediately resumed plotting with the Croatian opposition against the existence of the Yugoslav state.[38]

The contempt for the usual procedures and customs of diplomacy and the disregard of the rules which had been developed in international

[37] Ciano, *L'Europa verso la Catastrofe*, pp. 286, 338: "contrario allo nostro stile diplomatico per il suo carattere di Patto collettivo."
[38] Ciano, *Diario*, I, 34, 52, 61.

relations aggravated the difficulties of cooperation with those nations which placed emphasis on these rules and tried to reinforce them. Though Mussolini's Italy had never been friendly to the League of Nations, a working relationship had existed in the 1920's.[39] The completely negative and aggressively hostile attitude towards the League which had developed in the Abyssinian crisis and was maintained and accentuated by Ciano's foreign policy, rigidified the Italian position. By hardening the contrast between Italy and the West into a conflict between two opposite ways of life, it placed formidable obstacles in the way of eventual resumption of cooperation.

With increasing emphasis on the contrast between the democratic and the Fascist concept of foreign policy, Italy was naturally drawn to emphasize similarities with the other great anti-Western Power, Germany. Even in the earlier years of his regime, Mussolini had expressed the idea that a new world war was inevitable, and he had pointed to the 1940's as critical years. At that time, he regarded England and Russia as the great antagonists and believed that the conflict should be used by Italy to cut out an empire of her own.[40] With Italy moving close to Germany, the idea of an inevitable new world war persisted, but the perspective changed. The war became a war between totalitarian and democratic Powers; together with Germany, Italy would be one of the main protagonists, Germany destined to rule in the north, Italy in the south of Europe. One can see in Ciano's Diary how, in his discussions with Mussolini, the decadence of the democracies and the inevitability of war became recurrent themes.[41] It is true that the time of this war remained vague and in a not clearly defined future; but the feeling that the world would soon assume an entirely new aspect could only strengthen the tendency towards an irresponsible freedom of action in foreign policy.

It is hard to imagine Ciano achieving prominence in any other situation. In his pride of being the representative of a new, ruthless generation, he fitted perfectly into a *fin de siècle* atmosphere where everything that served to improve Italy's position for the future decisive clash seemed justifiable, and in which, under the threat of a coming world war, he could carry out actions which, in less critical times, would have been impossible for him. Ciano was not concerned with the slow and gradual strengthening and widening of the foundations which had been laid

[39] See Chapter 7, §v above.

[40] See the report about a conversation with Mussolini in Cantalupo, *Fu la Spagna*, pp. 42 ff.

[41] Ciano, *Diario*, I, 12; Ciano, *L'Europa verso la Catastrofe*, p. 375.

in the past. Instead, he groped in all directions where opportunity for gain or prestige and expansion of power seemed to beckon, becoming deeply involved in the military aspects of the Spanish civil war, and after Stojadinovic's fall, promoting plans to partition Yugoslavia and to bring Croatia under Italian control. But in Spain and Yugoslavia Ciano was dealing with situations which had arisen before he took office; the enterprises into which he put his whole energy were those which he conceived and planned personally: the actions against Albania and Greece.

Although the operation against Greece was probably conceived before 1939,[42] it was executed only after the European war had started, and it need not be considered here. In any case, the military action which led to the incorporation of Albania into the Italian empire is sufficiently typical of Ciano's methods.[43] There was no pretense, as in the case of Greece, of military or strategic considerations; and despite Ciano's later pride over having acquired Albania for the Italian crown, it still seems to have been a superfluous acquisition. Absorption of Albania by a more gradual procedure would have been entirely possible although even this seems unnecessary in view of the protectorate which Italy had acquired in the 1920's. Yet, when Ciano represented the Italian government at the marriage of King Zogu in May 1938, he decided that Italian policy should be directed toward complete and outright acquisition of Albania; and he obtained Mussolini's agreement and stuck to what he called the "integral solution." Ciano kept all the threads of this *coup* in his own hands; in the diplomatic sphere he agreed with Stojadinovic on compensating Yugoslavia by a strip of territory in northern Albania, but abandoned the idea of such a grant after Stojadinovic's fall. He prepared an internal revolt against Zogu's regime by organizing the distribution of money to the Albanian opposition leaders, and he supervised the military preparations for the enterprise. Finally, when the military action started, on Good Friday of 1939 (a day which to many people seemed hardly fitted for an action of this kind), Ciano himself flew to Albania to watch over his private experiment in empire building.

The Albanian annexation was achieved without raising more serious repercussions than paper protests. The Italian leaders regarded this enterprise as a sign of the freedom of action which Italy had achieved in the Mediterranean area. But actually this was an illusion and shows only

---

[42] Ciano, *1937-1938 Diario*, p. 44; *Diario*, I, 99.
[43] Ciano, *1937-1938 Diario*, pp. 118, 140, 150, 165, 170, 267; *Diario*, I, 24, 34, 35, 55, 64; *L'Europa verso la Catastrofe*, pp. 305-316, 409-412.

how little Ciano was able to conceive of Italian foreign policy as an integrated and coherent whole. Ciano once made a remark which shows how precarious the Italian position actually was. He said that one of the desirable consequences of the establishment of Italian power in the Balkan peninsula would be that it would create a balance against the growth of German influence there.[44] This was almost an admission that by conducting an expansionist policy which pointed towards the east, the south, and the west of the Mediterranean, and threatened the *status quo*, Italy had thoroughly disturbed her neighbors and greatly increased the possibility of interference by outside Powers in this area. By replacing a policy of clearly limited aims with a policy of unrestricted use of power within the whole of the Mediterranean area, Italy was in fact more deeply drawn into the vortex of European power politics and lost much of her freedom of action in her relations with the Great European Powers.

The advantages gained in the Mediterranean necessarily remained insecure because the fate of Italy depended on Italy's alignment in the constellation of the Great European Powers. The central issue of Italian foreign policy in the three years before the second world war was the relation of Italy to Germany and to Britain. As we have said before, in the summer of 1936, when Ciano took over the direction of Italian foreign policy, Italy had to decide whether she wanted to reestablish the traditional cooperation with Britain, disturbed by the Abyssinian war and to resume in the European state system the balancing role which she had played in former years.[45] When Ciano became Foreign Minister, not more than 15 months had passed since the Stresa Conference, at which Italy had aligned herself with France and Great Britain against Germany, and the increase in power which Nazi Germany had gained in the intervening period through the reoccupation of the Rhineland gave special urgency and importance to the decision which Italy would now have to make. The Western Powers tried to terminate whatever actions they had undertaken against Italian aggression, and efforts were begun to relieve the Anglo-Italian tension. The progress of negotiations was slow, cumbersome, and interrupted, however. A first positive result was obtained in January 1937 when the two governments published a dec-

[44] Ciano, *L'Europa verso la Catastrofe*, p. 311.
[45] For a discussion of the situation at the end of the Abyssinian war, see Maxwell H. H. Macartney and Paul Cremona, *Italy's Foreign and Colonial Policy 1914-1937* (London, 1938), chapter xv, and Donosti, *Mussolini e l'Europa*, p. 42. For the historical roots of the contrast between a rational and emotional-aggressive Italian foreign policy, see Federico Chabod, *Storia della Politica Estera Italiana dal 1870 al 1896*, I: *Le premesse* (Bari, 1951).

laration usually called the Anglo-Italian "Gentleman's Agreement," a reciprocal agreement to preserve the *status quo* in the Mediterranean.[46] But in the face of Italy's increasing military commitments in the Spanish civil war the value of such an assurance became questionable; and a bitter anti-British press campaign reduced relations to the previous state of tension. Even an exchange of messages between Mussolini and Chamberlain in the summer of 1937 did not revive the Anglo-Italian talks. It was only after Eden's dismissal in February 1938 that negotiations were resumed, resulting in the conclusion of a British-Italian Accord on April 16. This treaty reaffirmed the agreement of 1937 and regulated a number of issues in the Mediterranean and Near Eastern area connected with Italy's conquest of Abyssinia, but its real point was Britain's recognition of Italy's African empire and Italy's agreement to withdraw a substantial number of volunteers from Spain.[47] Once again, however, the Accord seemed to remain a piece of paper because Italy did not carry out the latter condition.[48] Nevertheless, after Munich, Chamberlain considered himself satisfied with a token withdrawal of volunteers, and the Accord finally came into force in November 1938. This was immediately followed, however, by violent anti-French demonstrations in the Italian Chamber and in the press; and Ciano showed little interest in the British attempts to improve Franco-Italian relations.[49] Nevertheless Chamberlain and Halifax carried out a visit to Rome in January 1939 to put the seal on the normalization of Anglo-Italian relations; but, as Ciano wrote, from the Italian point of view it was a visit "on a minor scale."[50]

In contrast to the hesitant course along which Anglo-Italian negotiations proceeded, Italy's advance towards friendship with Germany seemed smooth and steady.[51] Germany had been quick in recognizing Italy's African empire; and in October 1936 Ciano visited Germany and

---

[46] For the text, see Royal Institute of International Affairs, *Documents on International Affairs, 1937* (London, 1939), pp. 87-89.

[47] For the text see *Documents on International Affairs, 1938*, pp. 141-156.

[48] For a summary of the British complaints see the "Extracts from Foreign Office Memorandum on Anglo-Italian Relations" in *British Documents*, 3rd series, III, 812-815.

[49] *ibid.*, 478ff.; IV, chapter 4.

[50] Ciano, *Diario*, I, 20; see also the somewhat reticent tone of Mussolini's and Ciano's telegrams at the end of the visit: *British Documents*, 3rd series, III, 540.

[51] The basic work on the relations between Italy and Germany remains Elizabeth Wiskemann, *The Rome-Berlin Axis* (New York, 1949), but material which has come out since the publication of this book has now to be taken into account. Mario Toscano, *Le Origini del Patto d'Acciaio* (Firenze, 1948), is based on the Italian Foreign Office documents and gives an admirable presentation of the details of the diplomatic negotiations. The most recent survey is given by M. Magistrati, "Berlino 1939: da Praga al Patto d'Acciaio," *Rivista di Studi Politici Internazionali*, XIX (1952), 597-652.

saw Hitler. A few days later in a speech in Milan on November 1, Mussolini, in evaluating the importance of this visit, coined the famous phrase that the Berlin-Rome line represented "an Axis." Both countries, Germany and Italy, were quick in recognizing Franco and acted in concert in the London Non-Intervention Committee. Visits of Nazi hierarchs to Italy emphasized the maintainance of close contacts and Mussolini's visit to Germany in September of 1937 became an imposing demonstration of the closeness of Italian-German relations. By signing the Anti-Comintern Pact and by abandoning the League of Nations Italy increased the impression of Italo-German solidarity. On Hitler's visit to Rome in May of 1938 drafts for an alliance treaty were exchanged. These negotiations were interrupted by the Czech crisis, and, after their revival in October, were further slowed down by the attempt to include Japan in the treaty, but on May 6, 1939, after a meeting of Ciano and Ribbentrop in Milan, an announcement was made that a German-Italian alliance was concluded and on May 22 the Pact of Steel—a military alliance which did not even contain the usual escape clause restricting the obligations for assistance to the case of an enemy attack—was solemnly signed in Berlin.

During the tense years preceding the outbreak of the second world war, many people believed that an alliance had existed between Germany and Italy ever since 1936 and that they had conducted a concerted policy in which every move was carefully planned and agreed upon. This theory assumed that the leaders of the two countries denied the existence of an alliance treaty and pretended to act independently and on their own in order to obtain greater concessions from the Western Powers; that they did not want to lose the advantages to be gained by holding out as a bait the possibility of an alignment with the West; and that by maintaining contacts with Britain and France they were better able to prevent common action against aggression or at least to delay such action till the dictatorship had acquired enough strength to resist.

The documents which have been published since the war prove irrefutably the erroneousness of this interpretation. The Italian leaders were surprised by Germany's occupation of Austria, they were left guessing about Germany's true intentions in the Czech crisis, they had no previous knowledge of Germany's move into Prague. On the other hand, Germany was not previously informed about the Italian action against Albania. Both countries—Germany and Italy—did not feel sure that the other might not be willing to make a deal with Britain. Ciano prepared his famous dossier to incite Hitler against Britain; when the British-Italian agreement came into force Ribbentrop appeared in Rome with offers of an alliance. Behind the façade of public proclamations of German-Italian solidarity there appears lack of frankness and hidden doubts of the reliability of the partner.

Since the days when the myth of German-Italian solidarity was widely accepted, opinion has shifted and currently the view is often expressed that it would have been possible for the Western Powers to win Italy away from Germany and to prevent the conclusion of the German-Italian alliance. According to this view, Britain acted slowly and hesitantly; the Quai d'Orsay was haughty and prejudiced especially after the bitter Italian attacks against France in the winter of 1938-1939; feelers which one group in the French government put out were counteracted by another[52] so that the Italians could not be convinced of the seriousness of the French intentions; and these mistakes of the Western Powers drove Italy into German arms.

Ciano's Diary has been adduced as proof of the contention that Italy was not given a full chance to disentangle herself from the German embrace or at least to keep Germany at a respectable distance. The Diary shows irritation against the Germans after the *Anschluss* and particularly after the coup of Prague;[53] and it makes clear that the question of the South Tyrol and that of the Brenner frontier remained sore spots in Italy despite Hitler's solemn renunciations. Italy was deeply upset by the extension of German influence into the Balkans; after the occupation of Austria as well as after Munich, Ciano toyed with the idea of supplementing the horizontal Rome-Berlin axis with a vertical Rome-Belgrade-Budapest-Warsaw axis which was to form a barrier against further German penetration into Southeastern Europe.[54] Furthermore, various moves undertaken by the Italian leaders in 1938 are regarded as symptoms of Italian hesitancy. Despite the official assurances that the Anglo-Italian negotiations were not directed against Germany, Italy began to show serious interest in their progress at the very moment in February 1938 when Germany resumed an aggressive policy against Austria.[55] On Ribbentrop's visit to Rome in October 1938 Mussolini, despite an emphatically stated enthusiasm for a German-Italian alliance, mainly elaborated on the necessity of delay and of cautious procedure.[56] The quickness and willingness with which Mussolini

---

[52] See Chapter 12, §III above.   [53] Ciano, *Diario*, I, 55-58.

[54] Ciano, *1937-1938 Diario*, pp. 114, 263.

[55] See Ciano's instructions to Grandi in Ciano, *L'Europa verso la Catastrofe*, pp. 245-246.

[56] Toscano, *Patto D'Acciaio*, pp. 30-35.

grasped at the offer to act as mediator in the Czech crisis has been taken as a sign that he was glad to retreat from the exposed position into which Italy had advanced.[57] When Hitler had come to power in 1933, Mussolini had proposed a Four Power Pact and—it is said—this remained the true aim of his policy throughout.

Finally, the dramatic clash between Ribbentrop and Ciano in August 1939 is often regarded as decisive proof of the reluctance with which Italy had tied herself to Germany and of the divided mind of the Italian leaders.[58] If, then, we are to judge the strength of the thesis that Italy could have been detached by the Western Powers and the validity of the evidence which seems to support this, it might be well, first, to recapitulate briefly the circumstances of the Ribbentrop-Ciano meeting and the effect it had on Ciano's subsequent conduct in August 1939.

Attolico, the Italian ambassador in Berlin, had for some time been sending alarming reports to Rome, stating that the Germans had decided to take military action against Poland and were willing to risk a general war.[59] The ambassador suggested a meeting between Hitler and Mussolini at which Hitler would be forced to define his plans and at which Mussolini should, if necessary, exert a moderating influence. Ciano was displeased at being pushed into the background, and there seems to have been some suspicion in Rome that Hitler might persuade Mussolini to rash commitments, instead of Mussolini restraining Hitler. Thus, after some hesitation and delays, it was decided that Ciano should go to Germany. When he arrived in Salzburg on August 11, he seems to have considered Attolico's fears as exaggerated and to have felt reasonably sure that a common line leading to a conference of the Great Powers and to a peaceful international settlement could be worked out by Italy and Germany. After his first talk with Ribbentrop, however, Ciano's mood was grim. "We have come to blows," was his résumé of the interview and it is clear that Ribbentrop had admitted that Germany now in-

[57] The bellicose speeches which Mussolini made in September are explained as a means to maintain contact with Hitler so that Hitler would accept Mussolini's mediation.

[58] The most recent treatment is contained in Toscano, *L'Italia e gli Accordi Tedesco-Sovietici.* Ciano's reports are contained in *L'Europa verso la Catastrofe*, pp. 449-459, and in *Diario*, I, 140-141. Magistrati, Ciano's brother-in-law, who was a member of the Italian embassy in Berlin and present in Salzburg, has written two articles "Salisburgo 1939," and "Le Settimane Decisive," *Rivista di Studi Politici Internazionali*, XVI (1949), 479-509, and XVII (1950), 187-232, while Attolico's views are given in Leonardo Simoni, *Berlino Ambasciata d' Italia 1939-1943* (Roma, 1946), pp. 11-18. Important information is also contained in Donosti, *Mussolini e l'Europa*, pp. 198-201.

[59] See, for instance, *Documenti Italiani*, 8th series, XII, 263-264, 291, 378-381, 559-562.

tended to push things to the utmost. The luncheon following took place in an icy atmosphere; hardly a word was exchanged between guest and host. In further talks with Ribbentrop Ciano emphasized his conviction that Britain and France would support Poland if she were attacked and that the military outlook for the Axis Powers would be doubtful. Italy in any case would not be ready to participate in such an adventure. Ciano had the courage to maintain this position even against the prophetic assuredness of the Fuehrer.

Back in Rome Ciano began his fight to keep Italy out of the war which he now considered inevitable. The Duce was deeply disturbed by the idea that Fascist Italy—like the parliamentary Italy of 1914—should renege her word and become again a "traitor nation." One of the most violent discussions, wrote Ciano, took place on August 21: "Today I have spoken clearly, I have used up all my ammunition. When I entered the room Mussolini confirmed his decision to go along with the Germans. 'You, Duce, cannot and must not do it. The loyalty with which I have served you in carrying out the policy of the Axis warrants my speaking clearly to you now. I went to Salzburg in order to adopt a common line of action. I found myself face to face with a *Diktat*. The Germans, not ourselves, have betrayed the alliance in which we were to have been partners, and not servants.' "[60]

In his efforts to persuade Mussolini Ciano had the loyal and enthusiastic support of the professional diplomats, especially Attolico who traveled back and forth between Rome and Berlin and who worked hand-in-hand with him. Ciano had at long last become the protagonist of the traditional line of Italian foreign policy. But he was handicapped now by the carelessness of his own new diplomacy. In negotiating the alliance with Germany, the initiative was left to the Germans, and drafts which they submitted formed the basis of the treaty; a decisive weakness of the Italian position was the lack of written German assurances that the alliance had been signed with the understanding that action which might lead to war should be avoided for the next few years.[61] Because he had neglected to weigh carefully the reports about the German-Russian negotiations,[62] Ciano was surprised when the news of the Nazi-Soviet Agreement arrived; the situation seemed again transformed and the fight for Italy's neutrality had to be resumed. In the end Ciano

[60] Ciano, *Diario*, I, 146.
[61] This point had been made by Ciano to Ribbentrop in Milan and had again been stressed in the so-called *Memoriale Cavallero* of May 30. See Toscano, *Patto d'Acciaio*, pp. 186-191.
[62] See note 21 above.

succeeded in gaining Mussolini's agreement to Italy's neutrality. A professional diplomat put the final seal on this decision. On August 26 Attolico had been instructed to transmit to the German government a long list of military material which Italy needed to enter the war and which Germany was asked to provide. When the German officials wanted to know when the delivery was expected Attolico replied on his own initiative and without instructions "immediately before the beginning of hostilities," barring all possibility of further negotiations on the topic.[63]

There can be no doubt that, from the moment when Ciano met Ribbentrop at Salzburg, he was a changed man, thoroughly upset by the recklessness with which the Germans had violated the clause of the alliance providing for reciprocal consultation, and by the lightheartedness with which they embarked on a general war. And there is no question that, from this time on, he remained suspicious of the Nazi leaders and hostile to them. But, granted all this, what bearing does it have on the argument that Italy might have been won from Germany's side if only the Western Powers had been more intelligent in their diplomacy?

The answer to this question depends on our understanding of Mussolini's own position and upon an appreciation of the relations between Mussolini and his son-in-law.

The bulk of available evidence indicates that Mussolini was irrevocably set on a pro-German course of Italian foreign policy. He too may have had moments of doubt—particularly because he must have been continuously aware of Italy's economic deficiencies—but if so, he overcame his doubts quickly under the sway of Hitler's persuasive personality or under the impact of demonstrations of German strength. Ciano's Diary makes it quite clear that Mussolini's outbursts of irritation about German arbitrariness were short-lived—shorter than Ciano's; Mussolini always returned quickly to his pro-German course.[64] After Munich he scotched Ciano's plan of insisting on a common Polish-Hungarian frontier, in order to permit the formation of a vertical Axis.[65] Mussolini may have been utterly sincere when in October 1938 he justified to Ribbentrop his hesitation to conclude an alliance by citing the unprepared state of public opinion.[66] Soon after the meeting with Ribbentrop,

[63] Simoni, *Berlino Ambasciata d'Italia*, p. 17.

[64] Ciano, *1937-1938 Diario*, p. 134; *Diario*, I, 57, 60, 62.

[65] Ciano, *1937-1938 Diario*, p. 269.

[66] This differs from the interpretation given by Toscano, *Patto d'Acciaio*, pp. 33-34.

however, the Italian claims against France were announced and a bitter press campaign was unchained; and this widened the rift between France and Italy and served to demonstrate the usefulness of German support to the Italian public.[67] In comparison with the overwhelming amount of material which shows Mussolini's steady determination to arrive at a complete identification of German and Italian policy the few indications of doubt and hesitation can have no weight.

But could not Ciano himself, if given proper encouragement by the Western Powers, have prevented the full consummation of the German-Italian rapprochement? This would, in view of Mussolini's attitude, have involved an assertion of independence on his part. Was he capable of such a gesture? There is every reason to doubt it. The tone of his Diary in the years before the outbreak of the second world war was one of unreserved admiration for the Leader of Fascism.[68] The pervading theme is that "the Duce is always right." Doubts and criticism appear only later; it is possible that some resentment had already developed in earlier years and was then suppressed. The close family relationship may have had its drawbacks; Mussolini disapproved of his son-in-law's personal conduct quite as much as Ciano of his father-in-law's.[69] But if Ciano began to have some reservations they lay almost certainly in the purely personal sphere. There is no indication that before the summer of 1939 they extended into serious doubts about the Duce's political wisdom.

Moreover, in reshaping Italian diplomacy Ciano had been a true follower of the Duce. It has been shown[70] that Mussolini took over power full of contempt for the international system established at Paris and anxious to inaugurate an active foreign policy based on force, but he had been restrained by the adverse constellation in the European state system and by the impossibility of overcoming the resistance of the diplomatic bureaucracy. Ciano was the docile pupil who carried out the intentions of his master at a time when their realization was possible. The Italian diplomacy of the last three years before the war can be called Ciano's diplomacy less because the ideas of the new course were his own than because Ciano carried them out with an uninhibited and thoughtless energy, peculiar to this figure of a second-generation Fascism.

The transformation of the Italian diplomacy is an interesting example of the manner in which a revolutionary regime established complete

---

[67] Ciano, *Diario*, I, 104.

[68] Such expressions are collected by Namier, *Europe in Decay*, pp. 108-110.

[69] See Ciano's remark to Serrano Suñer, *Entre Hendaya y Gibraltar*, p. 317.

[70] See Chapter 7, §11 above.

control over a bureaucracy and reduced the professionals to powerlessness. But the reorganization to which Ciano subjected Italian diplomacy is also a decisive reason for rejecting the thesis that Italy's alliance with Germany could have been prevented, or that Ciano's views on this issue differed fundamentally from those of Mussolini. Ciano had fashioned an instrument to carry out a new course in foreign policy; it would have been a denial of what he had done if he had used the new instrument for carrying out the old, traditional foreign policy. Ciano loved to imagine himself as a free agent who could shape the world according to his will, and he liked to toy with plans and with projects. In moments of doubt and annoyance he may have played with the idea of siding with the French and English but actually he could not escape the momentum and weight of the movement to which he had turned the instrument of diplomacy. A time for reflection and choice arose only when the outbreak of the second world war created an entirely new situation.

Ciano's conversion at Salzburg in August 1939 was, then, not the result of a long evolutionary process in which he had nurtured growing doubts about the wisdom of the Duce's policy or during which he had seriously considered the advisability of returning to the traditional bases of Italian diplomacy. The important thing about the conversion was that it was sudden and, as such, in complete accordance with Ciano's characteristic approach to diplomacy. As we have seen, Ciano was little inclined to base his policy on considerations of permanent and underlying forces and interests. He approached policy in terms of personality, relying heavily upon his judgment of the leading figures of other countries. Thus, Ribbentrop's arrogant announcement of Germany's approaching military action against Poland, which revealed that the Italians had been trapped and overplayed, was a blow to Ciano's pride. He must have regarded it as quite a personal failure of his diplomacy, and turned now with vehemence against those whom he had misjudged.

III

There is irony in the fact that in September 1939, Fascist Italy with her proudly advertised first-rank-Power foreign policy ended up roughly in the same position in which parliamentary Italy had found herself at the beginning of the first world war. Likewise there is irony in the fact that from the summer of 1939 on Ciano developed into a practitioner of the policy of *combinazioni*—i.e. of trying to reap advantages from maintaining an undecided balancing position in the struggles of stronger Powers—a policy which in earlier years Ciano had regarded as char-

acteristic of the weakness of democratic Italy and condemned as undignified and unfitting to the reborn strength of Fascist Italy.[71]

But Ciano never learned to discern the real and concrete factors of
power behind the surface of appearances and his inability to see things
as they are played a role in his final fate. When he left the Palazzo
Chigi in 1943 he took over the embassy at the Vatican in the hope of
establishing contacts with the victorious Western Powers—strangely
unaware how little qualified he must have appeared to the democracies
for this task. Ciano also seems to have failed to realize that he was the
last who would reap benefits from taking an active part in Mussolini's
overthrow. And when he was in custody in Germany he moved heaven
and earth to be returned to Italy[72] where he seems to have hoped that
activity would again become possible for him; actually he gave himself
into the hands of his most implacable enemies.

When the ultra-Fascists who ruled Mussolini's Republic of Salò
condemned him to death in Verona, Mussolini did not interfere. He
decided that "sentiment" should not prevail over "reason of state"; he
was nevertheless profoundly moved by the events in Verona and, indeed, regarded them "as the most dramatic chapter in his restless life."[73]
Perhaps he felt that responsibility for this wasted life belonged also to
those who had raised Ciano into power without making him aware of the
limits of its possibilities and its uses. The German ambassador at the
Republic of Salò had great difficulty in restraining Mussolini from pub-
lishing the next day in his newspaper an encomium on the Conte Galeazzo Ciano.[74]

[71] Ciano, *1937-1938 Diario*, p. 52.
[72] Anfuso, *Roma Berlino Salò*, pp. 392, 451.
[73] Quotations from his letter to Serrano Suñer about Ciano's death, published in
Serrano Suñer, *Entre Hendaya y Gibraltar*, p, 323.
[74] Rudolf Rahn, *Ruheloses Leben* (Düsseldorf, 1949), p. 251.

17

Two British Ambassadors: Perth and Henderson

BY FELIX GILBERT

IN DEMOCRATIC STATES, it is generally considered that the making of policy is the responsibility of the Cabinet. In foreign policy, however, Cabinet decisions are necessarily influenced by the reports received from members of the diplomatic corps serving in foreign capitals, and the importance of such reports increases in times of emergency. In the years when Neville Chamberlain's appeasement policy was being inaugurated, the two most important posts in the British Diplomatic Service were Berlin and Rome. An appraisal of the work of the two ambassadors who represented Great Britain in those capitals—Sir Nevile Henderson and the Earl of Perth—is, therefore, of some importance if we are to understand the relationship of diplomacy and policy-making in times of crisis.

I

In the prologue of his book of memoirs, Henderson gives a brief definition of the principal functions of a diplomat. "The first commandment of a diplomatist," he writes, "is faithfully to interpret the views of his own government to the government to which he is accredited; and the second is like unto it: namely, to explain no less accurately the views and standpoint of the government of the country in which he is stationed to the government of his own country."[1]

It cannot be said that, during the years when Henderson had reached the high point of his professional career as British ambassador to Nazi Germany, he lived up to this formulation. Henderson was in Berlin from April 1937 till the outbreak of the second world war. During the first year of his mission, he was chiefly concerned with creating an improvement in the atmosphere of German-British relations; during the

[1] Nevile Henderson, *Failure of a Mission* (New York, 1940), p. viii.

last six months, after the German march into Prague, the British government had decided to take a firm line against the expansionism of Nazi Germany. Thus, the decisive year of Henderson's activities in Berlin, when his personal diplomacy came into its own, was the year 1938, which was dominated first by Hitler's annexation of Austria and then by the Czech crisis, ending in Hitler's triumph at Munich in September. It is precisely in this period that Henderson's conduct as diplomat is at variance with his own definition of the diplomat's duties.

Certainly, a reading of the British documents gives the impression of a tug-of-war between Henderson and his own Foreign Office rather than a picture of a diplomat anxious to act as "faithful interpreter" of the instructions received from London. On the one hand, we find examples of open censure, directed by the Foreign Office against the ambassador; on the other hand, and more frequently, we discover remonstrances on Henderson's part against the contents of his instructions, coupled with intimations of reluctance to execute them in the form in which they are presented to him.

Many illustrations of this kind of friction can be given. A direct clash between Henderson and the Foreign Office occurred immediately after Hitler's invasion of Austria. The ambassador was instructed to protest to Goering against this German action. In talking with the Field Marshal, however, Henderson agreed with Goering "that Doctor Schuschnigg had acted with precipitate folly"—a remark which led Lord Halifax to write subsequently that, by this admission, "you cannot have but diminished the force of the protest you were instructed to make."[2]

When the spotlight had shifted to Czechoslovakia, Henderson immediately took the line that the place where pressure would have to be applied was Prague: "I should be very loath to speak even unofficially to [the] German Government on the subject unless it was certain that [the] Czechoslovak Government meant to work on the basis of nationalities rather than on that of [a] national centralized state."[3] Consequently, Henderson was unhappy about the decision which the British and French governments had reached in their conference in London at the end of April,[4] namely, to make representations both at Prague and Berlin. As Hitler and Ribbentrop were in Italy at the time, Henderson was instructed to initiate the allied action by seeking an interview with Field Marshal Goering.[5] Henderson answered that he "had been gravely

[2] *British Documents,* 3rd series, I, 24, 29; see also L. B. Namier, *Europe in Decay* (London, 1950), pp. 210-212.
[3] *British Documents,* 3rd series, I, 115, also 110.
[4] *ibid.,* pp. 198-233, 243-245.   [5] *ibid.,* pp. 245-246.

exercised" in his mind "as to the expediency of making the communication in question to Goering rather than to Ministry of Foreign Affairs which would be more normal and recognized procedure"; and he succeeded in getting his instructions changed, so that his first discussion of the issue was with the Political Director of the German Foreign Ministry.[6] When, after Ribbentrop's return, the formal *démarche* was about to take place, Henderson asked for permission to have "a certain latitude in expression of personal opinion" in discussing the Sudeten matter with the German Foreign Minister. This time, however, the Foreign Office did not agree with Henderson's suggestion,[7] probably fearing that, if Henderson talked at greater length with Ribbentrop about the possibilities of a solution of the Sudeten crisis, he might, in accordance with his previously expressed views, suggest that the British government was in favor of a radical solution and thereby encourage the Germans to raise their demands.[8] For this apprehension there was some reason. It is evident that Henderson's concern about the manner in which the instructions for a *démarche* in Berlin should be carried out was inspired less by those reasons of formal correctness to which he alluded in his dispatches than by the wish to minimize the elements of urgency and pressure and to soft-pedal British opposition to German aims.

The inclination of the ambassador to accept the German point of view led to another implied censure later in the summer. In answer to a report from Henderson to the effect that the Germans declined any responsibility for the actions of the Sudeten party in Czechoslovakia, Sir Orme Sargent told him that "we do not really help ourselves if we allow the Germans to get away with these statements which we find hard to credit."[9]

Despite warnings of this nature, Henderson revolted again against instructions which he had received when the Sudeten crisis reached its climax in September. The ambassador was attending the Nazi Party Congress at Nuremberg, and Lord Halifax asked him to demand an interview with Hitler, in which he should leave no doubt that a world war was likely to start if Germany used force against Czechoslovakia. Against this instruction Henderson conducted an almost passionate campaign, in which he used the services of Chamberlain's confidential ad-

---

[6] *ibid.*, pp. 252, 256-257, 260.   [7] *ibid.*, pp. 273, 281.

[8] The suspicion of the Foreign Office had been aroused by Henderson's interview with the Political Director in the German Foreign Office; Henderson had indicated that Britain was urging a comprehensive settlement such as a state of nationalities. See *ibid.*, p. 260.

[9] *ibid.*, p. 592.

viser, Sir Horace Wilson; and in the end, he succeeded in getting the instruction rescinded.[10]

When Henderson returned to London in October for a leave of several months, he was indignant to learn that certain people in London believed that, by his behavior during the Sudeten crisis, he "had completely failed to impress upon the Germans the gravity of the position and the seriousness of Britain's determination."[11] Yet the charges of Henderson's critics seem to be corroborated by the documents that have been published since the end of the war. So far, in describing the ambassador's differences with the Foreign Office, we have cited only the British diplomatic papers. But the impression gained from these is strengthened by the abundant material on Henderson in the German Foreign Office files. This indicates all too clearly that, in his conversations with German statesmen, Henderson frequently made use of the diplomatic technique of "expressing a purely personal opinion"; and that, on the occasions when he indulged himself this way, he went very far in accepting the German point of view on Central European questions. In view of this, the Germans had every reason to question the "seriousness of Britain's determination."

Here again, a few examples may illustrate the point. In the summer of 1937, more than six months before the *Anschluss*, Henderson discussed the Austrian question with Franz von Papen and said that "he was convinced that England fully understood the historical need for a solution of this question in the Reich German sense."[12] Likewise, throughout the entire development of the Czech crisis, he was wholly uninhibited in expressing views which could only encourage the Nazi leaders in their plans. He was fond of expressing the opinion that Britain had not the slightest interest in fighting a war for Czechoslovakia and was often outspoken in his condemnation of the policy of the Czech government. After the May crisis of 1938, he accused the Czechs of spreading rumors of German troop concentrations "for the express purpose of serving as a pretext for planned partial Czech mobilization."[13] In August of the same year, he repeatedly emphasized in private conversation that "Great Britain would not think of risking even one sailor or airman for Czechoslovakia."[14]

Perhaps the greatest indiscretion of this kind was committed by Henderson at the Nuremberg Party Congress in 1938. Here, at a time when

---

[10] *ibid.*, II, 647-650.   [11] *ibid.*, IV, 590.
[12] *German Documents*, series D, I, 504. See also Namier, *Europe in Decay*, pp. 210ff.
[13] *German Documents*, series D, II, 449.   [14] *ibid.*, p. 536.

he was arguing in his reports to London that a special warning to Hitler was unnecessary since the German government must be fully aware of Britain's determination to stand with France and Czechoslovakia, he told a German S.S. leader that "he personally had no sympathy at all with the Czechs and moreover considered the placing of Sudeten Germans under Czech domination to be a grave mistake. He expressed his aversion to the Czechs in very strong terms."[15]

Such utterances cannot be justified by the fact that Henderson's views reflected more truly the attitude of leading men in the British government than did his official instructions. Although it may be said that the policy which Britain followed during the summer of 1938 was a policy of bluff, it was a conscious policy carefully worked out together with the French. Pressure was to be brought to bear simultaneously upon the two critical spots: Prague was to be threatened with withdrawal of support by the West; and Germany was to be warned that France and Britain would side with Prague in case of a military conflict. The Germans were not supposed to be encouraged to assume that the guns would not go off.[16] It was hoped that this double-barreled action would bring Germany and Czechoslovakia together on a middle line. In view of Hitler's decision to go the whole way, this policy probably never had a real chance of success; but it was not the function of the diplomat who was charged with the execution of this policy to counteract and undermine it by bandying around so freely his very different personal opinions.[17]

According to Henderson, the second commandment of a diplomat is to explain "accurately the views and standpoint of the government of the country in which he is stationed." The faults of the diplomatic technique which we have just discussed would weigh less heavily if they were not combined with a complete misinterpretation of the policy of Nazi Germany, of its general aims as well as its functional structure. Henderson's general conception of the objectives of German foreign policy was relatively simple; he thought about them in terms of nineteenth century nationalism. Henderson accepted the Nazi attacks against the Treaty of Versailles at their face value and regarded Nazism as a revolt against the Peace Treaty and as an attempt to right the injustices which had been done to Germany.[18] He believed that Nazi Germany

[15] *ibid.,* p. 768.

[16] *British Documents,* 3rd series, II, 56.

[17] In general, see *Survey of International Affairs, 1938,* II: *The Crisis over Czechoslovakia.*

[18] *British Documents,* 3rd series, II, 648.

was still struggling for the fulfillment of traditional national aspirations. He did not realize that the Nazi emphasis on race was a means rather than an end; instead he was convinced that an absorption of the German minorities into the Reich was the final goal of German foreign policy, that, after the achievement of this aim, Germany would become a saturated Power, and that the revolutionary fermentation would gradually disappear.[19] Henderson was not unaware, of course, that this development might imply a shift in the balance of power, through which Germany would become the dominant factor in Eastern and Southeastern Europe; but he regarded this as a natural development which could take place without changing the foundations of the European state system and without reducing the Western Powers to the status of German satellites.

It must be admitted that this misconception of German policy and of the dynamism of German expansion was shared by many influential people in Britain and elsewhere. "Doctrinaires" and "idealists," who base their conceptions of the policy of a country on an analysis of its economic policy or who conclude, from evidence of complete lack of morality in domestic policy, that cooperation in foreign policy is impossible, have always been regarded as "unsound" by the "realists" in governments and Foreign Offices; and Henderson was only one of many self-declared realists in positions of influence at this time. But, granted this, a more serious failure of Henderson as a political observer lies in his complete misjudgment of the mechanism by which decisions were made in Nazi Germany.

In Henderson's view, a continuous struggle was going on in Nazi Germany between moderates and extremists. He had little contact with those whom he considered to be extremists. His views about men like Himmler and Goebbels seem rather vague and shadowy. The only representative of the radicals whom he saw frequently, and whom he disliked intensely, was Ribbentrop. Henderson's main contacts in Germany were among the moderates, high officials of the German bureaucracy, and especially of the Foreign Office, like Neurath and Weizsäcker. The leader of this group and its most important and influential figure was, in Henderson's opinion, Hermann Goering. Henderson cultivated contacts with Goering; even after the war had broken out, he was still able to say that he found Goering "by far the most sympathetic among the big Nazi leaders" and that he had a "real personal liking for him."[20]

As for Hitler, in Henderson's view he could not be definitely as-

[19] *ibid.*, I, 108-112, 286-287.   [20] Henderson, *Failure*, p. 76.

signed to either of the two groups but rather wavered between the moderates and the extremists. In Henderson's eyes, the Fuehrer was a psychopath and a visionary, subject to bursts of rage and swayed by sudden intuitions.[21] We know now that the real Hitler was very different from Henderson's conception of him, that his vacillations were more apparent than real and that, in fact, he followed a carefully worked out plan in which the *Anschluss* and the annexation of Czechoslovakia were only the first steps on the way to German domination over Europe. Henderson, however, believed that the decision to realize the *Anschluss* was taken suddenly, as a result of anger over Schuschnigg's precipitate action of calling a plebiscite. "I do not believe," he wrote to Halifax, "that on the 11th March Hitler himself envisaged the complete assimilation of Austria to the German Reich."[22] This concept of Hitler determined the line which Henderson advocated during the summer of the Czech crisis. Fundamentally, the ambassador did not believe that Germany planned military action or wanted war. At the height of the Czech crisis in August and September, he was still saying that it was untrue that "Hitler has already decided on aggressive action against Czechoslovakia this autumn,"[23] and was still capable of writing about "Hitler's own love for peace, dislike of dead Germans and hesitation of risking his regime on a gambler's throw."[24] Henderson felt, however, that the catastrophe of a war might happen if "Hitler were pushed over the edge."[25] He reverted continually to the *démarche* which Britain and France had made on May 21 on the basis of rumors about the mobilization of the German army against Czechoslovakia; he believed that this action had had a most unfortunate effect on the Fuehrer, and had made him much more intransigent than he had been before. At all costs, the ambassador wanted to avoid a repetition of this performance, and he was most unwilling to undertake any step that might infuriate Hitler again.

Henderson became deeply involved in a complicated game designed to support the moderates in Nazi Germany. Because he hoped to strengthen their position and influence, he was inclined to recommend concessions which, the moderates told him, were necessary to restrain Hitler. And

[21] See Henderson's characterization of Hitler in *British Documents*, 3rd series, I, 97-100.

[22] *ibid.*, p. 99. Even the march into Prague a year later was not, in Henderson's view, premeditated, but again a reaction to sudden developments. *Ibid.*, IV, 595.

[23] *ibid.*, II, 133.

[24] *ibid.*, pp. 243, 245.

[25] In particular, see Henderson's letters from Nuremberg, September 1938, *ibid.*, pp. 649-654.

this was a view to which the ambassador held to the bitter end, arguing always that "everything depends on the psychology of one abnormal individual."[26] Even in his final report, he insisted that, if only unfortunate accidents had not upset Hitler and driven him to extreme measures, things might have worked out all right, a striking proof of his lack of comprehension of German realities. Henderson never for a moment suspected that he was wrong or that his failure to appreciate the purpose and the definiteness of Hitler's policy was really promoting the Fuehrer's aims. Yet his repeated argument that the moderates had a real chance of dominating German policy not only made it possible for Hitler to win major concessions from London but gave British policymakers a fallacious basis on which to plan their German course.

Analysis of Sir Nevile Henderson's activities in Berlin, then, shows that he can hardly claim to have carried out satisfactorily those fundamental tasks which he himself describes as the first two commandments of a good diplomat. Henderson may not—as *The Times* said after his death[27]—have been in the first rank of British diplomats; but, even so, it is strange that the man who had filled in a long and varied career a number of diplomatic positions[28] should have gone astray in what are, or are recognized by him to be, the most elementary duties of his profession. This is a problem which demands closer investigation, and the explanation of this paradox will be one of the chief purposes of this study.

II

In analyzing the reasons for Henderson's "failure," we have to acknowledge that he had to work on a particularly treacherous terrain: he was the ambassador of a democratic country to a totalitarian state. For this reason, a comparison of Henderson's diplomatic activity with that of the British ambassador in Rome has particular relevance. For the British ambassador in Rome had a very similar task, namely, that of improving the relations between the Western democracies and Fascist Italy.

Throughout the 1930's, the British ambassador in Rome was Sir Eric Drummond, who, in 1938, became the sixteenth Earl of Perth. Drummond had received his early political training under the most favorable auspices; he was private secretary to the most brilliant British states-

---

[26] *ibid.*, p. 296.   [27] *The Times* (London), January 4, 1943.
[28] After serving in Constantinople and Egypt, Henderson had been for one year at the British embassy in Paris. In 1928, he became minister in Yugoslavia, in 1935 ambassador in Argentina.

men of the early years of the twentieth century—to Grey, Asquith, Balfour, and Curzon—and he became their close friend. When, after the first world war, the League of Nations was founded, he was chosen as its first Secretary General and in this position he played a leading role in all the political crises and decisions of the postwar years, for fourteen years, until 1933.[29] It was he who was responsible for the important decision that the League Secretariat should not be staffed by officials in the service of the various member nations but should have its own international civil service; and it is chiefly due to him that this first experiment in an international bureaucracy was successful and was later followed when the United Nations was established. His handling of the political tasks of the League has been criticized as overcautious, but he did not lack courage for decisive action when such action was necessary for the maintenance of the authority of the League.[30] His slow and somewhat hesitant approach was useful in avoiding disappointments and setbacks and contributed to the League's steady gain in prestige.

Thus, the man who was appointed as ambassador to Italy in 1933 and who served in Rome until the eve of the war was one of Britain's most successful and experienced diplomats. For this reason, it is interesting to note that some of the features of Henderson's correspondence with London appear also in the reports of the Earl of Perth. His reports show the same concern with the mood of the dictator as Nevile Henderson's. He too argues that it is difficult to get close to Mussolini and that he has to be treated with great caution when he is in "a highly sensitive condition."[31] Frequently, Perth too seems to have had the feeling that the instructions sent him from London do not fit the special circumstances of the totalitarian country to which he is accredited, and he doubts that they may "produce any effect beyond irritation."[32] From Ciano's Diary, we know that Perth frequently gave to the Italian Foreign Minister his "personal views," which were apt to be sympathetic to Italian claims. In particular, Perth was inclined to agree with the Italian view that the French attitude toward Italy was unreasonable.[33] When, in the spring of 1938, Italian intransigence put obstacles in the way of the execution of the Anglo-Italian agreement of April 1938,[34]

---

[29] For Drummond's activities as Secretary General see F. P. Walters, *A History of the League of Nations* (2 vols., London, 1952), especially I, 75-80; II, 556-560.

[30] *ibid.*, I, 393 for his action in the conflict between Bolivia and Paraguay.

[31] *British Documents*, 3rd series, III, 319, 329, 358.

[32] *ibid.*, IV, 349.

[33] Ciano, *1937-1938 Diario* (Bologna, 1948), pp. 307, 313. *L'Europa verso la Catastrofe* (Verona, 1948), pp. 327, 355.

[34] See Chapter 16, § II.

Perth tried to keep the door open;[35] and, after the Munich conference, he pressed his government hard to put the agreement into force.[36] During these years, Perth seemed continuously concerned with demonstrating to the Italians that London was in a conciliatory mood.

In his reports to London, moreover, Perth frequently defended Italian policy. Ciano, who, because of the efficiency of the Italian secret service, was able to read many of Perth's reports, states in his Diary that the British ambassador, although opposed to the Fascist regime when he came to Rome, had developed into a "sincere convert" who "understood and even loved Fascism."[37] Though caution must always be employed when using Ciano's statements, Perth's reports suggest that there was a certain amount of truth in this remark. When, in November 1938, the Italians raised their claims against France, Perth certainly attempted to minimize the importance of the anti-French demonstrations.[38] His explanations of Italian aspirations in the Mediterranean suggest, indeed, that he was not immune to the historical arguments for revision pounded out by official Italian propaganda agencies. He considers the "grievances felt by Italy over the Peace Treaties" as "the crux of the matter"; "the feeling has grown in Italy that if the injustices inflicted upon the vanquished by the Peace Treaties are in process of swift revision, how much more ought the injustices suffered by one of the victors at the hands of her own allies to be repaired."[39] A consequence of this tendency to explain Fascist foreign policy as a result of Italian national aspirations was that Perth misjudged the decisive trend in Italian foreign policy: he underestimated Mussolini's eagerness to conclude an alliance with Germany[40]—an eagerness determined less by historical aspirations than by Fascist ideology.

These common elements in the diplomatic activities of Henderson and Perth, in Berlin and Rome, cannot have been accidental. They clearly derived from the difficulties of the situation in which democratic ambassadors found themselves in totalitarian countries. Since political decisions in these countries were exclusively in the hands of one man, and since this man was difficult to reach, the prognostication of political developments degenerated into a kind of psychological guessing game. Moreover, the methods in which diplomats had been trained to evaluate political trends in the country where they were stationed were of little use

[35] Ciano, *L'Europa verso la Catastrofe*, pp. 318-321, 327.
[36] *British Documents*, 3rd series, III, 322.
[37] Ciano, *1937-1938 Diario*, p. 309.
[38] *British Documents*, 3rd series, III, 463, 464, 466.
[39] *ibid.*, pp. 499, 506.   [40] *ibid.*, p. 322

in totalitarian countries. Diplomats are not schooled to base their opinions and recommendations on an intensive study and expert knowledge of economic developments and military budgets; they gauge the trend of future policy from an analysis of public opinion as it is expressed in newspapers, in political meetings, and in conversations with the various political personalities with whom they must keep in contact. In a country where there is a strictly controlled press which publishes only what the government wants it to publish, and where there are no political parties or people who express their opinions freely to the foreigner, this kind of analysis of political opinions is hardly possible. The slogans which government propaganda presents are, therefore, easily overestimated and regarded as an expression and reflection of long-lasting and deeply rooted national aspirations. Neither Perth nor Henderson was impervious to this kind of influence.

On the other hand, because the situation in totalitarian countries is so different from that in democratic countries the diplomat finds it necessary to emphasize and explicate the point of view of the totalitarian regime. The person who explains glides easily into the role of the person who justifies and advocates. It is an inherent danger of the diplomatic profession that representatives abroad tend inevitably to associate themselves with the government to which they are accredited, and to defend its policies; and this tendency grows in direct proportion to the resistance of the home office to such persuasion.

It should not be said that Perth succumbed to these dangers to the same extent as Henderson. Although Perth's reports show something of Henderson's eagerness to understand, and to make understood, the dictator's policy, he never displayed the enthusiasm which Henderson showed in this endeavor. Perth's reports to the Foreign Office were always marked by certain reservations, and he was always aware of the limitations set by circumstances upon Italian aspirations. His negotiations with the Italian government for an Anglo-Italian agreement had clearly defined and limited objectives. Italy was a much less powerful country than Germany, and there was not the same reason to pay for Italian friendship. Moreover, because the leaders of Italian policy had to act from a much more restricted power basis, their moves remained on a much more calculable basis. Perth may have misjudged Mussolini's attitude to Germany but, in the last analysis, even here he was not far wrong, for the limitations of Italian power made it impossible for Mussolini, in 1939, to carry out his intention of siding with Germany in the war.

Moreover, Perth had come to Rome with a sound basis of skepticism. In his post at Geneva, he must have felt little sympathy for the Italian leaders, who had been less than enthusiastic about the League of Nations. Soon after his arrival in Rome, he became involved in the Abyssinian crisis; and, perhaps still under the influence of the Geneva experience, believed that the Italians were bluffing and seems to have taken a rather strong line against them.[41] It is only natural that, when the League policy in the Abyssinian affair had proved to be a failure, and when the course in London had been changed, he should have been concerned with ending his diplomatic career with success and should have become a supporter of Chamberlain's "new course." Even so, the skepticism and the reserve remained; whereas, in contrast, Henderson—appointed to Berlin at a moment when the policy of London demanded the abandonment of all possible reservations and probably by nature the least skeptical man alive—had had no previous experience with the Nazis which could influence, or guide, his judgment and was rather proud of his "freedom from prejudice."

III

For both Perth and Henderson the decisive period of their embassies in Rome and Berlin were the years when British foreign policy was set on a new course, that of Chamberlain's appeasement policy. It is striking to read the word appeasement in the diplomatic reports of the time. The word is used in a matter-of-fact way which shows that it had a much more general meaning, and a much less invidious one, than it has now. Today appeasement has been entirely identified with the idea of buying peace by making concessions to aggression, whereas, in its original meaning, concession was merely one of several means which might be employed to attain a general easing of European tension. The truth of the matter is that Chamberlain's appeasement policy had a more comprehensive character than is now assumed.[42] It was directed towards the reestablishment of a concert of Europe which should be directed by the four Great Powers: Britain, France, Italy, and Germany. In a sense, it was an attempt to reestablish the Locarno policy, which had been destroyed by the Nazi rise to power and by the break between Italy and the League of Nations.

But the situation was now very different from that of the 1920's,

---

[41] Raffaele Guariglia, *Ricordi 1922-1946* (Napoli, 1949), pp. 236, 243, 248.

[42] For Chamberlain's concept of foreign policy see Keith Feiling, *The Life of Neville Chamberlain* (London, 1946), particularly chapters 23-24.

when Locarno had been concluded; and great difficulties now stood in the way of realizing Four Power cooperation. First of all, Germany and Italy had to be persuaded, by concessions of some kind, to cooperate once more with the Western Powers. At the same time, Russia, who had moved closer to the West, had once more to be excluded from Europe. Most of all, the whole concept of collective security and the League of Nations had to be abandoned. This policy would be a deviation from the line which Britain had followed since the end of the first world war. Despite the fact that certain aspects of League activity had been criticized by the Dominions, the League of Nations had become a useful instrument for harmonizing the policy of Great Britain with that of the Commonwealth, and the shift to a more exclusively European policy might place the relation between the mother-country and the Dominions under a severe strain. Although the United States was not in the League of Nations, the abandonment of collective security and of the idea of the League would certainly increase the difficulties of cooperation with that great Atlantic Power. In addition, the concessions which would have to be made to Germany would mean the break-up of the French alliance system and the weakening of the French position.

Finally, in addition to these considerations of power politics, there were certain moral issues. The abandonment of collective security and of the League of Nations would eliminate whatever progress had been made in the development of a peaceful system of international relations. It might bring war nearer because it would restore what has been called the period of "international anarchy." Considerations of morality and power politics could not be entirely separated. If Germany and Italy were promoted to full participation in the hegemony of Europe, would it not mean that ruthlessness and immorality were being rewarded? And could one not say that, if the violations of international law by Germany and Italy were condoned, it would be useless to expect permanent cooperation between the Four Powers?

Thus, Chamberlain's appeasement policy was an adventure and, as such, it met strong resistance in the Foreign Office. Against this, Chamberlain reacted sharply. In previous chapters, reference has been made to the interference of the Prime Minister in Foreign Office business, especially in the time of Lloyd George and Ramsay MacDonald. Neville Chamberlain carried this interference much further. His struggle with the Foreign Office falls roughly into two periods. The first one stretches from his coming to 10 Downing Street until February 1938, when Anthony Eden, who was, and remained, opposed to Chamberlain's concepts, was dismissed. During this time, Chamberlain constantly employed special emissaries who established contact outside the official channels of the Foreign Office. His confidants maintained close relations with the German and Italian ambassadors in London,[43] and their activities were coordinated by Sir Horace Wilson of the Department of the Treasury upon whom Chamberlain fully relied for the carrying out of his new policy. Chamberlain tried to break the resistance of the Foreign Office at the same time by establishing a more personal relationship with the dictators than had existed in the past. On the German side, his chief effort of this kind was the mission of Lord Halifax to Hitler in November 1937. A somewhat parallel development—the more sinister because less official—was the use which Chamberlain made of his sister-in-law, Lady Austen Chamberlain, to establish contact with Mussolini and revive the long-stalled Anglo-Italian negotiations for a Mediterranean settlement.[44] Through Lady Chamberlain, the Prime Minister assured Mussolini that he would recognize the Italian empire in Abyssinia, at a time when the Foreign Office was insisting that no such assurance should be made before the beginning of negotiations.

After Eden's dismissal, the situation was changed. Halifax, the new Foreign Secretary, was fully in Chamberlain's confidence, and the policy of appeasement now dominated the Foreign Office. Even so, Chamberlain and his friends remained distrustful of the permanent officials of that organization. As one of the members of Chamberlain's group said, the Foreign Office was dominated by a pro-French group, whose influence could be broken only slowly and gradually.[45] Chamberlain and Sir Horace Wilson, therefore, continued to interfere with the details of policy execution; and the lack of coordination in British foreign affairs administration went on.

It is clear that this development placed the two ambassadors at Berlin and Rome in a difficult position. Just as German diplomats under the Nazis were faced with the necessity of choosing between the Foreign Office line and the party line, so were Henderson and Perth forced to identify themselves either with the views of the Foreign Office or the policy of the Prime Minister. The decision was not difficult for Perth. He had been in Rome before Chamberlain came to power; he had been in close contact with the entire policy of the Foreign Office in the previous period; and, in any case, the mission of Lady Chamberlain showed that

---

[43] Ciano, *L'Europa verso la Catastrofe*, p. 251, where Sir Joseph Ball appears as Chamberlain's liaison man.

[44] Ciano, *1937-1938 Diario*, p. 87, 103.

[45] *German Documents*, series D, I, 223-225.

he did not belong to the group that Chamberlain fully trusted. Naturally, when the course was set on an understanding with Italy, he was pleased to assume this more responsible activity; but there was never any question of his failing to remain strictly within the functions assigned to him by the Foreign Office.

The position of Nevile Henderson was quite different, for his appointment had been intended to indicate and underline the inauguration of Chamberlain's new approach to policy. His predecessor, Sir Eric Phipps, had been a typical representative of the Foreign Office tradition and had aroused criticism and opposition among the Nazi leaders.[46] Although it must be denied that Henderson was appointed at the request of the Nazis, his selection had certainly been influenced by the fact that he was clearly untinged by anti-German or pro-French bias.[47] When he was in London before departing for Berlin, he had had a long talk with Chamberlain, who explained the principles of his new policy.[48] From that time on, Henderson considered himself less as a subordinate of the Foreign Office than as a personal agent of the Prime Minister, whose policy he was charged to carry out. Thus, he remained in constant touch with Sir Horace Wilson and directed appeals to him whenever he disapproved of the instructions which he received from the Foreign Office.[49]

The result was that Henderson was deeply involved in the planning of Britain's policy toward Germany. He felt entitled to give advice, and he was heard. In the various stages of the Czech crisis, he recommended definite policies and played an active role in all the decisive steps. The idea of the Four Power Conference appears first in his reports.[50] Although it is not clear to what extent the idea of Chamberlain's visit to Hitler was Chamberlain's own, or suggested to him by Henderson, he was one of the few who were informed of this plan in its early stages.[51] And Henderson insisted on the absolute necessity of agreeing to the separation of the Sudeten area from Czechoslovakia, once this idea had been launched.[52]

But it is also evident that the fact that Henderson played a policy-making role influenced and colored his views on Germany. He had gone

[46] See Chapter 16 above.
[47] Because he had spent much time in the Near East and the Balkans and hardly any in the great European capitals. See note 28.
[48] Henderson, *Failure*, pp. 6-8.
[49] *British Documents*, 3rd series, II, 647-650.
[50] *Survey of International Affairs*, 1938, II, 427-428.
[51] Feiling, *Chamberlain*, p. 357.
[52] *Survey of International Affairs*, 1938, II, 342.

there with a mission, namely, that of carrying through Chamberlain's policy, and he had a burning desire to win, not merely success, but what might later be described as a triumph. It is characteristic that one of Henderson's first thoughts upon being appointed to Berlin was of "the Latin tag about failure and success which ominously observes that the Tarpeian rock, from which failures were thrown to their doom, is next to the Capitol, where the triumph of success is celebrated."[53] But triumph depended upon finding in Germany a basis for cooperation; and Henderson himself admits that he set out to see the "good side" of Nazi Germany.[54] A critical or objective approach would have made the reasons for his appointment futile; his mission would have been even less than the fulfilment of a routine function and would, indeed, have destroyed the foundations of the Chamberlain policy to which he was fully committed.

IV

There remains a psychological question, namely, the question why Henderson felt he had to play this kind of historical role; why he was not content with the honorable but rather restricted role which a diplomat plays in the twentieth century; why he aimed at being a "great ambassador" in the style of the eighteenth or nineteenth century. It is sometimes said in explanation of Chamberlain's policy that the Prime Minister had a totally insular outlook and that this accounts for the shortcomings of his theory of foreign affairs. However this may be, it seems clear that Henderson had an insular outlook in reverse. He himself says that after he entered the Foreign Service he never spent more than three or four continuous months in England. The result was not that he became alienated from England but, rather, that he became more English than the English. Certainly the Germans saw in him the typical Englishman.[55] In the excitement and turmoil of the Munich Conference, he walked about unperturbed, immaculately dressed, with a red carnation in his buttonhole—always "the man with the flower," as Hitler called him.[56] But there was more to this attitude of studied calm than this. It was an external sign of the extent to which Henderson felt that, in contrast to the restlessness and vulgarity of his era, he had

[53] Henderson, *Failure*, p. 3.
[54] *ibid.*, p. viii.
[55] Paul Schmidt, *Statist auf diplomatischer Bühne* (Bonn, 1949), p. 390.
[56] Jacques Davignon, *Berlin 1936-1940* (Paris, Bruxelles, 1951), p. 88 and Filippo Anfuso, *Roma Berlino Salò* (Editore Garzanti, 1950), p. 79.

to represent the attitude of an older and better world.[57] From this perspective, he looked down on foreigners and was little inclined to become excited about special degrees of ruthlessness and cruelty in other countries.

But he felt separated not only from the non-English world; he began to feel out of step with developments in his own country as well. In England too, the world in which Henderson had grown up had begun to disappear.[58] He saw only the negative side of this process and had no understanding of the new forces which were coming into the foreground. The family from which he sprang had risen in the prosperity of the Victorian and Edwardian age, but, in Henderson's lifetime, this progress was halted. The estate which his father had bought, and on which Nevile had grown up, was sold; decline had set in before the family had been firmly established as part of the hereditary ruling group. These circumstances made Henderson something of a snob.[59] Because he was strongly attached to the values of a disappearing order, he felt uprooted in the 1920's, the time of the rise of the Labor party and of internationalism in foreign policy. Unintellectual, and traditional in his thinking, clinging to the values of the past—like many men of a conformist character in times of changing values—he grasped after a faith, an absolute. When he heard of his appointment to Berlin, he felt that God had granted him a special mission; he saw himself making a contribution to the salvation of society; in fulfilling this mission, his life would gain meaning.

For these reasons, it can perhaps be said that Henderson is more than merely a diplomat who failed. He is, rather, typical of the helplessness with which members of a declining ruling class faced the social transformation of the 1920's and 1930's.

V

Henderson's colleague in Rome did not have to face the bitter feelings of failure and futility in which Henderson's life ended.[60] The Earl of

[57] See Henderson's interesting remarks on aristocracy in *German Documents*, series D, II, 769ff.

[58] See, in general, Nevile Henderson, *Water under the Bridges* (London, 1945), a book of more personal reminiscences in contrast to his political memoirs, *Failure of a Mission*.

[59] It is characteristic of Henderson that, in *Water under the Bridges*, he recounts that, when he became nearly involved in a car accident while driving with Princess Olga of Yugoslavia, his "only thought was that, if one had to die, one might die in worse company than that of a Royal Princess." P. 18.

[60] In his last years, Henderson himself said that it was a mistake to have sent him to Nazi Germany, and he doubted his fitness for a diplomatic career.

Perth returned to Britain before the outbreak of the second world war. He could claim to have steered Anglo-Italian relations through a period of stormy weather into calmer waters, and the success of his diplomatic mission seemed confirmed by Italy's remaining neutral when the war broke out. His position in the highest ranks of the British aristocracy led him immediately into new activities. During the war, he performed useful services in the Ministry of Information, and he became deputy leader of the Liberal party in the House of Lords. In the upper chamber, he was an ardent defender of the diplomatic corps against criticisms made of it. Thus, he repudiated the accusation that the British "missions abroad . . . failed on occasion to inform the Government fully of the general trend of political movements in the countries to which they were accredited."[61] He denied sharply that "the members of the diplomatic and consular service can be held responsible for such failures, if failures they have been."[62] He insisted that "they surely must rather be attributed to our foreign policy, and foreign policy is primarily the concern of the Secretary of State for Foreign Affairs, though it ultimately must and should be the responsibility of His Majesty's Government as a whole."[63] There was, of course, a good deal of truth in these statements; but the special emphasis which Lord Perth placed upon them probably indicates some misgivings on his part concerning the role of Britain's representatives in the most important European capitals in the last years before the debacle.

[61] Parliamentary Debates: Lords, 5th series, CXIX, 610.
[62] *ibid.*
[63] *ibid.*

18

The Voice in the Wilderness:
Robert Coulondre

BY FRANKLIN L. FORD AND CARL E. SCHORSKE

IN A WORLD of bewildered and myopic makers of foreign policy in the last prewar years, Robert Coulondre stands out as a determined and clearheaded diplomat. History has given him stature by confirming the wisdom of his political judgment. To this it may be objected that history has as often sanctioned the prejudice of a fool as the judgment of a wise man; but this formulation would do less than justice to a remarkable observer. In Coulondre's political outlook, prejudice unquestionably played its part. During the critical years of his missions to Moscow (1936-1938) and Berlin (1938-1939), this Huguenot diplomat clung with dogged consistency to two simple ideas: first, that Germany must be stopped; second, that only a tight military alliance between the Western Powers and the Soviet Union could stop her. If he drew these conceptions from a well-established French tradition of foreign policy,[1] he tested and confirmed them by careful analysis of the modern international scene. If the course he advocated was not adopted by his government, it was not—insofar as we can judge from the sparse materials available—because of Coulondre's lack of skill in presenting his ideas. He exploited to the utmost the limited sphere of action open to the modern diplomat to make his policies prevail.

I

Coulondre was appointed to Moscow in the autumn of 1936 under the first Popular Front government of Léon Blum. With the government theoretically committed to an anti-Fascist foreign policy, the atmosphere might be thought favorable for the development of Franco-Russian relations. But the Popular Front was already suffering from internal tension

[1] Robert Coulondre, *De Staline à Hitler. Souvenirs de deux ambassades, 1936-1939* (Paris, 1950), p. 22.

and external pressure. The Communists, who had refused to enter the government, supported it in Parliament but kept their hands free for exercising pressure upon it from without. They participated actively in the intense labor struggles of 1936, which evoked fear in the Center and on the Right. In broad sectors of centrist and rightist opinion, the Soviet Union was held responsible both for France's domestic and social tensions and for the "red" civil war in Spain. Republican Spain was widely regarded as a beachhead for a revolutionary invasion of France. During the late summer of 1936, a strong resolution against Soviet intervention in French affairs was adopted by the Radical Socialist party congress. The red scare and the concomitant hostility to the USSR thus reached into the heart of the Popular Front itself.

In this atmosphere Coulondre prepared for his difficult mission. He was surprised to find the Foreign Office singularly lacking in information on Russia. The skimpy files showed him "that relations with the USSR, reestablished in 1924, had been neither very close nor very well cultivated since then, notwithstanding the pacts."[2] The political and governmental leaders whom Coulondre consulted were tinged by the prevailing mood of bitterness toward the USSR. Foreign Minister Yvon Delbos in particular was deeply suspicious of Soviet intentions. He suggested that the Soviets might be trying to drive the French into a preventive war against Germany. And if war should come, he asked, what aid would the Russians give France? By what routes could military assistance be provided? Concerning the value of the Franco-Soviet Mutual Assistance Pact of 1935, Delbos manifested the greatest skepticism. The Russians, he felt, were merely using it as a cover for their revolutionary propaganda in France and out. If this should continue, French public opinion "would force the hand of the government" into a thoroughly negative attitude toward the USSR. The fate of the Franco-Soviet agreement, he felt, "lies much more in their hands than in ours."[3] Thus the Foreign Minister, along with most of the leading politicians with whom Coulondre spoke, viewed Franco-Soviet relations primarily in terms of French domestic struggles rather than in terms of the European security problem. Only Blum, Reynaud, and Herriot assigned real importance to the strengthening of ties with the USSR.[4]

Whatever the prevailing sentiment in Paris, Coulondre was convinced that his primary objective must be the achievement of a tight military-political association between France and the Soviet Union to contain German aggression. If the attempt should fail, he felt, the only alterna-

[2] *ibid.*, p. 12.   [3] *ibid.*, p. 13.   [4] *ibid.*, pp. 14, 16-18.

tive would be a victory for those who sought the security of France on the dangerous road of collaboration with Germany.[5] What could he, a mere diplomat, do to create a more receptive attitude in his own government for a Soviet alliance? As he saw it from Paris, his mission was to make the Soviet government understand that it must cease its intervention in French affairs, that it must, in effect, choose between the promotion of French Communism and the protection of its vital security interests through a military alliance with France. Surely Coulondre's perspective was somewhat narrow. His unspoken assumption was that the French Right and Center would be adequately anti-German if only the Soviet Union would call off its Communist dogs. Was not social conflict in France too deep-rooted to be suppressed by the Soviet Union, even if the Soviets had had the will fully to curb their French following? There was something unreal about Coulondre's attempt to create the domestic basis for a Franco-Soviet military accord by diplomatic means. But the attitudes prevailing in official circles were those with which the ambassador had to work, and his only means were diplomatic. The alternative to the course he set for himself would have been inactive resignation.

In his initial interview with Foreign Commissar Litvinov, Coulondre ignored the customary diplomatic formalities to lay his cards directly on the table: "I have come here without prejudice for or against the Russia of the Soviets. I am, however, a convinced partisan of the assistance pact because I believe it to be one of the elements necessary to safeguarding the peace to which both nations are equally attached. . . . Well then, I come to tell you [that], if things continue as they're now going, there will soon be no more assistance pact. French public opinion is sick and tired of Comintern meddling in the domestic affairs of France —meddling which, we know . . . is inspired if not directly operated by the Soviet Government itself. . . ." Soviet interference, Coulondre continued, threatened not only to ruin the Popular Front, but also to swallow up the pact itself. "Either it shall cease, or the pact will become . . . a dead letter."[6]

Litvinov assured the ambassador that he would repeat previous orders to the Soviet embassy in Paris to stay out of French affairs. With respect to the Comintern, he could only make the customary specious denial that it had anything to do with Soviet foreign policy.[7]

The Soviet view of the problem Coulondre was to hear from President Kalinin. In accepting Coulondre's credentials, the President aired the Soviet grievances against France quite as bluntly as Coulondre had

[5] *ibid.*, pp. 22-23.   [6] *ibid.*, pp. 31-32.   [7] *ibid.*, p. 33.

[557]

spoken his to Litvinov. If intentions must be judged by acts, and the value of an agreement by its results, said Kalinin, then the French could not set much store by the assistance pact. Soviet efforts to acquire military supplies in France had met with resistance everywhere. Germany had offered to deliver the supplies on credit—even arms, Litvinov added. The Soviets had rejected these offers. But France had signed a pact of assistance with the USSR; it must also apply it.[8]

Coulondre had been aware of the reluctance of the French military authorities to supply the Soviets with equipment, but not of the depth of Soviet resentment against the treatment they had received. Kalinin's counteroffensive convinced the ambassador that his effort to win Soviet cooperation in the matter of noninterference in French domestic affairs must be paralleled by an attempt to make his government see the necessity of acquiescing in Soviet requests for military supplies. If the pact of 1935 were to be transformed into an effective military alliance, the deadlock would have to be broken more or less simultaneously in both capitals. The difficulty was that neither side was prepared to make the initial concession which might encourage a more accommodating attitude in the other.

How to extract a vital concession from either Moscow or Paris?—that was the problem which dominated Coulondre's diplomatic activity for almost two years. In the absence of any French documentary publications for the pre-Munich period, we can discover no more than the bare outlines of Coulondre's activity. We shall merely touch here on a few examples which illustrate the ambassador's situation and the methods by which he sought to break out of it.

On the Russian side, Coulondre quickly became convinced that Litvinov and his Foreign Commissariat had no power to produce any changes in Comintern behavior. Somehow, he must get the ear of Stalin. With neither instructions from his government nor any *quid pro quo* to offer the Communist dictator, the ambassador could not make a direct approach. He therefore utilized a GPU agent—one of the many who, with one or another official function, infested the diplomatic colony—to carry to Stalin his message on the Comintern. Stalin asked Coulondre, through the same intermediary, what he would propose. Coulondre replied that the Comintern should be, if not dissolved, then transferred out of Russia. Stalin answered that he could not accept this suggestion for the present. He made the unusual admission that the Comintern was a factor in the USSR's defense system; in view of the German situation,

[8] *ibid.*, pp. 33-34.

he could not let the control of it out of his hands. He stated that all he wanted of France was to be "strong and resolute in the face of Germany." As for internal affairs, Stalin cited the case of Turkey, with which he enjoyed excellent relations although its government was scarcely "soft" [*tendre*] with the Communists.[9]

Stalin's answer, though frank, was on the whole negative. Coulondre concluded from it that any French government, however rightist, would be an acceptable partner to the USSR if, as Litvinov said a few weeks later, it followed the "patriotic" policy of Poincaré and Clemenceau.[10] But the Comintern and the French Communists remained; as long as they did, and as long as they opposed any deviation by France from Soviet foreign policy, the French government would continue distrustful if not hostile. On the Soviet side, Stalin could not abandon the Comintern in the face of the Anti-Comintern Pact, concluded on November 17, 1936, only a few days after the delivery of his message to the French ambassador. Nor would he, as Coulondre realized, surrender his foothold in French domestic politics if it should ever become his policy deliberately to weaken France as a factor in European international life.

Having early struck bedrock in his efforts to effect a change in Soviet policy, Coulondre devoted most of his energy during the remainder of his mission to influencing his own government's attitude. In this shift in focus, he shared in a general tendency of diplomats who represented democratic powers in totalitarian countries. The monolithic structure of totalitarian government left a diplomat little room for maneuver. His only hope in influencing the omnipotent leadership abroad was through some change in his own government's policy. The divided counsels in the governing strata of the democracies strengthened the temptation for an ambassador who was frustrated in his host country to influence policy at home rather than merely to follow instructions.[11] In Coulondre's case, this natural penchant was reenforced by a conviction of the overriding importance of cementing the Franco-Russian alliance. The more conscious Coulondre became of the depth of Stalin's concern over the German menace and his fear of any internal challenge to his power, the more urgently he pressed the need for meeting Russia half way. Like his German colleague Schulenburg, Coulondre analyzed the purges in the context of the vast Soviet industrialization and militarization program. Although the internal upheaval might weaken Russia in the short run,

<hr />

[9] *ibid.*, pp. 39-40.   [10] *ibid.*, pp. 40-41.
[11] See above, Chapters 14 and 17, for instances in which ambassadors succumbed to this temptation.

it was nevertheless, in Coulondre's eyes, "a crisis of growth." Not, of course, growth toward democracy, but toward counterrevolutionary absolutism, nationalism, and—above all—industrial and military might.

Where the Western observers on the whole tended to interpret the era of the purges as reducing the importance of the Soviet Union in world affairs, Coulondre drew the opposite conclusion. Where many Westerners rejoiced in the increasing isolationism of Russia, Coulondre was frightened by it. He did not believe that the USSR would withdraw from Europe in fact, even if it could not find a *modus vivendi* with the democracies. The essential question for France to ask itself about Russia, Coulondre insisted, was not "Will Russia be with us or not?" but "With whom will Russia go?"[12] France was the first string to the Soviet bow, but if France should prove recalcitrant, the Soviets would not hesitate to try a German string.

Since 1935, the Russians had repeatedly made overtures for closer military ties with France, but had met, in the words of Blum, with responses of "a generally dilatory character."[13] In February 1937, Blum requested and received of Soviet ambassador Potemkin a Russian general staff estimate of the aid which the USSR could render in the event of a German attack on France or Czechoslovakia. General Gamelin, according to his own account, was not asked by Daladier, Minister of War, to comment on this memorandum until April 9, 1937.[14] In the Soviet memorandum, the difficult question of transit for Soviet troops through Poland and Rumania was already adumbrated. The French general staff commented that "the state of the conversations which France has had with these states does not permit an answer to the question." But the staff scarcely encouraged the search for an answer when it stated that, in any case, Poland and Rumania would need their railways for their own troop concentrations and could not spare them to transport Russian soldiers.[15]

Coulondre was in Paris during these April discussions, but there is no evidence that he was given an active part in them.[16] Although a program for a "military pre-accord" was drafted on April 15, it never reached the negotiating stage. General Gamelin's view that, because of the Polish-

---

[12] Coulondre, *De Staline à Hitler*, p. 44. For his views on the changes in the USSR during the era of the purges, cf. *ibid.*, pp. 43-45, 58-59, 72-125.

[13] *Commission d'Enquête parlementaire, Les événements survenus en France de 1933 à 1945, Témoignages et documents*, I, 90, 128-129, 272-273; Paul Reynaud, *La France a sauvé l'Europe* (Paris, 1947), I, 115-117.

[14] Général Gamelin, *Servir* (Paris, 1946), II, 285-286.

[15] *ibid.*, II, 287.

[16] Coulondre, *De Staline à Hitler*, p. 48.

Rumanian problem, a precise military accord could only lead France up a blind alley presumably prevailed.[17] Another attempt to inaugurate Franco-Russian staff conversations, made by Litvinov on a visit to Paris in May 1937, likewise came to nothing.[18] During the succeeding nine months, Coulondre was condemned to the role of an impotent observer while the ice gathered on the skeletal structure of the Franco-Russian alliance.

The rape of Austria and the threat posed by this event to the existence of Czechoslovakia infused a new vitality into the issue of France's relations with the Soviet Union. From March until May 1938, the international situation and the concomitant fluidity in French policy gave Coulondre both room for maneuver and grounds for hope that his project of an Anglo-French-Russian security bloc might be realized.

When Czechoslovakia became the nerve center of the European crisis, Coulondre advised his government that the Russian factor had now acquired its maximum importance for preserving the peace or, if war should come, for winning an armed conflict. Poland offered no comparable platform for joint resistance. If Hitler were to attack Poland, the Soviet Union could hardly be counted on as a reliable ally of France. The Czechs, unlike the Poles, were firmly committed to the European *status quo*. Above all, Czechoslovakia was "the only country on which the action of the three great peaceful Powers could be conjoined."[19]

We have no explicit evidence on the reception given to this advice in Paris, but the governmental atmosphere was certainly favorable to it in mid-March 1938. With the formation of the second Blum cabinet during the Austrian crisis, the weary and indecisive Yvon Delbos was replaced as Foreign Minister by Joseph Paul-Boncour. The first public diplomatic act of the new government was a demonstrative reception of the Czech ambassador by Blum and Paul-Boncour to assure him that "France would uphold its obligations to Czechoslovakia . . . effectively, promptly and completely."[20] To be sure, a meeting of the Permanent Committee of National Defense, summoned to consider what France might do militarily in the event of aggression against Czechoslovakia, revealed the usual pessimism on the part of the military authorities concerning French, Czech, and Soviet powers of resistance.[21] But the very bleakness of the

[17] Gamelin, *Servir*, II, 287.

[18] Vice Commissar Potemkin told Coulondre that the French ministries of air and navy favored the discussions, but that the ministry of war gave no answer. Coulondre, *De Staline à Hitler*, p. 127.

[19] *ibid.*, pp. 137-138.

[20] *British Documents*, 3rd series, I, 53-54; *German Documents*, series D, II, 217.

[21] Gamelin, *Servir*, II, 322-328.

military outlook confirmed Blum and Paul-Boncour in the conviction that the construction of an international resistance front was the more urgent. The Foreign Minister indicated unequivocally to the German ambassador that aggression against Czechoslovakia "meant war" with France.[22] He tried without success to induce the British government to take a similarly strong stand.[23] The British Foreign Secretary, Lord Halifax, replied that the British would honor their commitments to France under Locarno, but could not "see their way clear to adding to them."[24] Where Paul-Boncour urged a firm, overt stand against the Germans, Halifax counseled pressure on the Czechs. Halifax indicated, however, that Great Britain would not really let France succumb to Germany, and Paul-Boncour was prepared to take the risk that, if France took a firm position, Britain could ultimately be brought into line.[25] Meanwhile, however, it would be necessary for France to take the lead in Eastern Europe to reconstruct its disintegrating security system.

At the end of March, Paul-Boncour summoned the French ambassadors to the principal Central and Eastern European capitals for a conference to determine a consistent policy for the defense of Czechoslovakia. Very little is known about the course or outcome of this conference (April 5), except that there was sharp protest against the previous policy of drift and of shallow reliance on Geneva, and a general determination to place France's policy in Eastern Europe on a more realistic basis by applying all possible pressure to eliminate the conflicts of policy among France's eastern allies.[26] The Quai d'Orsay tried to enlist British support for this program.[27] The German ambassador in Paris described the projected French campaign in the Eastern European capitals as "a tendency which merits our most serious attention."[28]

Coulondre's role in the formulation of the new policy is impossible to determine from the sparse and contradictory evidence available.[29] On his

---

[22] *German Documents*, series D, II, 214.

[23] *British Documents*, 3rd series, I, 50-54.

[24] *ibid.*, I, 84.

[25] *ibid.*, I, 85; J. Paul-Boncour, *Entre deux guerres. Souvenirs sur la III République* (Paris, 1946), III, 83-84, 97-98.

[26] Léon Noël, *L'agression allemande contre la Pologne* (Paris, 1946), pp. 196-197; Paul-Boncour, *Entre deux guerres*, III, 93-94, 98-99; *German Documents*, series D, II, 215-217.

[27] In the aide-mémoire to London (April 9), the help of Britain was solicited in securing the cooperation of "the other countries of Central Europe and Danubian Europe" —a formulation which excluded the USSR. *British Documents*, 3rd series, I, 146.

[28] *German Documents*, series D, II, 222.

[29] Six weeks after the ambassadors' conference, Coulondre told the British chargé d'affaires in Moscow that "when he was in Paris last M. Blum was in power, and that he had felt constrained on that occasion to tender very moderate and guarded advice, of a

return to Moscow, however, he set to work to mobilize diplomatic opinion in support of an eastern containment front. Coulondre and his Czech colleague simultaneously advised their governments to launch an action in Bucharest and Moscow to solve the troop transit question. The Rumanians were to receive assurances concerning their continued possession of Bessarabia, which the Soviet Union had never recognized, in exchange for transit rights for Soviet troops to Czechoslovakia.[30] The French and Czech military attachés spoke to their British opposite as if Soviet intervention on behalf of Czechoslovakia were a foregone conclusion—a view which the British embassy hardly shared. On April 18 Colonel Pallace, the French attaché, told his British colleague that France would have "to speak very strongly to Poland and force her back to the side of France. For this purpose it was essential that M. Beck should be removed. Poland must be forced to allow Soviet troops to pass through their country."[31] Coulondre felt, "in that vague and intuitive manner in which one senses such things in Soviet Russia," that the new determination of his own government was paralleled by an increasingly earnest attitude on the part of the USSR. He was struck with Litvinov's change in manner, from sarcasm and skepticism to "the seriousness and moderation of one who has a sense of new responsibilities, who knew that the Kremlin would play its part in a European conflict."[32] A more tangible factor which led Coulondre to the same conclusion was the changed situation in the Far East. With stiffening Chinese resistance and Japanese military energies deflected into Central China, the Soviet government was relieved of anxiety in that part of the world, and could make "a correspondingly greater effort in the West."[33] Coulondre felt that the moment was extremely favorable for concluding the long-postponed military convention between France and the USSR. In early May, when he had just resolved on his own initiative to go to Paris to press his case, Coulondre was sum-

---

distinctly pessimistic nature moreover, in regard to Soviet affairs and the chances of the Soviet government taking a more positive part in counteracting German machinations . . ." (*British Documents*, 3rd series, I, 304). Coulondre states in his memoirs that, on his visit to Paris, he had stressed that the initiative and interest shown by the Soviets in the Czech question was a sign that they meant business; he had advised his government that it was "more useful and more urgent than ever to open military conversations with the USSR." (*De Staline à Hitler*, p. 135.) Coulondre's memoirs seem unreliable for this period: he states that he reported the above to Yvon Delbos, but the Foreign Minister at the time was Paul-Boncour, whom he does not mention.

[30] Coulondre, *De Staline à Hitler*, p. 137.
[31] *British Documents*, 3rd series, I, 172-173.
[32] *ibid.*, I, 304; Coulondre, *De Staline à Hitler*, p. 304.
[33] *British Documents*, 3rd series, I, 305. Cf. also Coulondre, *De Staline à Hitler*, pp. 139-140.

moned home by the new Foreign Minister in the Daladier cabinet, Georges Bonnet.

On the day of his departure from Moscow (May 16, 1938), Coulondre took an unusual step. He laid before the British chargé d'affaires and his military attaché an evaluation of the Soviet political and military position.[34] Coulondre was then under the erroneous impression that the British government had notified Berlin that it would regard a German attack upon Czechoslovakia as a *quasi casus belli*, and undoubtedly wished to associate his British colleague in his attempt to strengthen Soviet participation in safeguarding Czech independence.[35] His effort was a total failure. The British chargé, Mr. Vereker, expressed himself as "slightly mystified as to the motives underlying M. Coulondre's invitation, for I have always understood that he is usually reserved and uncommunicative." Vereker concluded that Coulondre's main object was "simply to clear his mind and be able to go to Paris fortified by an independent and unbiased third party opinion."[36] Vereker rejected out of hand Coulondre's contention that "one could in fact place some reliance on the Soviet government both in a political and military sense at this juncture." There was no reason for the Frenchman to feel "more optimistic of possible Russian intervention on the side of Czechoslovakia at the present moment than he had been heretofore."[37] The British chargé gave his "independent and unbiased" opinion "that the Russians were Asiatics . . . and that with the present Byzantine regime in the Kremlin anything might happen." But "there was no good hoping vainly that the Russians might be of some value as a counterpoise to the Germans when the balance of probability lay on the other side."[38] The conversation provided an accurate foretaste of the British attitude which was to play so large a role in the failure of Coulondre's Moscow mission.

During the interval between Coulondre's two visits to Paris in the spring of 1938, France had suffered another cabinet overturn. Rightist criticism of Paul-Boncour's energetic foreign policy had played no small part in the collapse of the short-lived Blum government, and the new premier, Edouard Daladier, decided to jettison Paul-Boncour in favor of the more flexible Georges Bonnet.[39]

The foreign policy which took shape under the new government deserves brief examination here, since it was to provide the background for Coulondre's activity. With Paul-Boncour out of the way,[40] Lord Halifax

[34] *British Documents*, 3rd series, I, 301-307.   [35] *ibid.*, 301.
[36] *ibid.*, 307.   [37] *ibid.*, 305.   [38] *ibid.*, 307.
[39] Paul-Boncour, *Entre deux guerres*, III, 93-94, 100-101.
[40] The British Foreign Office opinion of Paul-Boncour was perhaps characteristically

returned to the assault to dissuade the French from their drastic stand on Czechoslovakia, and warned the French government against persisting in too optimistic an interpretation of Chamberlain's hint that Great Britain might go beyond her legal commitments in defense of France.[41] In the Anglo-French conversations at the end of April, the French, unable to extract a commitment from Great Britain on Czechoslovakia, began the process of surrender to the British lead by agreeing to put pressure on the Czechs to make the "maximum concessions."[42]

Bonnet was not yet, however, prepared to shift the focus of French diplomatic activity from the reconstruction of a containment front to the mitigation of Czech-German tension *à l'anglaise*. In early May, he held conversations with Litvinov in Geneva. Litvinov again seems to have suggested staff talks in order to determine with precision the action to be taken by the allies in the event of hostilities.[43] Bonnet also sounded out Petresco-Comnène, the Rumanian Foreign Minister, on the ticklish issue of troop transit, although he did not go beyond mere inquiry to the exercise of anything like pressure on the Rumanians.[44] Bonnet later said that his policy at this date was first "to bring about a rapprochement between England and the USSR, then to conclude a military accord with Russia, finally to settle the question of passage for Russian troops through the [eastern] border countries."[45] The British documents supply no evidence that Bonnet pursued the first of these aims. His policy in May 1938 might better be described as according primacy to accommodation with Britain while exploring possibilities for a firmer foothold in Eastern Europe. Reduced to its simplest terms, French policy was teetering on the brink between appeasement and resistance.

On May 20, Ambassador Coulondre was received by his Foreign Minister. Bonnet detailed his conversation with Litvinov and expressed his readiness to inaugurate staff conversations with the Russians to deter-

---

expressed by Alexander Cadogan to Czech ambassador Masaryk (April 4, 1938): "Paul-Boncour was not a Foreign Minister who at so serious a moment could be a worthy partner in a discussion of the European crisis." *Documents and Materials*, p. 103.

[41] *British Documents*, 3rd series, I, 141.

[42] Royal Institute of International Affairs, *Survey of International Affairs, 1938* (London, New York, Toronto, 1951), II, 101-108.

[43] *ibid.*, II, 132; Coulondre, *De Staline à Hitler*, p. 142. Bonnet makes no mention of Litvinov's request for staff talks; cf. Georges Bonnet, *Défense de la paix* (Paris, 1946), I, 125.

[44] Bonnet, *Défense*, I, 126-127; cf. N. Petresco-Comnène, *Preludi del grande dramma* (Rome, 1947), pp. 37-40, where the Rumanian answer, though hardly encouraging, appears less absolutely negative than in Bonnet's account.

[45] Bonnet, *Défense*, I, 123.

mine the scale and modalities of Soviet aid. Coulondre was instructed to draft plans for the conduct of negotiations in Moscow.[46]

During the next two days, while Coulondre was preparing his memorandum, the Czech issue erupted into a major crisis. It was thought in the Allied capitals that Germany was about to invade Czechoslovakia. On May 21, Bonnet reaffirmed in a press conference that France would stick by Czechoslovakia.[47] Halifax instructed the British ambassador in Paris to dispel at once any illusions on the part of Bonnet: "If . . . the French Government were to assume that His Majesty's Government would at once take joint military action with them to preserve Czechoslovakia against German aggression, it is only fair to warn them that our statements do not warrant any such assumption."[48]

The military situation was such that the conquest of Czechoslovakia could not be prevented, "even," Halifax added pointedly for Paris, "with such assistance as might be expected from Russia."[49] By the night of May 22, after hearing Halifax's message, Bonnet was a chastened man. He told the British ambassador that "he would not dream of taking action . . . without ample consultation" with Great Britain. If Czechoslovakia were unreasonable, France "might well declare . . . herself released from her bond."[50] Daladier, on the same evening, was weeping on the shoulders of the German ambassador, begging the Reich not to compel him to go to war for an alliance which he "had not made . . . and was certainly not happy about. . . ."[51]

On the next morning, Coulondre returned to present to the Foreign Minister his draft plan for Franco-Russian-Czech military talks. Coulondre was astonished at Bonnet's change in attitude. Bonnet was hesitant; he feared, he told his ambassador, that the prospect of Soviet military support might "incite certain French elements to appear bellicose." "What had happened since May 20?" Coulondre asks in all innocence in his memoirs.[52] Despite his hesitation, Bonnet authorized Coulondre to submit his plan to Daladier. The Premier too was cautious, urging that the negotiations be conducted in the greatest secrecy in order to avoid any reaction on Hitler's part. Daladier felt that his doubts about the value of the Soviet army must be tested in staff talks, and gave his consent. Again Coulondre saw Bonnet, who expressed further doubts: the military unpreparedness of Britain and France, the attitude of Poland, the ambiguity of Soviet policy. Coulondre brought forth his battery

[46] Coulondre, *De Staline à Hitler*, p. 142.   [47] *British Documents*, 3rd series, I, 340.
[48] *ibid.*, I, 345-346   [49] *ibid.*, I, 346.   [50] *ibid.*, I, 357.
[51] *German Documents*, series D, II, 327.   [52] Coulondre, *De Staline à Hitler*, p. 143.

of arguments once more: Soviet policy was least ambiguous in Czecho-slovakia; France could not maintain indefinitely two contradictory alliances in the east, and must choose the USSR over Poland as the Power constituting the greater bar to Hitler's progress, etc. Bonnet agreed and finally approved the opening of military talks.[53]

Coulondre departed for Moscow with a real sense of achievement. It appeared as if his hopes were at last on the way to realization. He was soon disabused. During the last days of May, Bonnet tried in vain to persuade Poland to declare her support for Czechoslovakia in the event of a conflict. When Litvinov asked what France would do if Poland attacked Czechoslovakia and Russia in turn attacked Poland, Coulondre answered that France would stand by Czechoslovakia; Bonnet told the Soviet chargé in answer to the same question posed in Paris that the matter would have to be studied.[54] Understandably enough, Bonnet found it difficult to give up the Polish alliance in favor of a doubtful partnership with the USSR. But his equivocation did not help the cause of Czechoslovakia. With respect to that hapless power, French policy turned, after the May crisis, into a mere auxiliary of British policy. By May 29, Bonnet, under British exhortations, was already applying that pressure upon the Czechs which was to continue in a straight line until the "resolution" of the Czech question at Munich.[55] The corollary to that policy, in fact if not out of necessity, was the decision to stay with the Polish alliance rather than to strengthen the ties with Russia. Coulondre was not informed by Bonnet of these decisions. It dawned on him only slowly that the plans approved, however hesitantly, on May 23 were being abandoned. On July 1 he learned the full story—not from his own government, but from a dispatch of the Czech ambassador in Paris which his Moscow colleague Fierlinger gave him to read: "The French Government will not follow up Franco-Soviet military conversations for the present, in order not to offend the susceptibilities of the English conservatives."[56] An oversimplified analysis, but not without truth.

With French policy veering into other channels, Coulondre could do nothing but sit out the dog days in Moscow in frustrating inactivity. He smarted at French policy, which, rather unjustly, he held primarily responsible for reducing history in the summer of 1938 to "a kind of tragic tournament between two men, one of whom carried an olive branch, the other a knife."[57]

[53] *ibid.*, pp. 145-146. Bonnet's *Défense* contains no reference to the Coulondre visit or the contemplated action.

[54] Coulondre, *De Staline à Hitler*, pp. 152-153.   [55] Bonnet, *Défense*, I, 155ff.

[56] Coulondre, *De Staline à Hitler*, p. 153.   [57] *ibid.*, p. 154.

When the Czech crisis entered its final phase at the end of August, there was again a brief flurry of activity in Paris and Moscow. On both sides, however, suspicions ran too deep to be allayed by anything short of a dramatic gesture which neither side wished to take for fear of offending the Germans.

On October 4, it was Coulondre's unpleasant duty to inform the Vice-Commissar for Foreign Affairs officially of the content of the Munich agreement. Potemkin received the ambassador coldly and let him speak his piece. " 'I simply wish to state,' he said to me [Coulondre] when I had finished, 'that the Western Powers have deliberately kept the USSR out of the negotiations.' The silence weighed on us. Then his emotions gained the upper hand and, though a Slav and a diplomat, he spoke his thoughts freely to me: 'My poor fellow, what have you done? For us, I see no other consequence but a fourth partition of Poland.' "[58]

Potemkin's words provided Coulondre with the text for a brilliant dispatch in which he analyzed the consequences of Munich for Soviet policy. His analysis was not unlike that of his German colleague Schulenburg,[59] stressing the fact that the Soviet Union had now lost all confidence in collective security and would have to rethink her policy. As a Frenchman, however, Coulondre could go further than Schulenburg in pointing out that Russia, rejected by the West, and uninhibited by any ideological sentiments, had no choice but to try "to return to the policy of understanding with Germany which she had abandoned in 1931."[60] Less than two weeks after this last Cassandra cry, Coulondre received the news of his transfer to Berlin.

Coulondre's mission to Moscow could only be reckoned a political failure. The brief promise of the spring of 1938 was cut off by the May crisis and the shift in French policy which followed it; and the ground once lost could never be regained. Was Coulondre overoptimistic concerning the possibility of cooperation between Russia and the West? Did he rely too much on Litvinov, failing to realize the strength of other tendencies in Moscow or to see that Litvinov's position was already weakened by the failure of collective security in Abyssinia and Spain? Did he underestimate the costs of France's taking the diplomatic initiative out of British hands? Did he underrate the risks of placing too much pressure on Poland and Rumania, perilously receptive as they were to German blandishments and threats? There is no evidence to justify an affirmative answer to these questions. As far as we know, Coulondre never advocated rash or foolish commitments to Moscow. Even though

---

[58] Coulondre, *De Staline à Hitler*, p. 165.   [59] See above, Chapter 15, § v.
[60] Coulondre, *De Staline à Hitler*, pp. 165-168.

a firm alliance with the Soviet Union was his primary objective, his diplomatic methods were sober and cautious. He worked to keep the lines open between Paris and Moscow, and urged upon his government nothing more than to explore possibilities which could have been pursued if profitable but closed off again if too costly. Even such modest diplomacy toward Russia was too much for the timorous and prejudiced framers of French foreign policy after May 1938. Whatever one may think of Coulondre's positive aims, one must grant that he had the rare political virtue of asking the right question, which he permitted no sentimental considerations to obscure: "Not, 'Will Russia be with us?' but, 'With whom will Russia go?'" His superiors paid no attention to the question. As a result, Coulondre in Berlin was to have the bitter experience of seeing it answered at the expense of his country's vital interest.

II

Coulondre arrived in the German capital to take up his new duties on November 19, 1938. Even if there were not major gaps in the sources, it would be pointless here to recount all the details of what was in many respects no more than an epilogue to the ambassador's period in Moscow. What can, and should, be done with the materials we do have is to organize them around certain critical points between the autumn of 1938 and the outbreak of the second world war. The resulting discussion will call attention to some aspects of Coulondre's record as an observer and spokesman of France within the Reich, but it will place greater emphasis on his role as proponent of a definite line of action—a line which he would presumably have advocated regardless of his particular assignment. For dramatic as were the events of his nine and a half months in Germany, his personal importance consists much more in the continuation of his arguments with Paris over the general European power situation than in his specific functions as envoy to Hitler's government. This second ambassadorship was a continuation of the first, in that Coulondre brought to it, and never abandoned, the basic convictions he had formed while in Russia. Its special character arises from the fact that he had, while in Berlin, to restate those convictions in a constantly changing context of diplomatic developments.

For obvious reasons, Coulondre felt the lurch of suddenly shifted gears as he began his new mission. From 1920 until 1936, at the Quai d'Orsay, he had followed German affairs closely; and in 1931, he had been along on Laval's state visit to Berlin.[61] Between those experiences

[61] André François-Poncet, *Souvenirs d'une ambassade à Berlin* (Paris, 1946), p. 26.

and the autumn of 1938, however, had intervened the two years in Russia. "After having gone to Moscow to work for an entente against Hitler, I was now to go to Berlin to work for an entente with Hitler."[62] Despite his lack of enthusiasm for the latter prospect, he insists that he loved his craft too well to be completely pessimistic or cynical. "M. Coulondre told me," recorded Ribbentrop of their initial interview, "that, on taking up his appointment, he intended to do all he could to improve Franco-German relations. . . . He personally was not biased in any particular direction and was open to all suggestions."[63] The new ambassador's first statement to his own staff, as he recalls it, included the following: "Munich is our point of departure. Each of us is free to judge as he sees it the policy which led there. The fact remains that, to safe-guard the peace, the Western Powers went there. The question, the only question now before us, is whether peace can actually be found by this route."[64]

The possibility of a negative answer is clearly left open, as it had to be, given Coulondre's sentiments. His whole position while in the Soviet Union had been predicated on distrust of any deal with the Nazis, and he considered it quite possible that efforts at conciliation would only in-crease Hitler's appetite. "Policies of weakness, like others," he said later, "entail risks, generally the most dangerous."[65] Nevertheless, immersed as he was in day-to-day negotiations, he could not claim that Olympian perspective which would have justified his condemning appeasement without giving it a chance. Hence, throughout his dispatches of those winter months of 1938-1939 run conflicting tendencies. An official policy which he feared had to be tried. A stiffer line which he favored could not as yet be espoused save by indirection.

This opening period began when Coulondre presented his credentials to Hitler on November 22, 1938. The ambassador expressed his hope, based on a rereading of the Fuehrer's speeches, that France and Germany might reach a solid understanding. He alluded specifically to François-Poncet, whom Hitler had mentioned in flattering terms, and stressed the desirability of an early manifestation of mutual good will, as fore-shadowed in the former ambassador's farewell visit to Berchtesgaden the previous month. Hitler showed himself receptive, citing his exservice-man's horror of war and his belief that no change in the Franco-German boundary would justify the sacrifices it would entail.[66] Coulondre had

[62] Coulondre, *De Staline à Hitler*, p. 189.   [63] *German Documents*, series D, IV, 456.
[64] Coulondre, *De Staline à Hitler*, p. 204.   [65] *ibid.*, p. 195.
[66] *French Yellow Book*, pp. 29-31.

left Paris already in possession of a draft friendship pact which had been handed him at the Ministry of Foreign Affairs, and three days after his talk with the Fuehrer he was notified by Bonnet that this text had been approved by the Germans.[67] The Ribbentrop-Bonnet declaration, solemnly repudiating all cause for hostility between France and the Reich, was signed at Paris on December 6.[68]

Thus far Coulondre had figured as little more than an agent carrying out functions bequeathed by his predecessor. He appears as an observer in his own right only with the dispatch which he sent on December 15 as a summary of first impressions in Berlin. The German people, he stated, were genuinely opposed to war and relieved by the rapprochement with France. He added, however, that the Nazi party's aim was not general peace but rather enough security in the West to permit eastward expansion toward the Ukraine. "The integration of *Deutschtum* into the Reich has been carried out more or less completely," he pointed out. "Now the hour of *Lebensraum* has come."[69]

This apprehensive tone was intensified after Coulondre spent an hour with Ribbentrop early in February. In the course of a long monologue, the dependably arrogant Foreign Minister described German foreign policy as aimed at combatting Bolshevism and eventually regaining the lost colonies. In addition, however, he blustered about the Allies' alleged refusal to recognize vital German interests in terms which seemed to have little to do with either the Soviet Union or Southwest Africa. Concerning the Reich's eastern neighbors, Coulondre could only reply that "France had no intention of giving up her friendships or her interests in any part of the continent."[70]

What put the French ambassador in a particularly weak position at this time was the remarkable maneuver which his own government had just embarked upon, in an effort to divert Italy's territorial demands. This, it will be remembered, was the winter when shouts of "Tunisia! Corsica! Nice!" had erupted in the Italian Chamber of Deputies. While François-Poncet in Rome was seeking to convert Mussolini to four-Power friendship, Coulondre in Berlin had obeyed instructions to advise the Wilhelmstrasse of French concern over the Duce's impatience and the threatening presence of Italian troops in Spain.[71] Meanwhile, Paul Baudouin, President of the Banque de l'Indochine, had been sent to Rome and on February 2 had confidentially offered Ciano concessions in

[67] *ibid.*, p. 32. [68] *ibid.*, p. 35.
[69] *ibid.*, pp. 41-45. [70] *ibid.*, pp. 57-59.
[71] *German Documents*, series D, IV, 490-491, 492.

Tunis and Djibuti and the directorate of the Suez Canal.[72] Ribbentrop, who learned of these overtures through Ambassador Mackensen, immediately saw to it that they were made public; but Coulondre, operating in the dark so far as the Quai d'Orsay's gambit was concerned, obediently issued a formal denial to the press, on orders from Bonnet. Simultaneously, Count Fernand de Brinon arrived in Germany, introduced himself to the ambassador as merely a tourist, then went straight to Ribbentrop as a secret spokesman for the French government and "in a discreet manner suggested mediation between France and Italy."[73] The German Foreign Minister was certainly not interested in seeing France freed of Italian pressure, but in the process of defeating the move he had the malicious pleasure of asking Coulondre how he had brought himself to deny the true reports concerning Baudouin. The ambassador was understandably furious over Bonnet's deviousness and went to Paris on February 10 demanding hotly that in the future he be kept as well informed as the German Foreign Office appeared to be.[74]

If the Baudouin-Brinon incident underscored the difficulty and ambiguity of Coulondre's position in Berlin, the extinction of rump Czechoslovakia changed his whole definition of his task. As early as the preceding December he had pressed the Wilhelmstrasse for the joint guarantee envisaged at Munich for the revised Czech boundaries,[75] and in the *French Yellow Book* one may trace his futile efforts along this line during the ensuing weeks. When, in March, the Reich swallowed Bohemia and Moravia, Coulondre advised Paris that "the Munich agreements no longer exist," and that, although Hitler was still oriented eastward, the Allies should not overlook the danger that he might attack in the West at some future date if his lead in armaments seemed to be shrinking. France must rebuild her strength "to the limit of our capacity," but with as little publicity as possible.[76] To Weizsäcker, who became appropriately indignant, Coulondre spoke on his own initiative of "the contravention of the Munich Agreement, in contradiction to the relationship of confidence which he had expected to find here and to the aims

---

[72] Galeazzo Ciano, *Diario* (Milano, 1948), I, 32-33, 35, 61.

[73] *German Documents*, series D, IV, 495.

[74] The final editors of the *French Yellow Book* discreetly omitted any reference to this episode, and Coulondre himself treats it only briefly in his *De Staline à Hitler*, p. 233. It is discussed, however, by John W. Wheeler-Bennett, *Munich: Prologue to Tragedy* (New York, 1948), pp. 312-313; by André Simone, *J'accuse* (New York, 1940), p. 298; and by "Pertinax" (André Géraud), *The Gravediggers of France* (New York, 1944), pp. 234-235.

[75] *German Documents*, series D, IV, 483.

[76] *French Yellow Book*, pp. 102-106.

which he himself had set for his mission."[77] His assignment, he privately concluded, had now lost its positive aspects; henceforth he would remain in Berlin as a scout in an advance observation post.[78]

In this capacity he watched the Polish crisis begin to take shape in April, with Hitler's denunciation of the 1934 nonaggression pact, and reported each measure in the uneven crescendo of that spring and summer. He was sure that the critical test had come: to yield on Danzig would be to expose another nation to Czechoslovakia's fate, destruction in two stages. "It is not only the fate of the Free City," he wrote after the Reichstag meeting of April 28, "it is the enslavement or liberty of Europe which is at stake in the issue now joined."[79] Yet he was not enthusiastic over the Allies' sudden veering from appeasement to unconditional support of Beck. At the very least, he felt, Poland, "after its odious conduct toward Czechoslovakia," should now be required to seek an understanding with the Soviet Union, as its contribution to a general system of defense against Hitler.[80]

Throughout all his dispatches covering the first flareup over Danzig and the Corridor in April, the relative easing of overt German pressure in May and June, the tense, sultry atmosphere of July, up to the final outburst beginning in mid-August, Coulondre reiterated tirelessly his belief that the Allies must push their own rearmament swiftly but quietly and take a clear line with Berlin. In his eyes, the danger of war ultimately centered about three possible Nazi calculations: that the West might yet abandon Warsaw, that Danzig might be taken through a "spontaneous" rising within the Free City, and that if war did come Poland might be defeated before any help reached her. The Allies had the responsibility of disabusing Berlin on all three counts.

Concerning their readiness to resist direct aggression and their refusal in advance to be duped by a local *Putsch* in Danzig, Paris and London could, of course, clarify their position by their own statements and actions. Concerning the third point, the ultimate fate of the Polish army, however, they could scarcely impress Berlin unless the system of guarantees included some major Power east of the Rhine. This could only mean Russia. For Coulondre, there was no point in discussing resistance unless Hitler could be placed *between* formidable opponents.

At the same time, recalling the Soviet reaction to Munich, he was painfully sensitive to the threat of a Berlin-Moscow agreement. He noted with foreboding that Hitler had not attacked Russia in his *Reichstag*

[77] *German Documents*, series D, IV, 273.   [78] Coulondre, *De Staline à Hitler*, p. 274.
[79] *French Yellow Book*, pp. 134-135.   [80] Coulondre, *De Staline à Hitler*, p. 264.

address of April 28, though he believed the Fuehrer would await the outcome of negotiations for a military alliance with Japan before deciding on a future policy vis-à-vis the USSR.[81] A few days after that speech came the frightening announcement from the Kremlin that Litvinov was no longer Foreign Commissar. On May 7, the ambassador passed along the view of a well-placed German informant (it was Air General Bodenschatz) that "something is doing in the East" and that a fourth partition of Poland was not out of the question.[82] "The Reich would do its best," he wrote in late May, "to take advantage, to the detriment of France and Great Britain, of any failure, however veiled, in the [Allied] conversations now taking place with Moscow."[83]

So it went all spring and summer, the ambassador relaying each new evidence of an impending diplomatic revolution and adding to his admonitions his pleas for decisive counteraction. He was sometimes in despair over the resistance of the British government and his own superiors, including Lebrun; he was sometimes encouraged, as when Political Director Rochat assured him while he was in Paris in April that a way would be found to bring London and Moscow together.[84] Down to the last possible moment he was still urging the Quai d'Orsay, on its own and through pressure on Chamberlain, "to expedite to the very utmost the conclusion of the agreement with the Soviets. I can never repeat too often how important a psychological factor this is for the Reich."[85] The preceding statement was written only a week before Ribbentrop's departure for Moscow on August 22, 1939. Coulondre's series of dispatches on the Soviet issue ends with a laconic sentence in a message sent that day to Paris: "The announcement of the non-aggression pact with Russia has contributed powerfully to the strengthening of the Army's confidence in the success of German arms."[86]

The preceding night he had signaled the beginning of the final act: a German concentration of forces on the Polish frontier was underway.[87] The details of the next fortnight have already been published many times. So far as Coulondre's official activities during the war crisis are concerned, they can be summarized in a few words. He remained throughout in close touch with Sir Nevile Henderson and with the Polish ambassador,

[81] *ibid.*, pp. 267-269.

[82] *French Yellow Book*, pp. 145-149. Also, Coulondre, *De Staline à Hitler*, pp. 270-271.

[83] *French Yellow Book*, p. 164.

[84] Coulondre, *De Staline à Hitler*, p. 265. Coulondre later said (page 281) that this effort had in fact been made "with an intelligence and a tenacity worthy of a better fate."

[85] *French Yellow Book*, p. 269.   [86] *ibid.*, p. 287.

[87] *ibid.*, pp. 282-283.

Lipski. On August 25 he saw Hitler and received the latter's personal message to Daladier that France had no cause for war and should recognize that Polish behavior was intolerable for Germany—his own reply was that if war came the only winner would be "M. Trotsky."[88] The next day he was back at the Chancellery with Daladier's response, stressing Poland's willingness to negotiate and deploring the threat of another Franco-German conflict.[89] Coulondre reported late that night that Hitler had not reacted as hoped either to the Premier's letter or to the ambassador's own forty-minute plea: "Perhaps I moved him; but I did not prevail. His mind was made up."[90] On the 27th, however, Coulondre added that the *démarche* had been necessary and might yet bear fruit.[91] The same afternoon Ribbentrop gave him a copy of Hitler's formal reply and embellished its negative tone regarding Poland with his own comment that "we shall strike at the first incident."[92]

Not until the night of August 31 was Coulondre back at the Foreign Office, to receive from Weizsäcker a copy of Hitler's cunningly delayed "alibi" offer to Poland, communicated to the British and French ambassadors as though it had been ignored by Warsaw and had already expired.[93] Word of the German invasion reached the French embassy early on the morning of September 1, while Coulondre was in the garden with his staff, at work on air raid trenches. He went at once to hear Hitler's speech to the *Reichstag*. At 10 o'clock that evening he delivered to Ribbentrop the French government's affirmation of its intention to carry out its obligation's to Poland unless German military operations were suspended.[94] Thirty-six hours later, on the morning of the 3rd, he was ordered by Paris to notify the Minister of Foreign Affairs that if the German response to the *démarche* had to be taken as negative, France would fulfill her engagements to Poland as of 5 p.m. that day.[95] Shortly after noon the ambassador carried out these instructions, delivering the French declaration as soon as he had been assured that the German government had no intention of halting its military forces. "Well," Ribbentrop remarked, "it will be France who is the aggressor." Coulondre replied that "history would judge of that."[96] Next morning he and his mission left Berlin aboard the diplomatic exchange train.

Coulondre's recommendations to his own superiors during those final days had been consistent with his views as stated for months past. With respect to Poland, his personal hope lay in a population exchange.[97] He

[88] *ibid.*, pp. 302-305.   [89] *ibid.*, pp. 311-312.   [90] *ibid.*, p. 317.
[91] *ibid.*, p. 319.   [92] *ibid.*, p. 320.   [93] *ibid.*, pp. 356-357, 366-367.
[94] *ibid.*, pp. 376-377.   [95] *ibid.*, p. 399.   [96] *ibid.*, pp. 400-401.
[97] *ibid.*, pp. 307, 331. Also Coulondre, *De Staline à Hitler*, p. 296.

was, nonetheless, insistent that the Polish attitude should be firm and dignified, that no conversations should be entered upon until all threat of force had been withdrawn, that Beck should not come abjectly to Berlin, and that Warsaw's plenipotentiary, whether Lipski or someone else, should not open negotiations by merely receiving Germany's terms but should present the Polish viewpoint in a manner calculated to safeguard some balance in the talks.[98]

As for France herself, she must not repeat the Czech fiasco by accepting any settlement based on "vague undertakings and hypothetical promises in further matters."[99] "We cannot . . . expect a happy result . . . unless we are careful not to give the impression that we are on the watch for every possible compromise, whatever the cost may be."[100] Finally, in a personal letter which he wrote to Daladier on August 30 and which the Premier read to the Cabinet the next day in Paris, he opined that Hitler was weakening after having met resistance and that France must continue to call his bluff while avoiding any move which might push him to an act of despair.[101]

In order to comprehend this consistent hostility to appeasement, one must bear in mind two crucial factors in the ambassador's own conceptual scheme: the essential nature of Nazi foreign policy and the potential role of Soviet Russia. Coulondre's assessment of either or both could and still can be disputed. It cannot, however, be lightly dismissed, especially since it set him clearly apart from numerous other figures discussed in this book.

His analysis of German aims rested on his certainty that Nazi dynamism could not be accommodated or diverted, that it could only be checked by greater force opposing it. The Russian dictatorship, he believed, because of the geographical and social characteristics of the nation it controlled, might maintain a prewar economy indefinitely without being impelled toward actual conflict. The German dictatorship, he was equally sure, could do no such thing.[102] He conceded that there were differing degrees of impatience represented among the leading Nazis; but he could not, given his emphasis on the underlying

---

[98] *French Yellow Book*, pp. 308-309, 341-342, 354-355.

[99] *ibid.*, pp. 308-309.   [100] *ibid.*, p. 319.

[101] The text of this letter is given in Coulondre, *De Staline à Hitler*, p. 299, note 2. Paul Reynaud has written that the message "exercised a profound influence on Daladier." *La France a sauvé l'Europe*, I, 597. Coulondre, however, insists that it was delivered to the Premier while the Cabinet was in session, that the personal notes of Champetier de Ribes show that the decision to stand firm had already been taken and that hence his letter did nothing more than to confirm the ministers' resolve. *De Staline à Hitler*, pp. 304-305, note 2.

[102] *ibid.*, p. 247.

forces at work, interest himself as much as did most other foreign diplomats in the distinctions among various party chiefs or between the Nazi leadership corps as a group and the Foreign Office. He viewed Hitler's perfidy and rapacity as constants which would operate to the limit fixed by circumstances.[103] He considered Goering "at once ridiculous and formidable," even when espousing relative moderation. He found Hess uninteresting, Ribbentrop contemptible, Rosenberg pontifical, Goebbels —"ce petit diable boiteux"—not unimpressive in his amoral acuteness. Old acquaintances at the *Auswärtiges Amt*, such as Woermann, Ritter, and Gaus, proved incapable of talking candidly any longer, captives of the regime they served.[104] He was inclined to believe that Weizsäcker did not want war with France;[105] but his feeling for the Secretary of State never went beyond that to real cordiality or confidence, and nothing in the German documents suggests that it should have.

Coulondre's argument that Hitler would not stop of his own volition was matched by his claim that the Fuehrer could and would stop if faced by sufficiently great odds. One of the ambassador's more surprising statements, suggestive of a perhaps unavoidable degree of wishful thinking, was in a dispatch of June 1939 to the effect that Hitler "has never up till now undertaken any move which was not sure of success."[106] This judgment strained the history of the mid-1930's, but it was consistent with the view that Coulondre was still expounding in his August 30 letter to Daladier: Hitler might be bluffing and might yet be halted short of war if the Allies left no doubt in his mind concerning their determination to resist any further aggression.

This gamble Coulondre had been especially willing to accept while the Soviet Union could still be thought of as a possible ally against Germany. His belief that, even after Munich, Russia's self-interest would have made it cooperate with the Western Powers, had they been willing to talk business in Moscow, will doubtless always be a subject of disagreement. Whether or not he was deluded, however, this conviction, abandoned only with the coming of the Nazi-Soviet Pact, takes its place beside his view of Nazi dynamism as the second of his basic premises. Future historians will have to judge his position in the light of what-

[103] *ibid.*, p. 229.
[104] *ibid.*, pp. 217-221.
[105] *ibid.*, p. 314. Weizsäcker himself later complained of Coulondre that "he seemed not to realize—or perhaps he did not trust his own feelings—that in me he could have had an ally for the achievement of the higher interests we both had at heart." Ernst von Weizsäcker, *Erinnerungen* (Munich, 1950), pp. 210-211.
[106] *French Yellow Book*, p. 181.

ever further evidence may turn up concerning the Third Reich and the USSR, to sustain or to refute those premises.

The question will still remain: how did Coulondre's policy recommendations relate to his underlying sentiments? How can his insisting to the end that peace might be saved by calling Germany's bluff be reconciled with his view of the internal thrust behind Nazi expansionism and his characterization of Hitler as power-corrupted, increasingly irrational, "the monstrous specimen of a debased humanity?"[107] There are two alternative answers. One would be that Coulondre was sure that war was coming and could only hope that France would meet the test firmly, with a clear public awareness of the issues and without conceding the Nazis any further preparatory conquests. Calling Berlin's putative bluff would at the worst mean the Allies would be facing the issue. This explanation, framed in less sympathetic terms, is suggested by Weizsäcker's remark that "Coulondre spoke as if his words were to appear right away . . . in a Yellow Book."[108]

The other possible key to the ambassador's performance would relate less to a calculated campaign and more to the mind's ability to cushion terrible conclusions. Coulondre was unusually clearheaded in his assessment of the Nazi threat and the diplomatic flexibility required to meet it. He did not delude himself about Hitler's personality. He did not insist on patching up a Western European balance, regardless of cost, for the sake of the social *status quo*. But he would have had to possess an almost inhuman coldness of intellect not to seek an escape from his own prognosis. Might not a clear stand by the West force Berlin to count the risks and draw back from the fatal decision? The answer proved to be no. It would, nevertheless, be unjust to Coulondre not to consider carefully his reasons for posing the question.

[107] Coulondre, *De Staline à Hitler*, p. 326.
[108] Weizsäcker, *Erinnerungen*, p. 210.

19

The Diplomacy of Colonel Beck

BY HENRY L. ROBERTS

AMONG the public figures of countries overrun by Nazi Germany, Colonel Jozef Beck, Poland's Foreign Minister from 1932 to 1939, has probably received the least sympathy. Despite his determined resistance to Hitler's threats in the crisis leading to the outbreak of the second world war, he has been remembered as one of the Pilsudskian *epigoni*, as the man who refused to work with the Little Entente or the League of Nations, who pursued, in substance, a pro-German policy after 1934, who joined in the dismembering of Czechoslovakia, and, finally, as the man whose stubborn refusal to enter any combination with the Russians contributed to the failure of the Anglo-French-Soviet negotiations of the spring and summer of 1939.

After Poland's defeat and Beck's internment in Rumania the world heard little of him. He died in obscurity, of tuberculosis, on June 5, 1944. Less than a year after his death the war of which his country was first victim came to an end, but Poland soon fell under the domination of the Power that Beck always felt to be the ultimate enemy. This retrospective vindication of his Russian policy, the postwar publication of Polish, French, German, and British evidence bearing on his activities, and the recent appearance of Beck's own diplomatic memoirs[1] suggest a reappraisal of this controversial and rather elusive figure.

I

Although it has been said that Beck lacked diplomatic training,[2]

[1] Colonel Joseph Beck, *Dernier rapport: Politique polonaise 1926-1939* (Neuchâtel, 1951). Although these memoirs, three memoranda dictated between 1939 and 1943, are fragmentary and were intended as preliminary drafts, they are sufficiently complete to provide many insights into Beck's own view of his diplomatic role. Supplementing these, and of considerably greater value as a record of Polish foreign policy, is the journal of the Under-Secretary of State for Foreign Affairs: Comte Jean Szembek, *Journal, 1933-1939*, trans. by J. Rzewuska and T. Zaleski (Paris, 1952). This was published too late to be utilized fully here.
[2] L. B. Namier, *Diplomatic Prelude, 1938-1939* (London, 1948), p. 438.

it is doubtful whether his shortcomings as a statesman can be attributed to amateurishness. He did not, it is true, come to the Foreign Ministry from a career in the Diplomatic Service, but he was not lacking in experience. At the time of his fall, he was dean of European Foreign Ministers in terms of uninterrupted occupation of his post. Born in Warsaw in 1894, educated at the polytechnic school in Lwów and the *Exportakademie* in Vienna, he participated in the first world war as one of Pilsudski's legionnaires. During the period of confused fighting following the Russian revolution and the collapse of Germany he seems increasingly to have been chosen for diplomatic missions, official and clandestine. In 1922 Pilsudski sent him as military attaché to the Polish legation in Paris. After a year he was abruptly recalled under unpleasant but somewhat obscure circumstances with, perhaps, a permanent feeling of rancor for certain French circles.[3]

Following his return from France he entered the Polish War College and appeared to be moving toward a military career. As an active participant in the *coup d'état* of 1926, however, he entered the circle of Pilsudski's close collaborators and was the Marshal's *chef de cabinet* between 1926 and 1930. Some time before 1930 Pilsudski is reported to have said to an official of the war ministry: "Do not count on Beck; you will never have him. M. Beck is not going to make his career in the army. M. Beck will go to Foreign Affairs, to be charged with responsibilities of high importance."[4] In December 1930 he became Under-Secretary of State in the Foreign Office and in November 1932 Minister of Foreign Affairs, replacing August Zaleski. For the next seven years he directed Poland's foreign policy, as Pilsudski's agent until the latter's death in 1935, then largely on his own.

On the other hand, the French ambassador, Léon Noël, who found Beck "one of the most unusual, in certain respects one of the most mysterious, and above all one of the most interesting persons it has fallen to me to be associated with," was probably correct in his observation that Beck showed many of the characteristics of the young man who had climbed the ladder too rapidly and easily.[5] He was unduly confident in his own opinions and decisions. Moreover, he was of the generation of those who were twenty in 1914, a generation inclined to be self-consciously proud of its own "realism." Certainly, this tall, elegant,

---

[3] Léon Noël, *L'Agression allemande contre la Pologne* (Paris, 1946), pp. 106-107. Noël, French ambassador in Poland from 1935 to 1939, adds, however, that "it is not necessary to have recourse to this explanation to have the key to his policy in general and to his policy toward France in particular."

[4] Beck, *Dernier rapport*, p. xix.   [5] Noël, *L'Agression allemande*, p. 20.

and rather Mephistophelean figure conveyed an impression of hardness without depth.

Noël also felt that while Beck had a talent for diplomacy, his experience in military intelligence accentuated a tendency to employ *deuxième bureau* techniques in his conduct of foreign policy. All his fellow diplomats found him evasive, uncommunicative, and tortuous in his methods. One of Noël's colleagues remarked that when Beck had occasion to speak the truth, one noticed it at once.[6] His own memoirs, however, do not wholly support this impression of elaborate deviousness. Indeed, he seemed to operate on surprisingly simple premises, and was irritable rather than conspiratorial in his reluctance to explain or discuss his actions. Many of his more round-about maneuvers were made largely because they seemed to represent correct diplomatic form.

For, curiously enough, Poland, a new or at least resurrected state, displayed a distinctly old-fashioned diplomatic wardrobe. While the interwar diplomacy of the Western Powers exhibits the powerful impact of political and public pressures, and while the diplomacy of Poland's two great neighbors, Germany and the Soviet Union, was but one branch of the foreign activities of an ideologically imbued totalitarian order, Beck's diplomacy had Metternichean overtones.[7]

To a degree, of course, this continuation of cabinet diplomacy was a reflection of Polish society and government. Poland's rather hectic experience with untempered parliamentarianism was brought to an end with Pilsudski's return to power in May 1926. The constitutional structure remained for a time, and even some parliamentary activity, but under the stern supervision of the old Marshal. The new constitution which came into effect in 1935 was distinctly authoritarian. Following Pilsudski's death, his associates, the "Colonels," governed in a quasi-dictatorial fashion. The regime was not fascist or totalitarian but, as one Pole said, merely carried on the spirit of the former gentry, "We are Poland."[8] In the confused circumstances of Polish domestic politics after Pilsudski's death, it would be difficult to say what might have been the eventual outcome of this system. In any event, it is clear that the government was not responsible to the Diet, the *Sejm*, and that Beck was able

[6] *ibid.*, p. 22, note 1.

[7] Beck, for example, thoroughly admired the "meticulous British protocol" surrounding the coronation of King George VI, as the ideal atmosphere for diplomatic contacts and conversations. *Dernier rapport*, p. 128.

[8] Wladyslaw Grabski, *Idea Polski* (Warsaw, 1936), quoted in Raymond Leslie Buell, *Poland: Key to Europe* (3rd ed., New York, 1939), p. 99.

to retain his post, as were President Moscicki and Marshal Smigly-Rydz, throughout successive changes in the Cabinet.

The setting in which important decisions on policy were reached is described in a passage in Beck's memoirs: "Marshal Pilsudski, in the spring of 1934, suggested to the President of the Republic of Poland that he convoke a conference on foreign policy, chaired by the President himself, and at which all the public figures who, since 1926, had performed the functions of Prime Minister should take part. The conference was held in the Belvedere Palace. . . . By the wish of the President it was the Marshal who opened the conference; he declared that this form of conference, bringing together the men who had assumed the responsibility for all the affairs of the country, appeared to him to be very useful at moments of great decisions or important events. Comparing this sort of conference with analogous and permanent institutions of other countries, in particular with the privy council of the King of England, of which the members were designated and convoked by the King himself, he vigorously urged the President to institute the custom."[9]

Beck, who thoroughly approved of this procedure, continued the practice of calling together the inner circle from time to time to discuss the foreign situation and the action to be taken. Apart from these conferences and infrequent statements to the Diet, Beck directed his foreign policy as he saw fit. The outcries of the opposition seem to have carried little weight in determining or altering his line of action. To be sure, as in all such situations, there were tensions and conflicts within the ruling oligarchy: Beck had been a rival of his predecessor Zaleski; no love was lost between the Foreign Minister and the inspector general of the army Smigly-Rydz, upon whom the greater part of Pilsudski's mantle had fallen and who seemed much more aware of the German military threat; friction between Beck and his subordinates was not infrequent. Even these intramural clashes, however, do not appear to have influenced Polish foreign policy markedly in the years after 1932.

It would seem, then, that the rather perverse course of Polish diplomacy under Beck is not to be explained by the fumblings of the inexperienced or by the vagaries of public opinion and party politics. For an understanding of Beck's policy it is necessary to go further: to examine the extremely difficult and complex foreign problems which Poland faced in the second decade of its independence and to follow the line of Beck's reasoning in his effort to resolve or contain them.

[9] Beck, *Dernier rapport*, p. 61.

II

Without question, geography has set the most difficult problems for Polish foreign policy. While the term "natural frontiers" has been badly misused—after all, the Rhine was singularly unsuccessful in delimiting French and German territory, and the ridge of the Carpathians failed to bring agreement between Rumanians and Hungarians—it is true that, except for the comparatively limited stretches of the Baltic Sea and the Carpathians, Poland lacked any striking geographical boundaries. More important than the topography, however, were the confused historical background of Poland's political frontiers and the intermingling of nationalities and languages. It is simply not clear where Poland begins and ends.

Rendering perilous the confusion over frontiers was the fact that Poland was wedged between Germany and Russia, both much more powerful and populous states, both with a record of partitioning Poland, and both, in the interwar period, with open or suspected designs on territory Poland had acquired from them. It cannot be overlooked that Poland's existence as an independent state resulted from a coincidence which could not have been anticipated in 1914: the collapse through defeat and revolution of both Russia and Germany. In consequence, Poland's security was inevitably endangered by the recovery and growth of either or both of these Powers; if they should regain their strength and pursue a policy of close cooperation, Poland was, in all likelihood, doomed. In the last analysis, Poland's security as a state depended upon Russia and Germany being comparatively weak, as they were in the 1920's, or having hostile relations, as they did in the mid-1930's.

Poland, unfortunately, was not in a position to create or to maintain either of these conditions, which were determined by factors largely beyond its control. Hence, the task of Polish diplomacy was twofold: first, to seek where it could a means of counterbalancing the potential menace of its two powerful neighbors; and second, to render as secure as possible its position within the unstable framework of German-Polish-Soviet relations. The great question was whether these two lines of policy could be harmonized or whether the pursuit of one would threaten the attainment of the other.

In theory, protection against German and/or Soviet pressure might be obtained through an international order collectively securing the integrity of nations, through the creation of an intermediate bloc of states lying between Germany and Russia and similarly threatened by their recovery or rapprochement, or through alliances with other Great Powers. In theory likewise, Poland's relations vis-à-vis Germany and Russia might be best served by judicious balancing between the two, or by drawing closer to one or the other, depending on the circumstances. These possibilities and the position taken by Beck and the Polish regime toward them will be considered in the following pages.

III

Inasmuch as Poland's reappearance as an independent state was intimately associated with Wilson's Fourteen Points and the Versailles treaties, it might seem axiomatic that Poland should have been an ardent upholder of the Versailles system and of the League of Nations, which was to be the basis for a new international order. Such was not Beck's attitude, however. He regarded Wilson as an opinionated reformer who had contributed to the unfortunate practice of incorporating *exposés de motifs* in the treaties at the end of the first world war. An admirer of the "old diplomacy," he felt that a treaty should deal only with concrete issues: if a nation lost a war, it should be forced to make certain concessions, but without argument or justification. The Versailles treaties, however, which he saw as the work of parliamentarians, not diplomats, were filled with explanatory clauses open to rebuttal and debate. In Beck's view this weakness in the formulation of the treaties was important in paving the way to war in 1939.[10] While it can be argued that the Versailles phraseology dealing with such items as disarmament, "war guilt," and so on, did provide a convenient wedge for the German revisionist counterattack, this argument is not without danger to a state such as Poland, which had been dismembered by the old diplomacy and was brought back into existence, in part at least, because of a widespread revulsion against this method of carrying on international relations.

Beck's second major criticism of the treaty was "the complete absence of a well established hierarchy defining the degree of importance of the different clauses of the treaty."[11] Citing Pilsudski as his mentor, as he usually did, he contended that the territorial settlement was of the highest importance, limitation of German armaments next, and then, of much less significance, all the other clauses. Sanctions and collective measures should have been designed and reserved for the protection of the vital clauses; instead there had been a fruitless expenditure of energy on issues of secondary importance, and the indispensable portions of

[10] Beck, *Dernier rapport*, pp. 48, 251-252.
[11] *ibid.*, p. 252.

the treaty were gradually undermined. In retrospect this criticism appears largely justified.[12]

While Beck was critical of the Versailles treaties, he was definitely hostile to the League of Nations, to the "spirit of Geneva," and to the statesmen who rested their hopes in that organization, particularly the representatives of other successor states active in the League, Benes of Czechoslovakia and Titulescu of Rumania. The absence of the United States, he argued after his fall, had effectively deprived the League of its universalism and nullified its claim to represent a new international order. One may suspect, however, that this contention was a rationalization for the real basis of his dislike of the League: the pretensions of that body to concern itself with the internal affairs of the middle and small states, especially through such agencies as the ILO and the minority treaties. This meddling had the effect of disorganizing their internal stability and rendering them vulnerable to the propaganda of the aggressive Powers: "It is enough to study the political campaign and propaganda undertaken by the Third Reich while preparing the invasion of Eastern Europe to realize the support which it constantly found in the debates of Geneva and in the interpretations of the treaties on the protection of minorities."[13] Moreover, Beck felt that the League put the small and middle Power in a particularly difficult situation. It was forced by the Great Powers "to make unforeseen friends and enemies in connection with questions which had nothing in common with their own interests."[14]

It is not possible here to go into Poland's internal affairs, but there is little doubt that much of Beck's touchiness concerning the League stems from Poland's minority question, which was a source of continual friction with its neighbors and of domestic discord. About 30 percent of Poland's population was made up of non-Polish minorities, a large number of whom were Ukrainians. With the Soviet Union's entry into the League in 1934, Beck "deemed that the moment had come to finish with the question of the treaty on minorities. It was, in effect, inadmissible that the representative of the Soviet Union could discuss and decide the internal affairs of Poland."[15] With evident pleasure at causing a stir, Beck, in September 1934, announced to the Assembly of the League of Nations that, "pending the introduction of a general and uniform system for the protection of minorities, my Government is com-

[12] For a recent discussion of this point see R. F. Harrod, *The Life of John Maynard Keynes* (London, 1951), pp. 269-270.
[13] Beck, *Dernier rapport*, p. 256.   [14] *ibid.*, p. 266.
[15] *ibid.*, p. 71.

pelled to refuse, as from today, all cooperation with the international organizations in the matter of the supervision of the application by Poland of the system of minority protection."[16] Since he neither expected nor desired the minority treaties to be converted into a general system applicable to all countries, he was, by this unilateral act of denouncing an international obligation, flatly rejecting the competence of the League to concern itself with Poland's minorities.

Beck also resented another function of the League which intimately concerned Poland: its supervision of the Free City of Danzig, which the Treaty of Versailles had taken from Germany but had not given to Poland. The real danger to Poland here was, of course, Germany. Nevertheless, Beck was pleased with the difficulties the League High Commissioners were having with the growing Nazi domination of Danzig and proud of his ability to straighten out affairs by direct negotiation with the Third Reich. In reflecting on a minor crisis in 1936 Beck later commented: "The roles were thus reversed: It was no longer the League of Nations which protected Poland at Danzig, it was Poland which had to defend the League of Nations in the Free City. This corresponded, moreover, to the reality of things which Geneva, up to then, had so obstinately refused to see."[17]

By this policy on the minorities question and Danzig, Beck was, in effect, removing them from the sphere of international concern to that of direct German-Polish relations. In 1939 this transfer had dire consequences when Hitler began his assault on Poland with precisely these issues. Still, Beck could reply, "And what would the League have done to protect Poland in 1939?"

On the one occasion when the League undertook collective measures against aggression—its imposition of sanctions against Italy—Beck was lukewarm about the whole affair: the dispute was far from Poland; he approved of Laval's efforts to avoid a break in French-Italian relations; he wanted to maintain Poland's coal exports to Italy; he mistrusted the ideological overtones of collective security;[18] and he was bored and irritated by the tenor of Titulescu's anti-Italian tirades in the "little world" of Geneva. Indeed, Poland was the first Power to drop sanctions. In a letter to the President of the Council of the League, on June 26,

---

[16] League of Nations, *Official Journal, Special Supplement No. 125. Records of the Fifteenth Ordinary Session of the Assembly* (Geneva, 1934), p. 43.

[17] Beck, *Dernier rapport*, p. 123.

[18] In a conversation with Anthony Eden on October 9, 1935, Beck remarked that "sanctions should not lead to a reinforcement of the action of the Second International, which was patronized by the Third." *Ibid.*, p. 290.

1936, Beck, after emphasizing that the adoption of economic sanctions was a "sovereign decision" for each state to make, declared that since further measures were useless Poland was terminating its application of sanctions. In his memoirs he said that this action was not intended to hasten recognition of the Italian annexation, but was simply a response to the fact that "unfortunate Abyssinia had already ceased, *de facto*, to exist as an independent country."[19]

In retrospect the sanctions episode was a sorry one, which failed to check Italian aggression and contributed to driving Mussolini toward Hitler. It is painful, though, to hear a Polish statesman employ the "ceasing to exist" argument, when the soul of Poland's survival has been its obstinate refusal to admit the loss of national existence.

It is clear that the realist Beck placed very little confidence in the League of Nations as a defense for Poland. In considering the unhappy fate of those smaller states which did embrace the "spirit of Geneva" with such ardor, one may admit he had reason for his skepticism. After all, the League was not an independent, supranational authority, nor could it enforce the peace unless the Great Powers, France and Great Britain—not to speak of the absent United States—exerted their power on its behalf. This they did not do; a far greater responsibility for the failure of the League attaches to them than to Colonel Beck's scornful attitude. It cannot be said, however, that his activities in this field were of any positive value in the preservation of the peace or of international responsibility in those darkening years.

IV

In the absence of an international body, the maintenance of peace, in the century preceding 1914, had come to be regarded as a function of the "Concert of Europe," the Great Powers of the continent. During the interwar years one can follow a thread of attempts to reconstruct this concert, from the Locarno treaties of 1925, through the Four Power Pact of 1933, to the Munich Conference in 1938, attempts to settle major problems by consultation and agreement among Great Britain, France, Italy, and Germany (the Soviet Union was not included).

Beck's attitude toward this approach to international security is not difficult to guess. If he was scornful of the League, he saw these efforts as a positive menace in their aim of settling affairs to the satisfaction of the Great Powers, but in disregard of the middle and small states. He quoted with approval Pilsudski's blunt comment on Locarno that "every

[19] *ibid.*, pp. 107-108.

good Pole spits with disgust at the name." By the Locarno agreements, two categories of frontiers in Europe had been created, and in Beck's opinion Germany was thereby solemnly invited to attack to the East for the price of gaining peace in the West.

The Four Power Pact, while eventually reduced to a rather vague and innocuous statement,[20] aroused great indignation in Poland. Other middle and small states of Eastern Europe were equally alarmed, but upon learning of the eventual terms of the agreement, were willing to accept it. This compliance on the part of the Little Entente enraged Beck, who said that Europe had three categories of states: Great Powers, middle and small Powers with a will to pursue their own policy, and client states. Putting Poland in the second category—he always denied that Poland was a Great Power in the sense of having world wide interests—he was intent on maintaining an independent course against the infringements of the Great Powers and the submissiveness of the client states.

Since the Little Entente Powers had dropped their opposition to the revised pact, the Polish government felt obliged to show its displeasure alone; and Pilsudski and Beck consequently arranged that the newly appointed Polish ambassador to Italy should announce his resignation on the ground that Italian policy in pressing the Four-Power agreement was contrary to the international interests of his country.

This particular technique of taking abrupt action to indicate disapproval of some international move potentially affecting Poland became characteristic of the Beckian diplomacy and greatly contributed to his reputation for deviousness. In fact, Beck had a rather simple pride in this "style" of Polish diplomacy, fast ripening into a tradition. The sudden harshness of his last moves against Czechoslovakia in September 1938 were in part occasioned by this same intention to register a protest against the Four-Power decisions at Munich.

Unquestionably Beck had every reason to be suspicious of the "Concert of Europe." It was a danger to the independence of the smaller states. Nevertheless, to assume this attitude was to raise a difficult problem, for if both the old principles of the Concert and the new principles of the League were rejected, as they were by Beck, what alternatives remained for a state which was neither so situated nor so powerful as to be able to stand in splendid isolation?

Beck did not provide any satisfactory answer to this question. He insisted that states should mind their own affairs, and he spoke of the

[20] See above Chapter 4, §iv.

advantages of bilateral agreements between nations to settle mutual problems without infringing upon the rights of others. But quite evidently, such principles are only desiderata, which a professed realist like Beck could not find sufficient in a world of contending Powers, and on occasion he quite flagrantly contradicted his maxims. In practical terms, of course, the refusal to rely on the League or to admit the benefits of Great Power paternalism meant that Poland must acquire allies, either among the states of Eastern Europe or in the West.

V

That the states of Eastern Europe had much to gain from a policy of cooperation and mutual assistance against the German and Soviet dangers seems more than obvious. Unfortunately, throughout most of the inter-war period, Poland's relations with two of its immediate neighbors, Lithuania and Czechoslovakia, were far from cordial, and this condition made it impossible for Poland either to create a solid Baltic bloc or to cooperate with the Little Entente.

The conflict between Poland and Lithuania arose from the Polish seizure of Vilna after the first world war. Although its population was largely non-Lithuanian, Vilna had been the capital of the medieval duchy. Its loss was not recognized by the Lithuanian regime, which refused to establish diplomatic or economic relations with Poland. Despite occasional feelers, this anomalous relationship between two states once intimately connected continued up to March 1938.

The reestablishment of diplomatic relations with Lithuania is one of the oddest examples of Beck's diplomatic technique. While anticipating and accepting the German-Austrian *Anschluss*, Beck felt, nonetheless, that it would be "dangerous to remain entirely passive in face of the German expansion."[21] It was necessary to give proof that Poland was alert and able to react swiftly. At the same time, since the action in Austria did not directly affect Polish interests, "our response should be very prudent."

While mulling over these thoughts, he received word that, in a frontier incident, Lithuanian guards had killed a Polish soldier. He

---

[21] Beck, *Dernier rapport*, p. 149. In December 1936, in a conversation with Szembek, Beck said he was expecting a crisis to develop in central Europe. In such a situation, Poland had five choices, of which two were unacceptable: passivity or an alliance with Czechoslovakia against Germany. The other three were: (1) to occupy Teschen, permit Hungary to take Ruthenia, and gain a common frontier with the Magyars; (2) to take Kaunas; (3) to occupy Danzig. Szembek, *Journal*, p. 220. Apparently Beck felt he would have to do something, no matter in what direction.

grasped this occasion and, on March 17, 1938, arguing that in such tense times it was dangerous for Lithuania to refuse diplomatic recognition to Poland, sent a forty-eight hour ultimatum demanding, mildly enough, resumption of normal relations. Certain sectors of Polish opinion urged more extreme measures against Lithuania and the abrupt action raised further doubts about Beck as a responsible diplomat, but it appears that his real intent was the symbolic gesture of demonstrating that Poland, too, could issue ultimata. In actual fact, the action did not lead to further trouble, and Polish-Lithuanian relations showed signs of improvement. But by 1938 it was very late.

Much more serious was Poland's conflict with Czechoslovakia, arising out of the rival claims for Teschen. The Poles felt that the Czechs had obtained, in 1920, an unfairly large part of this district at a time when Poland had been fighting the Bolsheviks. While the Teschen issue was the focus of irritation, Beck had more far-reaching reasons for disliking the Czech state. He objected to Czechoslovakia's alliance in 1935 with the Soviet Union and claimed that the Comintern was using Prague as a headquarters for anti-Polish activities. Benes' work at the League aroused his scorn, and he held that the Czechoslovak regime's much advertised "liberalism" was but a façade for a classic "police state"[22] governed by an innately brutal nationality.[23]

Moreover, the existence of the Czech state as such did not appeal to Beck. Marshal Pilsudski was accustomed to say that there were two states which would not survive, Austria and Czechoslovakia; the only important point was to know which would disappear first. Beck obviously subscribed to this analysis. In December 1931, before he was Foreign Minister, he and Pilsudski decided to increase the aid sent the Polish minority in Czechoslovakia and to be more energetic in educating and organizing it.[24] There is little use in seeking consistency between Beck's own highly sensitive attitude toward external interference with Poland's minorities and this policy of aiding and propagandizing the Polish minority in Czechoslovakia. The divine right of one's own nationality is rarely a principle admitting of reciprocity.

When the Four Power Pact was under negotiation in 1933, Pilsudski did approve of some confidential negotiations with the Czechs, but this brief attempt at rapprochement collapsed with Czechoslovakia's willingness to accept the pact as finally drafted. In the following year he ordered practice maneuvers for Polish military operations to assure the

---

[22] Beck, *Dernier rapport*, p. 52.   [23] *ibid.*, p. 171.
[24] *ibid.*, pp. 9-10.

acquisition of Teschen in the event Czechoslovakia should disintegrate or capitulate in face of Germany.[25] The Polish regime was not interested in the maintenance of Czechoslovakia, regarded it as a doomed state, and was solely concerned with seeing to it that Poland gained its appropriate share of the remains.

With such an attitude toward Czechoslovakia, Poland was not likely to enter the Little Entente. Beck, however, had further objections to this bloc. He observed quite correctly that each of the Little Entente members was potentially threatened by a Great Power—Czechoslovakia by Germany, Rumania by Russia, and Yugoslavia by Italy—yet the Entente was, in fact, directed solely against Hungary, which was militarily weaker than any of its three neighbors. Consequently, the Entente provided for no united defense against aggression by a Great Power; and Beck had no desire to join an anti-Hungarian combination, since an improvement of Polish-Hungarian relations was a major aim of his foreign policy. He concluded that Poland had no reason to concern itself intimately with the affairs of the small Powers south of the Carpathians. The 1921 Polish-Rumanian alliance, directed against the Soviet Union, was the one Eastern connection which seemed to him to meet a real problem.

His attitude toward Czechoslovakia also influenced Beck in rejecting the French effort to create an Eastern bloc in 1934. While his major objection to this project, as will be seen presently, lay in his ambition to maintain a balance between Germany and Russia, he did not wish to enter any agreement which would oblige Poland "to guarantee the Czechoslovakian frontiers."[26]

Beck was not lacking in plans, however, for an organization of the Eastern European states. In the first place, he had hopes for a Baltic-Scandinavian bloc. Poland as a Baltic Sea Power should develop its ties with the advanced and more enlightened Scandinavian states: "The bridge which united Poland with the Occident and our western friends passed, for me, by way of the Baltic and the solid Scandinavian nations rather than by the artificial combinations of the Little Entente south of the Carpathians."[27] In pursuit of this project, he made several good-will tours, including one in the critical summer of 1938. The basic difficulty in the way of this bloc was, of course, that the Scandinavian states, for all their stability, were on the sidelines of the European power conflict and still pursued a policy of neutrality and non-involvement.

[25] *ibid.*, p. 83.   [26] *ibid.*, p. 73.
[27] *ibid.*, p. 154.

A second project, which Beck worked on when the expansion of Germany began to appear alarming, was the creation of a Rome-Belgrade-Budapest-Bucharest-Warsaw connection. In March 1938, on the eve of the *Anschluss*, he had several conversations in Rome with Mussolini and Ciano. After assertions on both sides that they did not intend to pull chestnuts from the fire for other Powers—a common figure of speech that passed for diplomatic sophistication in those years—there was mutual agreement that while an understanding with Germany was a necessary part of Italian and Polish foreign policy, the effort should be made to strengthen ties with Hungary, Yugoslavia, and Rumania, presumably as a check to overly great German domination.[28]

In support of this program Beck became increasingly anxious to establish a common frontier with Hungary. Just as the eastern prolongation of Czechoslovakia was, in part, strategically designed to give that country and Rumania common frontiers, so in the late 1930's, especially after Czechoslovakia's future seemed problematic, Beck's advocacy of Hungary's claims in Slovakia and Ruthenia was aimed at providing a geographical basis for increased cooperation between Poland and its "best neighbor."

A serious obstacle, of course, to Beck's rather jejune project was the fact that Hungary and Poland's ally, Rumania, were bitterly antagonistic. Beck did his best to patch up relations between these two states but without success. In mid-October 1938, after Munich, he proposed to the Rumanian ambassador that, in the event of Czechoslovakia's further disintegration, Hungary and Rumania should divide Ruthenia between them. A few days later, in a visit to King Carol, he elaborated on this proposal. While not overlooking Rumania's old ties with Czechoslovakia, he urged that, if Hungary and Rumania took such an action in concert, their mutual relations would improve, Rumania would gain an additional rail connection with Poland, and, incidentally, Poland and Rumania would be rid of a center of Ukrainian agitation unsettling to their minorities. Carol, however, declined the offer, and Beck was subsequently outraged to learn that the Rumanian Foreign Minister, Petresco-Comnène, had spread the story that Poland was attempting to lure Rumania into aggression against Czechoslovakia.[29]

---

[28] *ibid.*, pp. 145-148. See also Galeazzo Ciano, *1937-1938 Diario* (Bologna, 1948), pp. 127-129. While Beck found Ciano, underneath his theatrics, a precise and accurate agent for his father-in-law, Ciano felt that Beck was not very strong, rather rambling and imprecise.

[29] For Beck's account of this episode, see *Dernier rapport*, pp. 172-175; for the views of the Rumanian Foreign Minister, whom Beck called a perfect imbecile and who

Apart from such complications, Beck's scheme for an Italian-Eastern Europe bloc had two fatal drawbacks. In the first place, by basing his plans on Italy and Hungary rather than on the Little Entente, he was fostering the forces making for territorial revision of the Versailles system and weakening those defending the *status quo*. In so doing, he was undermining the very arrangement which had enabled Poland to make its reappearance as the largest state in eastern central Europe. In the second place, Germany was the most powerful and active of the revisionist nations. It is therefore difficult to see just how a Rome-Budapest-Warsaw axis—Belgrade and Bucharest in this connection merely represented the wreckage of the Little Entente—could be the instrument to check German ambitions.[30] By 1938 Germany was in a position to overshadow and outmaneuver any such combination, as was made clear by the absolute worthlessness of the common Polish-Hungarian frontier which was achieved by the Hungarian absorption of Ruthenia in March 1939.

But, if Beck's program may be dismissed, it must be admitted that in all probability no arrangement by the Eastern European states could have assured the security of the area, even had their statesmen been far wiser and more self-restrained. Apart from the internecine quarrels, which were perhaps an inescapable by-product of the same spirit of national self-determination which created these states from the destruction of the old multinational empires, this unhappy area, by its history, its geography, and its low economic and industrial level, was scarcely in a position to maintain itself against external aggression or internal strain. Beck may certainly be criticized for his contribution to the disastrous confusion which afflicted this area in the 1930's, but the fact remains that the responsibility for Eastern Europe ultimately rested with the victorious powers of the first world war.

VI

If Poland's defense against Germany and Russia was not to be obtained through association with other states in Eastern Europe, the remaining alternative was the support of other Great Powers. The United States in the interwar period was of little value. Great Britain's position until the spring of 1939 was summarized by Sir Austen Chamberlain's

---

suspected Beck of secret aggressive agreements with Germany, see N. Petresco-Comnène, *Preludi del grande dramma* (Rome, 1947), pp. 276, 283-294.

[30] See Chapter 16, § II above.

private remark in 1925, that, "for the Polish corridor, no British Government ever will or ever can risk the bones of a British grenadier."[31]

There remained France, upon which had been placed far too great a burden for the preservation of the Versailles system. A Franco-Polish alliance was, at the end of the first world war, an obvious development. France favored a strong state on Germany's east and had worked for a large Poland at the Peace Conference. France mistrusted the revolutionary intentions of the new Soviet regime and supported Pilsudski in repulsing the Red army from the gates of Warsaw in 1920. The two nations, in February 1921, signed an accord which included a provision for mutual assistance and contained a secret military convention covering a German attack against either signatory or a Polish-Soviet conflict.[32] When the Locarno treaties created a distinction between Germany's Eastern and Western frontiers, France attempted to compensate for this shortcoming by signing a further treaty of guarantee with Poland on October 16, 1925.

Poland, however, profoundly mistrusted the trend toward Franco-German cooperation during the Stresemann-Briand era and was not enthusiastic about France's support of the Little Entente. France, for its part, found the Pilsudski regime after 1926 a trying and truculent ally. These strains were greatly sharpened after Hitler came to power. Each state seemed to the other to be inclined to come independently to terms with the Third Reich, France through the Four Power Pact and Poland through its 1934 agreement with Germany.[33]

In April 1934 the French Foreign Minister, Louis Barthou, visited Pilsudski. The conversation turned to Germany:

"I have had enough of these concessions; the Germans must be made to feel that we will no longer yield an inch," M. Barthou declared.

"You will yield, Messieurs, you will yield," the Marshal answered; "You would not be what you are if you did not yield."

"How can you suspect us of such a thing, M. the Marshal?"

"Perhaps you yourself do not wish to yield, but then either it will be necessary to dismiss you, or parliament will vote against you and defeat you."[34]

Commenting on this visit Beck later wrote: "It was always the

---

[31] From a letter cited in F. P. Walters, *A History of the League of Nations* (2 vols., London, 1952), I, 284.

[32] General Gamelin, *Servir* (3 vols., Paris, 1946-1947), II, 225, 466.

[33] For a discussion of Poland's motives in signing the agreement with Germany see below, §VII.

[34] Beck, *Dernier rapport*, p. 59; Szembek, *Journal*, p. 5.

same thing: the Marshal wished to intensify the purely military cooperation in face of the German menace, whereas the French sought to drag
us into their own combinations in South-East Europe, combinations
which had scarcely any connection with the German problem, the only
decisive problem in the event of war."[35]

From the Polish point of view, then, the French were failing to stand
up to the Germans but at the same time were busy building elaborate
diplomatic constructions in Eastern Europe which the Poles could not
welcome and in which they refused to participate.

From 1934 on, as France sought to include Russia in its security
arrangements, this situation grew worse. Beck regarded Russia's admission to the League of Nations as a great mistake, since Russia lacked
practically all the qualities which were demanded of League members.[36]
The project for an "Eastern Locarno," which was in theory to be an
extensive pact of guarantee and mutual assistance organized by France
and Russia but open to Germany, was seen by Beck as merely a means
of pushing the states of Eastern Europe into the arms of Russia and
then to tie this group to French policy.

It is rather strange that, after criticizing the Locarno treaties for
creating a disequilibrium in Europe, Beck should have opposed a similar
system of guarantees for the East. His position, however, was expounded
at some length in a memorandum to the French government, drafted
in September 1934. In the first place, Poland had finally succeeded in
signing pacts with Germany and Russia; these, he hoped, would relieve
the *malaise* troubling Eastern Europe. The main point, however, was
that an Eastern Locarno required the presence of Germany: "Our principal thesis was that the participation of Germany in this pact represented
for us a condition *sine qua non* for the maintenance of our policy of
equilibrium between the two great powers which we had for neighbors."[37]
Since Germany refused to join, Beck was not going to endanger his new
pact by taking part in a combination that would have an anti-German
bias.

While Beck respected Barthou as the last of the French statesmen who
vigorously defended France's interests, he was somewhat relieved, after
the latter's assassination, to find that Laval put far less pressure on
Poland for an eastern pact. In Beck's view the real trouble-maker in
France was the "all powerful influence of the bureaucracy of the Quai
d'Orsay" for which he repeatedly indicated his dislike.

[35] Beck, *Dernier rapport*, p. 60.   [36] *ibid.*, p. 68.
[37] *ibid.*, p. 74.

After the project for an Eastern Locarno collapsed, France pursued the more restricted objective of a mutual assistance agreement with the Soviet Union, with which was associated a Soviet-Czech pact. When Laval passed through Warsaw in May 1935 on his way to Moscow to sign this agreement, Pilsudski was unable to see him; the old Marshal was dying. From that point on, Beck's and France's ways tended to part: France attempted in a rather halfhearted fashion to build up a defense system with Russia and Czechoslovakia, Beck relied upon the security given him by his pact with Germany.

The melancholy story of French-Polish relations during the next three years has been told at some length and with much feeling by the French ambassador in Warsaw, Léon Noël. In his view, Pilsudski, while having no respect for French democracy, was firmly attached to the principle of the French alliance. Beck, on the other hand, was definitely anti-French in his policy. He restricted the Franco-Polish alliance to the narrow terms of common action in the event of an actual attack by Germany but did not seek to concert with the French in the more general area of foreign policy.[38]

French criticism of Beck loses some of its point, however, if one considers the crisis of March 7, 1936, when Germany denounced the Locarno agreement and sent its forces into the demilitarized Rhineland. Seeing this move as a definite test of force by Hitler and also as a test of the value of the Franco-Polish alliance, Beck, without waiting for any word from Paris, summoned the French ambassador and requested him to inform his government that Poland intended to live up to her treaty obligations. So at this decisive moment, which was probably the dividing line between possible peace and eventual war or German hegemony, the Polish response was prompt and apparently unequivocal. Some French diplomats were of the opinion that Beck made this proposal because he anticipated no French action. This supposition, while quite possibly correct, is not wholly relevant.[39] France's failure—for which Great Britain bears her share of responsibility—to act on this fatal occasion gives a certain plausibility to Beck's subsequent actions. If France was unable to take measures to prevent the remilitarization of the Rhineland,

[38] Noël, *L'Agression allemande*, pp. 104, 115-116.
[39] Szembek, who saw Beck after the meeting with the French ambassador, recorded in his journal: "Beck then expressed the opinion that the violation by Germany of the demilitarized zone did not constitute for us a *casus foederis*. . . . He does not think that war will result. France, without the support of England, will surely not move, and Great Britain is neither sufficiently prepared nor sufficiently armed to risk a conflict with Germany." Szembek, *Journal*, p. 167.

a step which inevitably meant that Germany would eventually be free to strike in the East without fear of immediate invasion from the West, the states in Eastern Europe were unavoidably driven to an attitude of *sauve qui peut*. It must be added, however, that in his memoirs Beck says that it was difficult to believe that the Germans could be prevented, in the long run, from militarizing the Rhineland. He felt, though, that since Germany was taking a serious gamble, Hitler "was ready to accord significant political concessions to assure the success of his action."[40] In other words, Beck was less concerned with the strategic import of the act, which he felt the French could have accepted if given an adequate compensation, than with the diplomatic method employed. He feared that an unchallenged *fait accompli* would give Hitler inflated ideas.

The immediate consequence of the events of March 1936 was increased French-Polish mistrust. By the autumn of that year Noël was suggesting that Smigly-Rydz, who was to visit France to conclude a military and financial agreement, be told quite frankly: "The French Government is wholly disposed to aid you, but you know, rightly or wrongly, the French have no confidence in M. Beck; the Chambers and French opinion will refuse, we fear, to permit the grant of an important loan to Poland so long as he retains the foreign affairs portfolio."[41] Noël had reason to believe that Smigly-Rydz did not care for Beck's diplomatic policy, and the French government, apparently, was inclined to accept his suggestion. As it turned out, however, the French government did not press for Beck's removal, primarily, it seems, because of reluctance to make what would be construed as an anti-German gesture. This mood of rather irresolute hostility on the part of France served only to confirm Beck in the course he was following.

By the time of the Czechoslovakian crisis in 1938 France was in the unhappy situation of seeing one of its alliance partners, Czechoslovakia, increasingly threatened by another, Poland. Nevertheless, while the French were properly indignant over Beck's actions, France itself was guilty of forcing Czechoslovakia to yield to Hitler. Indeed, an extremely vicious circle had developed. A common Polish-Czech front of resistance to Germany in 1938 might have driven France to a support of its commitments; on the other hand, Beck's belief that France was not going to oppose Germany helped keep him on his anti-Czech course. Noël states that Beck had said to him several times during the first days of his stay in Warsaw: "We have no illusions, we know very well that our alliance

[40] Beck, *Dernier rapport*, pp. 113-114.
[41] Noël, *L'Agression allemande*, p. 140.

with you is unilateral; if you were attacked by Germany Poland would march to your aid, because it would be in its interest; but the reverse is not true; we do not forget the press campaigns in France on the theme: we shall not fight for the Corridor."[42] In May 1938, when the French government proposed that Poland join the French and British ambassadors in warning Berlin against the use of force, Beck, while refusing to associate himself with this move, referred to the Polish attitude of March 7, 1936 and declared that Poland "was ready to honor its obligations as an ally of France."[43] As the crisis became more acute, Beck, in a conference with other Polish leaders, gave the following analysis of the situation: 1) the Czechs would not fight; 2) the Western Powers were not prepared, either morally or materially, to come to their rescue. He went on to say, however, that "if my basic hypothesis was contradicted by the facts, it would be necessary, within a period of twenty-four hours, to modify completely the policy of Poland, for, in the event of a real European war against Germany, we could not be on the side of the latter, even indirectly."[44] As it turned out, both of Beck's premises were correct.

More fateful than this deterioration of the Franco-Polish alliance was the fact that the alliance itself, by the late 1930's, no longer had the strategic significance it possessed in the 1920's, when Russia was recovering from revolution and civil war, when Germany was disarmed and when France had the most powerful army on the continent. France alone was no longer able to counterbalance the growing power of Germany, nor, as it later proved, were France and Britain together. Consequently, Poland's security was more and more coming to depend upon the marginal influence it had in balancing itself between Germany and Russia.

VII

In a conversation with Pierre Laval, in January 1935, Beck explained the basic premises of Polish foreign policy by saying: "Polish policy rests on the following elements: it follows from our geographical position as well as from the experiences of our history that the problems to which we must attach decisive importance are those posed by the relations with our two great neighbors, Germany and Russia. It is therefore to these problems that we must devote the greatest part of our political activity

---

[42] *ibid.*, p. 252. On the other hand, in January 1935, Beck told Szembek that he did not think there was any chance that France might denounce her alliance with Poland, since such an action would amount to suicide on the part of France. Szembek, *Journal*, p. 32.
[43] Beck, *Dernier rapport*, p. 319.   [44] *ibid.*, pp. 162-163.

and of our modest means of action. History teaches us: 1) that the greatest catastrophe of which our nation has ever been victim has been the result of concerted action by these two Powers, and 2) that in this desperate situation there was not to be found any Power in the world to bring us assistance. . . . Another conclusion which imposes itself is that the policy of Warsaw should never be dependent upon Moscow or Berlin."[45]

To meet this difficult situation Beck, in theory at least, tried to pursue a policy of even balance between the two states. For example, in 1934 he timed a visit to Moscow to match the signing of the German-Polish pact. He insisted that his policy was clear and unequivocal and that having closer relations with one of the Powers than with the other "would fatally drag us into a political activity or even into armed conflict which would not be justified by any vital interest of Poland and the only result of which would be to transform our territory into a battlefield for foreign interests."[46]

While one may accept Beck's view that this was a reasonable position for Poland to take, the policy of balance leaves certain questions unresolved. It did not in itself prevent Germany and Russia from working together at Poland's expense. Moreover, while Beck contended that his diplomacy was based on "extremely simple" principles, it is not surprising that other nations found it increasingly complicated. The simple intention of riding two horses at once can lead to some exceptionally strenuous acrobatics. The real difficulty with Beck's desire to remain midway between Moscow and Berlin was its failure to indicate what should be done in the event one state was moving off on a clearly aggressive and revisionist tangent, whereas the other, for the time being at least, was not. In classical balance of power theory, a state trying to maintain itself between two more powerful states should move toward the less aggressive. In Beck's hands, however, the idea of preserving a balance seemed to mean that, if Germany took an aggressive action, Poland should respond by an act perhaps half as aggressive. There are several reasons for this rather peculiar behavior, which inevitably brought Beck closer to the Germans and farther from the Russians.

A number of authorities have said that in 1933, upon Hitler's coming to power, Pilsudski offered to join the French in an action against Germany and that, only after being rebuffed and after witnessing the conclusion of the Four Power Pact, was he impelled to turn to Germany for the nonaggression pact of January 1934. The evidence for this offer, reports of which began to circulate as early as the summer of 1933, is elusive, however, and the present author is doubtful of its authenticity.[47] A proposal for preventive war is not mentioned in Beck's own memoirs, nor does it correspond to his retrospective interpretation of Polish views at the time.

According to Beck, Pilsudski had attentively examined the "pros and cons and all the odds of a preventive war before taking the decision to negotiate with Germany. There were obviously many elements to consider in this connection. In the military field the Marshal estimated that the weakest point in our army was the high command. The weakness of our eventual allies at this period made us abandon the idea of a preventive war, and what happened later, at the time of the occupation of the demilitarized zone of the Rhine by German troops, amply confirmed the estimate of the situation."[48]

Apart from these negative considerations, it is unlikely that Beck or Pilsudski felt Hitler to be an immediate menace. Beck records that Pilsudski did not think Hitler's coming to power meant the pursuit of a more violent anti-Polish policy, and he advised Beck, in making a speech before the Polish Diet, not to attach importance to the excitement of the European press but to be calm, firm, and moderate.[49] In his speech of February 15, 1933, Beck confined himself to saying: "Our attitude with regard to Germany will be exactly the same as Germany's attitude toward Poland. Speaking practically, more depends on Berlin in this respect than on Warsaw."[50]

At the same time, however, the victory of the Nazis had increased tension in Danzig, the "barometer" of Polish-German relations. Pilsudski felt a vigorous step was needed and quickly moved to reinforce the Polish garrison at the Westerplatte. But, as Beck put it, the warning of this abrupt measure "was perfectly understood in Danzig and Berlin," which adopted a conciliatory attitude. The question then arose whether Poland was in a position "to profit from the internal revolution of the Reich to ameliorate our neighborly relations with that country."

The reasons for Polish optimism on this point appear in a memorandum Beck prepared in the autumn of 1933. His conclusions were as follows: (1) the National Socialist movement has a truly revolutionary

---

[47] For a further discussion of this point see the Note at the end of the chapter.

[48] Beck, *Dernier rapport*, p. 66.   [49] *ibid.*, p. 24.

[50] Jozef Beck, *Przemowienia, Deklaracje, Wywiady, 1931-1937* (Warsaw, 1938), pp. 58-59. The German translation, *Beiträge zur europäischen Politik, Reden, Erklärungen, Interviews, 1932-1939* (Essen, 1939) includes Beck's speeches up to January 1939.

character; (2) at all times reformers have wanted to reinvestigate old problems; (3) all reformers are primarily concerned with internal changes, and for that they need a period of external calm; (4) Hitler is more or less an Austrian, in any case not a Prussian; no Prussian figures among his direct collaborators; and this fact creates a new situation, since the old Prussian traditions were chiefly responsible for the anti-Polish feeling in Germany; and (5) the Hitlerian movement is the last act of the national unification of the German people. The conclusion drawn was that "we found ourselves before a unique occasion for redressing our situation in the European balance."[51]

In the spring and summer of 1933, Hitler, publicly and privately, gave reassurances to the Poles that he had no intention of violating existing treaties or stirring up trouble in Danzig. In November, the Polish government explained to Hitler that Poland's security was founded on direct relations with other states and on collaboration through the League of Nations. Since Germany had now withdrawn from the League, the Polish government wished to know whether there was any chance "of compensating for the loss of this element of security, in direct Polish-German relations."[52] From this opening, the path led directly to the signing of the nonaggression agreement of January 26, 1934; and there is no indication in Beck's memoirs that, after getting a favorable German response, Pilsudski turned once more to France before signing the agreement.

Without doubt, Beck himself was much pleased with the German pact, which he regarded as the greatest and most valuable achievement of Polish foreign policy.[53] After Pilsudski's death, he paid a cordial visit to Berlin and was able to reassure the Nazi leaders that Polish policy would not change with the Marshal's passing. Commenting on that visit, he wrote later: "It will doubtless be very interesting one day to study to what degree the complete reversal of German policy several years later

---

[51] Beck, *Dernier rapport*, p. 29. The same line of thought appears in the introduction to the Polish White Book: "There seemed a possibility that the National Socialist revolution might force German opinion to accept the idea of a rapprochement with Poland, though this had been impossible under the Weimar Republic. The Hitler regime transferred the power in Germany to men who had not come from Prussia, the land of traditional hatred for Poland." *Polish White Book*, p. 3.

[52] *Polish White Book*, p. 17. On October 1, 1933, Pilsudski called a conference to discuss the situation created by Germany's departure from the League. He ordered a report on the state of German rearmament. He also wanted to ask the French what information they had on the subject, and added: "It is necessary to draw the attention of the French to the fact that this work is secret, that we are not journalists nor in the service of journalists, and that we are not sounding the alarm." He concluded by saying that he had not yet formed an opinion with regard to German rearmament. Szembek, *Journal*, p. 2.

[53] *ibid.*, p. 41.

can or should be attributed to Hitler himself, in what measure eventually it was owing to the overly great ease with which his imperialist policy went from success to success, or, finally, if and to what point it had its origin in a reaction of the old Prussian spirit in the interior of Germany itself."[54]

Here seems to be the real clue to Beck's policy vis-à-vis Germany. While no pro-German, he was definitely attracted by, and had confidence in, what he thought to be the Hitlerian foreign policy.[55] He had no illusions that it was a static policy, but he thought it was based on nationalist principles. Consequently, he expected an attempt to take over Austria and, subsequently, action against Czechoslovakia; but he was quite willing to accept these developments as not imperiling Poland.

Beck never felt that he was becoming a German satellite or compromising the independence of Poland's foreign policy.[56] He did not join Germany in an anti-Bolshevik or anti-Russian crusade, although he was gratified whenever the Nazis told him of their dislike, not merely of Communism, but of any Russian state whatever its complexion. As early as the autumn of 1934, Göring had thrown out some hints that Poland might well join Germany in an anti-Russian agreement, but Pilsudski "cut short this conversation by declaring that Poland, a country bordering Russia, had to adopt toward that Power a moderate and calm policy and could not adhere to any combination of the sort to revive tension on our eastern frontiers."[57] Beck appears to have held to this view in face of subsequent hints and offers.[58]

---

[54] Beck, *Dernier rapport*, p. 101.

[55] In a conversation with Anthony Eden on April 2, 1935, Szembek remarked: "In any event, for the Poles there is no doubt that of all the possible regimes in Germany the present Hitlerian regime is the most satisfactory; the proof is that we have arrived at an understanding with it. A socialist or communist regime would inevitably entail a return to the Rapallo policy; the German Nationalists, . . . quite apart from their Russophile tendency, would, if they came to power, be most hostile to Poland. Hitler is the only German statesman who has wished, and known how to reach, an understanding with us. For these reasons, it is impossible for us, or at least very difficult, to join any action whatsoever which is directed against Hitler and the policy which he represents." Szembek, *Journal*, pp. 55-56.

[56] The difficulty, however, of maintaining this independence in practice is shown by a remark of Szembek to the Polish ambassador to Russia in December 1938: "It is exceedingly hard for us to maintain a balance between Russia and Germany. Our relations with the latter are entirely grounded on the belief of the leading personalities of the Third Reich that, in the future conflict between Germany and Russia, Poland would be the natural ally of Germany. In these conditions, the good-neighbor policy, which has its origin in the 1934 accord, could easily appear to be but a pure and simple fiction." Szembek, *Journal*, p. 386.

[57] Beck, *Dernier rapport*, p. 34.

[58] For example, in his conversations with Ribbentrop in January 1939, Beck explained the impossibility of Poland's joining the Anti-Comintern Pact. At the same time, he was

Some authors, Polish and of other nationalities, have gone so far as to argue that the chief fault of Beck's diplomacy was not the German connection, which was actually Pilsudski's responsibility, but the fact that, having achieved it, he did not then ride it for all it was worth. It is difficult to guess how such a venture might have turned out. In the short run, gains in the east might have compensated for the loss of Danzig and control over the Corridor. But, at the end of this road lay Machiavelli's warning: "A prince ought to take care never to make an alliance with one more powerful than himself for the purpose of attacking others, unless necessity compels him . . . because if he conquers, you are at his discretion."

Even Beck's unpleasant performance at the time of the Munich crisis was not planned in concert with the Germans. Western diplomats as well as many Poles felt, in the summer of 1938, that Poland's rapprochement with Germany was "degenerating into an undignified imitation of the small fish that seek their meat in the wake of the shark."[59] Nevertheless, Beck insisted he was pursuing an independent policy. As he later expressed it, "I formulated on the part of Poland a simple and at the same time very supple demand. I declared we demanded simply that, if the government of Prague decided to make concessions to other countries, our interests should be treated in exactly the same fashion. When the diplomats asked me to define our demands or claims, I categorically refused to do so and affirmed that Poland did not have the intention of dismembering the Czechoslovak state or of taking the initiative in an attack against this country, and that, consequently, it did not feel called upon to give a rigid precision to its claims. That if, however, the Czechoslovak state, a veritable mosaic of nationalities hitherto governed by methods of brutal centralisation, had the intention of revising its policy or its regime in order to take better account of the interests of a particular national group, we could not admit that the Polish minority, which was grouped in a very compact manner in a region situated on our frontier, should be less well treated than any other ethnic group."[60]

Having taken this "most favored nation" attitude, Beck was bound to be evasive when queried by the French or British ambassadors. The

---

on sufficiently close terms with the Germans to discuss with them the problems which might arise if internal pressures in Russia should lead to a war or if the Soviet Union should break up into national states. He did not, however, think that either eventuality was likely in the near future. Szembek, *Journal*, p. 413. On Ribbentrop's interest in Polish adhesion to the Anti-Comintern Pact, see Chapter 15, §v above.

[59] *British Documents*, 3rd series, I, 431.

[60] Beck, *Dernier rapport*, p. 159.

Germans, however, were equally uncertain of his intentions. On July 1, the German ambassador, Moltke, reported on a conversation with Beck: "As usual, when he wishes to avoid definite statements, M. Beck said a great deal without saying anything of importance." Moltke doubted that Poland would side with France if it intervened, but he would not assume that Poland would be on Germany's side: "Poland will . . . always act exclusively according to her own interests."[61] In September, Moltke denied rumors that he had been trying to influence Poland. "Practical cooperation already exists and great emphasis on this point would not be advisable in view of M. Beck's disposition. . . . It is correct to say that Beck attached great importance to achieving Polish aims as far as possible independently and that he is trying particularly to avoid giving the outside world any impression of dependence on Germany."[62]

The basic danger in Beck's "supple" policy was that the more Germany raised its claims, the more he was obliged to raise his. As the dispute moved beyond autonomy for the Sudeten Germans to the right of self-determination and plebiscites, Beck came to demand equivalent treatment for the Polish minority.[63] When the decision was reached to cede certain Sudeten territories without a plebiscite, the Poles in turn demanded frontier revision without plebiscite.[64] By September 21, the Polish government was pressing hard on the Czechs, denouncing the 1925 Polish-Czech convention dealing with minorities and demanding rapid action. To the Czech appeal for negotiation, the Poles responded even more peremptorily, in part because of a belief that the Soviet note of September 23, threatening to cancel the Polish-Soviet nonaggression pact, was somehow related to the Czech notes.[65]

Then came the Munich Conference at which the dispute was suddenly taken over by that old enemy of Polish diplomacy, the Four Powers. Germany gained its demands; Poland was not even invited to the meeting. Beck decided that an immediate reaction was in order and asked for a march on Teschen as a "protest against the Munich proceedings." On September 30, he sent a twelve-hour ultimatum to the Czechs, the text of which, as Benes subsequently remarked, was "almost identical with the ultimatum which Hitler sent to Beck himself a year later with respect

[61] *German Documents*, series D, II, 449-452.

[62] *ibid.*, pp. 973-974.

[63] *ibid.*, p. 811.

[64] *ibid.*, p. 849.

[65] Beck, *Dernier rapport*, pp. 163-164. It was agreed by British and German observers alike that the one thing likely to push the Poles explicitly into the German camp was the appearance of Russian interference.

to the solution of the question of Danzig."[66] This was not Colonel Beck's finest hour.

The first inkling that Polish-German relations were up for review came shortly after Munich when, on October 24, Ribbentrop proposed to the Polish ambassador a general settlement of issues between Poland and Germany. This settlement included the reunion of Danzig with the Reich, an extraterritorial road and railway across Pomorze, a guarantee of frontiers, joint action in colonial matters, and a common policy toward Russia on the basis of the Anti-Comintern Pact.[67] Beck's response was conciliatory but held that "any attempt to incorporate the Free City into the Reich must inevitably lead to conflict."

According to Beck, writing in October 1939, the turning point in his own mind concerning relations with Germany was his interview with Hitler on January 4 of that year. To his alarm he noted "new accents" in Hitler's remarks. The Chancellor, while continuing to propose German-Polish cooperation, now "treated with levity the ideas which he and German propaganda had hitherto elevated almost to the level of a religion."[68] Still unwilling to revise his estimate of Hitler, Beck thought that perhaps the Fuehrer was still inclined to be cautious but that Ribbentrop, "a dangerous personality," was urging a reckless course. Upon his return to Warsaw, Beck felt sufficiently alarmed to tell Moscicki and Smigly-Rydz that these shifts in the German mood might presage war. Ribbentrop visited Warsaw later in the month, but the conversations were not fruitful. Beck refused to give way on Danzig or Pomorze despite suggested compensation in Slovakia and even mention of the Black Sea.[69]

With the German occupation of Prague and Memel in March, the situation deteriorated rapidly. If Poland's Ukrainian problem had been relieved by Hungary's taking over Ruthenia, this gain was far outweighed by Germany's annexation of Bohemia and Moravia and its virtual military control over Slovakia, which, as General Jodl said, now made it possible to "consider the Polish problem on the basis of more or less favorable strategic premises."[70] By March 28 the German ambassa-

---

[66] Letter from Benes to L. B. Namier, April 20, 1944, in Namier, *Europe in Decay* (London, 1950), p. 285.

[67] *Polish White Book*, p. 47.

[68] Beck, *Dernier rapport*, p. 182. See also Szembek, *Journal*, p. 407.

[69] Beck, *Dernier rapport*, p. 186; *Polish White Book*, pp. 54-58.

[70] Cited in Royal Institute of International Affairs, *Survey of International Affairs, 1939-1946: The World in March 1939* (London, New York, Toronto, 1952), p. 291.

dor was accusing Beck of wanting "to negotiate at the point of a bayonet."
To which Beck replied, "That is your own method."[71]

Thus, Beck's efforts to maintain good yet independent relations with
Germany had come to failure. His basic error was a misreading of the
Nazi movement and of Hitler's personality. That he was deeply cha-
grined by this turn of events, which undid his whole diplomatic strategy,
is not surprising.[72] It was reported that, after his highly popular speech
of May 5, in which he courageously stood up against the German
menaces, "in a fit of rage, [he] had thrown a whole pile of congratula-
tory telegrams into a corner."[73]

Whatever Beck's personal feelings, it was clear that if he was to resist
Germany he had to look abroad. Britain, and secondarily France, were
the Powers to which he necessarily turned. But, as has been observed
above, by the spring of 1939 it was far from certain that Britain and
France were capable of rescuing Poland. Polish-Soviet relations now
assumed decisive importance.

VIII

Although Pilsudski and Beck declared that their policy was to keep
Poland evenly balanced between Germany and the Soviet Union, Polish
diplomacy was in practice perceptibly off-center. Pilsudski brought with
him the deep anti-Russian feelings of his revolutionary and wartime
career. To these were added a justifiable suspicion of Bolshevik intentions
and a concern about the large Ukrainian and White Russian minorities in
Poland's eastern provinces. As in many states bordering on Russia, the
outcome was a conviction on the part of the government, so pervasive as
to be almost unspoken and undebated, that no positive and fruitful relationship with the Soviet Union was possible.[74] In the 1920's, a Polish

[71] *Polish White Book*, p. 69.
[72] For an illuminating picture of Beck's mood and outlook at this time, see the account
of a train journey with him by the former Rumanian Foreign Minister, Grigore Gafencu.
Last Days of Europe (New Haven, 1948), pp. 26-53.
[73] According to the Polish Under-Secretary of State, Miroslaw Arciszewski, who is
reported to have given this information to the German ambassador, Beck was not happy
about the Anglo-Polish declaration of mutual assistance, was forced to make his address
of May 5 because of the Fuehrer's speech of April 28, and was exasperated by the Polish
public's enthusiastic reception of it. "M. Beck even now basically favors the previous
policy." *Vorgeschichte*, p. 253. It is difficult to tell whether this statement actually represented Beck's views, since it was designed for German ears. Moreover, on several occasions
Arciszewski seems to have gone beyond his instructions and acted on his own.
[74] The government's view was not identical with that of Polish opinion in general. In
March 1936, Szembek remarked, "Polish opinion is thoroughly hostile to Germany and,
in contrast, is favorable to France and even Sovietophile. I consider that it is indispensable
to make the principles of our foreign policy popular." Szembek, *Journal*, p. 172.

ambassador returning from Moscow reported to Pilsudski that he had not tried to settle conflicts of little importance but had rather sought to ameliorate general relations between the two countries. The Marshal interrupted him to say, "Now, that is curious. I should have done exactly the opposite."[75] While Beck always stressed the importance of an independent Polish policy and the value of bilateral negotiations, he was not enthusiastic about dealing bilaterally with the Soviet Union. When discussing in his memoirs the negotiations leading to the Polish-Soviet pact of 1932, he observed that Poland's traditional policy demanded "solidarity with all the western neighbors of Russia."[76] There was no equivalent sense of a need for solidarity with Germany's eastern neighbors when it came to negotiating with that Power.

Certain steps were taken, however. Poland (along with Estonia, Latvia, and Rumania) signed the Litvinov protocol on February 9, 1929, the Polish-Soviet pact of nonaggression of July 25, 1932, and—with Russia's other neighbors—the London convention for the definition of aggression of July 3, 1933; and, in 1934, Beck made his trip to Moscow to balance the signing of the German-Polish pact.

Within the next two years, however, Polish-Soviet relations fell off greatly. In July 1936 the new Polish ambassador in Moscow, Grzybowski, was received by Krestinsky, Litvinov's deputy, with blunt words: "The political relations between us could not be worse. We are working to increase the prestige of the League of Nations, and for collective security; we are combatting all forms of aggression and all forms of fascism. At the present time we are pursuing an anti-German, anti-Italian and anti-Japanese policy. Poland is pursuing a diametrically contrary policy, tending to weaken the League of Nations, combatting attempts to realize collective security, supporting Italy and sympathizing with Japan. Poland is within the orbit of German policy."[77]

Grzybowski, of course, denied this interpretation and his rather rueful comment on this meeting must sound familiar to those who have had occasion to deal with the Soviet Union: "Irrespective of Polish policy, the Soviets constantly interpreted it so as to contrapose it to their own policy."[78] Nevertheless, it is true that Beck disapproved of the Soviet entry into the League of Nations, regarded collective security as a Communist device, and was highly critical of France and Czechoslovakia for signing

---

[75] Beck, *Dernier rapport*, p. 6.   [76] *ibid.*, pp. 10-11.

[77] *Polish White Book*, p. 195.

[78] Grzybowski himself, however, was not pleased with Poland's Soviet policy, which he regarded as uselessly hostile. See his remarks in December 1938, Szembek, *Journal*, pp. 386-387.

treaties of mutual assistance with the USSR. Indeed, the more one considers the course of Polish diplomacy the more this deep-rooted and altogether natural mistrust of Russia seems to give a distinct flavor to Polish attitudes on almost all issues. Beck said at the end of his career, "In the course of the twenty years of my political activity in the field of foreign affairs, I acquired the conviction that the essential element which created divergences between Polish policy and French policy was not the German question but, invariably, the manner of viewing the Russian problem."[79]

Beck not only regarded the Soviet Union as a dangerous power but he denied that it could serve as a counterweight to Germany, notwithstanding the mutual hostility of these two powers in the 1930's. In 1937 he and Winston Churchill informally discussed this issue while relaxing at Cannes but were unable to agree. "I could not avoid the impression," Beck later wrote, "that this eminent statesman lived too much on his memories of the preceding war and that he was too inclined to consider Russia as a relatively important counterweight to German dynamism. I tried to make him understand that Europe could not have the least confidence in Soviet Russia and that we, its neighbors, had more evidence than anyone for judging the Russian phenomenon with skepticism."[80]

When Beck went to London in April 1939 to negotiate the British-Polish mutual assistance pact, he felt he should state Poland's position on having Russia as an alliance partner. Poland, he said, had no confidence in Russia or in the ends it pursued. It had had experience with Tsarist imperialism and with Communist imperialism, and they came to the same thing. However, in face of the German menace, there was no point in rebuffing Russia; one should at least be assured of its neutrality. Though doubtful of its achievement, he would not oppose an English-French-Soviet entente, but such an accord could not impose new obligations on Poland. He would be satisfied if an arrangement were made whereby, in case of war with Germany, arms could be sent to Poland via Russia and Russia could provide raw materials.[81]

The involved story of the unsuccessful efforts by the British and French to reconcile this position with the mounting demands of the Russians in the abortive negotiations of the spring and summer of 1939 cannot be told here. There is no question, however, that the Polish refusal to agree to the presence of Soviet troops on Polish soil was, as a

---

[79] Beck, *Dernier rapport*, p. 193.   [80] *ibid.*, p. 127.
[81] *ibid.*, p. 193. See also British comments on Polish attitude toward military cooperation with Russia, in *British Documents*, 3rd series, IV, 428, 453.

debating point at least, an important factor in the breakdown of the negotiations. The reluctance of the Poles to make this concession is certainly understandable, nor is it by any means certain that a greater show of cooperation on their part would have deflected the Soviet Union from its pact of August 23 with Germany. Nevertheless, the utterly negative quality of Polish-Soviet relations appears very clearly in a set of conditions laid down by the Polish ambassador in a conversation with Molotov in May 1939: "We could not accept a one-sided Soviet guarantee. Nor could we accept a mutual guarantee, because in the event of a conflict with Germany our forces would be completely engaged, and so we would not be in any position to give help to the Soviets. Also we could not accept collective negotiations, and made our adoption of a definite attitude conditional on the result of the Anglo-Franco-Soviet negotiations. We rejected all discussion of matters affecting us other than by the bilateral method. . . . I indicated our favorable attitude to the Anglo-Franco-Soviet negotiations, and once more emphasized our entire loyalty in relation to the Soviets. In the event of conflict we by no means rejected specified forms of Soviet aid, but considered it premature to determine them definitely. We considered it premature to open bilateral negotiations with the Soviets before the Anglo-Franco-Soviet negotiations had achieved a result." The ambassador continued, "M. Molotov made no objection whatever."[82] Indeed, there seemed to be very little to say.

Interestingly enough, Beck was quite pleased that Molotov had replaced Litvinov, whom he regarded as the "notorious enemy of our country." "It was possible to suppose that the anti-Polish complex peculiar to this man, who was by origin a *litwak*, had disappeared with him."[83] Just as Hitler, an Austrian, was to alter the anti-Polish bias of the Prussian tradition, so, presumably, Molotov was to rid Soviet policy of the anti-Polish prejudices of the *litwak* Litvinov.[84] Here again Beck's own nationalism was misleading him. By reducing foreign policy to such motives he was unable to grasp the basic drives of either the Nazi or the Soviet dictatorship.

For a brief period, it is true, Molotov adopted toward the Poles an attitude of "the greatest courtesy." The Soviet government offered to supply them with war materials; the Soviet press urged resistance to German demands. In retrospect, of course, this amiability, which con-

---

[82] *Polish White Book*, p. 208.

[83] Beck, *Dernier Rapport*, p. 200.

[84] Beck described the *litwak* as the "worst of the Jewish types, deported from Russia to the Polish provinces and who, at Vilna or at Bialystok, offended Polish ears with his Russian jabber." (*Ibid.*, p. 139).

tinued until the German attack, appears altogether sinister: intended at first to conceal the German-Soviet rapprochement and then, perhaps, to prolong Polish resistance in the event France and Great Britain failed to declare war on Germany.

In this instance, however, Beck's position did not change. To the last he refused to have Soviet troops on Polish territory;[85] and the most he would concede was that, after hostilities had started, he might agree to reexamine the question with a view to possible Soviet-Polish cooperation.

IX

Beck's diplomatic career ended in complete disaster. All his policies turned against him. The nonaggression pact with Hitler did not prevent a German assault; the disintegration of Czechoslovakia weakened rather then strengthened his southern frontier; his refusal to admit Russian soldiers to Polish soil did not keep them from overrunning eastern Poland in September 1939. Nor was this just bad luck. His views on the art of diplomacy, his estimate of the international situation, and his analysis of political motives were filled with inconsistencies that inevitably led to self-defeating policies.

He was not just an opportunist, though the charge of unprincipled opportunism has been laid against him. He adhered, rather arrogantly and purblindly, to a set of axioms which he took to be Pilsudskian heritage and which made up in their obvious preoccupation with the Polish national interest what they lacked in coherence and universality. But, unlike Churchill, who was fighting against the current and whose speeches of the 1930's have the real mark of prophetic insight, Beck was engulfed in the currents of his time, and his prophecies tended to be self-fulfilling ones which his own activities and outlook helped bring to pass.

Still, when all this has been said, an appraisal of Beck cannot be wholly negative. For all the errors of his policy, he was not one of the really malignant creatures of the decade. Contrary to widespread contemporary belief, he was not in league with Hitler, even though the two often appeared to be working in collaboration. Even in the case of his least defensible action, the ultimatum to Czechoslovakia, he was, to a large degree, the victim of his own "most favored nation" formula; the movement of events which drove him to such an unfortunate action came from the interaction of German aggressiveness and the wobbling retreat of the

---

[85] In mid-August 1939, Beck said to Noël, "Nothing assures us that, once they are installed in the eastern parts of our country, the Russians will participate effectively in the war." Noël, *L'Agression allemande*, p. 423.

Western Powers, France and Great Britain. He did not like Czechoslovakia, but he did not plot its destruction.

Nor can one say that he contributed greatly to the disaster that overtook Europe, except in the sense that his actions fed into a vicious circle which intensified and compounded the weaknesses of the existing international order. The League of Nations was indeed a weak reed, though attitudes such as Beck's helped make it so. Russia was indeed a dangerous and unpredictable Power, though Beck's policy toward Russia did nothing to make it less dangerous or unpredictable and seemed to provide a rationale for Soviet actions in 1939. In this respect, he is highly symptomatic of the 1930's. The feeling, so apparent in his memoirs, that there were no feasible alternatives, was characteristic of a general European mood which was creating, and being created by, the approaching catastrophe.

In one regard, however, Beck definitely deserves respect. When the final test came, he did not yield. In a desperate situation, partly of his own making, he took an unprovocative but courageous stand. The result, to be sure, was a horrible war, the outcome of which was not real peace and which had tragic consequences for Poland during and after the hostilities. For this reason there have been some to criticize him for not allying himself with Hitler, just as there have been those to rebuke Great Britain for not having been shrewd enough to let Poland fall as it had let Czechoslovakia fall. Whatever the results of such policies, one thing would have been missing in the future: the will to defy. Even in the painful situation of the world today, it is heartening to know that this value was not permitted to drain out of the life of nations as it threatened to for a time in the 1930's.

These considerations, however, extend beyond the horizon of Beck's career, which stopped in September 1939. By the end of his life he was far removed from politics and diplomacy. In August 1943, only ten months before his death, he wrote to his daughter-in-law: "Reading what you report to me, I have had the impression of a kind of doubling of my personality. Here am I, taking care of my lungs, which are in a pitiable state, and, there, a phantom moves about the world, another Jozef Beck with whom I have had no relations for four years. He goes this way and that, engages in conflicts, is attacked, is spoken of in books. He is a solid enough type, since he has moved about so long without my aiding him in anything. What a strange spectacle! I ask myself if someday I shall have the possibility and the desire to meet him again in this world or whether I shall abandon him to his own devices."[86]

NOTE ON POLISH PROPOSALS FOR PREVENTIVE ACTION AGAINST GERMANY

A number of writers and diplomats have referred to a proposal, or proposals, for preventive action against Germany which Marshal Pilsudski is said to have made to the French shortly after Hitler came to power. There seems to be no authoritative contemporary evidence, however, and the stories are not altogether consistent.

The Communist journalist "André Simone" stated that, in March 1933, Pilsudski informed the Daladier government of the alarming progress of German rearmament and proposed to France that the Hitler regime be crushed by a "preventive war." Daladier demurred, then refused. The offer was repeated in April, but there was no response. (*J'Accuse: The Men Who Betrayed France*, New York, 1940, p. 53). This account seems to be the source of substantially the same story which appears in J. W. Wheeler-Bennett, *Munich, Prologue to Tragedy* (London, New York, 1948), pp. 283-284. The emphasis here upon Pilsudski's concern over Germany's rapid arming is in conflict with Ambassador Noël's statement that Pilsudski believed Germany would require a generation before being ready to make war (*L'Agression allemande contre la Pologne*, pp. 67-68).

Pertinax stated that in April 1933 Poland proposed a preventive war, knowing that it would not be taken up, as a preliminary to its move toward Germany (*Les Fossoyeurs*, New York, 1943, II, 83).

The Polish journalist Stanislaw Mackiewicz wrote that in March 1933 Pilsudski deliberately tried to start a war with Germany. While granting that no evidence had been found in Poland of a memorandum addressed by Pilsudski to Daladier, he contended that Pilsudski's reinforcement of the Polish garrison on the Westerplatte was intended as a provocative act. (*Colonel Beck and His Policy*, London, 1944, p. 15) Beck, in his memoirs, interpreted this move as a warning to Germany of Poland's alertness, not as a provocation (*Dernier rapport*, pp. 25-27).

L. B. Namier has written that on three occasions, in March and November 1933 and again in March 1936, the Poles suggested to France armed action against Germany; he adds that Pilsudski's initiative in 1933, though authentic, cannot be easily documented (*Diplomatic Prelude*,

---

[86] Beck, *Dernier rapport*, p. xxiii.

1938-1939, London, 1948, p. 97, note 3). With regard to the November effort: "Pilsudski was sounding Paris once more about common action against Hitler. The talks were confined to military channels—the first approach was made through General d'Arbonneau, French Military Attaché in Warsaw. The result was negative . . ." (*ibid.*, p. 15). Apparently the source for this statement was Jozef Lipski, Polish ambassador in Berlin, who wrote to Namier: "After the German Ambassador, von Moltke, had on November 27 presented to Marshal Pilsudski the German draft of a non-aggression pact, I was instructed by Colonel Beck to keep the matter strictly secret, and that also towards the *corps diplomatique*. Pilsudski, who personally dealt with the problem, would not sign a pact with the Germans before sounding Paris once more about jointly taking decisive action against Hitler, which was a further reason for his instructing me to preserve absolute silence." (L. B. Namier, *Europe in Decay*, London, 1950, p. 282, note 1). Lipski elsewhere makes the same point: "Pilsudski se rendait clairement compte des possibilités militaires de l'Allemagne. La preuve en est qu'il me chargea d'employer devant le dictateur du Reich l'argument de la force. Hitler le comprit et proposa à Pilsudski un pacte de non-agression. Étant en possession de l'offre allemande, le Maréchal fit encore une fois des ouvertures à la France, suspendit les pourparlers avec Berlin, et partit pour Wilno. Cette fois encore Paris ne manifesta aucune volonté d'action." (J. Lipski, *Sprawy Miedzynarodowe*, No. 2-3, 1947, p. 15, quoted in Beck, *Dernier rapport*, p. 32, note 1).

Against this rather scattered evidence is the fact that there appears to be no mention of any Pilsudskian proposals in 1933 in the documents the Germans captured in Warsaw, in Léon Noël's memoirs, in the volumes thus far published by the French parliamentary commission of enquiry (*Les Événements survenus en France de 1933 à 1945*), or in Beck's three memoranda written between 1939 and 1943 (*Dernier rapport*). If Beck's interpretation of Pilsudski's point of view is to be trusted, the Marshal, in 1933, did not regard the Hitler regime as a serious threat, though he seems to have given some theoretical consideration to the advisability of preventive action. Apparently, military intelligence studies made in 1933 and 1934 (see note 52 above) led the Polish regime to believe that neither Germany nor Russia was in a condition to undertake any immediate military action. Beck, however, felt that of the two Russia was the more likely to risk an adventurous undertaking (*Dernier rapport*, pp. 65-66). His view was shared by Under-Secretary of State Szembek, who said to Eden in April 1935: "We have, however, arrived at the conclusion that the policy of Soviet Russia is to a certain degree hysterical, in any event less logical, and consequently less calculated than the policy of the Third Reich; it is for that reason that we consider we are threatened by surprises more from the side of Russia than from the side of Germany." (Szembek, *Journal*, p. 55.) If such was the case it would be both unnecessary and dangerous to move against Germany.

20

Yosuke Matsuoka and the Japanese-German Alliance

BY JOHN HUIZENGA

On July 22, 1940, Yosuke Matsuoka, who had been absent from the international stage since his dramatic performance of Japan's withdrawal from the League of Nations in 1933, suddenly reappeared in the role of Foreign Minister. With few exceptions Japanese Foreign Ministers had, since the inauguration of a professional diplomatic service in 1893, come from the ranks of career officials. It was symptomatic of the change in the control of Japanese foreign policy midway between the wars that Matsuoka, who had left the Diplomatic Service in 1921 after a successful career of almost two decades, should have found an entirely different route to the top of the Kasumigaseki.

The civilian career diplomacy, like the brief promise of genuine parliamentary government which developed in Japan after the first world war, fell victim to the increasing domination of political life by the military after 1931. It became the instrument rather than the maker of policy. Whereas in other countries party governments sometimes imposed handicaps on professional diplomacy, in Japan professional diplomats could have retained control of foreign policy only if parliamentary government had succeeded. The reason was, of course, that in Japan the alternative to disciplined party cabinets was government by bureaucracy. In a contest of bureaucratic factions the active military services, with their unique prerogative in Japan of providing or withdrawing Ministers of War and Navy, held the key position. By the simple expedient of withdrawing a service minister they could upset a cabinet if the Foreign Minister attempted to follow a line of policy disapproved by them. They could commit the government's policy by local action, as they did in the Manchurian incident in 1931, in the certain knowledge that Japanese

[615]

nationalist pride would not permit a civilian government to retreat. They could hamper negotiations with other Powers by staging local incidents prejudicial to negotiations, as was done frequently after 1937 when the invasion of China led to the violation of rights of third Powers there. They could conduct domestic propaganda, as the army did through controlled newspapers, especially the chauvinist organ, *Kokumin*. They could, if necessary, covertly sponsor and protect young officer fanatics in the employment of terror and assassination against opponents of extremist policies, as they did in the episode of February 26, 1936.

In March 1936, after the Okada Cabinet had been brought down by assassination in the February 26 Incident, the Cabinet of Koki Hirota, ironically enough a professional diplomat himself, set the pattern of military control.[1] It was not overt control, for an open military dictatorship was less desirable in the eyes of the military than effective control behind a façade of civilian government. Moreover, in view of the code of honor customary in Japanese public life it was dangerous, in the event that serious reverses of policy occurred, to be placed in the position of having to "assume the responsibility." With respect to foreign policy, military control did not become absolute, mainly because of factional differences within the services themselves. Nevertheless, no policy could be pursued by the Foreign Ministry without military approval, and in the end career diplomats were reduced to playing the game of faction and intrigue themselves.

On June 30, 1936, the Japanese War and Navy Ministers in the new Hirota Cabinet agreed on a "Basis of National Policy" which was "to consist in advancing toward and developing the South Seas as well as obtaining a firm position in the East Asiatic Continent." In detail it was stated that "Japan intends to get rid of the menace of the USSR, to prepare against Britain and the United States, and to bring about close collaboration between Japan, Manchukuo and China." Further, it was agreed that "in the execution of this continental policy, Japan must pay due attention to friendly relations with other powers."[2] Presumably the authors had in mind here the courting of Germany which had been carried on assiduously for some time by the military attaché in Berlin, Col. Hiroshi

[1] G. B. Sansom, *Japan in World History* (New York, 1951), p. 89; Royal Institute, *Survey of International Affairs, 1936* (London, 1937), pp. 894-895.

[2] *International Military Tribunal for the Far East* (hereafter cited as IMTFE), Exhibit No. 216. Most of the German and Japanese documents used in this study were introduced in the 1946-1948 Tokyo trial and may be found under exhibit numbers in the trial record.

Oshima, and was to result in November 1936 in the Anti-Comintern Pact between the two countries.

This outline of policy, which in broad terms charted Japan's course in the ensuing years, was then, on August 11, 1936, adopted by the Five Ministers Conference in which the two service ministers were joined by the Prime Minister, Foreign Minister, and Finance Minister. The procedure followed illustrated graphically that in Japan foreign policy, in consequence of the decisive role assumed by the military, had become inseparable from military policy. This fact was to condition profoundly Matsuoka's brief and stormy tenure at the *Gaimushō*.

I

Matsuoka had identified himself early with the military's foreign policy views. The South Manchurian Railway, of which he became Vice President in 1927, had been deeply involved in the Manchurian incident and had profited from the establishment of the puppet state of Manchukuo.[3] His associates in Manchukuo included members of what later became known as "the Manchuria gang," men like Tojo, who became Prime Minister of the war cabinet, Ohashi, who was to serve under Matsuoka as Vice Minister of Foreign Affairs, and Hoshino, who was later to occupy the key post of Chief of the Cabinet Planning Office. Matsuoka's role at Geneva in 1933 won him wide popular acclaim at a time when the military, who did not then exercise the control of public opinion which they later acquired, could only have welcomed a civilian hero personifying Japan's defiance of world opinion. "His fellow-countrymen looked upon him as a modern Horatius defending his people against the onslaughts of the world," Ambassador Grew reported. "His arrival home was the occasion for a public patriotic demonstration of a size seldom seen in Japan."[4] The significance of what Matsuoka had done at Geneva could not have been lost upon the military proponents of what in Japan was called a "positive" foreign policy. For by her withdrawal from the League Japan had declared her intention to repudiate the peace settlement for the Far East embodied in the Washington Treaties of 1922. In these treaties, according to the advocates of a "positive" policy, weak civilian diplomacy had betrayed Japan's victory in the first world war and her vital interests.

Not long after his return from Geneva in 1933 Matsuoka identified

[3] Report of Ambassador Grew to the Department of State, March 24, 1933, in *Foreign Relations, 1933*, III, 247-251.
[4] Report of Ambassador Grew to the Department of State, Dec. 14, 1933, *ibid.*, pp. 713-715.

himself publicly with another favorite theme of the military party. Although he had been elected to the Imperial Diet in 1930 and again in 1932 as a member of the Seiyukai party, he appealed for the abandonment of party government. "Western style party government," he declared, "does not conform to the conditions of our country nor the character of our people. . . . The time has come when the Japanese race must carry out its important mission in the interests of peace. . . . As a first step I advocate the dissolution of parties."[5] It was said in Japan at the time that his ambition had been fired by the public acclaim he had received, and that he repudiated his reputation as a political liberal because he expected a reactionary cabinet and hoped to be a member of it. He was correct in his judgment as to where the path to future power would lie, even if it was to be some time before he could set foot upon it. At least, in 1935, he was rewarded with the presidency of the South Manchurian Railway Company.

When in November 1936 the Anti-Comintern Pact with Germany was announced, "most of the comment on the Government's action was definitely critical."[6] The *Tokyo Asahi* wrote on December 2, 1936, that Japan "would not derive much benefit" from the association with Germany and warned that "if Japan should make an enemy of England, which holds much latent power in the Far East, it is not difficult to imagine that England, France, America, and Russia would cooperate."[7]

The Japanese Foreign Ministry itself accepted the Pact reluctantly. In a statement accompanying release of the Pact it was at pains to make it clear that Japan was not entering upon a relationship of alliance with Germany, but was "desirous of cooperating with as many Powers as possible for the purpose of perfecting their defensive measures against the Comintern menace, but for that purpose alone."[8]

The truth was that the military party had forced the Pact through against the better judgment of the Foreign Ministry. As the newspaper *Nichi Nichi* put it, "Foreign Office circles received the rapprochement

---

[5] *ibid.*, p. 714.

[6] *Survey of International Affairs, 1936*, p. 927. See also the comments of the German ambassador on the opposition of court circles and industrialists in Herbert von Dirksen, *Moskau, Tokio, London* (Stuttgart, 1949), p. 188. See also Chapter 13, § IV and Chapter 15, § I above.

[7] Quoted from a longer extract of the *Asahi* editorial in David H. James, *The Rise and Fall of the Japanese Empire* (London, 1951), p. 185.

[8] The English text of the statement is published in *Foreign Relations: Japan 1931-1941* (Washington, 1943), II, 155-157. Foreign Minister Arita promised the Privy Council in obtaining its approval of the Pact that the announcement would make it clear that the Pact did not mean that Japan would thereafter "act in concert" with Germany. IMTFE, Exhibit No. 484.

with Germany with much hesitation, but the enthusiasm of the Army was so strongly expressed that the Cabinet was obliged to conclude the agreement as national policy."[9]

It was characteristic of statements of public policy in Japan that they were so vaguely or loosely phrased that contending factions were allowed to preserve face. Opponents of the Pact had been allowed a statement which seemed to minimize the Pact's significance, particularly in terms of alliance with Germany. On the other hand, the military party had the Pact itself, including a secret protocol which amounted to a military arrangement with Germany against the Soviet Union.[10] It would be left to events or the efforts of the contending factions to resolve contradictions or ambiguities.

The military party began at once a campaign to win support for the Pact and at the same time to interpret it as an alliance with Germany. It was Matsuoka who now appeared as a principal advocate. In a speech delivered in Dairen on December 23, 1936, he attacked the lukewarm and apologetic attitude shown toward the Pact by the government and the press. He said that the meaning of the Pact was not to be found only in cooperation against the Comintern. "The historical significance of the Pact can be understood," he declared, "only if it is regarded as an alliance by which Japan, for the first time since 1922, entered upon an active foreign policy. And this alliance cannot be close enough; it must mean going together through thick and thin, and it must be based on complete loyalty and mutual self-sacrifice, as these find expression in Japanese *shinjū*."[11] Matsuoka was said sometimes to be quite carried away by his own impassioned oratory and on this occasion seems to have reached heights of true prophecy, for the Japanese-German alliance did indeed come to have something of the character of a suicide pact.

A formal alliance with Germany was to be long in coming, however. In 1937 when the Japanese began their invasion of China, the Germans resisted attempts to represent them as supporting the Japanese action, since the German Foreign Ministry and German army did not wish to sacrifice the considerable German interest in China.[12] Ribbentrop, then

---

[9] Quoted by Hugh Byas in his dispatch to the *New York Times* printed on November 26, 1936.

[10] The text of the protocol remained secret until after the second world war when it was found among documents captured by the Allies. It is printed in *German Documents*, series D, I, 734.

[11] The speech was printed in pamphlet form under the title "The Significance of the Japanese-German Anti-Comintern Pact" (*Nichi-doku Bōkyō Kyōtei no Igi*, Dairen, 1937).

[12] *German Documents*, series D, I, 742-744; Dirksen, *Moskau, Tokio, London*, pp. 185, 190-191.

the coming man in German foreign policy, felt no such hesitations, however. In January 1938, shortly before becoming Foreign Minister, he recommended to Hitler that an alliance with Japan be sought,[13] and discussed it with Oshima in the summer of that year.[14] In October he disclosed the plan to Mussolini, who gave his consent on January 3, 1939, to the signing of a triple alliance which it was then thought could take place within a few weeks.[15] In Japan, however, the army advocates of the plan met with resistance they could not overcome, for the opponents of the alliance now included the navy, which was willing to accept an obligation against Russia but was not willing to be committed against Britain as well, the only terms on which Germany would conclude.[16] The Japanese Cabinet remained in a state of virtual paralysis over this issue until Germany's surprise announcement of the nonaggression pact with Soviet Russia in August 1939. "This wholly unexpected turn of events, which the greatly embarrassed Hiranuma Cabinet described as 'intricate and baffling' . . . immediately brought to an end the life of the Cabinet itself as well as the whole scheme of an alliance against Russia."[17]

Marquis Kido, who became Lord Privy Seal in 1940, wrote in his diary on August 22, 1939 that he "was astonished at this extremely treacherous act, considering the existence of the Anti-Comintern Pact and the Secret Pact."[18] The really devoted adherents of the tie with Germany were only briefly shaken, however. In Berlin, Oshima, who at the army's insistence had been named ambassador, accepted Secretary of State von Weizsäcker's advice that "it was not legal technicalities that were of consequence, but realities as they were understood between men and soldiers," and withheld the formal protest his government had ordered him to present. He even informed Tokyo falsely that he had carried out these instructions. After the conclusion of the Polish campaign when, as he explained to Weizsäcker, "the step was no longer of so much consequence," he presented a version of the protest diluted on his own authority with the suggestion that it "be allowed to disappear in the archives."[19]

---

[13] ibid., pp. 162-168. [14] Oshima Interrogation, IMTFE, Exhibit No. 776.
[15] German Documents, series D, IV, 515-520, 543-545.
[16] An account of this episode based on the Tokyo trial exhibits is given in Herbert Feis, The Road to Pearl Harbor (Princeton, 1950), pp. 28-32. See also Documents on International Affairs, 1939-1946, I (London, New York, 1951), pp. 145-159, which prints English translations of relevant Italian documents.
[17] Memorandum by Prince Fumimaro Konoye, "On the Tripartite Alliance," IMTFE, Exhibit No. 2735A.
[18] Extract from Kido Diary, IMTFE, Exhibit No. 775.
[19] Weizsäcker's memoranda of conversations with Oshima on August 26 and September 18, 1939, are printed in Department of State Bulletin, June 16, 1946, pp. 1038-1039.

Despite a statement of the Japanese army expressing "disappointment" over the Nazi-Soviet Pact, activist elements were saying in the columns of *Kokumin* that the military alliance with Germany was still needed because Britain was the real enemy of "Japan's new order" in Asia. It appeared that what disturbed the army supporters of the alliance with Germany was not so much the fact that Germany had made a pact with the Soviet Union, but that they had not been informed of it in advance. There was no little loss of face—and in Japan "face" was an ingredient of power—in being thus cavalierly treated by the partner with whom they had proposed to enter into a brotherhood of arms.

Matsuoka was not officially involved in these events, although he moved closer to the center of the political stage during the period in which the alliance with Germany was under consideration. He was named member for foreign affairs of the Cabinet Advisory Council during Prince Konoye's 1937-1939 Cabinet, and in 1939 he resigned the presidency of the South Manchurian Railway Company to give his full time to political activity. A busy backstage pleader, he never wavered in his support of a German alliance on the army's terms during the 1939 deadlock, a fact which doubtless had much to do with his rise to power the following year.

The period of phony war in Europe was reflected in a period of phony truce in Japanese internal politics, with the active partisans of the Axis alliance obliged to efface themselves because of their "disgrace." The German attack in the West, the collapse of France and the Low Countries, and the peril of Britain threw the Japanese domestic scene into confusion once more, however. The prospects opened up by the sudden reversal of the balance of power in Europe led the military activists to raise a new clamor for the control of Japanese foreign policy. Not only did their earlier demand for closer ties with Germany seem to represent prescient wisdom, but the ambitious programs of expansion so long advocated by them seemed at last to be attainable. "The German military machine and system and their brilliant successes have gone to the Japanese head like strong wine," Ambassador Grew noted in his diary.[20]

The moderate Cabinet of Admiral Yonai made desperate efforts to save itself. On June 29 Foreign Minister Arita scheduled a radio address in which he proposed to announce his government's intention to consolidate its friendship with the Axis. The army, however, insisted on the revision of his speech, protesting that a "policy of sympathy for the Axis is not compatible with the policies hitherto pursued by the Cabinet," and

[20] Joseph C. Grew, *Ten Years in Japan* (New York, 1944), p. 325.

declaring that it would not allow the Cabinet to use "a sudden stress on friendship with the Axis as a maneuver to take the wind out of the sails of the opposition . . . and to save its own existence." The military police arrested the press officer of the Foreign Ministry who had revealed the army's action on Arita's speech to the newspaper *Asahi*.[21]

On July 5 the Chief of the Metropolitan Police in Tokyo uncovered an assassination plot, the victims of which were to have been Prime Minister Yonai and other government leaders.[22] The "plot" may have been serious or it may have been only the ritual by which the military party indicated that it meant to have its way by extreme measures if necessary. In any case, three days later the Vice Minister of War, General Anami, called on the Lord Privy Seal, the official who would be responsible for initiating a Cabinet change, and laid down the army's terms. He said that "the character of the Yonai Cabinet is not at all suitable for making negotiations with Germany and Italy and it might even cause a fatal delay." The army wanted Prince Konoye and would leave the choice of a Foreign Minister up to him.[23] On July 16 War Minister Hata resigned and the army refused to nominate a successor, thus forcing the Yonai Cabinet out of office. There followed the usual ceremonial consultations with elder statesmen, a title now assigned to former Prime Ministers, but it was noteworthy that no names other than Prince Konoye's were mentioned.[24] It seemed to be clearly understood that the army would not be denied.

Konoye's choice of Matsuoka as Foreign Minister was a natural one. He was an experienced professional diplomat and there were few if any diplomats who would have had the army's confidence at that moment. Only a man who had not opposed the Axis alliance in 1938-1939 would have been acceptable. In addition, Matsuoka, with his American education and experience of diplomatic service in Washington, may have seemed to Konoye the right man to handle Japan's difficult relations with the United States, relations likely to become more difficult as Japan drew closer to the Axis. The shifty vagueness of Japanese political language always left a great deal unclarified, and it is most unlikely that Konoye could have anticipated his later difficulties with Matsuoka on relations with America.

The government which took office on July 22, 1940, was perhaps as

---

[21] Telegram, Ambassador Ott to German Foreign Ministry, July 3, 1940, IMTFE, Exhibit No. 531.
[22] Kido Diary Extract, July 5, 1940, IMTFE, Exhibit No. 532.
[23] *ibid.*, July 8, 1940.
[24] *ibid.*, July 17, 1940.

unified in its foreign policy aims as any which Japan had had in some years. It had taken a radical realignment of the balance of power in Europe to accomplish this result. The reason was clear. The inherent limitations of Japan's power had always greatly restricted her freedom of action. Her whole forward progress as a Power had been based on association with a dominant Power or Powers in Europe. Her one serious humiliation and reverse, the Triple Intervention of 1895, resulted from her error in exposing herself in isolation to the united front of a combination of European Powers. The great debate in Japanese policy after the challenge of Nazi Germany had developed in Europe was between those who wished to link Japan's fortunes to this new Power, and those who preferred her traditional association with the Western Powers, or who at least did not regard Germany as a sufficient counterweight against Anglo-American naval power. During the Hiranuma Cabinet of 1939, the demand of the army for the former course had been staved off by a narrow margin. Now events seemed to have terminated the debate. And Matsuoka, long active in the shadow world of intrigue behind the façade of Japanese public life, qualified by his associations and his publicly expressed views, gained the opportunity to play the role which his ambition had so long coveted.

II

In the view of the new Cabinet the most urgent task which confronted it, a task in which delay might be fatal, as General Anami had said, was that of clarifying its relations with Nazi Germany, now suddenly by virtue of its dramatic victory the dominant Power in Europe. The impact of the German victory seems to have been, if anything, greater in Japan than elsewhere. "The world is now on the threshold of a stupendous historic change," were the opening words of a Cabinet policy statement approved on July 26, 1940.[25] Matsuoka later told an imperial conference that the defeat of Britain had seemed likely within the first ten days of the new Cabinet's existence.[26]

The gratification in Japan over the prospects opened up by a British defeat was mixed with genuine alarm and uncertainty as to the view which a victorious Germany might take of the new situation in the Far East. Would Germany acknowledge Japan as the inheritor of the remnants of Western empire in Asia or would she put forward successor claims of her own based on her military successes?

[25] IMTFE, Exhibit No. 540.
[26] On Sept. 26, 1940. IMTFE, Exhibit No. 550.

Foreign Minister Arita had already made some effort to deal with this problem as it emerged. On April 15, 1940, he issued a statement that "the Japanese Government cannot but be deeply concerned over any development accompanying an aggravation of the war in Europe that may affect the *status quo* in the Netherlands East Indies."[27] A German reaction was disconcertingly slow in coming and was obtained by specific request only after other Powers had at once acknowledged their support for the *status quo* in the Indies. At length on May 20 German Ambassador Ott was authorized to make an oral declaration to Arita of Germany's "disinterestedness in the Netherlands East Indies question."[28]

On June 19 Ambassador Kurusu received instructions in Berlin to suggest "a German declaration to the effect that Japan would have a free hand in Indochina."[29] No immediate reply was forthcoming and ex-Foreign Minister Sato, who was on a special mission to Italy, was sent to Berlin where he had a talk with Ribbentrop on July 8. He found the German Foreign Minister "non-committal" on the subject of the Dutch East Indies and Indochina. Sato said in his report to Arita that he was not prepared to conclude that Germany harbored "an ambition on the Southern colonies" but it must be recognized that German thinking had undergone a change in consequence of the great victory that had been won.[30]

The reserve shown by Ribbentrop, it is now evident, resulted from his confidence that the Yonai-Arita Cabinet was in its last days of life and that there was no need to assist its survival. There would soon be a government in Japan more to his liking, one dominated by men with whom he had dealt covertly for years in the expectation that they would one day rule Japan. Ott had reported on June 24 that "leading personalities of the Konoye circle are obviously trying to make contact with me" and that a new government under Konoye was indicated.[31]

Even the new government, however, was not entirely confident that the German attitude toward Japanese aspirations would be all that might be desired. Matsuoka himself said later, though perhaps in part to reflect credit on his diplomatic skill, that "German enthusiasm for cooperation

---

[27] *Foreign Relations, Japan*, II, 281.

[28] Telegram, Ribbentrop to Ott, May 20, 1940, IMTFE, Exhibit No. 517.

[29] Telegram, Ott to German Foreign Ministry, June 19, 1940, in *Department of State Bulletin*, June 16, 1946, pp. 1039-1040. Kurusu had replaced Oshima as ambassador in Berlin in 1939 and was replaced by him again in the winter of 1940-1941.

[30] Exchange of telegrams, Sato-Arita, July 13 and 15, 1940, IMTFE, Exhibits Nos. 525, 526.

[31] Telegram, Ott to German Foreign Ministry, June 24, 1940, IMTFE, Exhibit No. 523.

with Japan was generally at a very low ebb."[32] He was therefore careful
not to show excessive eagerness. Already on July 18, before taking office,
he had conveyed "confidentially" to Ambassador Ott his intention to
accept the post of Foreign Minister and his request for "friendly cooperation."[33] He waited until August 1, however, before inviting Ott
for their first political conversation. The delay may have seemed the
more justified since on July 22 Lord Halifax rejected Hitler's peace
offer of three days earlier and the collapse of Britain seemed, if not less
certain, at least less imminent.

The German ambassador appeared on August 1 armed with a bundle
of outstanding complaints. The Japanese had been insufficiently helpful
in facilitating shipments via Manchukuo of raw materials purchased in
Asia. Damage claims arising from Japanese operations in China had gone
unremedied. The English language press in Japan had carried on anti-
German propaganda. Japanese officials had impeded the repatriation via
Japan of German nationals stranded in the Americas. Ott "left the Foreign Minister with no doubt that Japan had much to make up for to bring
about even a state of benevolent neutrality toward Germany."[34]

Matsuoka was "most cordial" and promised to look into all these
matters. Then, indicating his distaste for diplomatic language and indirection, a formula he employed often by way of showing his honesty and
candor, he plunged into the business at hand. As the ambassador had no
doubt heard, there was a disposition in Japan to strengthen relations with
the Axis. The Cabinet had decided nothing, but he, Matsuoka, an old
advocate of closer relations with Germany, wished to explore the German
attitude with a view to urging such a course on his colleagues if possible.
What view would Germany take of Japan's proposed new order for
Asia, including the South Seas? What were Germany's expectations with
regard to relations with America and with the Soviet Union? How did
Germany anticipate that Japan's relations with these two countries should
develop?

The German ambassador wanted to know first what area was meant by
Matsuoka's reference to the South Seas. Matsuoka cautiously gave it as
his personal opinion that Japanese aspirations for the present extended
as far as Siam but might be enlarged if circumstances indicated. Ott raised
no objections to this and went on to say that Germany's views on the

---

[32] IMTFE, Exhibit No. 550.
[33] Telegram, Ott to German Foreign Ministry, July 18, 1940, IMTFE, Exhibit No.
535.
[34] Telegram, Ott to Weizsäcker, August 2, 1940, IMTFE, Exhibit No. 622.

South Seas region would, of course, depend on the further course of her war against Britain, and particularly on whether the struggle against Britain was prolonged into an effort to destroy the British empire. In this case, he implied, a Japanese contribution in some form might be expected. In the light of these perspectives he answered Matsuoka's other questions. Germany's relations with Russia were stable, and particularly since the German victory in the West, involved no danger. He thought Japan would be well advised to negotiate for improved relations with Russia and proposed German good offices. As for America, Germany did not expect her participation in the war. The tide of American opinion had turned against Roosevelt's efforts to involve the country. Germany had no intention of courting any future disputes with the United States and hoped for an eventual improvement of relations. He called particular attention to this point as it was important that a similar attitude be held in Germany and Japan toward the United States. Matsuoka agreed that Japan also hoped for peaceful relations with the United States.[35]

It was clear from this conversation that a meeting of minds was nearer than might have been hoped. The dispatch with which concrete negotiations were taken up confirmed this impression. Within a month a special negotiator had arrived in Tokyo. He was Heinrich Stahmer, in charge of Far Eastern questions in the *Dienststelle Ribbentrop*, and named minister for this assignment. For those familiar with Ribbentrop's working methods and his preference for circumventing his own Foreign Ministry in important negotiations, this was another sign of the seriousness of German intentions. When Konoye, Matsuoka, War Minister Tojo, and Navy Minister Yoshida on September 4 laid down the guiding principles for the negotiations, they noted that the sending of Stahmer indicated that the mission was likely to be more than exploratory.[36]

The four agreed that the principal object remained to obtain a recognition of the Japanese *Lebensraum* in East Asia, a convenient application of a German concept which showed that the Japanese had not lost their talent for appropriating Western ideas to their own uses.[37] The area of Japanese hegemony was to embrace India on the West and Australia and New Zealand in the South. The Germans were to be told for the present, however, that the outer limits were to be Burma and New Cale-

---

[35] Matsuoka's Memorandum of Conversation, August 2, 1940, IMTFE, Exhibit No. 545.
[36] IMTFE, Exhibit No. 541.
[37] Ambassador Grew noted in his affidavit presented at the Tokyo trial (IMTFE, Exhibit No. 1105) that the expression "Japan's New Order in East Asia" began to be employed in 1938. The German successes in that year obviously led the Japanese to believe that with similar slogans the walls of Jericho might fall for them, too.

donia, India being left to the Soviet sphere if necessary. It was recognized that German claims on the Dutch East Indies might be encountered and it was hoped at least to negotiate a "predominant position" there by "preferential supply to Japan of natural and material resources" while guaranteeing existing German undertakings.

It was further agreed that peace should be maintained with the Soviet Union and that the partners should join in "inducing the Soviet Union to bring her policy into line" with theirs. There should be cooperation in preventing the United States from interfering in regions outside the Western Hemisphere and United States possessions, and mutual assistance in the event that one of the partners became involved in war with the United States.

While it was recognized that "unless we are resolved on the employment of armed force, it will be impossible for us to carry on any useful talks with Germany" a request for military cooperation against Britain was to be met for the present only with an agreement in principle. It would be explained that, pending settlement of the China Incident, Japan felt obliged to confine herself to actions short of war, unless conditions took a decidedly favorable turn. Japan would, however, continue her political and propagandistic harassment of the British in Asia as a contribution to the German-Italian war against the Empire.

Matsuoka, still thinking it best not to show too much eagerness, allowed Stahmer to cool his heels in Tokyo for some days. When he finally saw Stahmer and Ott on September 9 the business proceeded with remarkable ease. After meetings on three successive days they were near to agreement on a draft. The Germans "did not ask any detailed questions" about the territorial limits of "Greater East Asia" and only asked that Germany's economic needs in that area be accommodated.[38] Further, Germany did not "look for Japan's military assistance at this juncture in connection with her war with England." The German attention was focused almost exclusively on the United States. "What she [Germany] wishes of Japan," Stahmer said, "is to have Japan play the role of restraining and preventing the United States from entering the war." This was an immediate and pressing objective for, barring American entry, the war might soon be terminated. Then there was the "long view," for even after the defeat of England there would be a "stupendous struggle against the British Empire, not to say the Anglo-Saxondom including America" and this struggle would "go on for tens

[38] Matsuoka Statement to Imperial Conference, Sept. 26, 1940, IMTFE, Exhibit No.

of years yet, in one form or another." By declaring herself at once Japan would assist the immediate aim of keeping the United States out of the war, and would assume in the longer view the posture which was in accordance with her interests, for "war between Japan and the United States cannot eventually be avoided."[39]

On September 19 Ribbentrop arrived in Rome to give his Italian allies their first information on the alliance which they would be expected to sign within a few days. No more than his spokesmen in Tokyo did he speak of the territorial limits of *Lebensraum* or haggle over the terms of Japanese hegemony in East Asia. He discussed the proposed pact entirely in terms of completing the victory over Britain. The invasion was prepared, he said, and would be undertaken after eight or ten days of good weather for air operations. The fact that the British in their desperate circumstances continued to be "particularly impudent" was, in the Fuehrer's view, due partly to "lack of comprehension" but also to the hope of outside intervention by Russia and America. "It is in order to meet this eventuality," the Italian record of the conversation continues, "and above all to paralyze America, that Herr von Ribbentrop has prepared, and now submits for the Duce's approval, the project of a tripartite alliance with Japan. . . . In German opinion, the formation of an alliance of that nature should have the advantage of reinforcing the isolationist reaction against Roosevelt's interventionist policy."[40]

This was the Duce's opinion, too. "One must bear in mind," he said, "that the Americans are very much afraid of Japan and of her fleet in particular, since the American fleet, while being quantitatively large, must be considered an amateur organization like the English army."[41]

Meanwhile in Tokyo the laborious machinery of Japanese policy making moved with unaccustomed speed. On the night of September 14 Marquis Kido sat with War Minister Tojo at the death watch for Prince Kitashirakawa and Tojo related to him secretly that the army and navy had that day given approval to the Axis alliance.[42] The Privy Council, which, as its history showed, could be extraordinarily obstructive and which surely still contained many opponents of the pro-Axis course, gave its consent on September 26. The great range of questions asked of Cabinet ministers suggested that a number of its members were more

---

[39] Japanese Foreign Ministry Memorandum: "Salient Points in the Informal Conversations Between Matsuoka and Stahmer," September 9-10, 1940, IMTFE, Exhibit No. 549.

[40] Galeazzo Ciano, *L'Europa verso la catastrofe* (Verona, 1948), p. 587.

[41] *ibid.*, p. 590.

[42] Kido Diary Extract, September 14, 1940, IMTFE, Exhibit No. 627.

cowed than convinced.[43] Matsuoka had glib answers for everything. Would the alliance drive the United States and Soviet Russia into each other's arms? There were no signs of it and he intended to take up Soviet-Japanese problems at once with German assistance. Was it not true that German-American relations were susceptible of improvement while Japanese-American relations were not, and hence was there "no fear of Japan alone drinking from the bitter cup?" Matsuoka replied that everything would be done to avoid war with America and to this end the German alliance would be helpful since there were 20 million Americans of German descent. Ribbentrop sometimes used this argument to discount the American danger but Matsuoka could hardly have been ignorant of its falsity.

The old Viscount Ishii, who had negotiated Japan's adherence to the Allied side in the first world war, and had written of the "shiftiness" of German policy under the Kaiser,[44] was full of warnings. Allies of Germany in the past had suffered only disaster; Hitler was a Machiavellian who had publicly stated that one should not hesitate to break alliances when convenient; he was known to have held anti-Japanese views in the past. Ishii would not oppose the pact because he believed that in terms merely of the balance of power the national interests of the three countries were parallel and Japan needed allies. But, he warned, "the national character of Germany is such as would suck the blood of others" and he hoped that after the pact was signed the government would not "neglect to take exhaustive and scrupulous care so that we need have no future regrets."[45]

If the men who now governed Japan were little inclined to heed this cautious voice of an older generation of statesmanship, they were still Japanese enough to hedge carefully the commitment they were undertaking. Article 3 of the Pact stated that the three Powers "undertake to assist one another with all political, economic, and military means when one of the three Contracting Parties is attacked by a power at present not involved in the European War or in the Sino-Japanese Conflict."[46] This seemed straightforward enough, but Matsuoka had obliged Ribbentrop to withdraw his original phraseology which required

[43] Protocol of Privy Council Investigation Committee on Tripartite Pact, Sept. 26, 1940, IMTFE, Exhibit No. 552.

[44] Kikujiro Ishii, *Diplomatic Commentaries* (Baltimore, 1936), p. 42.

[45] Record of Privy Council Meeting in Imperial Presence, September 26, 1940, IMTFE, Exhibit No. 553.

[46] The full text of the Tripartite Pact, signed at Berlin on September 27, 1940, is published in *Foreign Relations, Japan*, II, 165-166.

that aid take effect if one of the partners was attacked "directly or in-directly."[47] Moreover, he had obtained from Ott a letter which in-cluded the statement: "It is needless to say that whether or not a Con-tracting Party has been attacked within the meaning of Article 3 of the Pact shall be determined upon consultation among the three Contracting Parties."[48] He also assured the Privy Council that "in the event of the worst situation" Japan would "be able to choose the time and place to let the Japanese Navy participate in the war." The Japanese had shown great agility in the willful interpretation of written agreements; it could scarcely be doubted that in the fulfillment of this Pact, too, they would find ways to consult their own interests if necessary.

Despite the long period in which a German-Japanese alliance had been promoted in the two countries, the Pact which was actually made in 1940 had something hasty and impromptu about it, and it is doubtful that the participants looked very far down the long dark vistas which it opened up. As has been seen, in the minds of Ribbentrop and Hitler the Pact was prompted largely by the immediate concern to restrain the United States and Russia from intervening to defraud them of their anticipated early victory over Britain. It was a characteristic maneuver of Nazi diplomacy in the sense that its value was reckoned primarily in terms of immediate propaganda impact. For Matsuoka and his colleagues the first concern had been to accommodate themselves as quickly as possible to the prospects of a British defeat. This meant to obtain insurance that the vacuum which would be left by the collapse of British power in the Far East would be filled by Japan and that other potential aspirants would be excluded, among them Germany herself. The implications of the Pact, if it should prove necessary to implement it against the United States, were faced only reluctantly in the discus-sions which took place in the Privy Council. And the calculation on which both parties agreed, that the Pact would cause the United States to stand aside because it would strengthen those in America who opposed intervention, was in error. On the contrary, the interventionist case in the struggle to win American opinion was strengthened, for the danger to the United States, once given the shape of a worldwide con-spiracy of aggressors, seemed more real and intervention to forestall it more imperative. It was to this theme, that the United States faced a conspiracy of Powers which entertained unlimited aggressive aims, that the Roosevelt administration appealed in opening the campaign a few

[47] IMTFE, Exhibit No. 550.   [48] IMTFE, Exhibit No. 555b.

months later for Lend-Lease.[49] Far from deterring, the Pact accelerated the process of American involvement and widened the area of the contest, so that in the American mind the problem of peace or war with Japan became inseparable from the problem of peace or war with Germany. On November 1, 1940, Ambassador Grew noted in his diary: "Now that the Tripartite Alliance has been concluded, we can no longer regard and treat with Japan as an individual nation. She has become a member of a team, and our attitude toward Japan must be our attitude toward the team as a whole."[50]

III

As the Japanese leaders had agreed in laying down the terms of negotiation on September 4, the alliance with Germany and Italy was not conceived as an isolated maneuver but was linked with the intention to solve the problems presented by Russia and China. If attention was to be focused on an advance into South Asia and the South Seas in the wake of the collapse of the Western empires, it would be necessary to free Japanese forces from their commitment in China and to insure that Russia would not menace Japan from the rear.

Every Japanese Cabinet since 1937 took office with promises that first attention would be given to solving the China Incident, a festering sore which for the Japanese people was as psychologically disturbing as it was economically taxing. The new Konoye Cabinet was no exception. In its policy statement of July 26 it promised that its foreign policy would "be directed, first of all, toward a complete settlement of the China Affair."

Matsuoka, when he assumed Office, appeared confident of his ability to liquidate the China problem. He told the German ambassador on August 1 that Japan would be able to deal with it alone, and rather pointedly rejected a hint that German mediation could be of assistance. Obviously he was aware that a Japan which continued to flounder in the morass of China would be a less desirable ally in German eyes. Ott, who had long believed that Japan's value as a partner for Germany depended on disengagement of her forces from China,[51] pressed for an explanation of Matsuoka's plans and indicated that in his view negotiation with Chiang Kai-shek should not be excluded. Matsuoka replied that Japanese policy was committed to the position that Chiang had to be crushed en-

---

[49] See President Roosevelt's "arsenal of democracy" speech of December 29, 1940, printed in *Foreign Relations, Japan*, II, 173-181.

[50] *Ten Years in Japan*, p. 349.

[51] See his report of November 1, 1938 in *German Documents*, series D, IV, 685-689.

tirely. He did not believe that a military solution was the only possible one, however, and would not absolutely refuse to negotiate with Chiang.[52]

There was some suggestion in this conversation and in later statements he made to the Germans that Matsuoka would have liked to introduce somewhat more flexibility into Japan's China policy. He indicated during his Berlin conversations in the spring of 1941 that he was in personal touch with Chiang Kai-shek, and that the latter "knew him and trusted him."[53] Whatever the nature of these efforts may have been, Matsuoka did not succeed in altering the essential line of Japanese policy. During the first months of the Konoye Cabinet it was obviously hoped that the impact of British reverses, which had forced the British on July 18 to halt military shipments to China via Hong Kong and Burma, together with the threat imposed by Japan's incursion into Indo-China effected on September 22, would shake Chungking's resolution. In addition, there was Japan's alliance with the victorious Axis, which in the prestige-conscious Orient might set off a flight from the camp of national resistance. The only way held open to the Chinese, however, was by way of reconciliation with, or in effect submission to, the Wang Ching-wei regime at Nanking. Wang, who had departed Chungking at the end of 1938 to sponsor a peace movement, had been installed in Nanking on March 30, 1940, as head of a new "Central Government." This step, perhaps undertaken more as a maneuver of the weak Yonai-Arita Cabinet to improve its domestic position than as a well-considered measure of China policy, had only rendered a settlement in China more difficult. The Japanese, however, had refrained from giving full recognition to the Nanking regime, and Matsuoka, when he spoke of not refusing entirely to negotiate with Chiang, apparently thought that there was still room for maneuver. The reopening by the British of the Burma supply route on October 18, however, required a new gesture to document Japan's implacable determination in China, and on October 25 it was decided to give formal recognition to the Nanking regime. Before taking this step, however, resort would be had to German intervention. The German Foreign Minister was to be asked to give the Chinese ambassador in Berlin a final warning that the recognition move was imminent and to suggest that Chungking should "discontinue the useless war against Japan as soon as possible" if it did not wish to be "left behind in the advance of the new world situation."[54] Ribbentrop did oblige,

---

[52] IMTFE, Exhibit No. 545.　　　　[53] *Nazi-Soviet Relations*, p. 305.
[54] Japanese Foreign Ministry Memorandum, October 25, 1940, IMTFE, Exhibit No. 628.

though in somewhat more moderate language and with protestations that he had not been prompted by the Japanese.[55] The Chinese found Ribbentrop a no more plausible advocate for submission than the Japanese themselves, and on November 30 Japan was obliged to proceed with the recognition of the Nanking regime.

It is evident that Matsuoka, whatever hints he may have passed about secret negotiations with Chiang Kai-shek, either had no fresh ideas to overcome the stagnation of Japan's China policy, or was not in a position to bring them forward. Certainly the latter was likely to have been true in any case, for the views of the Japanese army on China were fixed. The prestige of the Japanese army, and therewith its claim to a dominant role in Japanese domestic politics, depended on the attainment of its announced objectives in China. The army well remembered the cloud under which it had fallen in consequence of the fiasco of the Siberian expedition. The result had been a loss of face which had much to do with the movement toward civilian control and even party government in Japan in the decade before 1931. There had been demands for cuts in military budgets and—as the military zealots put it—a traitorous abandonment of the Empire's sacred mission. The army's views on China policy had been fixed since 1937. At the end of that year an attempted German mediation had provided an opportunity to negotiate a settlement with Chiang Kai-shek, but pressure on Tokyo from the army command in China had led to the drafting of terms wholly unacceptable to the Chinese. The German ambassador learned that even the General Staff was deterred from an inclination to seek peace "in view of the radical opposition and the striving on the part of some Army groups to eliminate Chiang Kai-shek completely."[56] By the end of 1938, after the fall of Hankow and Canton, it had become the official determination of the Japanese Government, "to carry on the military operations for the complete extermination of the anti-Japanese Kuomintang Government."[57] The military had thus forced Japanese policy on China into complete rigidity. Matsuoka's formal recognition of the Wang Ching-wei regime was a further abdication of diplomacy to military policy. This was a bankrupt policy which insisted on ignoring the force of modern Chinese nationalism and proposed to subdue China by methods reminiscent of both the Mongol invasion and nineteenth century Western imperialism. Even if Matsuoka would have preferred

[55] *Nazi-Soviet Relations*, p. 224.

[56] *German Documents*, series D, I, 789-790, 799, 802-804.

[57] Statement of Prime Minister Konoye, December 22, 1938, printed in *Foreign Relations, Japan*, I, 482-483.

to preserve a more fluid situation in China, he had no real choice. It was precisely on this issue of no retreat from the positions staked out in China that in October 1941 Tojo broke with Konoye, and declared that war with the United States was preferable to repudiating the sacrifices of the Japanese army in China.[58]

IV

The alternative to negotiating with Chungking was, short of the total victory which the military wanted but could not produce, an attempt to further isolate it and to constrict its sources of outside aid. This, quite aside from the desire for a secure rear for the "Southward advance," was a principal motivation for the approach to Russia which it was agreed should follow in the wake of the Tripartite Pact. It was calculated not only that the Soviet Union might be induced to withdraw its support from Chungking but also that it would then take the Chinese Communist party out of the anti-Japanese front, and thus remove "the greatest obstacle to the rise of the influence of the advocates of peace in Chiang Kai-shek's camp."[59]

When Matsuoka presented the draft of the Tripartite Pact to the Privy Council he thus made it clear that an attempt to reach an understanding with the Soviet Union was an integral part of his foreign policy program. He held out no certain promise of success in the attempt, however. He put the chances at "fifty-fifty" and indicated that the outcome would depend entirely on the assistance that might be obtained from Germany.[60]

Ribbentrop had, in fact, ever since Germany's own pact with Russia, urged the Japanese to follow in his footsteps to Moscow. He saw Oshima in the opening days of the Polish campaign and told him that Germany was "quite capable and if desired also ready to mediate for a settlement between Japan and Russia."[61] In Rome on March 11, 1940, the German Foreign Minister solicited Mussolini's support. He asked the Duce to give his ambassadors in Moscow and Tokyo instructions to work for a Russo-Japanese settlement. He had found Stalin "very reasonable" on this subject, and pointed out: "The greater liberty Japan has vis-à-vis Russia, the better she will be able to exercise her useful function as a means of putting pressure on England and America."[62]

---

[58] Konoye Memorandum, "Facts Pertaining to the Resignation of the Third Konoye Cabinet," IMTFE, Exhibit No. 1148.

[59] IMTFE, Exhibit No. 628.   [60] IMTFE, Exhibit No. 552.

[61] Telegram, Ribbentrop to Ott, September 9, 1939, IMTFE, Exhibit No. 507.

[62] Ciano, *L'Europa verso la catastrofe*, p. 538.

The Abe Cabinet which assumed power at the outbreak of the war did succeed in terminating the Nomonhan incident which saw Soviet and Japanese troops engaged in full-scale battle on the Mongolian border in the summer of 1939. The Russian willingness to liquidate this affair, which was accomplished by Molotov and the Japanese ambassador in Moscow on September 16, 1939, was doubtless related to the activation of Russian policy in the West. On the morrow of the agreement Russian troops entered Poland in execution of the partition agreed upon with Germany. By the end of the year, however, the German ambassador in Tokyo was reporting that no further progress in Soviet-Japanese relations was to be observed. There had been desultory negotiations on border questions and on fisheries but the important political issue, the question of Soviet support for Chiang Kai-shek, had not been touched.[63] Like its predecessor, the Yonai Cabinet which followed in January 1940 was principally preoccupied with the problem of improving relations with the United States. It was perhaps also recognized that even if a political agreement with Russia could be obtained it would be likely to hinder rather than help a solution of the American problem.

On conclusion of the Tripartite Pact, however, the attempt to come to terms with the Soviet Union entered on a new phase. Ribbentrop now undertook to provide more active assistance, and it was this which was the principal reliance of Matsuoka's policy with respect to Russia. Molotov's visit to Berlin in November 1940 provided Ribbentrop the occasion to press the Japanese suit.

Already in his letter to Stalin of October 13, 1940, in which the invitation for Molotov to visit Berlin was extended, Ribbentrop raised the question of Russo-Japanese relations, arguing that "friendly relations between Germany and Soviet Russia as well as friendly relations between Soviet Russia and Japan, together with the friendship between the Axis Powers and Japan, are logical elements of a natural political coalition which, if intelligently managed, will work out to the best advantage of all the powers concerned."[64]

The character of this "natural political coalition" in which Russia would associate herself with the signatories of the Tripartite Pact was spelled out for Molotov in Berlin on November 12 and 13, 1940. The four Powers were to agree on a delimitation of their spheres of interest and were to aggrandize themselves jointly at the expense of the "Brit-

---

[63] Telegram, Ott to German Foreign Ministry, December 31, 1939, IMTFE, Exhibit No. 3503.
[64] *Nazi-Soviet Relations*, p. 213.

ish bankrupt estate," the defeat of Britain being, according to Ribbentrop, already an accomplished fact. They would all agree that their natural areas of expansion lay to the South, and Ribbentrop assured Molotov that in Japan, too, "*Lebensraum* policy . . . now was oriented not toward the East and North, but toward the South." Therefore, "just as it had been possible to delimit the mutual spheres of interest between Soviet Russia and Germany, a delimitation of interests could also be achieved between Japan and Russia."[65]

Molotov showed himself little interested in these grand perspectives. Far from dividing up remote regions of the British Empire, the talks became a near wrangle over "spheres of interest" in the immediate area of Soviet-German contact, particularly in Finland and the Balkans. Concerning a delimitation of areas of interest between Japan and Russia Molotov would only say that he found "quite vague" the idea of the "Greater East Asian Sphere" which had been assigned to Japan in the Tripartite Pact. He would have to obtain a "more accurate definition of this concept." Moreover, "Russia wanted to come to an understanding with Germany, and only then with Japan and Italy, after she had previously obtained precise information regarding the significance, the nature, and the aim of the Tripartite Pact."[66]

In one of his two talks with Hitler, Molotov made one other remark which would hardly have cheered Matsuoka, for it showed that Russia would not be likely to assist, as Matsuoka had planned it, in bringing Chiang Kai-shek to reason. Molotov said that "an honorable solution would have to be assured for China, all the more since Japan now stood a chance of getting Indonesia."[67] This was surely a plain enough hint that the inclusion of China in the "Greater East Asian Sphere" would be disputed. Matsuoka's conception had been that Russia, intimidated by the encirclement of the Tripartite Pact, despite the formal assurances given to her in its Article V, would withdraw support from Chiang Kai-shek and assist Japan to settle the China Incident. Molotov was far from intimidated at Berlin, either on Far Eastern or on other issues. German assistance to bring Russian policy into line proved to be an illusion. Matsuoka was wrong in supposing it might be possible to approach Moscow by way of Berlin.

It was in recognition of this error that, a little more than a month later, Matsuoka resolved to proceed to both these capitals in person. On December 19 he apprised Ott of his desire to accept an invitation to Berlin which the German Foreign Minister had extended at an earlier

[65] *ibid.*, p. 220.   [66] *ibid.*, p. 225.   [67] *ibid.*, p. 247.

date. Ott reported that Matsuoka emphasized "his need to make a strong gesture in favor of the Tripartite Pact and if possible to personally overcome the deadlock in the negotiations with Russia and China."[68] This was an acknowledgment, in effect, that the Pact had thus far failed in one of its main objects. Conceived as a gesture which, under the impact of the apparent German triumph over Britain, would cause Russia and China to fall in with Japanese plans for Greater East Asia, it now in turn required a new "gesture" to sustain its effect. There was a further revealing note in Ott's account of his conversation with Matsuoka on the proposed Berlin visit. He had the impression, he said, that Matsuoka "would like to enhance the weight of his policy and himself." Evidently Matsuoka felt the need for a "gesture" on his own behalf as well.

V.

By the time Matsuoka reached Berlin, toward the end of March 1941, there was much more involved than a ceremonial visit for purposes of prestige. On December 27, 1940, the German naval command pressed on Hitler the importance of operations against British sea power before the invasion of Russia, already in preparation, was carried out. It was suggested that the Japanese might be encouraged to undertake an assault on Singapore.[69] By the end of January Ott reported from Tokyo that there was some sentiment in favor of such a move in certain activist circles but he thought that the Japanese would probably agree to the attack only if it could be made simultaneously with a German invasion of Britain.[70] On February 23 Ribbentrop took up the matter with Oshima, who had just returned as ambassador to replace Kurusu. The attack on Singapore, to be made "with lightning speed, if at all possible without a declaration of war," would be a decisive blow which would force Britain to sue for an early peace, he said. He hoped that Matsuoka would bring with him "a final decision to attack Singapore soon."[71]

The conversations in Berlin which opened on March 27 brought together in Hitler, Ribbentrop, and Matsuoka the three foremost practitioners of the art of the statesman's monologue, that characteristic form of diplomatic intercourse among the Tripartite leaders.[72] In all their

---

[68] Telegram, Ott to Ribbentrop, December 19, 1940, IMTFE, Exhibit No. 567.

[69] "Fuehrer Conferences on Naval Affairs, 1939-1945" in *Brassey's Naval Annual, 1948,* p. 161.

[70] Telegram, Ott to Ribbentrop, January 31, 1941, IMTFE, Exhibit No. 562.

[71] Telegram, Ribbentrop to Ott, February 28, 1941, IMTFE, Exhibit No. 571.

[72] Five lengthy memoranda on the Berlin talks are printed in *Nazi-Soviet Relations,* pp. 281-316.

discursive speeches, however, Hitler and Ribbentrop returned to the same theme: Britain was tottering on the brink of defeat and only a final push was needed to bring all the Tripartite partners into their inheritance; the time had come for Japan to act and what Germany wanted was an attack on Singapore.

Considering that six months earlier, at the conclusion of the Tripartite Pact, it had been stated that no Japanese help against Britain would be expected, a Japanese statesman might have been given pause by the new line. Not so Matsuoka; he declared himself fully in accord with the German suggestion. He hastened to add, however, that he was not in a position to commit his government. "According to his idea," he said, "the attack should come as soon as possible. Unfortunately he did not control Japan . . . at the present moment he could under these circumstances make no pledge on behalf of the Japanese Empire that it would take action."[73]

It was typical of the indecisive ways of Japanese diplomacy that Matsuoka had undertaken his long and arduous mission without any clear authority to commit his government on the principal issue which concerned his German ally. In a memorandum written while en route to the Berlin talks Ambassador Ott set down the views of the Japanese military on the question of attacking Singapore. Both the army and navy were rushing preparations, but the Chief of the Navy's General Staff expressed "misgivings" because of possible British and American countermeasures. The Chief of the Army's General Staff was equally uncommitted although for a different reason. The army demanded that it be freed first from the danger of Russian intervention.[74]

The accomplishment of the latter object by diplomatic means was in fact the only concrete objective of Matsuoka's mission.[75] It was the issue of relations with Russia which made of the Berlin talks a comedy of double duplicity. Hitler and Ribbentrop did not tell Matsuoka that planning for a German attack on Russia had been going on for months, but he was given the broadest hints that relations were not cordial between Berlin and Moscow, and that anything was possible. "The Russians," according to Ribbentrop, "had for some time demonstrated their unfriendliness to Germany wherever they could." He did not think that Stalin "was inclined toward adventure, but it was impossible to be sure. The German armies in the East were prepared at any time. Should

[73] *ibid.*, p. 295.
[74] Ott Memorandum of March 25, 1941, IMTFE, Exhibit No. 576.
[75] This is confirmed by Toshikazu Kase who was a member of Matsuoka's delegation. See his *Journey to the Missouri* (New Haven, 1950), p. 156.

Russia some day take a stand that could be interpreted as a threat to Germany, the Führer would crush Russia."[76]

There cannot be any doubt that Matsuoka understood the significance of this startling intelligence well enough, but he did not press too closely for an explanation. He said that his talks with Stalin and Molotov en route to Berlin had been the result of Russian initiative.[77] He added that he would probably have to take up the matter of a nonaggression treaty and other pending questions on his return trip to Moscow and asked "whether he should go very deeply into these questions or treat them only superficially."

Ribbentrop replied that "in his opinion only a purely formal, superficial handling of these points was advisable."[78]

When on his return visit to Moscow Matsuoka did sign a Neutrality Pact with the Soviet Union, the Germans were surprised and annoyed. This annoyance was not decreased by Matsuoka's bland assertion to the German ambassador in Moscow that he had explained in Berlin that "he would be compelled to do something in case the Russians were willing to agree to Japanese wishes" and that Ribbentrop "had agreed in this point of view."[79]

While Ribbentrop may have been entitled to some pique for a certain lack of candor on Matsuoka's part, the Germans had in no way indicated that the deterioration of Russo-German relations at which they so broadly hinted would lead to a request for Japanese assistance against the Soviets. On the contrary, Ribbentrop had said that "if the Russians should pursue a foolish policy and force Germany to strike, he would—knowing the sentiments of the Japanese Army in China—consider it proper if that army were prevented from attacking Russia. Japan would best help the common cause if she did not allow herself to be diverted by anything from the attack on Singapore."[80] In another connection he had said that "one thing was certain: if Russia should ever attack Japan, Germany would strike immediately. He could give this firm assurance to Matsuoka, so that Japan could push southward toward Singapore without fear of any complications with Russia."[81]

All this was in strict accord with German military plans of that date, which specifically excluded any expectations of Japanese assistance in the attack on Russia. A Hitler directive on military cooperation with Japan, which called for technical assistance to the Japanese in encouraging operations by them against British forces in Asia, stated that "Bar-

[76] *Nazi-Soviet Relations*, p. 285. [77] *ibid.*, pp. 296-297. [78] *ibid.*, p. 309.
[79] *ibid.*, pp. 322-323. [80] *ibid.*, p. 309. [81] *ibid.*, p. 303.

barossa," the planned German attack on Russia, would itself provide "militarily and politically a favorable basis" for a Japanese attack on Britain in the Far East. It also stated: "No intimation of any sort is to be given the Japanese concerning the Barbarossa operation."[82]

If, as has been indicated, the principal object of his mission was to secure Japan's rear for the anticipated "Southward advance," Matsuoka had succeeded magnificently. Not only did he obtain a guarantee in the form of the Neutrality Treaty at practically no cost,[83] but he also obtained verbal assurances in Berlin that Germany would vouch for Japan's security vis-à-vis the Soviet Union. Actually these gains, so favorable to the military plans then being made in Tokyo, fell into his outstretched hands without very much effort on his part. The Germans were eager to guarantee Japan against all dangers if she could be persuaded to attack Britain in the Far East. Stalin, alerted to the German danger by Berlin's silence following the ominous note struck during Molotov's visit there, as well as by specific warnings received from the United States and Britain, was only too glad to enter into the neutrality arrangement. While he surely would not have placed much confidence in the paper guarantee of neutrality, he could not have been unaware at that critical moment of the advantage of setting the Japanese in motion to the South.

It is impossible not to have some sympathy with Matsuoka in the difficult position in which he found himself on his European visit. His German ally was hinting broadly that there might be trouble between Germany and Russia, but being at the same time most vague as to the time when such a contingency might develop, and also telling him that Japan must ignore this possible development and proceed with her assigned task, which was to assault Singapore. On the other hand, his Russian hosts had adopted a cordiality most strange indeed considering the belligerent tone which had been customary with them for some years past, particularly since Japan's invasion of China. A pact with the Soviets would constitute a personal triumph of a kind most important to Matsuoka's prestige in the shifting sands of Japanese internal politics. In the circumstances Matsuoka reached out and took what the Soviets offered him, and trusted that his explanations to his German friends would not be found wanting. It is hard to say whose was the shabbier role in this low

---

[82] OKW Directive of March 5, 1941, printed as document 075-C in *Trial of the Major War Criminals*, XXXIV, 302-305.

[83] Matsuoka told the German ambassador in Moscow that he refused to pay Stalin's price—abandonment of Japanese concessions in North Sakhalin—and Stalin gave in. *Nazi-Soviet Relations*, pp. 322-323.

comedy, but it must be conceded that if Matsuoka was less than candid with his allies they had hardly deserved better of him.

VI

During his European visit Matsuoka had seen his stated policies threatened with confusion, but his homecoming was to bring him new troubles in another quarter. While the Germans in Berlin were threatening a reversal of Tripartite policy toward Russia, some of Matsuoka's colleagues were exploring a possible change in the Pact policy toward America. On April 16, attempts which had been made for some time by private persons to initiate negotiations between Japan and the United States bore fruit in the presentation of a proposal by the American government.[84] Despite the Axis alliance and the far-reaching and officially approved plans for expansion in Asia at the expense of the Western Powers, there remained influential elements which hesitated to execute these plans at the risk of a clash with the United States. Court circles, certain business interests, some leaders of the navy still welcomed an attempt to reach an agreement with the United States.

In present perspective it is clear enough that these negotiations never had any prospect of success, both because the gap between the positions from which the two sides proceeded was too wide to be bridged by any verbal formula, and because those men in the Japanese government who really desired an agreement did not have control of that government. Matsuoka at once sensed the danger of such negotiations to his personal position, recognizing that what they implied was an attempt to detach Japan from the Axis. In this he was correct, for as the American record states: "This Government was impressed . . . by the consideration that the hope of defeating Hitlerism in Europe would be greatly enhanced if the more conservative elements in Japan should succeed in what was represented as their effort to divert Japan from courses of conquest and to cause Japan to withdraw—even though gradually—from the Axis camp and align itself with the United States."[85]

Matsuoka resorted first to tactics of delay, and gained two weeks by a convenient illness with which he came down in consequence of the exertions of his European trip. When he saw the German ambassador on May 5 he said that he was using the interval to arouse activist groups

[84] A full record of the Japanese-American negotiations thus launched is printed in *Foreign Relations, Japan*, II, 325ff.
[85] *ibid.*, p. 335.

of younger officers against the proposals for an understanding with the United States.[86]

His next step was to attempt to prejudice the negotiations in advance by sending a preliminary reply to Secretary of State Hull in which he stressed that Japan could undertake nothing which might adversely affect the position of Germany and Italy, to whom her honor was engaged as their ally in the Tripartite Pact. He reported the full confidence of his Axis allies in victory and their conviction that American entry, although it might prolong the war, could not alter its outcome. In a second message he proposed a Pacific nonaggression pact.[87]

The first of these messages Ambassador Nomura made only a half-hearted attempt to deliver, and after indicating his disagreement with its contents, readily accepted Mr. Hull's suggestion that he exercise his "discretionary authority" to withhold it. The nonaggression pact Mr. Hull simply "brushed aside" as incompatible with the basis of negotiations on which the talks had begun.[88]

As a result of the American negotiations Matsuoka was soon menaced by the mistrust both of his own colleagues and of his allies. He could not refuse altogether to pursue the negotiations with the United States, and on May 12 he was obliged by the Cabinet to send off a reply to Washington without awaiting the German comment which he had requested.[89] Oshima warned from Berlin that the Germans were strongly suspicious that they were being betrayed and he himself protested against what he called "two-faced diplomacy."[90]

The negotiations which Admiral Nomura now proceeded to carry on in Washington were to drag on in an endless exchange of drafts and counterdrafts, and they did not therefore force an immediate choice between a settlement with America and loyalty to the Axis. But there was no doubt where Matsuoka stood. He may have been sincere enough in his often-expressed desire to avoid war with the United States, but he had no policy for dealing with the American problem beyond that laid down in the Tripartite Pact: the United States was to be neutralized by the threat of that alliance and was to withdraw its interest from all those extensive regions which the Tripartite partners claimed for their own. This was a policy of bluff, and the diplomacy by gesture which

---

[86] Telegram, Ott to Ribbentrop, May 6, 1941, IMTFE, Exhibit No. 1068.

[87] "Konoye Memoirs" printed in *The Investigation of the Pearl Harbor Attack*, Senate Document 244, 79th Congress, Pt. 20.

[88] *Foreign Relations, Japan*, II, 412.

[89] "Konoye Memoirs," *Pearl Harbor Attack*.

[90] Telegrams, Oshima to Matsuoka, May 20, 1941, IMTFE, Exhibit No. 1075.

Matsuoka preferred to coming to grips with the realities of Japan's situation.

While he was engaged in these maneuvers to prevent loss of control over Japanese policy to those who wished to negotiate with America, and at the same time to prevent the Germans from discerning his weakness, Matsuoka was evidently increasingly uneasy about the development of Russo-German relations. In one of his first conversations with the German ambassador after his return he gave Ott an opportunity to enlighten him. He ventured the opinion that the possibility of American intervention and a long war "could induce the Fuehrer to resolve upon a solution of the Russian question by violent means in order firmly to secure areas of supply." He also added: "In this case, Japan would be driven by the force of necessity to attack Russia at Germany's side." Ott did not rise to this bait, but continued to stress the importance of the Singapore action.[91]

In the end the Germans did not give Matsuoka much time to accommodate himself to the drastic turn of events signalized by their attack on Russia. On June 6 a telegram from Oshima reported an interview with Hitler in which the latter announced the German decision, although he did not yet specify the date.[92] Matsuoka represented to Marquis Kido, however, that in his opinion "the conclusion of an agreement was 60 percent possible and the outbreak of war 40 percent in spite of Ambassador Oshima's observations."[93] On June 21, however, he repeated to Ott his earlier promise to join in a Soviet-German war but expressed the hope that this development might come in such a manner as to "ease his own position."[94] His position was now deteriorating rapidly, for Konoye, Kido, and the powerful Interior Minister, Hiranuma, were on that day discussing ways to be rid of him. These three had no intention of allowing Japan to be dragged in the wake of Germany into an unplanned war against Russia, clearly now Matsuoka's purpose.[95]

As always, the decision really lay with the Japanese army. When on June 28 War Minister Tojo told Kido that the army's policy toward the German-Soviet war was that they should be "calm and prudent,"[96] Matsuoka had lost the argument. On the same date Ribbentrop appealed for the first time for Japanese aid against the Soviets, arguing

[91] Telegram, Ott to Ribbentrop, May 6, 1941, IMTFE, Exhibit No. 1068.

[92] Kase, *Journey to the Missouri*, p. 160.

[93] Kido Diary Extract, June 6, 1941, IMTFE, Exhibit No. 1084.

[94] Telegram, Ott to Ribbentrop, June 21, 1941, IMTFE, Exhibit No. 635.

[95] Kido Diary Extract, June 21, 1941, IMTFE, Exhibit No. 781.

[96] *ibid.*, June 28, 1941, IMTFE, Exhibit No. 1098.

that an opportunity for a "total solution" of the Russian problem was offered and promising a quick victory which, by making available oil and raw materials, would also insure the subsequent defeat of Britain.[97] This argument changed nothing and the decision of the Imperial Conference of July 2 was to stand aside and await the progress of events, with a reservation that intervention might be undertaken "should the conditions of the German-Soviet war progress favorably to Japan."[98] Meantime Japan would continue its effort to dispose of the China Incident and would pursue the "Southward advance." Matsuoka was obliged to confess to Ott that, although he himself shared entirely the German view that Japan should attack Russia at once, he was unable to prevail on the Cabinet.[99]

Matsuoka now found himself almost completely isolated within the government, but instead of accommodating himself to the views of his colleagues he adopted an increasingly provocative course which virtually invited his ejection from power. In addition to advocating war with Russia he sought to impose conditions on the continuation of negotiations with the United States which all other members of the Cabinet, including the military, believed would cause a breakdown of the talks. When he went so far as to send instructions to Ambassador Nomura without getting Cabinet approval, the Konoye Cabinet, on July 16, resigned for the specific purpose of jettisoning the Foreign Minister.[100]

It seems evident that Matsuoka would not have invited his expulsion from power without good reason. There is every indication that he calculated that he would soon be able to return. On June 23, in his first conversation with the German ambassador after the German attack, he had asked to have an inquiry made in Berlin as to whether an early collapse of the Stalin regime was to be expected.[101] In a personal message on July 1 Ribbentrop replied that German armed forces had succeeded in eight days in "breaking the backbone of the Russian Army." He promised further: "The coming operations of the German Army will, I have no doubt, destroy the remaining forces of the enemy in the same manner and it can be counted on that perhaps even in only a few weeks Russian resistance over the whole European area of the Soviet Union

---

[97] Telegram, Ribbentrop to Ott, June 28, 1941, IMTFE, Exhibit No. 1096.
[98] IMTFE, Exhibit No. 588.
[99] Telegram, Ott to Ribbentrop, July 3, 1941, IMTFE, Exhibit No. 796.
[100] Kido Diary Extract, July 15, 1941, IMTFE, Exhibit No. 1115.
[101] Telegram, Ott to Ribbentrop, June 23, 1941, IMTFE, Exhibit No. 795.

will be broken. It is very likely . . . that this in turn will result shortly in the total collapse of the Bolshevist regime."[102]

When Matsuoka defied his Cabinet colleagues he was gambling that this forecast would prove correct, that Japan would surely then take the course he was urging, and that his faithful advocacy of unwavering collaboration with Germany would be vindicated. Matsuoka was both very ambitious and convinced that world power relations were undergoing revolutionary change. "I think the days of small things are now definitely over," he told the America-Japan Society in a speech on December 19, 1940. "We must think big and act big. It is no time to deal in small change."[103] And at Berlin in congratulating Hitler on the "decisiveness and power" with which he was leading the German people in "this great period of upheaval, a period without parallel in previous history" he added significantly: "The Japanese people [have] not yet found their Führer. He [will], however, certainly appear in time of need and with determination take over the leadership of the people."[104] It is not excluded that Matsuoka saw himself in this role. It is certain at least that he was opposed by conservative politicians of the type of Hiranuma, Kido, and Konoye for reasons in addition to his foreign policy views. They mistrusted his brazen disregard of the conventions of Cabinet politics in attempting to by-pass the Prime Minister and influence the Emperor directly, and beyond this they mistrusted in him his talent for frenzied demagogic oratory and his pretensions to popular leadership.

VII

These qualities of opportunism and ambition are likely to figure as largely in any historical evaluation of Matsuoka as they did in the mistrustful appraisal of his contemporaries. In terms of the history of modern and Japanese diplomacy, however, he deserves notice for other reasons.

In his methods he was above all representative of the school of totalitarian diplomacy as it flourished in the years before the second world war. The leading characteristic of that school was its application of the techniques and apparatus of propaganda to the purposes of diplomacy, its reliance upon the immediate impact of the dramatic or seemingly dramatic gesture to bring opponents to terms. Matsuoka himself was

[102] Telegram, Ribbentrop to Ott, July 1, 1941, printed in *Department of State Bulletin*, June 16, 1946, p. 1040.
[103] Full text in *Foreign Relations, Japan*, II, 123-128.
[104] *Nazi-Soviet Relations*, p. 298.

much more practiced in public statements, usually carrying vague overtones of menace, than he was in the private art of negotiation.

It was true, of course, that Japanese foreign policy, committed as it was to upsetting the whole order of power in the Far East, had little use for the art of negotiation, for to negotiate seriously would have meant a willingness to reach agreements on the basis of existing treaty relationships. Matsuoka was more acute than his Cabinet colleagues in recognizing the futility of negotiations with the United States, given the objectives which Japan had set for herself. On the other hand, he did not appear to discern that these objectives exceeded the limits of Japanese power, or if he did, he blandly accepted a policy of desperation. In this he was representative of almost the whole of his generation of Japanese leaders, men who, perhaps because they were dazzled by what they conceived to be the breakup of the European system of Great Powers and its hegemony in the Far East, launched Japan in pursuit of undefined goals beyond her capacity to attain. They showed themselves to be mere technicians of power, men who were deficient in those qualities of imaginative statesmanship which had enabled the leaders of the Meiji Restoration, by a nice balance of daring and caution, to bring Japan into the circle of the Great Powers in less than a half century.

It would be too much to say, however, that Matsuoka for all his opportunism and heedless pursuit of power, both for himself and for Japan, was entirely without any systematic conceptions of foreign policy for Japan. One idea to which he held fanatically was that Japan must not allow herself to be isolated, that her aims could not be fulfilled except in alliance with a European Great Power. In his Dairen speech of December 1936, cited above, he rebuked those in Japan who had taken pride in the "honorable isolation" which had followed the Manchurian Incident and the withdrawal from Geneva. He said that for twenty years prior to the Washington Conference Japan's entire diplomacy had been based upon the Anglo-Japanese alliance, that with its termination Japan had become a rudderless vessel, and in the Manchurian affair had therefore "struck a reef." "The vessel of Japan," he added, "has now obtained a new rudder in the form of the agreement with Germany, and so this agreement must be made the basis of the Empire's future diplomacy." To this conception he was absolutely faithful and it doubtless explains his readiness to follow the Germans when in June 1941 they changed course without, as was their way with their allies, the courtesy of an advance warning.

Matsuoka not only believed in a policy of alliance for Japan, but specifically in a German-Japanese alliance, and in a German-Russian-Japanese bloc if that should prove feasible. As a young man Matsuoka had been a protégé of Count Shimpei Goto, Japan's Foreign Minister for a time in 1918 when Matsuoka was serving in the Foreign Office and as secretary to the Prime Minister. The South Manchurian Railway Company had been organized under Count Goto as its first president in 1907, and it was under his sponsorship that Matsuoka became a director of the company in 1921, at which time he also left the Diplomatic Service. As Foreign Minister in 1918 Count Goto had been an active proponent of the Siberian expedition, but in the early 1920's he became an equally active supporter of Soviet-Japanese friendship, and played a part in launching the negotiations which led to the resumption of relations between the two countries in 1925. At the same time, however, he was a friend of Germany. He had studied medicine there as a young man and after his return had founded the Japanese-German Cultural Institute in Tokyo. He was regarded in Japan as the author of the conception of a Japanese-German-Russian bloc. The formulation of this theory commonly attributed to him was that "Germany, Russia, and Japan are a three-horse team, but the Russian horse must proceed in the middle so that it cannot break lose and upset everything." To the extent that Matsuoka was able to plot a course in terms of systematic ideas, these were derived from Count Goto.

It was consistent with these ideas that the system of the Tripartite Pact anticipated an adjustment of Soviet-Japanese relations. Russia was to be a passive participant in that system, assigned to proceed quietly between German-Japanese traces. When Molotov visited Berlin in November 1940 he made it clear that the Soviets would not accept this role. "The participation of Russia in the Tripartite Pact appeared to him entirely acceptable in principle," he said, "provided that Russia was to cooperate as a partner and not be merely an object."[105] Hitler was not accustomed to dealing with others as partners and chose to regard the Russian behavior as dangerous and unruly. When he then decided to attack the Soviet Union, Matsuoka was confronted with an awkward situation, but not one which was basically inconsistent with his conceptions. It may be that he thought of his nonaggression pact in Moscow as an attempt to check a too headlong shift of the German course, but in the end he was willing to accommodate himself to it. He was doubtless the more willing since he believed that the Communist danger

[105] *ibid.*, p. 233.

would have to be dealt with sooner or later. In Berlin he had suggested to Ribbentrop that the Anti-Comintern Pact, due to expire in 1941, be renewed.[106] Even before the Tripartite Pact was signed, when there was no hint of any break in Soviet-German friendship, he told the Privy Council in his justification of the Pact on September 26, 1940, that he regarded any settlement which might be reached with Russia as only temporary. "Even though the Russo-Japanese relation may be readjusted it will hardly last for three years. After two years, it will be necessary to reconsider the relations among Japan, Germany, and Russia." And on the same occasion he stated flatly: "Japan will aid Germany in the event of a Soviet-German war, and Germany will assist Japan in the event of a Russo-Japanese war."[107] These were the conceptions to which he held firm in the divided councils of the Japanese government in June-July 1941, and for which he allowed himself to be expelled from power in the conviction that his vindication would not be long in coming.

No Foreign Minister was the master of Japanese foreign policy in the years before Pearl Harbor. The plague of faction was endemic in Japanese political life and, persuasive as he was said to be, it was quite beyond Matsuoka's powers to win consent and unified support for his policies. Above all, however, it was his error to place himself at odds with the military. Early in his tenure of power Matsuoka told Ambassador Grew that it "had been a *sine qua non* of his taking office that he was to direct Japan's foreign relations," and that he would not allow the military to "dictate to him."[108] This remark was at the time tailored to Grew's special pre-occupation with the military's violation of American rights in China, but Matsuoka doubtless meant it in his own sense. If so, it was a presumption which no Foreign Minister in prewar Japan could allow himself, and because of it, Matsuoka passed from the scene as suddenly as he had appeared a year earlier.

[106] *ibid.*, p. 305.
[108] Grew, *Ten Years in Japan*, p. 345.

[107] IMTFE, Exhibit No. 552.

21

Two American Ambassadors: Bullitt and Kennedy

BY WILLIAM W. KAUFMANN

WINSTON CHURCHILL has characterized the recent international conflict as the unnecessary war. By this, presumably, he means that if the Powers threatened by Germany, Italy, and Japan had acted together early enough and boldly enough they could have thwarted the aggressor states without the fearful costs and consequences of a second world war. Whatever one may think of Mr. Churchill's hypothesis, it is certainly true that the effort to test it was not forthcoming largely because of the policy of isolation followed by the United States in the interwar period.

That policy had never won complete acceptance in the public mind. Ever since 1919 powerful groups had advocated American participation in the work of the League of Nations and the World Court, but it was not until 1938 that the basic premises of isolation were called into question and a broad discussion started about the role of the United States in European affairs. The debate that followed was in many respects partisan and uninformed; for two years it proved inconclusive. That was to be expected: the problem was new and complex. What seems more surprising in retrospect is the discovery that at the same time a similar situation prevailed within the administration itself. Despite far-flung information services, an elaborate bureaucracy in Washington, and expert consideration of the problem, the American government lay virtually paralyzed in the realm of foreign affairs. It is true, of course, that the President and Secretary Hull eventually progressed to all-out aid for Britain and a firm stand against Japan; but these decisions matured very painfully over a period of three years, and the final act of war against the Axis resulted, not from some tortured and secret plot, but from the attack on Pearl Harbor.

[649]

No doubt the reasons for this funereal pace are many and complex; probably not all of them have as yet been divined. Certainly the role and responsibility of American diplomats remains to be assessed. In this connection two men—William Christian Bullitt and Joseph Patrick Kennedy—present particularly intriguing problems for the student of history. They occupied the key diplomatic posts of Paris and London, they witnessed the unfolding of the Czechoslovak crisis with all its sinister overtones, and they remained on duty until after the fall of France. Finally, as a result of these experiences, they came to urge utterly divergent points of view on the President and Secretary of State. What, one wonders, was their influence during this difficult period, how did they exercise it, and what explanations can be found for the positions that they took?

Neither man fits comfortably into the category of professional diplomat, although Bullitt probably comes closer to it than does Kennedy. Born in Philadelphia of a wealthy and socially prominent family, he inherited all the qualifications considered appropriate to the American foreign service. These he improved upon by spending four years at Yale and one at the Harvard Law School. After serving as foreign correspondent and associate editor of the Philadelphia *Public Ledger*, and making the acquaintance of Colonel House, he became a special assistant to the Secretary of State during the Wilson administration, went to Paris as a member of the American peace delegation in 1919, and from there paid his celebrated visit to Lenin and Chicherin as an emissary of the President. The mission was to have a fateful influence on his career. It convinced him of the necessity of reaching an early agreement with the Bolsheviks, and he returned to Paris with this recommendation. When the Big Four ignored his advice he resigned his post and later, before the Senate Foreign Relations Committee, denounced the whole peace structure of Versailles.[1] For that act, and for what was regarded as his disloyalty to Wilson, the Democratic Party virtually ostracized him. During the next fourteen years Bullitt occupied himself with an interest in the motion picture business, a novel, marriage to the widow of the American communist, John Reed, and a good deal of travel.

The election of Roosevelt in 1932 brought him back into the government service, where he was to remain for twelve exciting years. Once more he started as special assistant to the Secretary of State, and again he participated in negotiations concerning the Soviet Union. This time, however, his efforts, combined with those of the administration, resulted

---

[1] Bullitt's testimony before the Senate Foreign Relations Committee is conveniently available in *The Bullitt Mission to Russia* (New York, 1919).

in American recognition of that country, and his own appointment as the first postwar ambassador of the United States to Moscow. It was with this varied and unorthodox experience that Bullitt reached the Place de la Concorde in the autumn of 1936, thoroughly disillusioned with the Soviet Union, to take up his duties as the American envoy to France.

Kennedy's interests and career had proceeded along somewhat different lines. A Bostonian, educated at Harvard, like Bullitt a lifelong Democrat, he quickly involved himself in the world of business and finance. His experience ranged from shipbuilding and investment banking to the motion picture business and the intricacies of corporate finance. It also included the accumulation of a large fortune and the rearing of nine children.

Kennedy's interest in Franklin Roosevelt began early. He was a supporter of the President and a contributor to his campaign before the Democratic convention in 1932, and at Chicago is reported to have used his influence with William Randolph Hearst to bring the California delegation into the Roosevelt camp.[2] His rewards followed rapidly. In 1934 he became the chairman of the newly created Securities Exchange Commission; in 1937 he received the chairmanship of the Maritime Commission; and early in 1938, following hard upon the rumor that he would succeed Henry Morgenthau, Jr., at the Treasury, he replaced the ailing Robert Bingham as American ambassador to the Court of St. James.[3]

II

The scene that greeted Bullitt and Kennedy in the Europe of 1938 was a turbulent one. The precarious equilibrium so casually constructed at Versailles was teetering on the verge of collapse. Not only had Germany regained a goodly portion of her armed strength; she had won the Saar by plebiscite and the Rhineland by a skillful *coup de main*. Civil war was flaming in Spain, Austria was about to fall, and Czechoslovakia was coming under the guns of the Wehrmacht. France, the principal guardian of the latest statute of Europe, meanwhile appeared to be slipping into a permanent decline, while Britain, still outwardly powerful, contented herself with the role of the impartial spectator. All of Wilson's early schemes had been tried, however ineptly, and had failed; the ideas and

[2] For this, and other sidelights on Kennedy's relations with Roosevelt, see James A. Farley, *Jim Farley's Story* (New York, 1948); Edward J. Flynn, *You're the Boss* (New York, 1947); and Raymond Moley, *After Seven Years* (New York, 1939).

[3] For indications of Roosevelt's attitude on the Treasury, see *Jim Farley's Story*, pp. 115, 126.

mechanisms of the League of Nations lay discredited. Europe was not the idyl of contented, democratic, and cooperative nations envisaged at Versailles, but the very cockpit of competing states which the peacemakers of 1919 had hoped to banish forever from the earth. The problem no longer was one of adopting measures to enhance the contentment of Europe; it had resolved itself into one of determining at what point, and by which means, the competition for power launched by Germany was to be resolved. For the nations in the Western camp two major alternatives lay open: the classic policy of the balance of power so recently disguised under the anomalous heading of collective security, and the equally ancient though less venerated policy of concession and appeasement. To the statesmen in Paris and London each had its drawbacks. Appeasement, with all its indubitable attractions, might lead to aggrandizement without a corresponding change in attitudes. A policy predicated on the balance of power was both difficult and dangerous to operate; and, without the cooperation of the United States and the Soviet Union, it might not suffice to deter or subdue the aggressor states.

Although this, essentially, was the dilemma plaguing Paris and London in the spring of 1938, its outlines had not yet become wholly clear either to the statesmen of the two capitals or to Bullitt and Kennedy. In part the obscurity resulted from the traditional difficulties in Anglo-French relations. But the dilemma also found concealment in a variety of other issues. Powerful groups both in France and in England sympathized with many aspects of the Nazi and Fascist regimes, and this sympathy, combined with an intense dislike of the Soviet Union, led them to underestimate the consequences of a further increase in the power of Hitler and Mussolini. Moreover, parties of both the Left and Right questioned the propriety of the Versailles settlement. Doubting the nature and expression of the values embodied in the treaty of 1919, they found it difficult to oppose the ideals advanced by Germany and Italy, however brutally these might be stated. Leading public figures such as Flandin, Bonnet, Baldwin, Simon, and Chamberlain had thus reduced their credos to a single value: peace—peace at almost any price. And they were encouraged in the search for peace by their own military weaknesses, by the comparative remoteness of the objects that Hitler was seeking (why fight for Danzig?), and by their unwillingness or inability to appreciate the true character of the Nazi regime.

Nevertheless there were occasions on which this fantastic structure of complacency and delusion was suspected of containing fatal defects. Although governing circles in France and Britain leaned toward appeasement, they often peered over their shoulders and yearned after the promise of collective security. The trend was by no means irremediably in the direction of wholesale surrender. Chamberlain might reject the tentative overtures of President Roosevelt in the winter before Munich; the French might speak, quite justifiably, of the American capacity for words rather than deeds; but both London and Paris were, for the most part, more than anxious to obtain the good will of the United States.

In these circumstances the position of the American ambassador in either capital was one of great potential importance. Whoever the individual, he was bound to be sought after and consulted. As the official representative of the United States his words, however informally spoken, could not help but carry great weight. He was also bound to be well informed. The Foreign Offices of both countries, in their efforts to win the support of the United States, were willing to reveal to the American envoys much of their most highly classified information. Leaders of contending parties, diplomats from other countries, refugees, businessmen, all were anxious to provide a fact or discuss a point of view. The data were inexhaustible. The gregariousness, ambition, and interest of Bullitt and Kennedy were such that they took full advantage of the opportunities open to them. Bullitt established extremely confidential relations with French political and military leaders of all stripes; Kennedy, who had won a special place in British hearts by shooting a hole-in-one at Stoke Poges shortly after his arrival in England, frequented the great country houses of the Cliveden Set and became an intimate of Prime Minister Chamberlain. Both men entertained lavishly and reported back their impressions to Washington with an equally free hand.

Their position in relation to the Roosevelt administration was similar in many respects to the one that they occupied in France and Britain. For in Washington as well as in Paris and London there was debate and confusion in the realm of foreign policy. The choices open to the Executive admittedly were limited at this stage by isolationist sentiment, the intransigence of the Congress, and the neutrality legislation. The military establishment, moreover, was in a deplorable state. Had it not been for the existence of the Navy, the United States would surely have ranked as a third-rate Power in its ability to influence contemporary events. Nevertheless, even with these constraints, there remained much that the President and State Department could do. The work of clarifying their own views, educating Congress and the public, bolstering national defense, and organizing bold and forthright leadership presented great opportunities for action despite the complacency of the country. And

Bullitt and Kennedy could play a significant role in persuading the Executive to grasp them.

This was so for a number of reasons. Although the President was becoming increasingly preoccupied with problems of foreign policy, his views on the subject had by no means matured. His love of analogy, his tendency to think in Wilsonian terms, until recently his concern with the domestic program of the New Deal, and, above all, the overwhelming mass of business that crossed his desk, prevented him from obtaining a very profound understanding of international relations.

The thinking of Cordell Hull and Sumner Welles was of a similarly fluid character. The idea that the United States might formulate a comprehensive program of action and then bring influence to bear in order to implement it was quite alien to the principal inhabitants of the State Department. Intimates of high officials have in fact expressed perfectly their philosophy during this period by saying that policy was the product of cables received from abroad rather than of a dynamic conception of American interests. In part, such thinking was due to the tradition of isolation and a lack of experience on the part of the professional diplomats. They had had so little to do for so many years. But it was also a consequence of inadequate political analysis. The Secretary, and many of his advisers, tended to depict other nations in their own image. Being satisfied with the existing degree and scope of American influence, and having economic problems uppermost in their minds, they found it difficult to believe that the states of Europe could be discontented for other than economic reasons. Their world was static, rigidly divided by oceans, yet peopled largely by foreign-speaking Americans. The result was that prior to Munich their thinking ran to trade agreements, lectures on international morality, and efforts to bring together the heads of the great European states in order to resolve around a table the differences that divided them.

Despite these preconceptions, the President at least was open to argument. Those who suspect him of having engaged in some vast and complicated plot to drag the United States into war overlook completely the uncertainties that beset him between 1938 and 1941. He knew that the situation in Europe was deteriorating rapidly, but before and even after Munich, what this condition portended for the United States, and what action he should take, were still matters of intense personal debate. The consequence was that American emissaries in key posts abroad could exert a considerable influence on the development of his thought. This was particularly true of men like Bullitt and Kennedy, for the President distrusted foreign service officers as a class. He referred to them sarcastically as the profession of perfection, and on one occasion he wrote to Cordell Hull: "I am reminded of a remark made to me by an old career service man—'You can get to be a Minister if (a) you are loyal to the service (b) you do nothing to offend people (c) if you are not intoxicated at public functions.' " In the same memorandum he remarked that there was "a lot of dead wood in the top three grades that should never have got there."[4]

All of his ambassadors were authorized to communicate with him directly, but, in view of this feeling about professional diplomats, it seems likely that he gave the closest scrutiny to the reports of his personal appointees. To a man of Roosevelt's temperament, Bullitt and Kennedy were bound to inspire more confidence than the supposedly apolitical foreign service officer. Both men were avowed Democrats; they had contributed liberally to the party's campaign chest; and they had participated wholeheartedly in the implementation of the New Deal's domestic program. Their ideological credentials thus were very much in order.

Bullitt maintained a particularly close relationship with the President. He advised him on foreign service matters generally and exercised considerable influence in the determination of diplomatic appointments. His embassy in Paris became the channel through which a great deal of the information from Europe passed on to Washington; and Bullitt himself was something more than the American ambassador to France. He acted as both a roving emissary, reporting on his experiences in Britain, Germany, and Poland, and the informal inspector-general of the Diplomatic Service. He was in constant communication with the President by letter, cable, and telephone. The two men had even worked out a special code for their transatlantic conversations, and talked cryptically about Yale-Harvard baseball scores and the ages of the President's elderly relatives.[5]

Although Bullitt and Kennedy were nominally subject to the control of the State Department, their status in the Democratic party and their relations with the President gave them a freedom of action not ordinarily accorded to professional diplomats. These considerations, together with the uncertainty that reigned in high official circles, endowed them with

[4] Elliott Roosevelt, ed., assisted by Joseph P. Lash, *F. D. R., His Personal Letters, 1928-1945* (2 vols., New York, 1950), II, 913-14.

[5] Bullitt's connections with the President are discussed briefly in Joseph Alsop and Robert Kintner, *American White Paper* (New York, 1940); *Jim Farley's Story*; Bertram D. Hulen, *Inside the State Department* (New York, 1939); and William L. Langer and S. Everett Gleason, *The Challenge to Isolation, 1937-1940* (New York, 1952).

the opportunity to affect policy in Washington as well as in Paris and London. How then did they employ this opportunity?

III

Until after Munich they allowed themselves to be swept along by the current of thought then prevalent in France and Britain. A great deal of information about German intentions had already become available by this time. There was not only the evidence of *Mein Kampf*, the statements of leading Nazis, and the record of internal persecution, rearmament, the Rhineland, Spain, and Austria. There was also the whispering gallery of Europe—composed largely of the aristocracy and prominent refugees, and supplied with data by such prominent German officials as Weizsäcker in Berlin and Schulenburg in Moscow—which gave forth an extraordinary amount of accurate information about Nazi intentions. Unlike the Soviet Union of today, the Germany of 1938 was a comparatively open society. Colonel Lindbergh and General Vuillemain were treated to intimate and detailed views of the growing might of the Luftwaffe. In June 1938, Mr. Churchill was able to ascertain that the Wehrmacht had at its disposal at least thirty-six infantry and four armored divisions; estimates that M. Daladier in Paris confirmed.[6] There was, in other words, a large volume of concrete evidence about the Nazi threat awaiting employment, yet neither Bullitt nor Kennedy appears to have assimilated or evaluated it.

To the extent that Bullitt had formulated a consistent and harmonious view about the situation in Europe, he permitted it to be dominated by his distrust of the Soviet Union. He had gone to Moscow full of enthusiasm and hope; he left for Paris, three years later, disgusted and disillusioned. Like all but one of his successors he had become convinced that "the aim of the Soviet Government is, and will remain, to produce world revolution. The leaders of the Soviet Union believe that the first step toward this revolution must be to strengthen the defensive and offensive power of the Soviet Union. They believe that within ten years the defense position of the Soviet Union will be absolutely impregnable and that within 15 years the offensive power of the Soviet Union will be sufficient to enable it to consolidate by its assistance any communist government which may be set up in Europe. To maintain peace for the present, to keep the nations of Europe divided, to foster enmity between

[6] For this and other items of intelligence about Germany collected by Mr. Churchill, see Winston S. Churchill, *The Gathering Storm* (Boston, 1948), pp. 118-119, 121, 123, 144, 145, 189, 236-237, 338.

Japan and the United States, and to gain the blind devotion and obedience of the communists of all countries so that they will act against their own governments at the behest of the Communist Pope in the Kremlin, is the sum of Stalin's policy."[7] In order to counteract such a policy, the United States should instruct its "diplomatic representatives in Europe to use all opportunities in personal conversations to point out the danger to Europe of the continuation of Franco-German enmity and to encourage reconciliation between France and Germany." Above all, Bullitt concluded, "we should guard the reputation of Americans for businesslike efficiency, sincerity, and straightforwardness. We should never send a spy to the Soviet Union. There is no weapon at once so disarming and effective in relation with the communists as sheer honesty. They know very little about it."[8]

After a year and a half in Paris Bullitt remained more or less constant to this view. His reception in France was precisely what he must have hoped for, and failed to obtain, in Russia. Whereas polo equipment for the Red army, baseball games and zoo parties for Bolshevik functionaries had failed to soothe the Soviet beast, elaborate fetes and a superb chef at the Place de la Concorde brought him the most intimate confidences of high French society. Lord Chilston, the British ambassador to the Soviet Union, is reported to have said, "It is not what an ambassador can do in Moscow but what he can stand." Bullitt, who undoubtedly nourished similar sentiments, found Paris and all her celebrities a glittering and bewitching contrast. So great was his popularity, especially in governmental circles, that the wits dubbed him minister without portfolio in the kaleidoscope of French cabinets. And in this atmosphere Bullitt responded with affection, devotion, and trust. Just as the Soviet Union was the implacable enemy, so France became the cherished friend. It followed from this, first, that the Franco-Soviet alliance should not develop beyond the innocuous limits set by the treaty of 1935; and, secondly, that the French position should be strengthened by a rapprochement with Germany. What Bullitt had advocated in the spring of 1936 he continued to favor until after the debacle of Munich.

Ambassador Dodd in Berlin suspected him of pro-Nazi inclinations, although precisely on what grounds it is difficult to say. In his reports to the President and State Department Bullitt took pleasure in mocking Goering's "German tenor" proportions and repulsive mannerisms. On

[7] Bullitt to Hull, Moscow, July 19, 1935, *Foreign Relations: The Soviet Union, 1933-1939* (Washington, 1952), p. 227.
[8] Bullitt to Hull, Moscow, April 20, 1936, *ibid.*, pp. 294, 296.

one occasion he even informed the Reichsmarshal that in the event of
trouble there were enough trees in the United States on which to hang
the five million German-speaking Americans, if that should prove necessary; and by 1937 he was calling the atmosphere of the Wilhelmstrasse
"as cocky as before the war."[9] Nevertheless, despite these appraisals, or
perhaps because of them (for they were not particularly profound), he
remained an advocate of improved Franco-German relations and even
suggested to Bonnet that "such a reconciliation would have the full bene-
diction of the United States."[10]

That such an accord might involve a heavy sacrifice for France did not
seem to occur to him, and he became intensely annoyed with the English
when they began to show some awareness on this score. He confided to
Dodd that he cared "not a damn" for Britain, and, after a conversation
with Sir Eric Phipps in Paris, he concluded that the British ambassador
had instructions "to prevent the French from having any tête-à-tête conversations with Germany; that the policy of Great Britain is still to keep
the Continent of Europe divided . . . and that little or nothing is to be
expected from Great Britain in the way of support of the policy of reduction of barriers to international commerce and restoration of the economic
life of the world."[11]

If the *bête noire* of Bullitt was the Soviet Union, with Great Britain
playing the role of minor villain, the ghost that haunted Kennedy was
war. As befitted a former chairman of the Securities Exchange and Maritime Commissions, his primary interest lay in economic matters, and the
problem of promoting business recovery in the United States governed
all his thinking. As he looked out on the world from Grosvenor Square
it was only natural, therefore, that he should have established a direct
correlation between peace and prosperity. At times he also linked up the
survival of free institutions with the existence of these two conditions.
Thus, if peace could be preserved, prosperity would follow, and only in
a setting of peace and prosperity would free institutions flourish. However, if war should break out in Europe, with all its accompanying costs
and uncertainties, economic recovery would be wrecked and free institutions stifled. The obvious inference from this line of thought was, first,
that the avoidance of war was worth almost any sacrifice, and secondly,
that whatever might happen in other parts of the world, the United

[9] *F.D.R., His Personal Letters, 1928-1945*, I, 489; *Trial of the Major War Criminals*,
XXXVII, 594-601; Charles Callan Tansill, *Back Door to War* (Chicago, 1952), p. 361.
[10] Tansill, *Back Door to War*, p. 321.
[11] William E. Dodd, Jr., and Martha Dodd, eds., *Ambassador Dodd's Diary, 1933-
1938* (New York, 1941), p. 309; Tansill, *Back Door to War*, p. 330.

States must strive to remain aloof from conflict. If she did not, her economy would crumble and bring down with it all of her democratic traditions. Kennedy thus started his mission in London with the conviction that peace in Europe was necessary and therefore possible. This preconception inevitably colored all his analyses of the continental scene.

The revolutionary character of the Nazi regime was not a phenomenon that he could easily grasp in these circumstances. It was far simpler, and more in accord with his own premises, to explain German aggressiveness in economic terms. The Third Reich was dissatisfied, authoritarian, and expansive largely because her economy was unsound. Let her gain dominion in southeastern Europe and she would either achieve prosperity and shed her dictatorial mannerisms, or become crippled and helpless with indigestion. Kennedy was not sure which would be the likelier eventuality, but either was preferable to an effort to block the expansion.[12]

There may have been other reasons for Kennedy's unwillingness to interpose obstacles in the way of German ambitions. It is difficult to say. The German ambassador in London, Herbert von Dirksen, held a number of conversations with him during the summer and autumn of 1938. He reported to the Wilhelmstrasse that Kennedy was not only sympathetic to a great many of Hitler's policies, but also anxious to visit Berlin and discuss with the Fuehrer measures for improving German-American relations. Among other things, he had learned that the Nazis were doing "great things for Germany and that the Germans were satisfied and enjoyed good living conditions." He "repeatedly expressed his conviction that in economic matters Germany had to have a free hand in the East as well as in the Southeast. He took a very pessimistic view of the situation in the Soviet Union."[13] An effort by Kennedy to be tactful and conciliatory may have been mistaken by Dirksen for a genuine expression of his views. But, whatever the case, the American saw in Nazi Germany not something to be frustrated by all available means, but rather a force to be satisfied and tamed.

Bullitt had become interested in sponsoring a Franco-German rapprochement as a way of thwarting Soviet ambitions. Kennedy, for his part, favored an Anglo-German entente, partly as a means of preserving peace, and partly as a means of preserving England. He liked the British; he enjoyed particularly the relations he had established with Chamberlain and Halifax; he sympathized with the view that they and

---

[12] For one expression of Kennedy's reasoning on this subject, see *British Documents*, 3rd series, II, 213.

[13] *German Documents*, series D, II, 368-369; I, 714-718.

their associates took of European affairs. Although his principal duty lay in sparing the United States from the rigors of war, he came increasingly to include the England governed by these friendly people within the circle of his goodwill. So solicitous of their welfare did he in fact become that at the height of the Czechoslovak crisis Roosevelt reportedly exclaimed: "Who would have thought that the English [the Cliveden Set] could take into camp a redheaded Irishman?"[14]

With preconceptions such as these it was only natural that Bullitt and Kennedy should have had difficulty in providing the President and State Department with comprehensive and accurate reports of prevailing trends in Europe. They were not looking for the data that mattered, as, for example, was Churchill. But then, Churchill had started with some hypotheses about the nature of international politics which bore considerable relation to existing reality. Bullitt and Kennedy did not have this advantage. To a very large extent their dispatches were in the classic diplomatic tradition. That is to say, they consisted, more often than not, of gossip, accounts of conversations with prominent officials in Paris and London, scraps of unassimilated information, rumors, horseback opinions written at the gallop, and predictions. In many respects the two men were reporters rather than analysts, and so much of their data came from official sources that they tended to adopt the interpretations of the governments to which they were accredited. The influence at their disposal in Paris and London they therefore employed largely to confirm and reinforce the views already held by Daladier and Chamberlain.

The tendency to become subject to the prevailing trend of French and British thought was particularly evident throughout the Czechoslovak crisis. In May 1938, Bullitt expressed the opinion that eventually the existing conflict of ideologies would seem as idiotic as the old wars of religion were now considered to be. Americans, he said, could not accept the idea that war was inevitable; reason and understanding might yet prevail.[15] As the German pressure on Czechoslovakia increased he became more pessimistic, as did Daladier, and estimated that the chances of war and peace were about evenly balanced. Nevertheless he told the British ambassador on September 2 that "Hitler had invited M. Herriot and M. Piétri to Nuremberg and that he gathered they were accepting the invitation. This seemed to be a slightly more hopeful sign." What he feared almost more than Hitler's fanaticism was some desperate action

---

[14] Henry Morgenthau, Jr., "The Morgenthau Diaries," *Collier's*, October 18, 1947, p. 16.

[15] *New York Times*, May 30, 1938, p. 4.

by German or Russian "agents provocateurs." Meanwhile he held to the optimistic belief that "the last word lies with Lord Runciman, against whose summing up Germany will hardly dare to act."[16] He still toyed with the possibility of bringing France and Germany together, and only excised the suggestion from a speech he was to give early in September when the French Foreign Minister informed him that this was not the appropriate moment for such a proposal. As the tension reached its pitch in the last week of September, his fear of war came to match that of Bonnet and Daladier; and after the signature of the agreement at Munich he rushed to Bonnet's apartment, with tears in his eyes and his arms full of flowers, to convey "le salut fraternel et joyeux de l'Amérique."[17]

Kennedy's emotions followed a similar course. The ambassador was at the Foreign Office almost daily during the heat of the crisis, and consulted frequently with Chamberlain. Until the end of August he was unable to see any dispute or controversy in the world that might warrant the sacrifice of his or anybody else's sons. When the Prime Minister informed him that Germany might actually invade Czechoslovakia he seemed surprised, but loyally agreed that Britain was in no position to stop Hitler and that, in the circumstances, it would be unwise to utter threats. He thought that the consequence of any German action would be absolute hell, and asked whether there was anything that the President could do to avert the catastrophe. For example, should Roosevelt make another speech? When the Prime Minister said he thought that would be unnecessary, Kennedy seemed relieved and expressed the conviction that the President had decided "to go in with Chamberlain; whatever course Chamberlain desires to adopt he would think right."[18]

By September 10, when the nature of German intentions had become fully apparent, and the Prime Minister was reluctantly assuming a belligerent posture, Kennedy articulated the view "that it was essential to take every possible step to avoid misunderstanding in Herr Hitler's mind and that only overwhelming argument" should suffice to prevent the British from giving the Wilhelmstrasse a final warning against aggression. He thought that the alerting of the Royal Navy had been fully justified and even wondered "whether over the weekend it might not be possible for the Soviet Government to make some movement that would compel attention, such as concentration of aeroplanes near the

---

[16] *British Documents*, 3rd series, II, 218-219.

[17] Georges Bonnet, *Défense de la paix* (2 vols., Geneva, 1946-1948), I, 294.

[18] *British Documents*, 3rd series, II, 213.

frontier."[19] By the 29th, however, all the fight had gone out of him. Chamberlain was in Munich, and Kennedy told Halifax that "he himself was entirely in sympathy with, and a warm admirer of, everything the Prime Minister had done." While hoping for the best from the negotiations he recognized "all the dangers and difficulties that still had to be surmounted. The situation, in his view, was one that had to be faced in a spirit of realism by those on whom the responsibility rested, although . . . there was nothing easier or more attractive than to pursue ideals with small regard to hard realities when no responsibility [was] attached to doing so."[20]

The role that the two men envisaged for the United States during the Czechoslovak crisis was the product of a variety of factors. Kennedy, because he wanted peace, Bullitt, because he feared the Soviet Union, consistently underestimated the nature and imminence of the German threat during the summer of 1938. Kennedy, admiring Chamberlain yet isolationist, Bullitt, following faithfully in Daladier's footsteps and probably confused by this latest turn of events, therefore pictured the United States as the disinterested peacemaker who would bring together the contending factions in Europe. On this score they were in virtual accord. Where they differed was on the concrete steps by which the President and the State Department should act out the mediatory part. Kennedy was by far the less forward of the two. He had a tendency to see in Europe a kind of Miltonian Hell, inhabited by selfish politicians, fighting eternally for petty objects. Starting with such a view, he could hardly understand why the United States should become involved in the competition, however much he might sympathize with men like Chamberlain. He was not convinced that a common interest existed between the American people and any other nation, and he opposed any kind of alliance with a foreign state, even though such an arrangement might be temporary and designed to prevent war. The only activities that he regarded as legitimate on the part of the President were the tendering of advice and the emission of ambiguous statements about the intentions of the United States in the event of a European war.

He himself was willing, as he told Lord Halifax, to encourage Roosevelt to make another speech, to pay an ostentatious call on Chamberlain at the height of the crisis, even to think of manufacturing publicity out of the arrival of several American cruisers in British waters. But he was also willing—perhaps without appreciating the significance of what he was

[19] *ibid.*, pp. 284-285.   [20] *ibid.*, p. 625.

doing—to tell the counselor of the German embassy in London that he intended using all his influence to keep the United States out of war.[22] Such an indiscretion, however well-intentioned, was bound to negate the admittedly small effect of his other actions. Whatever else he might say or do, however the State Department might instruct him, Kennedy was irresistibly tempted to reduce American influence abroad to the sum of zero. He might desire peace, but faced with the complexities of the Czechoslovak crisis he could not see how or why the United States might contribute to that end. The paradox was, and remains, startling.

Bullitt, by contrast, ended up by urging a fairly active role upon the President. Already in July he was castigating certain nations for resorting to the "murder of defenseless men, women and children"; he also asserted that without "international morality as without national morality, there can be no human life worth living."[22] But by early September he had grown cautious again. His opinion was that the anti-German sentiment in the United States not only did not imply an early American entry into some future war, "but that it did not even imply any alteration of the Neutrality Act favorable to the Powers fighting Germany, at the very earliest, till after the meeting of Congress in January." As he reminded his listener, against the anti-German feeling "must be set a very definite objection on the part of the American people to be involved again in hostilities in Europe only twenty years after the last war, with the likelihood that they would again get more kicks than ha'pence for their help." He had already explained himself on this score to the French government and felt that they were not laboring under any illusions.[23]

Only two days later, however, Bullitt coupled the timeworn American nostrums for peace (trade and disarmament) with the statement that if war should break out in Europe no one could predict whether or not the United States might become involved.[24] As the crisis over Czechoslovakia deepened, his interest in an active American policy underwent a corresponding growth. On September 13 he advised Hull that Chamberlain and Daladier were considering a three-Power conference with Hitler and that they might like to have other states join them at the table. However muted the hint, it sufficed to send the Secretary off on an evening of croquet and anxious thought.[25]

More revolutionary suggestions were yet to come. On the 24th, Bullitt

---

[21] *British Documents*, 3rd series, II, 213, 296; *German Documents*, series D, II, 744.
[22] *New York Times*, July 9, 1938, p. 4.
[23] *British Documents*, 3rd series, II, 218-219.
[24] Bonnet, *Défense de la paix*, I, 207.
[25] Alsop and Kintner, *American White Paper*, pp. 7-8.

became bolder and actually urged the President to make a concerted effort to preserve the peace. Admittedly, his thoughts as to how the President should proceed were of a conventional order, and possibly inspired by Daladier and Bonnet. At first he wanted the President to summon a meeting of the Great Powers at the Hague, and send an American delegation to the conference. Shortly thereafter, he recommended that Roosevelt offer himself as arbitrator of the dispute and issue a warning against the dispatch of troops across any European frontier.[26] But this was overly strong medicine for the State Department, and the net result of Bullitt's efforts was a series of Presidential appeals to the heads of the Powers immediately involved in the crisis. These had no effect on the summoning of the Munich conference; and, as Chamberlain departed for his particular Canossa, the best that Roosevelt could muster by way of advice was a terse "Good man!"[27]

Nevertheless, Bullitt had at last stepped down from that pedestal of righteous aloofness occupied by so many American diplomats during the 1920's and 1930's. Not only had he pushed the threat of the Soviet Union temporarily into a corner of his mind; he had actually begun to cast about for measures by which the President could shape the European situation according to the requirements of American interests. The change reflected itself in a rapid revision of his sentiments about the Munich settlement. Already on October 3 he was reporting that "Daladier sees the situation entirely, clearly, realizes fully that the meeting in Munich was an immense diplomatic defeat for France and England, and recognizes that unless France can recover a united national spirit to confront the future, a fatal situation will arise within a year."[28] Ten days later he was in Washington to urge upon the President himself the desperate nature of the French and British positions.

Kennedy reacted more gradually. He quoted Chamberlain as saying that Hitler was "uncouth and certainly not the kind of fellow one would like to go around the world with on a two-wheeled bicycle."[29] But, in a speech delivered at a Trafalgar Day dinner, he still proclaimed as a theory of his "that it is unproductive for both democratic and dictator countries to widen the division now existing between them by emphasizing their differences which are self-apparent. . . . After all, we have to

---

[26] Cordell Hull, *The Memoirs of Cordell Hull* (2 vols., New York, 1948), I, 590; Langer and Gleason, *The Challenge to Isolation*, pp. 33, 34.

[27] Langer and Gleason, *The Challenge to Isolation*, p. 34.

[28] *ibid.*, p. 37.

[29] Tansill, *Back Door to War*, p. 432.

live together in the same world, whether we like it or not."[30] Only in December did he acknowledge publicly that things were in bad shape and that the situation was changing every day, "and not for the better." Indeed, so pessimistic had he become at this point that he even informed reporters of his retirement from the field of prophecy, despite a record of accurate forecasts about the prospects of peace and the stock market.[31]

By December, then, both men had given full marks to the German menace. Where they still differed was on the extent to which American interests were endangered, and on the kind of action that the United States should take. The problem, admittedly, was a difficult one, raising as it did the costs of alternative types of policy. It was particularly difficult to resolve when threats to the established order were emanating from so many sides—from Japan and possibly the Soviet Union as well as from Germany and Italy. Indeed, the situation was almost out of hand from the standpoint of making rational and calculated decisions. There were so many imponderables to evaluate and equate, including the relative power of the democracies and Germany, the full extent of Hitler's ambitions, and the costs of continued appeasement as compared with the risks of war. Such are the problems which, despite the daydreams of experts, make politicians necessary.

Rules of thumb in such circumstances are always dangerous. Nevertheless, history appears to indicate that, where alternatives cannot be carefully weighed for relative merit, the statesman can do worse than to define broadly the interests of his country and act boldly for their protection. That at least gives him a share in the government of events. The alternative of withdrawal involves surrendering the shape of an unknown future to other and perhaps unfriendly hands. Yet this was the course that Kennedy now advocated for the United States.

It was comparatively easy for him to fall into a position of extreme isolation. Throughout the Czechoslovak crisis he had remained steadfast in his belief that wars solve nothing and that whatever ailed Germany could be cured by infusions of peace and prosperity. Therefore, while regretfully acknowledging the Nazi threat, he strove manfully to fit it in with his preconceptions. Between Munich and the outbreak of the war his efforts on this score took several different forms. One conception which greatly interested him involved the creation of four or five great spheres of influence dominated by Britain and France, Germany, Japan, the

[30] Royal Institute of International Affairs, *Documents on International Affairs, 1938* (2 vols., London, 1942), I, 421.
[31] *New York Times,* December 16, 1938, p. 13.

United States, and possibly Russia. Each sphere would be more or less self-sufficient economically. Each would achieve military security at relatively low cost. And each could obtain what it needed in goods and services from the outside either by barter or by free trade. Such a system might bring about the conditions in which free institutions would develop once more. It would involve, admittedly, the surrender of most of Europe to Germany, and all of the Far East to Japan, but that was a condition that was long overdue anyway. Another conception, which Kennedy regarded less enthusiastically, was predicated on the outbreak of war in Europe and the defeat of Britain and France. Given this situation, he was willing to have the United States expand its sphere of influence to include a number of British and French possessions. Such a move, while hardly desirable, would be necessary in order to counteract the increase in power of Germany that the collapse of Britain and France would entail.[32] Still a third conception, and one to which Kennedy became increasingly addicted, required Britain and the United States to stand with arms folded while Hitler obligingly marched eastward and collided with the Soviet Union. The mutual destruction of the two great totalitarian Powers would then resolve once and for all the problems of the democratic world.[33]

In this search for a rational justification of his deepest convictions there was one point of consistency: all three conceptions permitted the United States to stay out of war. Each argument in effect demonstrated that American interests either would not be affected by what was occurring in Europe, or could be maintained successfully without resort to violence. This conclusion did not imply, however, that Americans should remain idle spectators of the approaching storm. The experience of the Czechoslovak crisis had convinced Kennedy that, whatever the outcome of Germany's struggle for power, the United States must rearm. However much he might desire American isolation from Europe, and the creation of an island of peace and prosperity in the Western Hemisphere, however much he might worry about the stock market and the stability of America's financial structure, he acknowledged the need of the United States to prepare militarily against any contingency. He had a similar admonition for the British. As long as Chamberlain remained in Downing Street he could apply many of his prescriptions to England as well as to the United States. Not only did he wish the British well from a dis-

[32] Franklin D. Roosevelt Library, Hyde Park, N. Y., President's Secretary's File, 1938, Box 39.
[33] Langer and Gleason, *The Challenge to Isolation*, pp. 122-123.

tance; he actually encouraged the President to consider repeal of the Neutrality Act and became the advocate of limited financial aid to Britain. With Chamberlain in power, England was worth helping, provided that the cost was nominal and the effort did not include American military action.

For the most part, however, Kennedy's attitude was akin to that of the weather prophet. He saw clouds on the horizon and he correctly predicted rain; but he hoped that the storm would either dissipate itself or blow off in another direction. It never seems to have occurred to him that politics, unlike the weather, are man-made, the product of multiple influences and subject to a measure of control. He was content to watch, pray, keep his distance, and urge the purchase of umbrellas. His credo forbade him to advise a more active course for the United States even though bold and firm measures might possibly have forestalled the very war which he so greatly and understandably dreaded.

The consequence of this outlook was that in the last dreary months before the war Kennedy's reports had something of the frantic inconsistency that one associates with accounts of mysterious natural phenomena. The omens were uniformly ominous, yet he hoped that events would take a turn for the better, and he grasped at every straw in the wind. In his blacker moments he thought that the British and French were "putting coal into an engine that is not going any place, but they are just keeping it up because there doesn't seem to be anything else to do."[34] After the signature of the Nazi-Soviet Pact he found Chamberlain similarly discouraged. Kennedy reported that, according to the Prime Minister, "the futility of it all is the thing that is frightful; after all they cannot save the Poles; they can merely carry on a war of revenge that will mean the destruction of the whole of Europe. . . ." He himself felt that the Poles should be encouraged to make a deal with the Nazis so that Hitler could continue uninterrupted his eastward march.[35]

On other occasions, however, his mood was bullish. In February 1939 he relayed the opinion that England was on her way and that Germany would not attack. A month later, after a visit to Italy, he expressed the belief that the United States could "accomplish much more by sending a dozen beautiful chorus girls to Rome than a flock of diplomats and a fleet of airplanes. . . . Every time the President says anything, nobody in the Cabinet or Government in Rome is fit to talk with for the rest

[34] Arthur Krock, "How War Came: Extracts from the Hull Files," *New York Times Magazine*, July 18, 1943, p. 34.
[35] Langer and Gleason, *The Challenge to Isolation*, pp. 196, 76.

of the day."[36] This, he apparently regarded as a hopeful sign. There were other good omens as well. Hitler might yet attack the Soviet Union instead of Poland; the thought buoyed him up even through the agonies of the Anglo-Russian negotiations. As he told Joseph E. Davies, "Russia would have to fight for Poland and Rumania anyway, and regardless of whether there was a formal agreement with France and Britain or not, because it was vital to Russia's self-interest."[37] Even after Stalin had discredited this analysis by signing a nonaggression pact with Hitler, Kennedy clung to shreds of hope. On August 29 he reported that the door to Berlin still was open and that the Fuehrer was merely trying "through blackmail . . . to squeeze the last drop of possible advantage out of Poland without war." The next day his news was even better. The British Cabinet felt it had "Hitler on the run," and Halifax had found it advisable to soften a note to the Wilhelmstrasse for fear of provoking Hitlerian ire and Polish stubbornness.[38]

When, on September 1, Germany invaded Poland, the reaction set in and Kennedy crashed into the darkest kind of foreboding. All was over, the party was on, it was the end of the world, the end of everything. So bleak was his despair that the President, burdened as he was with new responsibilities, felt obliged to comfort him a little.[39]

Henceforward, Kennedy was to be a prophet of unrelieved gloom, even though this attitude would cost him his position with the administration. As long as Roosevelt had remained of two minds about foreign policy, Kennedy's reports had probably left their mark. But now that the President was groping toward an active policy for the United States, he began to ignore and by-pass his ambassador. Missions went abroad to observe and report independently of Grosvenor Square. Negotiations between Britain and the United States had their locus in Washington more frequently than in London, or, after Churchill's accession to power, took place directly between Prime Minister and President. The policy of isolation that Kennedy had advocated for America was to be applied with increasing rigor to himself.

Nevertheless he continued to perform his duties to the best of his abilities for yet another year. Britain, he persuaded himself during this time, was going to lose the war. Already in September 1939 he had announced that she did not have a Chinaman's chance. "England and

[36] Tansill, *Back Door to War*, pp. 449, 517.
[37] Joseph E. Davies, *Mission to Moscow* (New York, 1943), p. 440.
[38] Arthur Krock, *New York Times Magazine*, July 18, 1943, p. 37; Langer and Gleason, *The Challenge to Isolation*, p. 198.
[39] Alsop and Kintner, *American White Paper*, pp. 59, 68.

France can't quit, whether they would like to or not and I am convinced, because I live here, that England will go down fighting. Unfortunately, I am one who does not believe that it is going to do the
slightest bit of good in this case."[40] Later in the year he declared that
morale in England and France was low, economic conditions wretched,
and that the people yearned for an early peace.[41] Communism was just
around the corner. He had very little idea what the war was being
fought for, he told one British journalist, and nobody else seemed much
more enlightened in this respect.[42]

His thoughts seemed to turn rather frequently to the past. The British people did not adequately appreciate Chamberlain; they should
erect a bust to him for the services he had rendered at Munich. After
all, the time won by the sacrifice of Czechoslovakia had given Britain
the opportunity to rearm. Still, he doubted whether enough could be
done to turn the tide. The Nazis were too clever, British industry too
inefficient, the air raids too disruptive. In each phase of the war he predicted the direst consequences for England. In 1939 he discovered that
the Germans were building submarines faster than the Royal Navy
could sink them; the Luftwaffe, for its part, was outstripping the RAF
both in quality and in quantity.[43] During the Norwegian campaign he
discanted at length on the lack of preparedness in the military establishment and the inefficiency of the government. On the eve of Dunkirk he
announced that only a miracle could save the British expeditionary forces
from being wiped out.[44] When the miracle occurred he began to evoke
the nemesis of the Luftwaffe. So heavy did the gloom become that the
President felt impelled to write him: "when the real world forces come
into conflict, the final result is never as dark as we mortals guess it in
very difficult days."[45]

But Kennedy was beyond the reach of comforting words. Hitler's
progress merely deepened his conviction that American interests would
be most effectively served by a policy of neutrality and isolation. He
became increasingly vocal on this score as the war unfolded and Allied
fortunes deteriorated. Only by making the Western Hemisphere an
isolated fortress, set off from the madness of Europe and Asia, was there

[40] Langer and Gleason, *The Challenge to Isolation*, pp. 251-252.

[41] *ibid.*, p. 345.

[42] George Bilainkin, *Diary of a Diplomatic Correspondent* (London, 1942), pp. 58-60.

[43] Langer and Gleason, *The Challenge to Isolation*, p. 345.

[44] *Memoirs of Cordell Hull*, I, 763; Langer and Gleason, *The Challenge to Isolation*, p. 466.

[45] *F. D. R., His Personal Letters, 1928-1945*, II, 1020.

any hope of preserving the values to which he was so deeply attached. The idea permeated his dispatches, speeches, and conversations; but only later did it come to dominate him wholly. In 1939 and 1940 Britain was still more important than Iceland. He had stayed too long in England not to be affected by the struggle; the thought of abandoning so many friends must have tormented him often. His relations with Chamberlain remained excellent; one of his last acts before retiring from the embassy was to call on the dying statesman.[46] Even Churchill, that "raconteur of history," so different in temperament and outlook from his predecessor, could occasionally arouse Kennedy's sympathy and enthusiasm. The ambassador admitted that the United States must show consideration for its friends; and, although not much consulted, he found it in himself to advocate measures of aid to Britain from time to time. Rifles and ammunition after Dunkirk, and fifty destroyers, were not too much to give, and principle might be abated in favor of limited lend-lease.[47]

For the most part, however, his heart was not in the fight. Peace remained his goal, even if it meant the domination of Europe by the Nazis. Just as he had proposed isolation for the United States, so he favored a compromise peace between Britain and Germany. Only eleven days after the beginning of the war he opined that "this situation may crystallize to a point where the President can be the savior of the world. The British Government as such certainly cannot accept any agreement with Hitler, but there may be a point when the President himself may work out plans for world peace."[48] The German attack in the West only increased his interest in the subject; but now he feared that opinion in England had so hardened against Hitler that the populace would gleefully reject any German offer of compromise. An even more horrifying thought struck him. The British, buoyed up by aid from the United States, might go on rejecting a settlement in anticipation of eventual American intervention. With this in mind he repeatedly warned Washington: "Don't let anybody make any mistake; this war, from Great Britain's point of view, is being conducted from now on with their eyes only on one place and that is the United States. Unless there is a miracle, they realize that they haven't a chance in the long run."[49] His warnings went unheeded. By July 1940 the great swing in American sentiment and policy had already occurred. The Destroyer Deal was

---

[46] Bilainkin, *Diary of a Diplomatic Correspondent*, p. 214.
[47] Langer and Gleason, *The Challenge to Isolation*, p. 493.
[48] *ibid.*, p. 249.   [49] *ibid.*, pp. 491, 711-712.

about to be consummated and Lend-Lease lay just over the horizon. Kennedy had lost his battle and he appeared sick and disillusioned. In October he relinquished his post and returned to the United States, there to observe and protest. By the time that Winant replaced him in London a new era in Anglo-American relations had opened. To Kennedy's dismay and disappointment the United States was becoming far more than merely considerate of its friends.

Bullitt, too, ultimately joined the ranks of the dissenters from Roosevelt's foreign policy. But his loss of faith and influence was to occur much later on and for wholly different reasons. From the autumn of 1938 until well after his retirement from the French embassy in the summer of 1940, he acted as one of the most enthusiastic supporters—and, on occasion, initiators—of the administration's policy. In retrospect this is hardly surprising for it is clear that where Bullitt differed from Kennedy was in the character of his perspectives. They were more cosmopolitan.

It is probably true that Bullitt lacked any studied and reasoned conception of international politics; he therefore had difficulty in evaluating the trend of events before the crisis over Czechoslovakia: there were too many conflicting strains to disentangle and comprehend by intuitive means. But intuition, intelligence, and wide experience enabled him to see clearly after the rude shock of Munich. The situation had suddenly simplified itself; Hitler's excursions assumed an orderly if ugly pattern. The threat to his beloved France now stood forth in stark and ominous outline; a great many of his most influential acquaintances were turning their backs on appeasement; the days of illusion had passed. In fact, Bullitt saw the new dispensation so clearly that he fell prey to every rumor about German intentions and sent clouds of excited dispatches to Washington. His perturbation was understandable. The time left to practice the arts of diplomacy was uncommonly short.

Although Bullitt still nourished the hope that a peace with honor might yet prevail, he now appreciated that its realization would depend, not on the kind of mediatory gestures that he had advocated before Munich, but on the organization of a strong front against Germany. He was also becoming aware of the shortage of materials with which to accomplish the task. French ties with Britain needed strengthening; the British themselves required prodding, particularly in the matter of conscription; and the Anglo-French coalition cried out for accretions of strength, even if that involved an approach to the Soviet Union. He doubted that one could rely much on treaties with the Russians but agreed with Daladier that no stone should be left unturned, "even though one might expect to find vermin under it." His personal feeling was that if Herriot went to negotiate a treaty in Moscow he should be accompanied by someone as unscrupulous as the Bolsheviks.[50]

Bullitt combined this interest in the foreign relations of France with a growing concern about her military capabilities. During the Czechoslovak crisis he had believed that, despite the quality of the German air arm, the French army was the finest in the world.[51] Now he was no longer so sure: the disparities in aerial strength disturbed him. He had begun to delve into the problem of French plane production as early as the spring of 1938. After Munich he attacked it with all his great vitality. The French obviously could not mobilize sufficient resources to match the Luftwaffe at an early date, and the British would be unable to fill the gap by themselves. The Spitfires and Hurricanes were only beginning to come off the assembly lines in quantity and the RAF had gaping holes in its own organization. The only other source of supply lay in the factories of the United States. Bullitt plunged into the business of making these resources available as quickly as possible. He saw the President in Washington on October 13 and presented the case for expanded plane production by the United States. Roosevelt immediately endorsed his view, and in December a French purchasing mission slipped into New York, the first of what was soon to become a plethora of such agencies.[52]

The effort to overcome French deficiencies in the air may well have suggested to Bullitt a conception of the role that the United States could play in relation to Europe. He told the President that Britain and France constituted the first line of American defenses. Since the policy of appeasing Germany no longer offered any possibility of success, it would therefore be to the interest of the United States, not only to denounce Nazi aggression and rearm, but also to act as a military arsenal for the democracies. Roosevelt, who was becoming increasingly impatient with the passive role envisaged by the State Department, happily accepted Bullitt's reasoning and indicated to Congress, in his message of January 4, 1939, that, in the event of war, he would throw America's material support to the side of Britain and France.[53]

The German occupation of Prague and Memel, and the Italian seizure of Albania, left Bullitt feeling that even this position might not suffice

[50] *ibid.*, p. 70.
[51] *British Documents*, 3rd series, II, 218-219.
[52] Langer and Gleason, *The Challenge to Isolation*, pp. 37-38.
[53] *ibid.*, p. 58.

to protect American interests. He had tired of the moral strictures with which Roosevelt, Hull, and Welles were raking the enemy and wanted action of a more concrete order. Here, however, he was on uncertain ground. He knew, as he continually told the French, that the likelihood of American participation in a war against Germany was very small. It is not clear, in fact, whether he yet saw the need for the United States to throw all its power and energy into the balance. As late as March 1939, he still seemed to think of the problem of deterring Hitler primarily in European terms. The task of actually standing up to Germany lay with Britain, France, and the Soviet Union.[54] But the consequences of their not doing so, he realized, would be serious for the United States. He therefore begged the President to denounce the latest Nazi aggression and ask Congress for repeal of the neutrality laws.[55] After Mussolini's occupation of Albania he urged that Italian funds in the United States be frozen; he also warned that the time for words had passed. The only response of the administration was the Haydnesque "Saturday surprise" message of April 15, a symphony of words in which the President asked Hitler and Mussolini to guarantee the independence of certain European states believed to be in immediate danger.[56]

It was a discouraging prospect for Bullitt, who had at last realized that for Americans "the acceptance of war is a less horrible alternative than the acceptance of enslavement."[57] But what was there left for him to do? He turned his energies to the improvement of Anglo-French and Anglo-Soviet relations and to the prognostication of impending catastrophe. In the final crisis of August 1939, he contented himself with getting the last-minute Presidential messages to the various heads of states phrased in such a manner that the onus for starting the war would fall squarely on Hitler.[58] Although occasionally, even at this late date, he may have slipped back into the contemporary delusion that diplomatic gestures would somehow alter Hitler's purpose, for the most part he stuck to the position that the contest had resolved itself into a struggle between the big battalions, of which France and England had too few. But since Washington refused to look this fact directly in the face, he could do no more than await the arrival of a new set of events to prove his contention.

[54] H. L. Trefousse, *Germany and American Neutrality, 1939-1941* (New York, 1951), p. 20.
[55] Langer and Gleason, *The Challenge to Isolation*, pp. 66-67.
[56] *ibid.*, pp. 81-82, 84.
[57] Louis Fischer, *Men and Politics* (New York, 1941), p. 592.
[58] *Memoirs of Cordell Hull*, I, 662.

Once the war had started these were not long in forthcoming. The pace of the Nazi blitzkrieg, the Soviet occupation of eastern Poland, and the massing of the victorious German armies on the western frontiers of the Reich were ominous enough. Even worse was the showing of the French forces when they took the field. Their mobilization and deployment, combined with a winter of stagnation, showed how far the finest army in Europe had deteriorated since the first world war. General Gamelin remained serene and confident but Bullitt could not share his optimism. The havoc wrought by the German panzers in Poland, a tour of the Maginot Line, and the confused state of the French services of supply left him more than ever persuaded that the Allied cause would fail without large-scale assistance from the United States. At one point he even expressed the fear that Britain and France might collapse before American production could be brought into play.[59] Unlike Kennedy, however, he did not permit this conclusion to cool his enthusiasm for a bold American policy. He encouraged the French to follow more aggressive purchasing policies in the American market; at the same time he was in the forefront of those advising repeal of the arms embargo. The matter of plane production remained a source of continued interest to him. So did the awakening of his countrymen to the dangers that surrounded them. On his return to the United States late in 1939 he complained that Americans were "still in the state of mind of England before Munich."[60] Although he may have hoped that American material aid, however late in arriving, might yet shift the balance of power in favor of Britain and France, and that American military intervention would not be necessary, he no longer doubted that the United States should be ready and willing to act outside its own backyard. Even if the British and French managed to make their way alone, it would be a close-run thing.

An awareness of this delicacy of balance, and of the odds working against the Allies, did not prevent him from reviving his bitter hostility to the Soviet Union. Although the policies of the Kremlin had done much to precipitate the German invasion of Poland, it is not clear, even in retrospect, that any hostile act short of an attack on Russia itself would have brought the Soviet Union into the war. In 1939 and 1940, however, it seemed that Stalin might yet choose sides, and many well informed and experienced people therefore believed that it would be well to act with discretion toward Moscow. Bullitt did not share this view.

[59] Langer and Gleason, *The Challenge to Isolation*, p. 219.
[60] Davis and Lindley, *How War Came*, p. 51.

When the Red army invaded Finland he sprang into action. Despite his knowledge that Germany by herself was almost more than a match for Britain and France, he was instrumental behind the scenes in having the Finnish case brought before Geneva; and he urged the United States to participate in the act of expelling the Soviet Union from the League.[61] The expulsion, in which Hull refused to share, left no apparent mark on the armor of the Soviet mind; but it was a daring step to advocate at a time when another weight on the Nazi side of the scale might have proved fatal to the cause in which Bullitt was now inextricably involved.

On the subject of Italy he adopted a more calculated attitude. Although Mussolini was bedazzled by Hitler's success, and far more likely to support him than was Stalin, Bullitt continually harped on the desirability of keeping the Italians out of the war. His own ideas as to how this should be done took shape in a wide variety of proposals. At first he thought that measures such as repeal of the arms embargo might suffice to deter the Duce.[62] But after the German attack in the West he moved into bolder spheres. "It occurs to me," he cabled in May, "that nothing would have a greater restraining influence on Mussolini than a genuine fear that the Pope might leave Rome and take refuge in a neutral country."[63] Another thought was that the Pope might be persuaded to threaten the Duce with excommunication.[64] His interest, at a more mundane level, centered on the American fleet in the Atlantic. At various times he suggested sending it on courtesy calls to Greece, Lisbon, and Tangier. On May 29, with the French position growing desperate, he pleaded directly with the President: "Al Capone will enter war about fourth of June, unless you can throw the fear of the U.S.A. into him. About U.S. opinion I know nothing, but the only hope in my opinion is for the rest of the Atlantic Fleet to follow" the three ships which had already gone to Lisbon. "There are United States interests in Tangier, after all. If, as I believe, Al Capone is going to try to get to Tangier, why not get there before him with something good?" Unfortunately, Mussolini had no intention of going to Tangier and the President was unwilling to spare the Atlantic Fleet.[65] On June 10, when Italy declared war on France, Reynaud commented to Bullitt: "What really distinguished, noble and admirable persons the Italians are, to stab us in the

[61] Langer and Gleason, *The Challenge to Isolation*, p. 333.
[62] *Memoirs of Cordell Hull*, I, 693.
[63] Langer and Gleason, *The Challenge to Isolation*, p. 459.
[64] *Memoirs of Cordell Hull*, I, 781.
[65] Langer and Gleason, *The Challenge to Isolation*, p. 462.

back at this moment." Beyond promising all material aid to the Allies, and a rapid increase in the pace of American rearmament, Roosevelt could do no more than turn this phrase into his celebrated denunciation of Mussolini's act.[66]

American assistance to France herself was of a similarly limited character. The German breakthrough at Sedan on May 14 had exposed those weaknesses in the French military machine which Bullitt had so accurately foreseen. In a frantic effort to stave off disaster the ambassador pleaded once more for planes, ships, and denunciations. But everything was in short supply except words, and they proved useless against Rundstedt's armored spearheads. Sumner Welles complained that the flood of suggestions from Paris was "something fantastic."[67] And so it must have seemed to one not so closely identified with the struggle as Bullitt. To him the collapse of France was more than a catastrophic loss to the Allied cause; it was a personal tragedy. Even so, once it became clear that defeat was certain, the ambassador acted with remarkable energy to salvage what he could from the wreckage. He succeeded in getting a portion of France's gold reserve out of the country; he also obtained pledges from Reynaud, Pétain, Darlan, and others that the French would not surrender their fleet intact to the Nazis. And, despite the pain that such a duty must have caused him, he obeyed his instructions from the State Department to inform Reynaud that a declaration of war by the United States, or even the clouds of planes that the Premier had demanded, were out of the question.

The last days of free France must have proved especially agonizing. The surrender of the Belgian army under King Leopold, the British evacuation at Dunkirk, and the final collapse of French resistance followed one another in quick succession while Bullitt stood helplessly by. In angry frustration he lashed out at the British. Their refusal to send more planes to France was more reprehensible than the defection of Leopold. To Roosevelt and Hull he even communicated the suspicion that the British were conserving their air force and fleet as bargaining counters for future negotiations with Hitler.[68]

One last gallant gesture nevertheless remained. Over Hull's protests he stayed on in Paris, after the French government had fled, in order to receive the conquerors and prevent the sack of the city. After two weeks of Prussian correctness, he went down to Clermont-Ferrand, ob-

[66] *ibid.*, p. 515.   [67] *ibid.*, p. 489.
[68] William L. Langer, *Our Vichy Gamble* (New York, 1947), p. 18; *Memoirs of Cordell Hull*, I, 774.

served the beginnings of the Vichy regime, and then departed for home. He arrived in time to find Frank Knox appointed Secretary of the Navy in his stead, to help formulate the American policy toward Pétain, and to support wholeheartedly the measures by which the United States began to project its weight into the tottering European balance.

IV

Although the views and recommendations of Bullitt and Kennedy thus came to diverge sharply, it is the similarity between them rather than the differences separating them which is most interesting for the historian. This, of course, is particularly true for the period before Munich. Both men had difficulty in evaluating the German threat; both found it hard to believe that the traditional methods of diplomacy might fail of results. And, although they both placed a high value on peace, neither envisaged a role for the United States in its preservation. By the time that they had become fully cognizant of the gravity of the European situation, the chances of deterring Hitler had declined radically. Yet even so, Kennedy never, and Bullitt only tardily, acknowledged the need for an active and forceful policy by the United States. With the contacts that they had, the incomparable sources of information at their disposal, and positions of influence in Paris, London, and Washington, they had many opportunities to accelerate American appreciation of and adjustment to the increasing responsibilities of the United States. It is not unfair to say that they did not make the most of their opportunities. To make such a judgment, however, is to say very little. More important, and more interesting, are the reasons why their perceptions were so tardy, their points of view eventually so divergent, and their recommendations often so little related to what, in retrospect, appear to have been the exigencies of the situation. Here, of course, we can only speculate.

No doubt the personalities, temperaments, and previous experiences of the two men played their part. Kennedy, coming from the specialized atmosphere of the business world, found it particularly difficult to adapt his thinking to the complex discourse of international politics. His tendency, naturally, was to apply to the new game the rules and techniques he had learned in another arena, however impracticable in the long run they might prove to be. But even Bullitt, with a wider range of interests and the advantage of greater experience in the field, encountered similar difficulties of adjustment. He has been variously described as a *Childe Harold*, a romantic revolutionary, a lover of causes:

impatient and inclined to be governed by his emotions.[69] Perhaps these characteristics prevented him, as a business background may have prevented Kennedy, from appreciating the nature and extent of Europe's danger.

Their location in London and Paris, and the volume of business which confronted them in their embassies, surely must have contributed to their confusion. They moved, for the most part, in a society that thought in terms similar to their own, and they both tended to assume the coloration of their environment. Churchill might describe Chamberlain as a town clerk looking at the situation in Europe through the wrong end of a municipal drain pipe, but Kennedy found in him a congenial and sympathetic personality. Bullitt seems to have thought equally well of Daladier until the disasters of 1940. Instead of influencing they were influenced, took their cues from the heads of the governments to which they were accredited, and issued reports and recommendations in much the same style as did Whitehall and the Quai d'Orsay. There is, in fact, an extraordinary similarity between their views in 1938 and 1939 and the views of the British and French governments. The failures of vision on the part of Chamberlain and Daladier almost seemed to transmit themselves through Kennedy and Bullitt to act as a serious constraint on the President.

The reliance of Kennedy and Bullitt on these sources is understandable. They were both executives, accustomed to rapid decision—men of action rather than contemplative students of affairs. Their duties were diverse, imposing, and never-ending. In the constant stream of reports, speeches, social calls, and receptions there was little opportunity for reflection and analysis. The demands upon their time were already enormous. Moreover, the situation which they had to evaluate was extremely complex. The problem of Germany, while the most urgent, was not the only one that confronted them. Italy barked at their heels; the Soviet Union loomed menacingly across at them; and, in the distance, Japan stretched out a grasping hand. By contrast, Britain and France were weak; they suffered from internal differences, confused leadership, and doubts about the justice of their cause. The United States was aloof, disarmed, and preoccupied with domestic problems. So disorderly was the perspective, particularly before Munich, that even a simple and stable personality like Lord Halifax suffered from nightmares reminiscent of Kafka. As Kennedy lamented, there were no perfect plans, no

[69] See, for example, Alsop and Kintner, *American White Paper*, p. 13; and Martha Dodd, *Through Embassy Eyes* (New York, 1939), pp. 178-180.

simple solutions. To every course of action there was attached the possibility of an undesirable consequence. Bullitt and Kennedy had both breathed the political atmosphere long enough to be conscious of the pitfalls inherent in long-range planning and unpopular policies. It was only natural, therefore, that they should have eschewed such modes of thought. The short-run, the tentative, and the popular were bound to attract men who had risen by political preference, particularly if they aspired to rise still higher.

But these were not the only factors. The American tradition of isolation hung over them like a cloud; it obscured their vision and shackled their thought. Kennedy never was able to break with the tradition, and even Bullitt, with all his sensitiveness and quick intuition, found it difficult to do so. Europe, the eternal battleground with its interminable quarrels, seemed so remote and so incomprehensible. Why should America intervene, and what could she accomplish if she did? The answers, in 1938, were neither simple nor obvious and the question died hard.

The State Department did little to kill it. The men in the upper reaches of the departmental hierarchy were for the most part intelligent and able public servants. But during this period they had become the prisoners of a doctrine that had little sense and less utility. This doctrine, repeated as an article of faith by all good foreign service officers, proclaimed that the State Department made policy, but that policy was a function of the reports coming in from abroad.[70] The idea had theoretical merits: it defined areas of responsibility, gave the State Department ultimate control over policy formation, and at the same time assigned a key role to the foreign service officer. In practice, however, the doctrine produced two unfortunate consequences. The first was that the State Department and President awaited events from abroad to formulate their policy. They rarely initiated a strategy dictated by some conception of American interests; rather were they the pawns of situations created by others. Foresight, the definition of objectives, planning, all were impossible as long as American foreign policy was a tail wagged by a European or Asiatic dog.

This meant, inevitably, that the diplomat abroad, as the principal source of information for the State Department, was in a position actually to shape policy; for what he said, and how he said it, would influence the nature and orientation of departmental thought. Yet doctrine ex-

[70] Typical expressions of the doctrine may be found in Alsop and Kintner, *American White Paper*, pp. 3-4; and James Rives Child, *American Foreign Service* (New York, 1948), pp. 35-36.

pressly forbade him to make policy; his duty was to report and perhaps to evaluate the information that he purveyed. Here, then, was the doctrine's second consequence. Since policy was made on the basis of the cables, no criteria existed by which the diplomat could determine what was relevant to put into the cables. In an immense sea of fact and supposition, without a sense of direction, without any indication of what they ought to look for—with the admonition merely to observe and report—is it any wonder that Kennedy and Bullitt should have had difficulty in orienting themselves to their respective situations? They could obtain little or no guidance from the State Department, except in matters of detail, because for the most part the Department did not know where it was going. The result was the interlocking confusion and paralysis that characterized American foreign policy in the period of Munich. Lacking in direction from above, Bullitt and Kennedy could only rely on their own sense and intuition to report back what might prove useful. And the State Department, depending on the cables to give it impulse, found itself beset with chitchat, rumor, and irresponsible prediction. These were hardly propitious circumstances in which to cope with the dynamism of Germany and Japan.

In default of guidance from above, Bullitt and Kennedy might have expected to receive competent advice from below. Both were served by staffs of professional diplomats presumably skilled in observation, analysis, recommendation, and tactics. Could they not find here a fund of knowledge and experience that would compensate for their own shortcomings and the deficiencies of the State Department? The answer, generally, is no. With the exception of a few skilled professionals like Henderson, Grew, and Messersmith, the foreign service officer had remarkably little to offer in the way of useful advice and assistance. Indeed, most of the faults attributable to Bullitt and Kennedy derive from the sterility which characterized the thought of the professional diplomat during the interwar period. No doubt his exclusion from a significant role in the events of the 1920's and early 1930's had prevented him from refining his craft. But his problem was more complicated than that. One of the great tragedies of both Europe and Asia, as well as of the United States, during this period was that the professional diplomat had lost contact with the world in which he lived. His universe was that of the eighteenth and nineteenth centuries, and it bore little relation to the revolutionary cosmos of which Nazi Germany, Fascist Italy, Soviet Russia, and Imperial Japan were parts.

The failure for so long to grasp the true nature of Hitler Germany, the tragic voyages of Chamberlain to Godesberg and Munich, the unworldly belief of Sumner Welles that a conference on norms of international behavior might alter the trend of events, the suggestion that the President and Prince Konoye might resolve Japanese-American differences by meeting somewhere in the Pacific, the frantic search for peace by Kennedy, Bullitt's recommendation that the Pope should be brought to the United States as a means of preventing Mussolini from entering the war—all this was symptomatic of something more than stupidity, wrongheadedness, or ideological blindness. In more instances than not, the good intentions were present; what was lacking was the boldness of vision and conception to convert these intentions into effective policy. Professional diplomats, despite the many rebuffs that they suffered in the interwar period, were in positions everywhere to provide the political leaders with effective advice on this score. That they did not do so is ample testimony to the low estate into which their art had fallen.

In view of the factors militating against a rapid and vivid appreciation of the situation in Europe, what is surprising about Bullitt and Kennedy is not that they performed so badly, but that they did not do worse. Although theoretically they were in positions to exert great influence on the State Department and the President—if not in shaping basic trends, at least in clarifying issues and indicating directions in which it would be desirable to move—in practice this was too much to ask or expect of them. The obstacles raised by personality and background, the complexity of the situation, the milieu in which they moved, and the American tradition of isolation: these might have been overcome, as Bullitt eventually overcome them, if only the theory of statecraft and diplomacy had kept pace with the times. Without such a theory, without a tested device by which Americans could measure and protect their interests, without even a tradition such as the one that lifted Churchill to such brilliant heights, the United States could only grope and fumble, first as a spectator, then as a cautious partisan, until Pearl Harbor projected her into the fray.

INDEX